phuket to everest
dancing in the rain

PHUKET TO EVEREST
DANCING IN THE RAIN

CATH SHINTON

2014

FIRST PRINTING: 2014
C.B. SHINTON
EVEREST
DY14 0NR

ALL PROFITS FROM THIS BOOK WILL BE DONATED TO
PROSTATE CANCER UK

Dedication

*This written account of my husband's illness was born out of
anger, frustration and upset. It is dedicated, with all my love, to
my soul mate, Alan - my man who has suffered somewhat
unnecessarily in my eyes, through negligence initially, and then from all
the complications associated with not one, but two,
terminal prognoses plus other medical conditions. However, his
fortitude has been admiral, commendable and mostly good
humoured. We continue to fight every obstacle together, which cements
our love and devotion to each other. This type of love
in one's very soul is a rare privilege .. and one which will never die.*

Acknowledgements

Living through this type of challenging trauma without family and friends would be unthinkable, and our daughter, Givvi, and her husband, Percy, have been with us every step of the way and have been of tremendous help and support. Our very special friends - Janet, who I have known for some 57 years ... and Mark and Lynn, have been at the end of a phone and prepared to drop everything to come to our rescue when needed. We love all of them dearly and without their support we could well have crumbled.

Finally, but by no means least, this literary attempt and offering is also an expression of thanks to a very special young man ... Declan, who is an extraordinary talent in his chosen role, and who, over time, has become our friend. We were so lucky to meet him when we did, even though the circumstances could have been better! Without his devotion, care and attention, our lives together would no doubt have been somewhat shorter, and for that, we will be eternally grateful. His devilish black humour matches Alan's, and this has been their bond. Declan is forward thinking, but with old fashioned values, prepared to go that extra mile. We put our trust in him completely, and in return he put his trust in me to care for Alan to the best of my ability. In Alan, he met a challenge he could never have envisaged, and the rule book was thrown out of the window very quickly! His compassion and care for us both will never be forgotten.

'Thank you' is such a short phrase, but, no doubt, it will be one that will be repeated forever and a day, to all these special people.

Preface

A devoted wife's personal diary of every-day life since my husband was diagnosed with terminal prostate cancer whilst on holiday in Thailand during March 2011 – the negligence of our own GP during the previous six years and my fight to get the justice so much deserved by my husband. It follows his treatments and their side effects, including the sudden onset of life limiting acute heart failure, and much later, the onset of diabetes. Together we have successfully fought our corner against certain medics – had dealings with the GMC – and for the past three years, I have thoroughly researched the disease in an effort to support our litigation case. Incidents and situations have arisen along the way which, had we not been personally affected, would have been considered works of fiction - involving hospitals, drugs, family, police, social workers, hospices, care homes … to mention but a few.

It's been sad, harrowing, and traumatic - but mostly borne with black humour and dogged determination to defy not only this hideous disease, but also the medics who gave us such a poor outlook As autumn 2014 looms, my beloved husband continues to fight his unbeatable war, with some successful battles behind him, and with me continually at his side.

Contents

Introduction

The story about my life with Alan goes back to 1993 when we met on a blind date. We had both recently divorced, 44 years old, two children and car owners. It was a reasonable starting point as we had things in common!! We had a very complicated love affair – not exactly a ménage à trois, but very unusual to say the least, which culminated in our marriage in 1995. We lived happily together in Worcester in the house that I owned, and spent the next few years redecorating the house and putting our own stamp on it. We scrimped and saved in order to have cheapie holidays in Turkey and Portugal in 1996 and 1997.

In 1998, my lovely Dad won a competition, the prize being a holiday for four to the Far East. He asked Alan and me if we would like to accompany my Mum and him on this trip. We visited Hong Kong, Phuket and Bangkok. Phuket made a very big impression upon us and we were determined to return there on our own as quickly as possible. This is when our annual pilgrimage to Phuket started and continued until 2011.

During the Queen's Golden Jubilee celebrations In June 2002, my Dad died, suddenly and unexpectedly. Although devastated, we had to deal with my Mum who had been taken into hospital that very weekend suffering from anaemia. However, this diagnosis, made years earlier, turned out to be so very wrong. She was actually suffering from raging Myeloma, which took her life some 20 days later. Their legacy to me enabled Alan and me to consider a move out into the country, and in September 2002, we moved to "Everest", a refurbished bungalow on the top of the Clee Hills in South Shropshire. What a challenge that turned out to be!

We spent the next eight years working all year round to achieve the type of property that we really wanted to live in, including the landscaping and planting of a third of an acre garden. We socialized, had days out ... generally a very nice life. There were some medical problems along the way and we had numerous visits to the local surgery, but nothing of a very serious a nature – or so we thought

In 2009 and 2010, we had attended the Cenotaph in Whitehall on Remembrance Sunday to be part of the Veterans' Parade. During the 2010 visit, Alan had become virtually paralyzed with pain in his right hip and had to accept help in   walking back to our coach. Nothing out of the ordinary showed up on an X-ray and our GP suggested that exercises would help. The problem faded away before Christmas, but we had no idea how significant this event would turn out to be ... eventually!

In February 2011 we are ready for our annual trip to Phuket, Thailand - and thereby lays this tale ...

Chapter 1: Welcome to Vienna .. and Kuwait!

Tuesday 22nd February 2011. I was up early and in the shower allowing plenty of time to get my hair done. Alan never wakes until I take him a cup of tea, but he's ready to move a little quicker this morning. All the doors and windows are locked and checked. Beds made and suitcases in the kitchen. We're just waiting for Wayne to arrive to take us to Birmingham Airport by taxi. The spare room is now clear of the clothes and supplies we will need for our long awaited return to our beloved Thailand, Phuket in particular – for the previous month I have been gathering things together, all essential bits we'll need for a good holiday, which totally overrun the spare room. We can't possibly have anyone to stay for the last month before the holiday! For the first time ever we have decided to have an extended stay of a full six weeks in the sun. We are both looking forward to it. Alan has been tired lately and the break will do us both a lot of good. We think six weeks is just about the longest time we could cope with ... even though we both love the place, there is no way either of us would actually want to live there.

As usual, Wayne arrives a few minutes early so that we will be on time to get away at 9am. Alan considers the suitcases weigh a ton and must be well over-weight. They are both under-weight in reality, it just seems he doesn't have his usual strength today. I had one final quick check around the house before setting the alarm. Passports, money, tickets, handbag, tablets, inhalers ... phone! All present and correct. We expect the whole journey to take a total of 26 hours from now ... nevertheless, the excitement of what is in store at the other end always keeps me upbeat – shame Alan does not feel the same way. My holiday starts now. Alan feels his doesn't start for another 26 hours! Oh dear!

The journey to the airport is a fairly sedate affair as Wayne can't risk being picked up for speeding and in any event, we have plenty of time. We always prefer to be early rather than rushing and panicking. He has taken us so often now we are comfortable having light-hearted conversations with him. He talks about the school runs in which the taxi firm is involved ... the weather and the state of the roads at this time of year. Why on earth does he think we choose this time of year to disappear out of the UK and avoid most of the snow?

When you live as close to the top of the Clee Hills in Shropshire, as we do, then the first 1" of snow will bring the hill to a standstill. We have been known to be housebound for up to six weeks in previous years with absolutely no chance of getting our car out or back in again. Our steeply sloping driveway joins the main A4117 in a 40mph limit ... however, 70 or 80 mph is not unheard of by some maniacs. However, as the driveway turns into an ice rink, the thought of floating out of control onto the road is not a thought we relish ... safer staying put in the warm. It's at times like these that the benefit of internet shopping for groceries comes into its own ... even if the delivery van can only get to the bottom of the drive. The drivers are well prepared and arrive with a sack truck to get the supplies up the last 20 yards.

Before we know it, we are arriving at the airport. Even taxis have to pay to make drop offs since the slip road adjacent to the terminal doors was closed to all but buses and emergency service vehicles. It's just one more minor inconvenience in the name of prevention of terrorism. The suitcases are loaded onto a trolley (which also needs to be paid for these days!), Wayne is paid, and we're off to start our long and tiring air journey

. The plan we work to is to get all the baggage checked in immediately, and get our boarding passes. We have booked with Emirates again as their service splits the journey quite nicely in Dubai, where we have time to stretch our legs and have a break. We haven't used a travel company for years! Our hotel booking is on a rollover basis from year to year ... never pay anything up front ... just deal with the bill at the end of the holiday. At check-in with the suitcases on the conveyor, Alan can no longer complain about their weight! 28 and 27 kilos .. both just under the baggage allowance. All the usual questions answered, passports and tickets checked, we are given our boarding passes and we're now free to do as we please for a couple of hours. Upstairs in the terminal is a very pleasant café/restaurant where we routinely have our last 'full English' before flying out to the sun. We can relax. There are no time pressures. Pots of tea and coffee are delivered to the table, quickly followed by the very welcome seven chosen items, which make up our breakfast.

Now that our stomachs have been satisfied we can take a leisurely look around the terminal. We decide to go through all the security checks early so that we are able to peruse the duty free section. I really don't know why we bother to look as we never buy anything in there. We seem to spend our time commenting that items are not bargains at all and we will find much more tempting prices in Dubai. Now is the time to get a supply of mints, sweets and chocolate for the journey along with a couple of magazines, which can be flicked through in a moment of boredom. My shoulder bag is now starting to bulge with all the in-flight essentials .. iPods, camera, wet wipes, inhalers, tablets, tissues and newspapers ... all that I just bought added into the mix as well, and it's becoming a weighty item, which has to be carried - by me - unlike the hand luggage suitcase, which Alan takes control of ... as it has wheels!

Finally, the time arrives for us to make our way to the pigpen, laughingly known as the departure lounge. Passports checked yet again - and no upgrades going begging! If you are lucky enough to get a seat in the lounge then it is usually one of the most uncomfortable ever produced. We always choose seats at the rear of the aircraft and one of the advantages of this is that the rear 10 rows get called to make their way to the plane immediately after the 'first' and 'business' passengers. As we leave the lounge, our passports are checked just one more time and then we are able to make our way down the gangway and onto the plane. As in 99% of our journeys, we have to turn right into 'cattle class'. We've been able to turn left into the posh end just a few times in the past ... however, we do have that to look forward to when we get to Bangkok this time around!! We have to get all the way to the back of the plane and it always amazes me that folks can't just get into their seats quickly, rather than faffing around with overhead luggage and deciding they want something out of the case whilst the remaining 200 passengers stack up in the aisles behind them! We stand, smile ... stand, smile ... until finally, one of the stewards asked them to take their seats. Just like a cork being taken out of a bottle, the stationary queue suddenly flows again. I quickly slot myself into the window seat of our double position and start depositing everything I'm carrying around my feet. Alan gets rid of the small suitcase in the overhead space and sits down beside me, depositing his pillow, blanket and anything else he doesn't want onto my lap! The plane fills up quite quickly and soon the lovely ladies and lads are making their final checks and then we're ready to go.

Unlike many people, I have no fear of flying ... an obvious small amount of apprehension ... but generally, I enjoy flights. I wish Alan could too! Push back. We're off! The plane follows its appointed route to the end of the runway and makes the 90 degree turn to line up with the mile or so of smooth tarmac. I like to watch the progress from the external cameras on Emirates' planes, especially on take-offs and landings. As the engines roar and we start moving, Alan and I always turn to each other and say "Happy Christmas ... Happy Birthday". We always sacrifice gifts from each other on these occasions so that we can boost the holiday fund! Feeling the rotation and take off, I can now watch the screen and see the houses and roads getting smaller and smaller and then suddenly we are into thick cloud from which we finally emerge to the bright blue sunlit sky. Oh, sunshine .. how lovely it will be to feel warm again on the beach.

The trolley dollies are now in action with the drinks' trolley, making their way half way up the plane and working their way backwards. That's the problem with being at the back of the plane ... you get served last! Never mind, I can wait. Alan never drinks alcohol on a flight ... but I do! Love to have a couple of nice brandies ... all part of the holiday to me! He has something obnoxious like tomato juice! Once the drinks are away then those lucky people who are having a special meal are served ... the entire vegan, vegetarian, low fat, sugar free concoctions! We've been given the menu and have made our choices, but quite regularly by the time we are being served, there is no choice!! Becomes a 'take it or leave it' option! Have to say, though, Emirates meals are normally very good and, let's face it, we were having 'full English' less than 4 hours ago! By the time the drinks' trolley comes round again I can manage another brandy and then with a bit of luck I may even fall asleep for a few hours.

All goes well for about the first couple of hours of the flight, and then it becomes very apparent that we are descending. Now either my watch has stopped or there is something not quite right Finally, the captain's voice comes over the speakers ... there is a medical emergency, we need to land as soon as possible, and therefore, we are diverting back to Vienna! Big sighs all round ... can't see any activity near to us, so have no idea where this sickie person is sitting. The captain advises that there will have to be a fuel dump carried out as the plane was too heavy to land, and this was plainly obvious when we could see something venting out of the back of the wing! Quite eye catching ... had never seen that before! And so this is how we ended up at Vienna airport. The plane was directed to a quiet part of the airfield and there we parked and waited for the attending ambulance. A nurse came on board to assess the patient who was eventually removed to the ambulance. In view of the fuel dump, we now had to wait for the re-fuelling truck to arrive. Luckily, when you fly with Emirates there is no need for a whip round to pay for the fuel .. unlike some Russian airlines! As time goes on, what was an exciting diversion becomes a boring pain in the arse ... quite literally. After two hours or more on the ground the pilot announced that we would be on our way shortly and everyone's mood lifted somewhat. However, we were all aware of the engines being cut for a second time and a further announcement was made. There was a second medical emergency and we were waiting for the arrival of a second ambulance. Unbelievable! Everyone is scouring the darkness outside for any hint of flashing blue lights heading in our direction .... yes, here they come. This time around, the patient was removed very quickly ... thank goodness. All this time on the ground and the stewards had not been allowed to serve drinks!

Finally, the engines restarted and almost immediately, we were taxying to the end of the runway for a quick getaway. Vienna is very pretty from the sky at night ... just the same as any other city really. Having done some quick calculations I estimate that we still have another 5 hours flying time to Dubai. Things are going to be very tight, if not impossible, to make our connection to Bangkok, but we'll worry about that when we get to Dubai!

Everyone settles down after this little adventure and are contentedly dozing, watching films, playing games or listening to music. However, after some four hours, it is obvious we are descending yet again. Had I miscalculated the journey time from Vienna to Dubai? ... I didn't think so. Had the pilot found a following wind and saved quite a bit of time? Apparently not! Next thing we all know is that the captain's voice is in our ears again. There is yet another medical emergency on board and the plane is being diverted a second time - this time to Kuwait. We have since learned that this situation has never arisen before in Emirates' history on a medium haul flight of just seven hours. What can we do? Absolutely nothing! But is it now obvious that there is no way we can make our connection in Dubai. We're not on our own ... there's another 250 people in exactly the same situation and we will all need to be accommodated once we reach Dubai. So it was that we called in to Kuwait where the plane was made to park up at some isolated corner of the airfield in the pitch black with nothing to see other than a couple of other aircraft. By this time, apart from the sick patient who was waiting to be removed from the plane, there appeared to be half a dozen other passengers on oxygen and lying in the aisles! What on earth was going on here? They were dropping like flies! You would have thought that we should have considered that all of this disruption was not a very good omen about this holiday we had so looked forward to ... but it never occurred to us at the time. All we were interested in was actually getting to Dubai and progress from there. An ambulance duly arrived and the passenger was removed to their care.

Of course, the added problem with this type of incident is that the sickie's luggage also has to be identified in the hold and removed from the plane. A time consuming exercise! As explained to us, the sickie may not be genuine and feigning illness could easily be a ploy to

8

depart the plane leaving a device on board. Everyone remaining on the plane has to identify his or her overhead luggage to the stewards so that every piece is accounted for and 'attached' to a remaining passenger. This is the third time we have been through this exercise now and it is all getting somewhat tiring. The captain was eager to get going as his crew were now running out of hours, but as the delay continued arrangements had to be made to replace the crew. As luck would have it, there was a crew available in Kuwait who were quickly rounded up and summoned to the plane. Again, a time consuming exercise, none the less. Patiently we all wait for the handover of staff ... then, again, we are ready to be on our way.

Dubai is yet another 2 hours away from Kuwait in flying time. It really was an absolute pain in the arse, and we were all grateful when we were on our final approach into our respite stop. By the time we landed this first leg of our journey had taken a total of 13 hours ... some six hours late!

The hub terminal at Dubai was a nightmare. The distances to be walked are huge and it is such a confusing place - we have gone in the wrong direction two or three times in the past when trying to find the transfer gate. There were just so many people! The Brits all queued quite calmly - unlike some other nationalities but I suppose in view of what we'd been through, we all managed to get through their very strict security regime without too much of a delay. The security staff are well over the top here ... but everyone has to accept these days that it is for his or her own benefit. We were directed to the transfer desk and for once, we didn't get lost!! This is where we were told that we were booked onto another flight to Bangkok, which was due to take off in 25 minutes. Great! We should make our way to gate number whatever, which is a 25-minute walk from here. OMG! Not so great! We were handed new boarding passes ... obviously not our chosen seat numbers - but who cares at this stage? No chance of a decent coffee ... no chance of seeing their wonderful duty free ... no chance of a cigarette in the smoking room ... no chance of getting to a toilet ... no chance for anything except a brisk walk in the direction we had been sent!

Just before our allotted gate in the terminal, there was an Irish pub, of all things. Folks were smoking in there! With minutes to spare we dived in and ordered one drink between us and started to light up cigarettes. Phone in hand I am desperately attempting to phone the hotel to advise them not to send the taxi to the airport for us in Phuket as we will miss the Bangkok connection as well. Having made contact I told them that I will phone them again from Bangkok when I know what plane we are going to be boarding. Very brief. Very quick. I only hope they understood. Ciggies out. Time to go.

We arrived at the departure gate at the final call, passports checked again and straight down the gangway to the plane where we have been allocated the window and middle seat within a set of three ... and there is nobody sitting in the aisle seat. We are so late getting on the plane, perhaps we are going to be lucky and have an extra seat to share. No such luck! Whom do we get ... the weirdo! There's one on every plane ... and we have him! Six hours of him is going to be interesting!

Alan does the only sensible thing and pretends to be asleep! By comparison, this leg of the journey is very uneventful ... we have the drinks ... and then the meal ... try to have a sleep for a couple of hours and even though time was dragging, we did eventually arrive in Bangkok. The plane was directed to one of the gates on the furthest point away from where we needed to be. With swollen ankles and stiff legs, this long walk is going to be a trauma.

Being our arrival point in Thailand, rules are rules, and apart from getting through immigration, our luggage must be collected from the carousel before we can make our way to the Thai Airways check-in desk some two floors up from arrivals! Bangkok airport is huge and the walk seems endless. No doubt, it is the best part of a mile. Neither of us is in the mood for this but I have to keep a cool head as Alan's temper is somewhat frayed at this point. There must be 25 carousels if there is one! Having found the board, this notifies us of what number carousel we need ... oh, yes, of course, the furthest one from where we are actually standing! Suitcases retrieved we can now make our way out through customs and make a beeline outside into the fresh air. Wrong description! There's nothing fresh about Bangkok air! However, it does give us two minutes to have a quick cigarette before making our way upstairs to the check-in desks. (It was at this point on a previous trip that we were arrested! None declaration of excess cigarettes and tobacco! Oh dear, never mind! That's another story - which cost us an arm and a leg in front of a magistrate in central Bangkok! We missed our connection that day too!) Luckily, we have 'business' tickets for this portion of the journey and therefore the Thai Airways staff just can't do enough for us. We had been looking forward to spending some time in the Thai Airways lounge ... a benefit of the ticket, but we were told that our plane was due to take off in 20 minutes and the departure gate was approximately a 20 minute walk. Oh dear .. here we go again!

Tired, fed up, with swollen feet and legs, we do our best to walk briskly in the direction of the gate. We were just about the last to arrive at the departure lounge and were directed straight onto the plane where the two of us were the only passengers in 'business'! Whilst we were walking, I had desperately tried to contact the hotel again. This flight would only take an hour and that's how long it would take the taxi to get from the hotel to the airport to collect us. Could not get through on my phone – it had decided that it wasn't going to 'roam'. I spoke with the purser who very kindly went and got her own personal phone and made the call for us, and she told us that the taxi would be waiting for us when we arrived in Phuket.

For this final hour of our flights, we were able to relax in something like a decent seat. One day, I thought, we must try to do the whole journey in 'business' ... it would make life so much easier. They only serve drinks and snacks on this short jump down to Phuket ... but the snacks are not that appetizing! Both of us managed to get about half an hour's sleep, which I suppose is better than nothing. It was no time at all until we were landing. We were first off the plane and therefore first to arrive at the luggage carousel ... the walking distances at Phuket being about one tenth of those in Bangkok. One of our suitcases came out very quickly, but the second one arrived when everyone else had left the airport! How do they manage to be split up like that?

At last, we can leave the airport building and hopefully be able to have a more leisurely cigarette, but not every best-laid plan on this journey is working. The rep from the hotel is in immediate view and he greets us with a 'Welcome home' ... ah, bless! He gets on his mobile and summons our driver to make his way to the pick-up point and quite literally, within a couple of minutes he is pulling up. They load up all the luggage and are ready to go .. well, you'll just have to hang on one minute. Actually, it's a mini bus, not a taxi, so the seats are not that comfortable. Our chosen hotel is at the furthest point on the island from the airport - wouldn't you just know it - and both of us are now suffering, with yet one more hour to go. Alan is worse off than I am and his back is giving him quite a bit of trouble. The driver speaks little or no English and we are able to have a quiet journey, only broken by the offer of the occasional Polo.

I don't think we have ever been so delighted to arrive at the Kantary Bay Hotel. It has taken some 33 hours to get here! We know all the staff and the welcome is lovely. Cold drink, cold flannel! The luggage is dealt with by the lads and all we need to do is hand in our passports, say hello to everyone, collect our key and make our way to our room. We don't even need to be taken. We know the way. This has been our home for four weeks every year for the past seven years. Quick shower ... change ... and we're off out for food before the restaurants close for the evening! And then, not a minute too soon ... we hit the sack.

We don't ever want a repeat of the last 33 hours!

Chapter 2: Relax, chill out and enjoy our 'second home'

I always love the first morning in our second home. The sun rises at about 6.30am and will be shining on the white marble Buddha statue a few miles away on the top of a mountain, which can be seen from our balcony. It is already very warm and we have no plans other than to rest for the whole day on the beach at the neighbouring and sister hotel ... Cape Panwa - which is where we spent eight fabulous holidays before moving down to the Kantary (where we get double the time for the same price!). I take the first tablets from the many packs I have to have with me and it is a visible reminder of just how many days we are going to be here.

This is no ordinary hotel room. This is a substantial apartment with views across the bay to a neighbouring island.   We are on the fourth floor but a palm tree still obscures one of the windows!   The décor is plain with dashes of colour in cushions and bed linen, mostly made of Thai silk.   The lounge area has a 'comfy' settee and chair, coffee table, along with a television and DVD/CD player. The dining area has a large table and four dining chairs, which over time will become covered with all sorts of purchases we will no doubt be making! The double bedroom has fitted wardrobes and drawers with ample room for storage.   The inclusion of a digital safe is also useful for the safekeeping of passports and travellers' cheques. The provision of a hair dryer on the dressing table is unnecessary in view of the speed at which hair dries in these temperatures! This area is usually reserved for gifts we will be buying throughout the trip ... and sunglasses. That way we always know where they are! The bathroom is sizeable and has a separate enclosed shower.   The self-contained kitchen has a fridge, microwave, a small hob, kettle, toaster, cooking utensils, crockery and cutlery. We won't need most of the equipment, but it is good to be able to have an ample supply of cold drinks, and be able to start the day with a good cup of tea! And there has been a wonderful addition in recent years ... a washing machine! This saves a fortune on the hotel laundry bill.

The lads have delivered a very large laundry bag to our room ... this holds all our Thailand possessions. Rather than drag the same items backwards and forwards each year we have an arrangement whereby our bag will be put into storage and kept safely for us. There's snorkelling gear and sandals, sun cream and talc, hairbrushes and Paracetamol, sarongs, shorts and t-shirts, playing cards and paperbacks ... and our very own steam iron! With everything unpacked and put away whilst Alan gets through his first couple of cups of tea, we put our swimming costumes on under our clothes, collect everything together that we'll need for the next few hours and head off .. our first port of call being the breakfast room. It's just 8 am.

On day one of our holidays, we know that breakfast will be a lengthy session. The staff are pleased to see us and come to greet us. We then need to work our way through about a dozen couples, all friends by now, who stay here during similar weeks each year. We don't communicate with any of them throughout the year and always have so much to talk about during our month together. Not everyone has arrived at the hotel yet and we are expecting more friends in the next week or so. Breakfast needs to be finely timed ... no one wants to be up too early when on holiday, but it is better to have chosen your breakfast before the arrival of the Chinese visitors who descend en-masse to devour the food like locusts. They put everything on the same plate ... eggs, bacon, noodles, rice, cakes ... you name it, they have it. The Russians and East Europeans are interesting, needing to build up the contents of their plates until there is a need for scaffolding, only to leave half of it when they decide to disappear from the room. Of course, there are also the folks who do not intend to pay for a lunch anywhere, so must sneak as many bread rolls, butter, cheese, cakes and pieces of fruit into their carrier bags thinking that the management have not noticed! This is a great place for 'people watching' and we've spent many a leisurely hour watching an assortment of nationalities come and go.

9am sees the arrival of the shuttle bus which travels between the two hotels every half hour or so. The bus is not required for the long distance between the two, far from it (the total distance wouldn't be a quarter of a mile) ... but the incline to be climbed to get to Cape Panwa is known amongst the holidaymakers as 'cardiac hill'. I don't know the percentage figure but it is very, very steep. As mere 40-somethings on our first ever trip here, we did walk the hill – maybe twice! Now as ageing 60-somethings, the thought of walking doesn't even enter our heads ... always the shuttle! As the bus crawls up the hill there is an array of tiny shop units filled with dresses, or sandals, cosmetics or crisps. There are a couple of restaurants and massage parlours. None of these is accessible to the ageing holidaymakers so small, private arrangements are made with the shuttle drivers who, acting against hotel rules, will drop you off at the summit so that the only direction needed to be walked is downhill. They will oblige most of the time for extra pocket money!

The façade of the Cape Panwa Hotel is a welcome sight. Again this is a lovely friendly hotel where we know most of the staff, but it is a little more formal than The Bay and of course, they have atypical hotel rooms, albeit large ones, rather than apartments. The reception area is huge, an open air space with a massive horseshoe shaped welcome desk. The bellboys spot us the moment we get off the bus and again the welcomes are genuine and friendly. The assistant manager Tim is also there to greet us. He was originally employed to teach the staff English some 12 years ago, but that didn't seem to work out and he finally ended up in the AM's position, is now in charge of all the beach weddings, and acts as a celebrant.

All greetings done we can now start to make our way to the beach. Following a well-trodden route we walk through 'The Roundhouse' which is a beautiful quiet lounge area used for 'meet and greet' by large parties of tourists, or a place to use computers and access the internet free of charge. There are newspapers and the paperback exchange. A beautiful floral display fills the middle of the area and there is a wonderful view of the main swimming pool and poolside restaurant. There is a series of steps leading down to a motor housing. This huge motor is required to control the tram-like lift, which operates non-stop all day, every day, to ferry guests down the steep slope to the beach area. Believe me, it is a nightmare if this ever breaks down or requires maintenance. Travelling slowly down in the tram you can see one of the main hotel blocks and the Jacuzzis on each balcony along with day beds. Many of the curtains are still shut at this time in the morning. To the other side the gardens are pristine with a team of gardeners at work all year round. The plants and flowers are vibrant colours, some of which we recognize as being seen in the UK as pot plants, which may flower occasionally ... but these are so profuse! The individual guest bungalows are staged down the hill, each with its own small infinity pool. These are always popular but their cost well beyond our reach and we always tend to comment, "oh, one day!"

As the tram comes to a halt it never quite lines up with the exit barriers and mostly there is the need to distort your body in order to get out without crunching your hips on the woodwork! There is a seating area here where guests can wait for the tram, and a few more steps down onto the beach area. At this point, the area is covered in some strange type of Thai grass, with an abundance of palm trees and loungers. This is an area preferred by those wanting a quiet time where they can read in peace undisturbed and away from the beach itself. The pathway leads us towards the beach bar area where the beach boys and girls are waiting to attend to the guests' needs. Suddenly from somewhere in the palm trees comes the call "Alaaan ... Ma Cat" ... it's Sandie, our regular beach girl for so many years. She comes running over to us, delighted to see us ... big hugs, etc. etc. Once upon a time, we may have had the cynical opinion that we were a walking tip .. but things have moved on from there. Sandie picks up half a dozen towels and directs us to the sea edge part of the sandy beach which she knows is our chosen favourite spot, puts two beds together, finds us a couple of small tables and, most importantly, at least three sun umbrellas! The towels are duly laid out in regulation fashion and for the first time this trip I can stare out to sea and take in the beauty of this very special place and see again "Cath's Island" which sits directly in front of us but looks so tiny at this distance. There are many other islands in view, but that particular one means so much to me, having thought and wondered about it for so many years. Why it should be such an important constant for me on these trips to Phuket, I have no idea ... but that's the way it is.

The sun is already strong and the temperature is up in the 30's already ... the beach is clean and the water looks so inviting. Depending on the tide, the water here is either brilliant or rubbish for swimming and messing about. There really isn't any middle ground with it. Sandie tells us she will see us with elevenses and leaves us to settle ourselves into our routine. However, the first thing I must do is go and get my feet wet, which involves haste in negotiating across the hot sand to reach the final relief of the beautiful cool water. This is it! We're here! I've landed! Such a fabulous feeling.

The wooden loungers are not the most comfortable in the world but if you double up on the mattresses, it becomes manageable. The two tables between us are covered with a sarong acting as a tablecloth onto which the contents of the beach bag are duly emptied! Hats, sunglasses, iPods, Polo mints, sun cream, inhalers and headache pills, cigarettes, lighters and the all-important bean bag pillows. The brollies have been strategically placed so that I am completely in the shade. Unlike Alan's, my skin doesn't do sun well!

Very close to 11am, Sandie arrives carrying a tray. She has a pot of boiling water, a tiny milk jug along with two cups and saucers. She does this for us every day and saves us a fortune as no charge is made for hot water and she sneaks the tiny amount of milk onto the tray for us. I always take a supply of Tesco tea bags (well, what else?!!) and a supply of sugar packets (which I spend the whole holiday collecting) with us to the beach! By this time, I have bought a supply of individual coffee pouches which are pre-milked, so we both have our drink. I take the water first and then load the pot with the tea bags! Sorted!! One cup of tea a day on the beach would cost us about £1.50 per day ... it's not a lot but when you're there for at least 30 days (and this holiday about 44 days) the cost soon mounts up. What we save here we are able to give to Sandie as a tip at the end of the holiday. This way everyone is happy!! Normally a tip is given every day for the beds to be set up but we include everything together and give Sandie a lump sum at the end of the holiday, which she can actually do something with ... rather than the few pence a day which 'tourists' tend to give.

By this time, I will have been in and out of the sea several times to cool down providing that the tide is OK and there is a decent depth of water. I truly love the sea ... be it calm or rough. We have certainly seen the best of both here. Now it is time for me to start socializing! We have been very lucky over the years to have met so many lovely people who also agree with us that this is the only place to take a holiday. So many of them we see every year, but there are some we've not seen as yet. We even know where they sit on the beach so there is no need to search ... just head off and go directly to them. Alan tends to stay on the lounger and enjoy the sunshine. I can only meet up with two couples during each trip away from the lounger, otherwise I am scalded by Alan for deserting him! When I return this is about the time when I'm able to persuade Alan to come into the sea with me. If it's rough at the time, I have no chance. He has never been a great lover of the sea, is not a strong swimmer and will only go out as far as he has 'floor'. 'No floor' means we have to head back in the direction of the beach! We have spent some memorable times together in the sea.

As lunchtime approaches, we decide that as it's our first day we will eat at the beach café. This is a private beach. There is never a fear of anything going missing from your loungers and tables when you leave them. This makes life very relaxing and there is never the need to leave someone behind to look after everyone's belongings. The beach café is all of 30 yards from where we sit and consists of about 20 tables with brollies, set out on slabs adjoining the shack-like bar and kitchen. Again, we are known to the majority of the staff ... they remember what we like to drink, and most of the time can make a very good guess at what we will choose from the never changing menu! So it's a cheese sandwich and chips for Alan and a 'Mongolian' for me. A 'Mongolian' is a 'pick your own raw ingredients' stir fry which one of the cooks then prepares for you with either noodles or rice. My choice doesn't vary too much ... some chicken, 3 or 4 massive prawns, a little beef, baby corn, cauliflower and mange tout ... a touch of crushed garlic and some chopped ginger along with a good helping of sweet and sour sauce. With everything collected into a dish, I hand it all to one of the cooks and within minutes a beautiful stir fry with rice is produced. Now why can't I do that at home? We tend to eat lunch here just a couple of times a week. No cash changes hands on the beach (other than paying tips or when buying something from the tiny beach shop). Satisfied and full to capacity we can now return to the loungers for a quiet dozing session. As the afternoon progresses, there will be more jaunts in and out of the sea before we make a move and think about going back to the apartment at about 4pm. By that time, we've both had enough of the sun and will enjoy the coolness of the air conditioning in the rooms. Having cleared everything back into the bags we stroll back across the beach area to the tram, which takes us back up to the hotel. There may be a wait now for the shuttle but it is of little consequence as we chat to the staff in reception and play up, much to their delight. When the bus arrives, even if there is only the two of us waiting, the driver will normally just turn around and make his way back down cardiac hill and deliver us safely to the front of our hotel.

By this time, Alan's back is painful and the 20 odd steps to be negotiated up into the reception area seem to be somewhat of a trial today. No doubt, this has something to do with the discomfort of the long flights. After collecting our key, we make our way up to the lift and head for the fourth floor. Our room is as always in pristine order and welcomingly cool. We take advantage of this time to relax, watch a film, have a snack and take a nap. By the time we awake all that's left to do is jump in the shower and get ready to go out for dinner. What a life!!

Being so close to the equator, sunset is always at about 6.30 pm and sets behind the Big Buddha sitting on top of the hill, which we can see from the balcony. At this time of year, the sunsets are absolutely stunning ... every colour you could associate with sunsets is in evidence. I try to make sure that I see this every day during our holidays and even get quite emotional just thinking about it now. Many a time we have been together on the balcony just mesmerized by the view. We have taken so many photos of the scene and you would swear there had been serious colour adjustments made when viewing the printed photos. I really don't have enough words to describe the whole event.

The Thais who live locally to the hotel set up market stalls during the late afternoon and this makes for a very pleasant diversion during the evening stroll along the sea front promenade. There are five restaurants within two or three minutes' walk away from the hotel and three or four others, which can be reached with the help of a friendly shuttle driver! The little Thai restaurants, quite comically, copy each other's menus ... it then becomes a choice of which cook you prefer! Therefore, there are some restaurants we only visit once during the holiday in favour of those where we have enjoyed our meals. Our favourite happens to be the one right on top of the hill so we have spent many years befriending the shuttle drivers!

Next door to our favoured eatery is a small massage parlour ... again our favourite of the half dozen available near the hotels. As it is our first night, then we'll treat ourselves to a foot and leg massage. The girls are pleased to see us again and make us completely welcome. First on the agenda is to have our feet washed before we make ourselves comfortable on their reclining chairs. The lights are dimmed ... relaxing music is being played softly in the background and for the next hour, we are in the hands of experienced masseurs as they ease the aches and pains of our feet and legs. We both regularly fall asleep here!! Included, and always part of the routine during the last 5 minutes, is a head, neck and shoulder massage which just finishes off the evening nicely. I have no idea what this would cost us at home, but know it would be far more than the £6 each we pay here for the service. We know we will be returning several more times during the holiday ... and they know that too!! We sit outside with the girls until the shuttle bus re-appears and gesticulate madly for the driver to stop and deliver us back to the hotel.

We've brought with us a small computer and it is time to let everyone know back at home that we have arrived safely. Our friends Mike and Gerry are due to arrive in just over a week so we really have to send them a quick email to let them know that the weather is wonderful and we're looking forward to seeing them again. After a quick cup of tea, it's time for bed and we are really ready for it now! Sleeping the night through is never a problem for either of us in Phuket.

The days of the next week follow a very similar pattern as the first day. We are becoming so relaxed we can't even be bothered to venture into town and look at the shops ... we are still happy with the beach days and can save up all our shopping needs for when Mike and Gerry arrive. The problem with Alan's back is not easing and we are quickly getting through our supply of Paracetamol, which had been brought to quell the occasional headache. Luckily, it will not be difficult to re-stock as there is a pharmacy about a mile up the road.

Chapter 3: Life will never be the same

Thursday, 3rd March, 2011 ... 7.45 am: Yet another beautiful morning. We've been up a short while. I've taken my daily tablets and I think we're about ready to go for breakfast. Everything we need for the day is in the beach bags and Alan is in the loo.

"I've just passed some blood as I've had a wee ... and like an idiot, I've flushed the toilet! I should have shown you". Oh! We decide that it's probably nothing more than a urine infection and maybe the backache has something to do with this. We decide that the best course of action is to get Alan to drink as much as possible and to collect a sample. We don't have a suitable bottle with a lid. I leave Alan in the apartment and nip down to the local hotel supermarket and buy a small bottle of fruit juice. On the way back, I see Bob, one of our old friends here. He is waiting for the shuttle over to the beach. Asking if we are OK I tell him we are about to go to the hospital as we think Alan has a water infection. We'll catch up with him later.

Back up in the room I boil the kettle so that the emptied bottle can be sterilized before using it for a sample. Quite quickly, Alan needs the loo. He disappears with the bottle. He pees in the bottle but there is something else in the sample. He felt it as he had passed it! It looks like two grains of rice joined together. Very odd. We definitely have to get this checked out. The girls in reception organize for us a hotel taxi to take us to the hospital.

Phuket International Hospital is somewhere we have found a need to visit before during various holidays ... in fact, we both carry a registration card issued on a first visit. It's just a 20-minute run in the taxi. This is a large, state of the art, hospital, which is, of course, fee paying and therefore is only attended by better off Thais and tourists. The overwhelming impression when walking in through the front doors is its space and cleanliness. At the reception desk, we ask to see a doctor and hand over Alan's registration card. Unbelievably it is over 5 years since our last visit and therefore the registration process must be completed again. It was lucky we had taken his passport as this is an essential document they need to see. Paperwork complete we were asked to wait in the A & E triage seating area. A nurse comes to take Alan away for weighing and to have his blood pressure checked. She also takes brief notes of the problem. We are escorted to a separate area where samples of urine and blood are taken and then asked to wait in the triage area again. Within minutes, we are called in to see the doctor and explain to him what has happened. He takes Alan away into a cubicle and asks him to remove his pants and get up onto the bed. He gives him a rectal examination. Whilst Alan is dressing, the doctor returned to where I was sitting, and it was at this time I showed him 'the alien' in the sample bottle. As Alan returned he told us this was something not seen often ... it was a blood clot. The sample test results were now available and the doctor started to talk to us in somewhat broken English.

"I am sorry. This is cancer. Prostate very big and very hard. No soft bits. Cannot operate. Too old." Although his command of the English language was very acceptable, the Thais don't know how to 'wrap things up' as the doctors would at home. There were no full explanations or talk of what treatment was envisaged.

You could have knocked us over with a feather. The shock. The horror. This was the last thing we had expected. "Too old ... am I too old for an operation?" Alan asks. *"No, no cancer is too old"* came the reply. Both of us by now are in a mental daze but understand that an appointment will be made for Alan with a specialist in a few days' time. We are given an appointment for 9.30am on Sunday 6th March ... just a couple of days away. A prescription for painkillers is given in view of Alan's continuing back problem. The procedure after an examination and prescription is to attend the pay desk to settle the bill. Alan's bill for all that has taken place today is under £100, which we pay in cash. The cashier directs us to the pharmacy area when the prescribed drugs are being dispensed. Once these have been collected, we are free to go. Drugs duly handed over we make our way back outside. We had been at the hospital less than one hour! Standing outside the hospital on such a beautiful morning ... what can we do? Hug each other and cry.

I cannot put into words the devastation we both felt ... the shock ... the doctor's words going round and round in our heads. After all, we had been expecting to be told Alan had a urine infection and to be given antibiotics for a few days. We weren't programmed for this! We're 6000 miles from home and the realization of all the implications we immediately think of is frightening.

The taxi driver spots us outside and trots off to fetch the mini bus for the trip back to the hotel. We are both very emotional as we talk about the whole experience on the journey back. In the company of another man, Alan tries valiantly to fight back the tears but I have no control as the tears come over me in waves. There is a lot of handholding going on! Delivered back to the hotel we are too upset to chat with the reception girls and just make our way to the lift and back to our room where again we can embrace each other, each of us trying to convince the other that 'everything will be fine'. Does either of us believe this? I don't think so! There is little we can do except wait for Sunday's appointment to learn a bit more about our situation.

In very sober mood and continually fighting back the tears, we decide that we may as well make the best of the day and decide that we will go to the beach and try to make sense of the news we have been given, and which is obviously going to take some time to sink in properly.

As we arrive on the beach the first people we encounter are Bob (who I had spoken to earlier) and Sandra, his wife. Obviously, they want to know how things have gone at the hospital. We sit down with them on their loungers and relate the whole sorry story. We don't want to upset other people on their holiday with this news but they have to understand why we may not be the best of company for the time being. Alan and I have always been known as a fun loving couple who will tease, set up false rumours, which spread like wildfire, and generally have fun with everyone. Not so today! Having wished they hadn't asked in the first place, both Bob and San are visibly shocked and very sympathetic. As part of the beach jungle drums, we ask them not to impart this information to any of the other couples ... we would prefer to tell them ourselves, in our own time. This they promise.

Alan and I can talk of nothing else between us on this particular day. He admits to me that for some weeks before we came on holiday that he had feelings and sensations deep inside his body, which had made him think something was going wrong but had decided this could be dealt with after the holiday. During the day, we see many of our other friends and impart the news. Everyone is shocked, but surprisingly many of the men folk admit to having had prostate problems in the past, which have been dealt with without too many problems. Perhaps it's not as bad as we fear and not to worry about it too much ... try to enjoy your holiday until things are made clearer on Sunday. We hadn't questioned that an error may have been made at the hospital, but would get the whole situation dealt with by the specialist on our next appointment. At one stage, Alan disappeared into the sea on his own, and I cried. I could see he was struggling to come to terms with what he now knew. A solitary figure with the weight of the world on his shoulders. Just heart-breaking to see, and in this moment I feel tremendous pain of my own, thinking of what life may hold for us in the future. This is just the most dreadful feeling. Actually, I feel physically sick. Why us? Why now? I just want to hold him, love him and make things better, but am very upset at the prospect that, in fact, I will be unable to do anything much to help. We just need to get through the rest of today and tomorrow before we may learn more on Sunday.

By the end of Saturday all our friends on site are aware of our situation and are being very supportive, and are more than happy to try and talk things through with us in an attempt to lessen the load. People are very kind when there's a problem. Anything they can do to help ... day or night ... they will be there if we need them.

Alan's backache is being particularly stubborn and as yet, the painkillers are not doing their job. We decide to buy a lilo, which can be used as an extra mattress on the beach lounger. Sandie is quite happy to keep it at the beach in its blown up state so that we can pick it up each day we are there. The topic of conversation between us varies very little during Saturday. The more we talk the more questions there are to be answered. We arrange a hotel taxi for the next morning and try to get some sleep.

Sunday 6th March, 2011 – at last - the day we have waited for and we face it with some trepidation. The taxi is booked for 9am so we make sure that we give ourselves time to have a decent breakfast before this time. Having said that, our appetites have not been great since we were given the news.

At the hospital, we go through the same triage procedures again ... weight, blood pressure, etc., and asked to return to the seating area to wait for our turn to see the doctor. We are getting used to the quirkiness of the system and the language, so when the call goes out for Mr. Aran (the Thais have real problems with the sound of the letter 'l' in the context of Alan's name) we know who they mean!

We are taken to a private room where a young doctor is already going through Alan's notes from last Thursday. He asks Alan how he is feeling today and we explain that the back pain is still the worst thing being suffered. Usual problems using the loo, but nothing much has changed. The doctor tells us he wants to repeat some of the tests previously done and to carry out some others. Today he would be taking blood, a urine sample and carrying out an ultrasound scan. He would be making an appointment for Alan to have a special bone scan. We are taken away to the samples room so that these can be worked on whilst Alan is seen again by the doctor. Unfortunately for Alan, the doctor feels there is a need to repeat the rectal exam so that he can judge the situation for himself. By now Alan is feeling totally 'abused'! In order to carry out a successful ultrasound scan Alan is told that he must drink as much as possible and not use the toilet. We are told to report to the imaging department. However, we decide to take a short break outside and have a cigarette before any further 'abuse' has to take place! The taxi driver thinks we're ready to go, but is waved away. Cigarette finished, nerves settled we head off back into the hospital and

26

go to the imaging department where the staff are busily handing out drinks to everyone in sight. Alan complies even though orange juice is not normally part of his daily intake! He jokes with the nurses by gesticulating that he is going to disappear to the toilet but the nurse shakes a finger at him *saying "No!! Cannot"*. The wait seems endless and Alan gets to the point where he is bursting for the loo. *"No .. Cannot"* is all we hear!! He's getting tetchy now and I'm relieved when his name is called to take him into the scan room. I wander around staying in sight of the department until Alan emerges and I show him where the toilet is that I found during my wanderings. Now he feels better! We return to triage and we are told to come back in an hour for all the results. There is nowhere for us to go other than to the hospital café where we can have a decent drink and a snack. We then saunter off into the sunshine, still clock watching, traffic watching too on the busy dual carriage way in front of the hospital, and just generally count the minutes until we are expected inside again. The taxi driver is still hovering, but we have to tell him it will be 'long time' before we are ready to leave. He's getting a bit disgruntled now as this is a fixed fee trip .. we've learned that using a hotel taxi is the best option with their fixed fee system. Local taxi drivers may have a meter but mostly they will just charge you for the amount of time taken on a visit like this.

Finally, the hour is up and we can return to triage. We are taken back in to see the doctor. His English is somewhat better than the doctor we saw on Thursday. He is also very sorry but he can only confirm everything we have previously been told. The scan shows that Alan's bladder and kidneys are not involved and there is no evidence of tumours showing there. Alan asks if this tumour is capable of moving. *"Where, show me?"* Alan lowers his trouser and points to a raised area just below his appendix scar. The doctor smiles. *"No. Not tumour. New hernia!"* Oh, well that's all right then? You must be joking! What the hell else are they going to throw at us? The doctor tells us that he has decided against the bone scan, it can be done when we return to the UK. He tells us he is happy for us to continue our holiday and make arrangements for treatment when we get home. Alan has concerns. "How long dead?" he asks the doctor. *"No, no!! Not dead. May be long time OK!"* May be? That description's not too encouraging! The doctor prescribes a low dose of morphine in an effort to rid Alan of the back pain, but he confirms that he feels this pain is definitely cancer related. Oh dear! Alan asks if the doctor will see him again the following week just to make sure everything is OK. This is agreed and an appointment made. We now have to go through the same procedure as before by paying the bill and waiting for drugs. However, on close inspection of the paperwork, we note that the doctor we have just seen is a Urologist Specialist and his name is Dr. Inwa Innachit. You couldn't make it up, could you? We certainly feel 'in a shit'! We decide the credit card should be brought into play now as it would seem that an insurance claim is likely at the end of this as there are going to be further visits. Alan wants to see the doctor every week, for continuity, for the duration of the holiday ... and this is what we'll do.

Now we had definitive confirmation of prostate cancer, the emails between our UK GP's secretary and ourselves started. Janet is a lifelong friend and was very shocked and upset by the news. She passed all the details on to our GP and we asked advice as to whether we should be considering flying home early or would the GP be happy that we carried on with the rest of our holiday. Janet would start making appointments with UK consultants in readiness for when we got home. The decision came back to us that we should stay in Phuket for the duration and enjoy the rest of our holiday as much as we could. At this stage, I also asked Janet to prepare a copy of all of Alan's medical records so that they would be available to us as soon as we got home. We offered to pay whatever fee was chargeable.

The pains in Alan's back had become acute and there was one particular night when I thought I would have to call an ambulance for him, but luckily, the pain subsided. He described the pains as something he had never experienced before and had they continued, he was convinced he could have easily have jumped off the balcony in order to stop them once and for all. To have such extreme thoughts made me realize just what he was suffering. Although he had been prescribed Morphine at the hospital it was probably the language barrier which had stopped us from understanding that these tablets should be taken each and every day continuously rather than taking them as if you were treating a headache! At this stage, we had such a lot to learn about pain management!

We broke the news to Givvi and close friends and between them they had every eventuality covered should there be a need to fly home quickly, and may be end up at some distant airport. Obviously, they were all totally gutted and very concerned … but felt so helpless at such a distance. We then had to keep in touch with them all by phone and email to update them regularly.

During the next few days, I got into conversation with a couple on the beach, of similar age. The conversation came around to where we had flown from and what a coincidence we had both used Emirates out of Birmingham. An even bigger coincidence was the fact that they lived just four miles down the road in Cleobury Mortimer! We'd lived just outside the village for eight years or so and I had never clapped eyes on them before! They had heard my husband was not too well and enquired about the problem. The biggest coincidence was that this man too had also had a prostate problem and had undergone green laser surgery to solve his problem, with a consultant at The Priory in Birmingham and he would be more than willing to recommend him. He gave me the phone number of the consultant's secretary and thought it would be worth a call as this consultant was at the top of his field in dealing with prostate problems. After discussing the whole matter with Alan, we decided that there was nothing to be lost by attempting to get an appointment with this Mr. D on a date soon after our return to the UK. I telephoned his secretary the following evening (don't forget the 7 hour time difference!) and was able to make an appointment for Tuesday 12th April – almost immediately after our return to the UK. Somehow, it feels a little better knowing that something has been done and plans are being put into place.

We were joined by friends in Phuket a week later. We had spent several holidays in the company of Gerry and Mike and after the initial upset of having to go through the whole story, we managed to have a very enjoyable two weeks in their company. It certainly helped to take our mind off things for a while. The weather was great and no one was interested in doing much other than being on the beach every day. The only diversion from the beach was the day we had the hotel yacht - this privilege given to guests who have returned to the hotel on more than 10 occasions. We took about a dozen friends with us and the highlight of the afternoon was when Alan was allowed to pilot the yacht under the watchful eye of Somchai who we have known for many years. Although the weather was really good when we set out it seemed that we were being followed by storm clouds the whole afternoon and we finally arrived back at the pier in the pouring rain. Nevertheless, we had all had a very enjoyable time – a memory we won't forget in a hurry.

Every day we did our best to keep Alan's pains under control and to enjoy ourselves. As we said a sad goodbye to Mike and Gerry, unbeknown to us we were also saying goodbye to the good weather we had enjoyed for the past four weeks. We had a further two weeks in which to enjoy ourselves and each and every day we hoped that the rain would stop!! We bought ourselves plastic capes and decided to explore Phuket on the new Pink Bus circular service on which you could travel any distance for a matter of pennies. Generally, Alan was very uncomfortable as their buses are nothing like those we are used to ... they just have wooden benches down each side.

On one of these trips, we called in at the hospital to pick up a 'fit to fly' certificate for Alan, with an added proviso that he was given wheelchair assistance at every airport. All that was needed once we had this piece of paper was a quick phone call to the airlines to make them aware of the situation.

As we moved into April many of our friends who had been on long stays at Kantary Bay were now preparing to leave and head for home, leaving us very much on our own. Three days before we were due to fly back home, the weather changed yet again. Several times during the wet period, there had been horrendous electric storms ... black clouds, which descended to make it appear that the end of the world was coming ... and thunderstorms like you have never heard before!! We had watched the little boats in the bay being tossed around mercilessly. One local man's boat was thrown against the promenade and badly damaged, but all that could be done at the time was to secure it against the wall in the hopes that it might survive.

The weather was now beautiful again and allowed us back onto the beach to enjoy the last chance of relaxation in the sun for our final three days.

It's **Thursday 7th April 2011** and it's time to start our journey home. As in years gone by, we start our journey home during the early evening, catching our main flight in the early hours of the next morning. The manager of Cape Panwa Hotel arrived at our door acting as bellboy. All the staff on duty at the Kantary Bay came to wish us farewell. I don't think either of us wants to leave and return to the UK to face the realities of this disease ... but obviously, we have no choice. However, I was in tears as we left the hotel, not sure whether or not we would ever be able to return. At the airport, we are met by a porter, wheelchair at the ready. After check-in, we are deposited in the Thai Air Executive lounge as our short trip to Bangkok is in Business Class. The porter returns in time to escort us to our departure lounge and on to the plane. At Bangkok Alan is collected by another wheelchair attendant. The Emirates' flight to Dubai is a six hour journey, which we have done many times before, in comparative comfort as we always choose and books our seats wisely. However, there has been a change of aircraft and it was with some excitement that we went on board the new double-decker 380. A new plane looking superb ... but the comfort element during construction apparently comes very low on the manufacturer's list! Alan is in pain; we are both very uncomfortable and whereas we would have been used to just two seats, we were now stuck in a row of three with some obnoxious stranger in the aisle seat. It was a long six hours!

Once in Dubai and Alan is installed into a wheelchair, the first stop had to be the smoking lounge ... we both needed one! After a coffee or two, it's time to board our flight to Birmingham. Luckily, it is the aircraft we are expecting and therefore our preferred seats belong to us! Although still very uncomfortable, Alan did manage to sleep the majority of the seven hour flight, which was completed without further event. The use of a wheelchair at airports is certainly the way to travel in order to get through airport formalities at the fastest possible speed. Having collected our luggage we were soon out in the beautiful Birmingham sunshine and warmth, which was very welcome when compared with the dreadful conditions we have arrived back in on past holidays.

Our taxi driver has, in the past, been waiting for us in the arrivals hall. Today there was no sign of him. Deciding he had been delayed we sit outside in the sunshine waiting patiently. I phoned him when he hadn't appeared after a few minutes ... only to be told that we had not booked the taxi for our return journey! Of course, I had ... I always book the two journeys together. Anyway, he was unavailable and we would have to make our own way back home. I asked one of the local taxi drivers for a price, and was told the price would be £100!!! As a last resort, I telephoned a friend in Birmingham who was able to come out to the airport and bring us home. Luckily, he was more than happy to accept the fee we would have been paying our taxi driver. We now have the weekend to recover before we start on the dreaded journey involving all manner of tests and examinations with the involvement of hundreds of miles in the car.

Chapter 4: Sammy – a strange coincidence

Some things in life just cannot be explained. Between us, Alan and I have four children but for one reason or another, we were only in touch with one daughter, Cordelia (always known as Givvi). She had told us that during the previous year she had accidentally bumped into Sammy, on the estate where she lived, when he was making some collections from houses in his truck. Sammy is Alan's number one son! Whilst we were in Thailand, Sammy had turned up at her door with a letter for Alan and asked if she would deliver it for him. She explained that we were away but that she would deliver it as soon as we got home. She did this at the very first opportunity.

Reading the letter, Sammy explained that at the beginning of March he suddenly found that he was unable to sleep and was thinking a lot about his Dad. He became very concerned that should something happen to either of them he would never forgive himself if he had not tried to put things right between the two of them. He had almost forgotten what they had fallen out about, but felt that life was too short to continue like this. He was now a father himself and understood a little more about life. He had obviously matured a great deal since the last time we saw him. He included his phone numbers and address and said that he would very much like to be back in touch with his Dad It is spooky when you think about the timing of all of this ... it would seem Sammy was having all these thoughts at the very time Alan was getting his initial diagnosis on holiday.

A phone call was made to re-establish contact and it was no time at all until Sammy visited on his own to have a good chat with his Dad and put behind them the disagreements of the past. Soon afterwards, we were able to meet his wife Zoe, who like Sammy, had a child from a previous relationship, and she and Sam had a little girl together. Zoe was also pregnant again with her third child.

Chapter 5: From bad to worse ...

Our first appointment on this journey was with Mr. D at The Priory in Birmingham during the evening of Tuesday 12th April. He took a brief history of what had been happening to Alan and raised his eyebrows at the fact that symptoms had been reported to our GP over a period of almost 6 years without any sort of test or examination taking place. He examined Alan and confirmed without doubt the diagnosis given to us in Phuket. He told us *"if this hasn't got to the bones, then we are laughing – so to speak"* ... words which have stayed with us ever since. We asked if he would consider transferring Alan to his NHS list and luckily, he agreed. Alan would need to have urgent tests carried out including bloods, urine, biopsies, MRI and full body bone scans. He asked that I text him the next morning to remind him to instigate these tests through his secretary at the Queen Elizabeth Hospital. Twenty minutes consultation – £200 – thank you and good night!

During the following weeks, all the tests were carried out. The biopsies were done first and turned out to be the most traumatic of all those to be done. Blood and urine samples were taken first at this appointment. Although the biopsy procedure injects local anaesthetic into the prostate before the samples are taken, it became apparent during the taking of the biopsies that this had been ineffective in view of the tumour's size and density. With each sample that was taken, Alan suffered excruciating pain. At one point the nurse who was watching the screen, which followed the biopsy tool, suddenly told the doctor to stop and not attempt to take another sample. The biopsy needle could not puncture the prostate as it was so hard, and the needle was actually bending. Of course, had this needle broken then we would have been in all sorts of trouble. In view of this situation, the doctor felt unable to attempt to take any further biopsy samples ... the normal number would be a dozen – but he had only managed to get eight. Eight will have to do! Alan could not get out of the place quick enough ... he was in pain and felt dreadful.

The MRI scan and the full body bone scan had been arranged for the same day and would involve being out for a full day! Again, we made our way to the Queen Elizabeth Hospital and our first call was to the Imaging Department for an MRI scan. This process took in excess of an hour. Some way into the scan Alan's back had become most painful and although he reported this to the technicians they told him there was only a few more minutes to go, stay still and it would all be over soon. Half an hour later, they had to help him off the table as he was totally unable to move. He came out of there in a far worse state than he had gone in!

Next port of call was to the Nuclear Medicine Department where Alan was to be injected with a small amount of radioactive liquid, which would take approximately two hours for complete body circulation. In the meantime, we could go and have lunch and a walk outside in the beautiful sunshine. We were not the only ones enjoying the sunshine and having a smoke outside that day. There were half a dozen 'squaddies' from the Military Ward sitting outside in their wheelchairs laughing and joking together. We became aware of helicopters overhead and certain restrictions being placed on vehicles turning up at the front of the hospital. Bollards were being put into place to stop anyone parking. This all continued for about half an hour. Quite suddenly, an entourage of very smart cars arrived and parked. Prime Minister David Cameron gushed across the paved area and into the hospital on one of his visits to the Military Unit. He did whatever it is that he does on these occasions and was gone again within the hour! I had the undistinguished privilege of talking to his bodyguard in the queue for coffee!

At the prescribed time, Alan and I made our way back to the Nuclear Medicine Department where the full body bone scan was to take place. This scanner seemed to be a little more comfortable than the MRI table and within minutes Alan had fallen asleep. I sat in the room with him whilst the machine did its business. There were two monitors hanging from the ceiling which started to show images. I asked the technician what it was that I was seeing and it was explained that one was the front view of the progressing scan, the other being the view from the back. I sat watching intently as the images grew on both screens. Little white spots starting appearing at various places as the scan continued but it was when it reached the pelvic area that I knew we had severe problems. Alan's hipbones were lighting up like a Christmas tree. The spots on his head, chest, and ribs were nowhere near as dense as these. I decided to keep this information to myself as I considered Alan already had enough on his plate. At the end of the scan, we had to wake Alan and get him off the bed. By this time, we were both more than ready to make our way home.

A letter arrived in the post to advise us of an appointment on 19th May when we would be given all the results and the plan of action on treatment. Almost three weeks to wait ... that's a long time to wait when you are living in turmoil.

During the many hours we spent alone on the beach in Phuket, we had talked about what had happened during the past few years in respect of symptoms, which we had reported to our GP over a period of some five years, or more. He had never conducted a single test or carried out an examination. He had been very dismissive at times. Rightly or wrongly, we concluded that had he done his job properly, a diagnosis of cancer would have been given many years previously. Our confidence and trust in the man had disappeared. We decided that on our return home we would change to another doctor.

Having seen the most senior partner of the practice on our return home, we were due to see him again a week later. We arrived at the surgery only to be told that he was on holiday and our original GP was covering for him. It will be of no surprise that Alan refused point blank to see him, and I arranged an appointment with a new doctor to the surgery and we would travel to the other location to see him. This is how we first met Doc M. He is young, Irish, and quite a character. The first thing he did was to get Alan on the bed and examine him from top to toe. This type of examination had not taken place during all of the nine years we had been with the practice. Hearing of Alan's continuing pain he asked if he had been taking the prescribed morphine. Alan told him 'no'. *"Then it's your own fault that you're in pain!"* That was all it took for Alan to form a bond with this young doctor and admire his forthrightness. Now that he had been told exactly what was to happen with his medications, Alan was totally accepting of the situation.

19th May, 2012 – the day of the long awaited appointment to get all the test results was finally upon us. We parked up our car at a friend's house not far from the hospital and we were given a lift to the door ... and our friend would park up and wait for us. (You may recall that in Thailand after just 20 minutes we had been told that this cancer was inoperable and 'old'). By this time, Alan's pain was not easing particularly and he had to use a stick for walking. We were a little upset not to be seeing Mr. D himself on this occasion – rather Alan's notes had been passed on to one of his registrars. We were not totally prepared for what we heard. In laymen's terms, it was confirmed that this was, most definitely, Prostate Cancer ... but not only that, the cancer was at the most advanced stage, aggressive, had spread via the lymph system to bone sites all over Alan's body, it was not curable ... it was terminal. I think that final word is the only one Alan remembers from the whole appointment. Chemotherapy and radiotherapy were considered inappropriate in Alan's case, and therefore, the route to be taken was that of hormone therapy. By now, Alan had his head bowed and leaning on the top of his walking stick. I was not completely sure how much more bad news he could take. The registrar gave us some facts and figures relating to the test, all of which were worse than the results we had in Thailand from tests carried out just 6 weeks before the current tests. I felt we needed to ask the most obvious question ... the reply to which was 18-24 months. We were given a prescription to collect from the pharmacy and an appointment with a specialist nurse two weeks later. We were told there were leaflets available in a nearby room and we could help ourselves. Thank you and goodbye!

Well, I think if there had been any feathers floating around, they would easily have knocked us both over. *This just has to be the worst day we have ever experienced.* As we walked away from the door, I asked Alan if he had understood the same as I had about what we had just been told. Yes, we agreed. We had just been told that Alan had 18-24 months left to live. We were devastated by the news we had been given in Phuket ... but this had moved things to a whole different level and we were utterly numb. I think it is outrageous that people can be given this sort of news and then ferried out of the door as the doctor is so busy, without someone waiting outside, knowing what news you have just received and to pick up the pieces of the shattered lives which have just been created. We collected the prescription from the hospital pharmacy and made our way back to the car. The ride back to our friend's house was silent. Our friend, who was also a cancer sufferer, no doubt realized how serious this now was. Back at the house, I dissolved into tears as I related the details to our friend's wife. There were lots of hugs and tears, but nothing was going to make any of this easier. We had a quick cup of tea ... that's all ... we needed to get home. Driving is never a great idea when you are upset but it is something I am beginning to get used to by this point.

The following day Alan started on his hormone treatment, which, just for now, meant taking only one tablet a day - Casodex. These tablets apparently will prepare the body and the cancer for the 'main event'. Our heads are reeling with things that need to be done and the first one Alan wants to tackle is the updating of our wills and the gifts to be left for others. I draft and re-draft the list until he is completely happy with things and produce the final article - only for him to change his mind yet again forcing me back to the drawing board! Eventually the job was done.

In an attempt to plan ahead, we had talked about buying a wheelchair and walking frame. We had no idea the need would be so soon. The wheelchair was delivered on 26th May and it will have to be put into service immediately as Alan is no longer capable of walking even short distances.

As the days and weeks progressed Alan was becoming increasingly 'poorly' – he could not sit comfortably and was certainly not comfortable in bed anymore. Doc M would call in often and also asked the local MacMillan nurse to become involved. Jenny is a lovely lady and very concerned about Alan's comfort and pain issues. He explained his objections to the amount and regularity of the prescribed painkillers, but once more it was all explained to him – even when the pain has gone you must continue with all the medication to keep your body pain free. Finally, this was accepted and understood ... but not without a fight. Mac nurse Jenny was able to source a special cushion for Alan to use on his chair, which made life far more comfortable. She then suggested a mattress of the same composition may be very useful. Within a couple of days the mattress was delivered and, although it was only a single size, I placed it in the middle of the king sized bed. Alan could not believe the improvement in his pain levels in bed! It was like magic. I think he thought he was sleeping on a cloud. The only downside of course, was its size and the fact that he kept rolling off the edge of it. We had a chat with the Mac nurse and explained that we didn't want to appear ungrateful, but was there any way this mattress could be exchanged for a double sized one ... she didn't think there was such a thing as a king size! Within another couple of days, the replacement mattress arrived and since then comfort in bed has not been a problem. It has made the bed that little bit higher meaning that Alan now has to clamber to get in! Well, you can't have everything, can you?

Doc M, during one of his visits, wanted to talk about 'end of life' and wanted Alan to consider where he would like to be on his death and it was suggested that we chat about this together, having been told the options, and let him know the next time we saw him. This is certainly not the type of conversation you relish but there was no doubt in Doc M's mind that Alan's cancer was progressing and he was in decline and these decisions, difficult though they were, had to be dealt with now rather than later. Without prompting, he also brought us a form for the fast track application of Disability Living Allowance based on the doctor's opinion that the patient had less than 6 months to live. Another part of this conversation had to do with 'resuscitate or not' in an emergency situation. Huge decisions which were not taken lightly. Alan decided that he would prefer not to be resuscitated based on the information we had about the disease, and we were duly given a completed form which should be kept in the house and given to any paramedic or doctor who attended here in an emergency situation. Really scary stuff. Once all these delicate issues had been dealt with we felt able to relax a little knowing it was an area of conversation we would not need to make a return visit.

In total contrast to the conversations with the medics, Alan's friends could only make black jokes about the whole situation. A friend in South Africa wanted to lay claim to our car when Alan died and would we be kind enough not to put too many miles on the clock! Another would be quite happy to take possession of Alan's favourite chair in the conservatory!! To be honest, it is this type of humour that has kept us going through all the tough times! Many people can't cope with it ... but it does Alan good to have this type of banter with his friends!

The time was upon us for our first visit to the specialist nurse at the QE (8th June) who was to administer the main part of the hormone therapy. It is called Zoladex and is in the form of a pellet to be implanted into the flesh on Alan's stomach. (I would liken these implants, and their application, to the chips currently implanted into pets for identification purposes!! Only difference is the location!) Zoladex is a slow release drug that would last just four weeks. At the end of this time period, the second implant would be administered but this would be three times the dose and would remain active for 12 weeks. The larger version would then form the main part of the continuing treatment for the foreseeable future. At the end of 28 days, the initial tablets would cease.

This nurse was able to tell us some of the finer points of the test results and also tell us things we were not made aware of at the 19th May appointment. In medical terms, the stage of Alan's cancer was at Stage IV – the most advanced stage, and thought to be aggressive. His PSA had risen to 310 (normal range is 0-4!). His Alkaline Phosphatase result was on the rise and at the outer 'norm' limit of 130. The cancer was classified as T4N2M1 meaning a Stage IV cancer, with the involvement of 2 lymph nodes, and which had spread to the bones, called metastasis, in five separate sites ... skull, ribs, spine, pelvis and right hip. The Gleason score was (5+4)=9 (the highest score being 10) - this relates to the positive cancer cells and their type - these results coming from the biopsy samples taken. The extra piece of information, which we had not previously been told, was that the tumour was already making in-roads to the rectal wall. This was just about the worst diagnosis anyone with Prostate Cancer could possibly have. Again, we were plunged into the depths of despair - but at last, we felt we had the full story and knew exactly what we were dealing with.

I don't think I have ever survived on so little sleep as I did through the summer months of 2011! All I can tell you is that when the sun rises before 4.30am it is absolutely beautiful to watch ... not that most people would choose to be up at that time. This wasn't my choice either, but I was having extreme difficulty getting my head around what was happening to us and there were numerous mornings when I would be pacing around the garden at stupid o'clock. I would do this rather than watching the monotony of overnight shopping channels on the TV, whilst trying to come to terms with all the dreadful news and prospects that had been thrown at us. Alan, by contrast, and being new to all the painkilling medications seemed able to sleep like a baby most of the time. The drugs just knocked him out, I think. Maybe that was the best thing for him.

It was during this time that my research into the disease began in earnest ... I was like a sponge, soaking up all the information I could from books, leaflets, the internet, and support groups that I had now joined. Knowledge is power and gives you a greater understanding of the problems, options and the solutions. I would never again allow myself to be present at one of Alan's consultations without knowing what would be the most useful and sensible questions to ask.

Chapter 6: "Bucket Party"? - What *is* that?

Our friends and family are spread far and wide. Everyone is concerned about Alan's health and would like to visit. Rather than having a continual dribble of visitors, Alan and I decided that the best plan of action was to throw a party in the garden and invite everyone along. This would be his (Kick the) 'Bucket Party' – he would rather enjoy his friends' company in this life rather than miss all the drinks at his wake!! We decided to put all our plans into action and have a thoroughly good day ... we decided it would take place on 6th August.

On 7th July, Alan's second Zoladex implant was due - slow release will last for 12 weeks. Doc M has decided that for the time being he will administer these at home rather than sending Alan to the QE at Birmingham which only causes distress and discomfort. In an effort to make this more of a social occasion tea and cakes are on offer! We are not sure Doc M has carried out many of these implants before, but he will certainly be getting more practice as the months go by!! Alan went and lay on my bed for the implant to be done. Suddenly I can hear laughter and urgent calls for tissues! Alan is bleeding - everywhere ... the bed, the carpet, but more particularly his clean t-shirt! You would have thought he had been shot! The laughter continued as they both returned to the conservatory. It's nice to have a doctor with a warped sense of humour!! We have affectionately christened our new Doc M "Buddha Doc" as there is such a striking resemblance to a four faced Buddha head that we have!! Truly terms of endearment!

The following week Doc M returns to take blood samples in readiness for the forthcoming appointment with the consultant Oncologist at the QE, Professor J. This will be the first set of results since the treatment started and there is no doubt that we are both very concerned about what the results might reveal. Luckily, we are given permission to phone Doc M's secretary a couple of days later to get the results so that we are prepared with the knowledge before attending the appointment.

15th July: Today is our wedding anniversary - 17 years. Now I know neither of us has been out to the shops ... so no cards. I sent a lovely e-card for Alan to have this morning. He looked at it and swore ... profusely! Yes, of course he had forgotten! Five minutes later, he emerges from the bedroom ... card in hand! How does that work then? It's pink, has roses on, says 'Wife' on the front. Inside - Happy birthday, with the word birthday crossed out, but nothing to replace it! Well, we roared ... couldn't make it up, could you? Seems he couldn't make up his mind between two cards last birthday and had bought both! It's the thought that counts!

19th July: Today turned out to be one for a bit of a celebration. *PSA down from 310 to 8.1* - absolutely sensational! The treatment is working! Yippee! Alan says that he can now feel that the tumour is shrinking - certain internal pressures have eased.

On the specified day, we made our way to the QE in Birmingham. Professor J's clinic was running particularly late and Alan and I sat for the best part of two hours in the waiting room. Alan's pain was getting out of control to the point that I asked the staff if they had any pain relief that he could be given. Of course, there was nothing they could do and eventually we got to meet Professor J. He was delighted with the blood results. He showed us the MRI scan and in particular the area of the right hip joint which was completed engulfed by the secondary cancer. It was his opinion that Alan could be receptive to hormone therapy for many years and probably had a life expectancy of some 6-8 years. He suggests that Alan's cancer has been in progress for several years and therefore is not as aggressive as we had been led to believe, and sees no reason why, after such an excellent initial response to hormone therapy, Alan should not respond to treatment longer than we were at first advised. After this meeting we have absolutely no idea what to expect! Our whole world is turned upside down, yet again.

He offered Alan a place on the Stampede Trial where he commented that Alan would be put on a randomly selected arm of the trial and would not know until chosen which drug treatment would be given. He told us that as part of the trial, Alan would be monitored far more closely than during regular appointments for the condition. This actually sounded quite unfair to us. Why couldn't everyone be monitored with the same care? We said we would rather go away and think about this option. In all honesty, we had been made aware of Stampede and had already decided against it in view of the fact that Alan did not want to be a guinea pig during the last two years of his life. In view of Professor J's ideas, should we now be reconsidering this route if Alan had so much longer to live? But whom do you believe? Did we have two or eight years left? There is a big difference in these time frames and it's the sort of information that plays havoc with your mind. We now have absolutely no idea how long we have.

During conversations with Doc M and Mac nurse Jenny as to the likelihood of the correct prognosis, taking into account the current state of Alan's health, it was generally accepted that we were looking at something closer to the two years rather than the eight. Should Alan get passed the two year marker, then perhaps we should accept any time beyond that as a bonus.

As we had received such confusing information from the team at the QE and the total inconvenience of having to travel to such a difficult location for appointments, we asked Doc M to refer us to more local consultants who could be seen at either Kidderminster or even more locally. The last visit to the QE had become a 'day trip' of pain, distress and delays that we find unacceptable and would prefer not to have to endure something like that again. Referrals were duly sent to more local consultants.

Saturday 6th August, 2011: Friends rallied round in helping get everything ready for the 'Bucket Party'. There were marquees and tents to be erected – food to prepare – furniture to be moved – bunting to get up – b'b'q to prepare - the day was very busy!! And somehow we had to get power from the bungalow to the tents! Friends started to arrive early in the afternoon and some were pitching tents in the garden ready for their overnight stay. There was an array of decorated buckets given to Alan as gifts – plastic squeaking chickens – buckets decorated in 'Kiss' style – plastic sheep (don't ask!) and all manner of joke items brought along. As a release of all the recent tensions, I was totally inebriated by about 4 o'clock to the amusement of Doc M when he called in for a drink!!!

One of our best jokes in preparation for the day had been sending letters to four of our friends informing them that they had been nominated to take part in the Queen's Diamond Jubilee 'Torch Relay'. The typed letters looked genuine enough, courtesy of certain computer programs!! They would be required to attend an interview at a hotel in their locality where hopefully, they would qualify for the relay. As a test of loyalty, these appointments would take place on 6th August. Now they would have the dilemma of should they come to see Alan at his party and give up the chance of a lifetime … or be totally selfish and attend the interview. We never expected to fool all of them … and we didn't! Just one of our friends fell for this - hook, line and sinker! Generosity of heart made him come to the party. Alan had constructed a 'Jubilee torch' and I had rescued the Union Jack flag, which had been replaced that very morning from the garden flagpole. It was with great ceremony that Alan presented our friend with the lit torch and wrapped the flag over his shoulders and sent him on his way running around the garden!! He was cheered all the way by the appreciative crowd who congratulated him on taking this cruel joke so well. It's something none of us will ever forget … and he has a torch and flag to remember it!!

The highlight of the afternoon was totally unplanned and unexpected. To the delight of everyone present, the Red Arrows display team flew directly over the top of us at low level. The noise was a bit of a shock! Alan commented something like "right on time!" as if this was all pre-arranged. In fact, someone even asked him how much it had cost to organize the display!! You have to be joking!! Suspect it would be telephone numbers possibly only affordable by huge lottery winners – so that rules us out!

In all we had about 50 people come and go during the day, including Doc M … some calling in for an hour or so … others for the duration. The weather was cruel so the chiminea was commissioned into the marquee and quickly lit in order to get a bit of heat going!! It promptly smoked everyone into a choking fit!! We had prepared a huge curry to serve in the evening and it was very much appreciated as the weather was really chilly by this time. The final event of the evening was the release of 'wish lanterns'. Now living so close to the top of a hill like this, you would think that a nice gust of wind would lift these lanterns up above the level of the summit and disappear into the distance, wouldn't you? Absolutely no chance!! The lanterns briefly ascended but were then swept downwards in the direction of the valley below ... and the village hall car park opposite in particular! Filled with cars owned by locals attending the local bingo session, suddenly the panic set in as lanterns started to disappear in amongst the cars, and the sprinters in our midst shot off in an attempt to save the cars and the village hall roof!

By now it was really too chilly to stay outside and everyone started to leave or make preparations for sleeping over. We had folks sleeping in all the beds, in the conservatory, three tents in the garden, and four friends had decided to stay in the marquee for the night. We had given them a huge polythene ground sheet that became a skating rink when mixed with the wet shoes coming off the damp grass. One of the ladies slipped, took a heavy tumble - noisily passing wind at the same time, which caused massive hilarity within the marquee, so much so that one of the lads caught an airbed with his cigarette, which instantly deflated. It can't be said that they had a comfortable night and they were trying to get back into the house by about 5am!

The morning sunshine was warm and pleasant as we all sat out on the patio drinking tea and coffee. What a shame the weather couldn't have been this good yesterday! It was then decided to make bacon baps for everyone and the party continued. Later that morning everyone did what he or she could to help with the clearing up process and by lunchtime it was all over bar the shouting. Everyone had had a memorable and enjoyable weekend and I think it had done the power of good to lift Alan's spirits. Eventually there were just four of us remaining and we were able to sit down and reflect on the weekend and how much fun it had been. It was decided that if Alan made it through the next 12 months, we would do it all again!

Chapter 7: Necessary evil

During these summer months, Alan had categorically made up his mind that we would not be going to Phuket in the February of 2012. Not because he didn't think he would be well enough, but because he felt we must make certain alterations within the house that would be needed for our convenience in the future. We have two bathrooms in the bungalow ... a family bathroom with a full sized bath, and a shower en-suite off the main bedroom. We had installed an over-bath shower in the past, as neither of us liked to take a bath and it had been used for its correct function just once in nine years! Its only other use had been for washing duvets or curtains! His plan was to rip out the bath and replace it with a walk in shower unit big enough to have a second person present when help was needed. The en-suite shower room had the smallest shower cubicle imaginable and a little imagination was going to be needed to make this more user friendly.

In view of Alan's illness, we approached the local council as we knew grants were available if bathrooms needed to be converted for a disabled person - which was now how Alan was officially classified. However, once a financial assessment was made it was obvious that we qualified for absolutely nothing! They could offer us a loan, but their interest in the property would need to be logged with the Land Registry in the form of a Land Charge so that in the event of Alan's death, they would have first access to his estate to recoup their outlay! Not a chance, pal! We would somehow fund the alterations ourselves. We did enquire through the British Legion and Alan's old Regiment as each have funds available for such needs ... but we were told that if the local council was unable to help us on financial grounds, then they too would be unable to help us. We were disappointed but as with everything else in our lives ... we'll do it alone. The Council occupational therapist, although totally unable to help us on a financial level, would very much like to help with the planning of the new bathroom and the choice of fitments! You really think so? What a cheek! She was sent away with a flea in her ear!

To be honest, I was in my element with this sort of challenge. I scoured the internet specialist outlets and after weeks of having samples sent, looking at colour schemes, I had come up with the plan for both bathrooms. I knew how much everything was going to cost to source ... all we needed to do was find a tradesman who would do justice with our plan. We attempted to get quotes from four local firms, three responded, but only two turned up to assess the work involved and give us a quote. Obstacles and regulations were pointed out to us, which made us alter our choice of tiles and lighting, but then we had to sit and wait for the quotes to arrive. They were a bit of a shock! One of the contractors had a local web page listing where previous customers had been able to leave comments. They were all very favourable and we decided to go with that choice. The fact that he had produced the cheaper quote was a bonus!

Stuart was a total lunatic ... told terrible jokes ... couldn't sing ... and could get through as many cakes as you could put in front of him! He started work on the main bathroom on 1st September. He worked alone, didn't cut corners, and found problems which needed to be rectified ... made a mess every day but cleared up before he went home and by 30th September we had a totally brand new bathroom which would not have looked out of place in any 5* hotel. Black and beige with an Art Deco feel about it. We were absolutely delighted with the result.

Stuart knew that we couldn't afford to have the second bathroom done immediately and we arranged with him to come back during his 'quiet' time – shortly after Christmas.

Although we had planned this work in what we thought was plenty of time, it so happened that Alan's deterioration by this time was total justification for getting it done. All that was needed was a stool for him to sit on as, not only was he having trouble standing for any length of time, he was becoming breathless. It was wonderful to be able to have a shower without your backside touching all the sides as you turn around! This shower cubicle is huge!

Whilst work on the bathroom was in progress, Alan had another blood test. His PSA had dropped even more down to 0.6 but his Alk Phos (ALP) figure had remained high at 130. His Testosterone level had dropped out of sight at less than 0.1. All in all we have to be delighted with these results. So on 21st September we had Alan's first appointment with the new consultant Urologist at the Cottage Hospital, having moved hospitals to be closer to home. Mr. S is more than happy with progress and suggests Alan's next appointment should be in three months, and to repeat blood tests before that date (especially the ALP). We discussed the hot flushes that Alan was suffering - occurring many times each hour and so severe you would think he had been in a sauna as the sweat drips off him. The Urologist agrees that the drug Cyprostat, which had been recommended to me, may be the solution to this problem and immediately starts Alan on a course of tablets. On 29th September it was time for another implant which Doc M administered at home – no blood loss this time!

Chapter 8: Complications set in

When Oncologists look at the blood results of PCa patients, one of their main concerns is the PSA result, as it is the best indicator as to whether treatment is working. They calculate how quickly the number doubles and this gives them an appreciation of how quickly the cancer may be advancing or spreading. It doesn't matter how big the PSA number is at the start of the process. Obviously the shorter the time it takes to double up, the worse the problem.

Alan's blood results in the middle of October were very disappointing. His PSA figure had not doubled … it had trebled in just four weeks. All sorts of warning lights are flashing in my head. Nothing will happen at this stage and we will have to wait another month before the next blood test is done. We would be seeing the new Oncologist then and we would learn more about what was happening.

During my research into the progress of this disease, I had learned much about courses of chemotherapy and radiotherapy. Alan and I had talked at length about the "what if's" we may need to face. We talked at length with friends who had experience within their circles of these types of treatments and also sought 'off the record' medical opinions from those with whom we were in contact. Chemotherapy would be administered over a period of several months and at worst the patient is totally debilitated between treatments and their reactions could include vomiting, sickness, tiredness, mood swings and lack of appetite. However, there are other patients who sail through the whole experience with hardly a problem, but in all honesty, how often do you hear about or experience this type of patient? In general terms the consensus of opinion was the same as we had formed for ourselves … this line of treatment is unlikely to be 'a walk in the park' and best avoided.

So then we considered all the pro's and con's in relation to a course of radiotherapy. In view of the position of the prostate gland the possibility of complications relating to the treatment are pretty well guaranteed at one level or another. These could present themselves as something quite mild, such as occasional incontinence, or at worst could result in permanent and total double incontinence. Was Alan prepared to take these risks? The usual course of treatment would be carried out on every weekday for a period of 7 weeks. Our nearest radiotherapy unit is some 50 miles away and we talked through how difficult and tiring this regime would be ... and how costly it would be for the 100 mile round trip five times a week. Alan was no longer driving so the transport responsibility would fall on my shoulders and, quite honestly, I didn't know if I had the capability or stamina to do this journey in busy commute traffic for the length of time involved. We could envisage a period of time when life would involve sleeping and travelling ... and little else.

Of course it was possible Alan may need to undergo both treatment regimes thus consuming some 11 precious months of whatever time we had left together. And for what gain? Maybe three months would be added to his expected life span was the figure given to us. Not enough! We were convinced that someone reaching an end of life situation probably doesn't have a very desirable final three months, anyway!! I have always been a 'numbers' person and the maths of this equation just didn't add up. Why on earth would a person put himself through this torture, for that length of time, for so little gain? No ... this option was clearly not for us! We talked for hours on the subject and came to the conclusion that we would by far prefer to choose 'quality' over and above 'quantity'. We could do all sorts of things during those 11 months to make more memories together, providing Alan was generally well enough to enjoy the experiences. So that was it. We had made up our minds.

More bloods were taken from Alan just prior to the Onco appointment in November. Our immediate impression of our new oncologist in Kidderminster was not great. It would appear that you are a file, not a human being!! Yet again the numbers were not good. The PSA figure had doubled in just four weeks and his Alk Phos figure had also increased. The Alkaline Phosphatase results give the medics an indicator as to whether the bone lesions are increasing. It would appear from these results that Alan was no longer responding well to the hormone therapy. Oncologists have the power to throw all the tools in the box at a patient without thought – and most patients just accept as gospel what they say is going to happen. Not us, I'm afraid. Somewhat surprised, he had to accept that Alan was not prepared to undergo the type of treatment he would like to put in place for him. He suggested that we had another talk about it at the next appointment. However, he did suggest that Alan should accept a monthly infusion, which would help repair and strengthen his bones against the attack of the metastasis. There were very few side effects to this particular treatment, most of which were inoffensive, and, therefore, Alan was prepared to accept this. It was also suggested that in view of the crippling pain being experienced in his coccyx that Alan should undergo a one-off blast of palliative radiotherapy specifically pinpointing the coccyx and which would help alleviate the pain for several months … hopefully. Alan agreed to try this. The Onco would make the necessary arrangements.

Five days later we returned to Kidderminster hospital and made our way to the chemo unit, which is where the infusions would take place. The nursing staff were lovely and greeted us in a very friendly manner. The infusion process and possible side effects were fully explained to us. It's a process that takes about half an hour from start to finish and would be carried out every four weeks. There were not a specific number of treatments … it would just continue forever! A blood test would be required prior to every treatment, carried out just long enough before the infusion that the results were available to the nurses. It was suggested that we should organize the blood tests with Doc M rather than having to make an extra journey to the unit just for these tests. Alan's tiredness has been increasing and all the excitement and travel during the previous couple of weeks have only added to this!

Within a couple of days we were heading for Wolverhampton to the Radiotherapy Department. This first visit covered all the paperwork involved and the technical issues of 'mapping' where the beams were to be aimed, and for Alan to have a minute tattoo pinpointing the actual spot that could then easily be lined up with the equipment. Long journey in heavy traffic ... short appointment followed by even heavier traffic during the journey home. A week later we were on our way back to Wolverhampton for the actual treatment. Again it was a wearying journey to spend just 15 minutes in the hospital before hitting the road yet again. I immediately knew that I would have been totally incapable of making this journey every weekday for a period of 7 weeks!! Couldn't even contemplate it! But for now, there were no more journeys to think about and we are hoping that this one blast will help Alan with his pain levels. Apparently it could take a little while for the effects to 'kick in'.

Chatting to Doc M about the need for regular blood tests, he suggests that arrangements are made with the district nurses to call at the house on a four weekly basis in order that these samples can be taken. This seems a very simple solution so I made a phone call to the senior district nurse and made a year's worth of appointments. My next move was to ask the local surgery for a supply of 'blood' envelopes upon which I could write all the basic details required. This would save the nurse a bit of time on each visit. I just need to be organized! I have lists and calendars for everything!!

Before we know it the scheduled blood test date is upon us. The district nurse duly arrives to do the business. We are hoping for, but not expecting, an improvement in the results. We should have had more faith! The PSA and ALP results have both dropped – which is extremely good news. Alan's PSA is down to 2.5 and his ALP down to 58. As we enter Christmas week we return to the Millbrook Suite (official name of the chemo unit) at Kidderminster Hospital where Alan undergoes his second bone infusion. All goes well but it would seem that this treatment does add to his tiredness. Just a couple of days later Doc M visits us at home to administer the hormone implant. This done we can now concentrate on Christmas.

We have absolutely no idea whether or not this will be the last Christmas we will have together. Alan has never liked Christmas – doesn't want decorations put up – would rather not have to think about presents – and just wants to spend the day quietly on our own. However, this year he has insisted on buying a new tree and decorations. He wants everything to be special and rather than spending the day on our own he invited our Telford friends to come and spend the day with us. We have a turkey, which may fit in the oven … and all the trimmings.

25th December – Christmas Day: Our friends duly arrived and we exchanged gifts. Unfortunately Alan is not feeling great but manages to enjoy the day. The dinner was delicious, but you wouldn't have thought so seeing Alan's plate. He made a valiant effort at the meal, but really was not feeling well at all and by mid-evening decided that the best place for him would be in bed.

26th December - Boxing Day - Alan's 63rd Birthday: As the day turns out, it's probably his worst birthday on record. I feel upset inside as I have no idea whether this is likely to be his last birthday and he has to spend it in bed. He is the colour of calico and vomiting on a regular basis. Eventually, I place a call to the 'out-of-hours' service and request a doctor's visit. Giv and Perce have always celebrated Christmas and Alan's birthday together by spending the day with us. They arrived armed with presents and cards. There was nothing we could do about the day. I was backwards and forward to the bedroom, cleaning up vomit and generally just making sure that Alan was comfortable. The on-call doctor visited and felt this was a local bug and to make sure Alan was kept warm and well hydrated. Giv and Perce stayed until well into the evening in the hopes that they would be able to spend some time with him. I encouraged Alan to come up to the lounge if only for a few minutes to see them. Big mistake … big, big mistake!! He managed to get to the lounge in his dressing gown and slippers, sat down and was promptly sick all over the floor! Oh dear … back to bed. By the time I had him settled and comfy again, Giv was already mopping up and cleaning the carpet. Oh, what a wonderful day we've all had!!! It was at this point that Giv realized just how poorly Alan was … a fact that had not been readily accepted prior to this incident. She now vows to herself that she will do everything in her power to visit him at least once a week, as the penny drops that he may not be with us very much longer. He really is very poorly just now.

This gastric episode is akin to the Norovirus and Alan has to have a doctor out twice more during the next 5 days in an effort to help him get well. Not a great end to a year which started without a care in the world, and which ends up with Alan being sick and in bed following a very traumatic and life changing 10 months.

Chapter 9: When the going gets tough in 2012

1st January: Alan's very nasty gastric episode is over for now. He feels much better but is very weak and his weight has dropped to 12st. 11lbs – almost unheard of since we have known each other. So today he is able to open his birthday cards and presents at last. Such a shame it couldn't be the special celebration we had planned for Boxing Day.

9th January: Stuart arrives to make a start on the en-suite. By the end of the day the tiny room is totally gutted, dust and rubbish everywhere ... but guess what? I don't really care. Very soon we will have two lovely bathrooms. To make financial savings we have decided to use the same coloured wall and floor tiles as there would be considerably less wastage. I have jiggled the layout so that we are able to get another huge shower cubicle installed, which could also be used by two people if Alan needed help showering. The colour scheme is going to be somewhat different from the first Art Deco-type styling ... I have gone for scarlet to create "The Tart's Bathroom". I've never in my life had the chance to design a bathroom to my own specification without thought for what others may think or like. Alan didn't want to interfere with this one and told me 'just get on with it'! I had sourced a scarlet and black marble effect shower tray ... no one, but no-one has ever seen anything like it before! I settled on a counter-top frosted red glass basin with a matching waterfall tap. I did have trouble sourcing the base cupboard unit as the size was so unusual ... but a flash of genius led me to look at over-wardrobe bedroom cabinets, which happened to be the exact width required. Just buy a set of legs to go on it and, hey presto, correct width and height! Sorted! The doors are a dirty pinkish red and it will look fabulous.

The wall mirror was very difficult to source. I had seen the design I wanted, but when I contacted the retailer they were out of stock and not expecting any more. However, he felt he could get one made in the same design for the old advertised price. The first attempt he made at this manufacture was a total disaster - so after waiting many weeks, I was still without a mirror as I had flatly refused to accept what I had been sent. I ended up having to draw the design for the manufacturer, putting precise measurements and angles onto the design for them to follow. Not exactly rocket science and they should have been totally capable of this themselves. When the second mirror arrived it was absolutely spot on, thank goodness! With everything he needed to hand, Stuart was able to continue his work without interruption ... up until the day he decided that we were going to run out of wall tiles and sent me off to Stourbridge to collect the deficit! The feature tiles for the en-suite are red/black mottled mosaic bordered in black. Everything was so unusual; in my mind's eye I just knew it was going to be stunning.

16th January: This was going to be quite a big day for us as Alan had an appointment with the oncologist following his Zometa infusion. In view of the last two good PSA results it was decided to delay any further chat about chemo or radiotherapy. I asked if it would be possible for Alan to be put onto a new drug should the need arise. This was the drug Abiraterone, which had been used successfully on the 'Lockerbie Bomber' giving him an extra two or three years over and above his predicted life expectancy. This drug would normally only be given after failed chemotherapy ... even if that only amounted to one session. The answer came back as a 'no' as without the chemo aspect, funding would not be made available. However, the licensing details of this particular drug are due to be changed during the summer of 2013, removing the need for chemo, and, therefore, it could possibly be made available to Alan at some time in the future. So it was not all bad news. The Onco decided he would like to see Alan again in a month's time to see how things were going. The thought of repeating the MRI and full body bone scans was not discussed in view of the more positive blood results.

By the **3rd February** Stuart has completed his magic in the en-suite. "The Tart's Bathroom" looks spectacular and it becomes very obvious that the best use of space has been achieved. I'm thrilled to bits and Alan has to agree that it is stunning!

We had a quiet celebration for my birthday on the 5th and at the end of the day ended up with a Chinese takeaway. My goodness, we really know how to push the boat out!

Stuart was back first thing on **6th February** – now it's the kitchen's turn for a bit of a makeover. The plan is new wall tiles, worktop, sink and cooker. The cupboards are all still good and so is the floor. Let battle commence. Again, everything has been sourced at the best possible prices and we can leave Stuart to get on with things. The job is only going to take a few days, so although inconvenient - it won't take long.

By **13th February** all the work that we anticipated doing in the house is finished and our pockets are many thousands of pounds lighter! It was a necessary evil and the improvements will stand us in good stead for many years to come. The kitchen also looks beautiful as the new colours have given it a real lift. Yet again I am delighted with Stuart's work.

It was about at this time that Doc M had a new 5th year medical student come to work with him for 3 months before final exams. He is a mentor for students at Keele University. She was a very pleasant young lady called Harriet. Doc M suggested that she should come to the house on her own and talk to Alan and myself about his diagnosis and the treatment received since.

When questions started to be asked as to why Alan had not reported any of the symptoms prior to diagnosis, we found it difficult to answer without knowing whether or not this conversation was covered by 'doctor/patient confidentiality'. Harriet confirmed that this was definitely the case. We were then able to explain to her the circumstances of having been to see our previous GP (within the same practice) on numerous occasions over a period of nearly six years complaining of different symptoms and that nothing had been done about it. We also told her of the terrible attitude this particular GP had with patients and how he would belittle them, be sarcastic at times and even bully on occasions. She listened intently and also commented that

59

she had been asked to sit in with this particular GP and had been horrified by his attitude and lack of diagnostic skills. She had specifically told Doc M never to make her go through the same exercise again. She had found the experience totally embarrassing. Therefore, in a way, she knew that what we were telling her was the truth. She spent about two hours with us that afternoon.

However, unbeknown to us, the burden of this knowledge must have weighed heavily on her inexperienced shoulders and she felt compelled to sit down with Doc M and relate the whole story to him ... including the fact that we were angry, upset, frustrated and felt that this GP had robbed us of many years together in view of the prognosis. We had explained that we would very much like to make a complaint - had wanted to from the start - but didn't want to damage the relationship we had built up with Doc M or jeopardize any future treatment.

On this same day Alan is due another bone infusion and again we have had good results from the bloods taken on 9th February. His PSA is down again to 1.3 and his ALP at its lowest ever number of 48. This will be his last infusion at Kidderminster Hospital as Doc M felt it was appropriate for him to continue to supervise these and in which case they could be carried out at our local Cottage Hospital ... just five miles from home and so convenient, thus making better use of the local facilities. We were quite happy to go along with that thought.

Following on from the infusion, Alan has an appointment with the Onco's Registrar - Alan informed her that chemotherapy would not be considered (which would also exclude him from Abiraterone, the new drug treatment) on the basis that we were looking for quality of life over and above quantity. We asked if it would be possible for all further treatment to be supervised by Doc M at our local community hospital. In view of this request, Alan has been discharged from the oncologist's care and handed over to Doc M who will take total control of all palliative care, plus the supervision of future Zometa infusions and Zoladex implants.

It's a big decision to discharge oneself from the care of a Consultant but as the months have gone by and Alan's relationship with Doc M has grown, he feels far more comfortable to be under his care alone. We have had the impression for several weeks now that Doc M truly wanted to be in sole charge of Alan's care - for whatever reason ... (but our MacMillan nurse told us that Doc M has a very soft spot for us both and really wants to do the very best he can to make life easier for us). Well that's comforting to know.

Chapter 10: Making complaints official

17th February: I have been trying to deal with the anger and frustration I have felt ever since Alan's diagnosis in Phuket. We spent many hours on the beach recalling all the times we had attended our GP when Alan was displaying symptoms we now know to be classic Prostate and/or Prostate Cancer symptoms. During the timescale of 2005 to 2010 we attended the doctor approximately 20 times repeating several different symptoms and yet no tests were initiated or examinations undertaken. Had a simple PSA blood test been carried out in 2005, or even a bit later, then we would not be in this situation now. Alan could have been cancer free had he been caught early enough and suitable for the prostate to have been removed. I cannot keep quiet about this situation any longer as I feel so aggrieved about the negligence and lack of duty of care given by our then GP.

Doc M has been made aware by Harriet that something is bothering me and asked me to go and see him in surgery. I told him of my anger and frustration at being powerless to right the wrongs I felt had been laid upon us. Without hesitation he told me that I must do whatever it took to deal with these feelings as I was going to need to be extremely strong to deal with what laid ahead for us in the future. If this meant making a complaint about another doctor or healthcare worker, then so be it. But I must deal with it.

Therefore, I felt I had been given the green light to deal with things my way. I have raised my concerns about our ex-GP (now forever known as "Dodgy Doc") in a formal complaint to the General Medical Council ... a process, which we understand, can take some considerable time for them to investigate. Hopefully it will be worth the wait. I have also vowed to Alan that whatever the outcome of this complaint, I will accept the matter as dealt with - without any more fretting, worry or heartache. I felt this was a fair request for him to make and promised that I would accept the GMC's decision.

So here we are at the end of the first 12 months dealing with this dreadful disease. It has been a very traumatic time … some very big decisions have been made regarding treatment versus quality of life. We are uncertain as to whether this is a date that should be celebrated … but we decided to mark the date by taking ourselves out for a meal. It was really nice to be able to get out together on our own for something other than hospital appointments. However we are saddened by the fact that on this date we would normally be in our beloved Phuket and this is the first time in 15 years we have been unable to take a holiday. We have now put our trust into the hormone therapy to which Alan has finally responded so well, and Doc M … but as we start our second year dealing with this disease, we do wonder what the future holds for us.

Chapter 11: When life's complications become complicated

March starts with another round of blood tests … the results of which are again really good. PSA is 1.0 and ALP is 58. We attend the Cottage Hospital for Alan's next Zometa infusion that will be supervised by Doc M and would normally be administered by one of the nurses. However, as Harriet was working with him, she was tasked with setting up and controlling the infusion. Harriet is a 5th year student so has quite a bit of experience with cannulas and the like. She carries out the work very confidently. It is also time for Alan's next Zoladex implant but this is something she has never even seen before. After being given a full explanation as to how the applicator works and where the implant is to be deposited, she felt confident that she would like to attempt the administration of the implant. She handled it very well and was actually dancing round the room afterwards when she realized that she hadn't hurt Alan at all and hadn't even drawn blood. Alan is now always very supportive of all the students Doc M has under his care from Keele University. During their stay we do have chance to see them on more than one occasion which is good for them to see the continuity with one patient

Time goes by quickly and before we know it the April blood tests are due. Again the results are very favourable – PSA at 0.6 and ALP at 78. Although the ALP figure is up it is still well within the acceptable scale – the top of which is 130. The next Zometa infusion is carried out by Nurse Tara at the community hospital and she becomes our regular contact for these. So it would appear we have no problems at the moment with the prostate cancer as it seems to be behaving itself. However, it is when we got these results and everyone is pleased with them, Alan comments that he doesn't understand how the results on paper look so good … and yet he continues to feel most unwell. He can't remember the last time he actually felt anything like 'well'. No one has an answer to this … at that time.

Mid April the weather suddenly breaks and spring is here ... or is this summer? The sunshine is wonderful and the temperature is rising daily. Alan wants to get outside and see what little jobs he is capable of doing for himself. On 29th April and after several weeks of feeling generally unwell and even more fatigued, today saw an incident of total breathlessness almost to the point of collapse. I have to say that it frightened him. It happened during a non-active period (not that there has been much activity for months!) when he was taking a gentle stroll back from the garage. Alan had experienced something similar last November, but not to this extreme. Next day, we visited the surgery and Doc M initially treats the episode as a possible chest infection and prescribes antibiotics and steroids. He took more blood samples for some more specific tests to be made.

By the **4th May** there is no improvement in symptoms, and standard blood tests are all OK. I ask the question as to whether this could possibly be a heart problem! Doc M's immediate reaction was 'No', but, just in case, diuretics and angina spray were prescribed. Whilst in the surgery Alan's heart rate is 115 at rest. The plan of action is to have a chest x-ray scheduled (to identify possible metastasis in lungs) and I ask if he will carry out a BNP blood test (as an indicator of a possible heart failure). This test was suggested to me by a friend who is a nurse. X-ray and blood test can be done the following Wednesday when Alan will be at the hospital for his scheduled Zometa infusion. Alan has now deteriorated to a point where he is incapable of any physical activity - even very slow walking is a problem. We have found it necessary to ask the District Nurses to supply a 'monkey pole' which will help Alan pull himself up in bed and be able to move and turn over more easily. This will be delivered within a couple of days. Alan's deterioration has been so quick; it is actually quite frightening as we don't really know what has caused the problem or how it is going to be resolved.

9th May: We attend the Cottage Hospital where blood is taken for the BNP test. This is followed by the Zometa infusion. When that is complete we make our way to the X-ray department for the chest X-ray.

Everything was completed very quickly. There has been a passing thought, which we had discussed with Doc M that the cancer may have spread to the lungs, and if any mets were large enough they would show up on x-ray. It would be several days before we had the X-ray results as they have to be sent to Worcester for analysis. We made our way back home.

Doc M was on the phone before lunchtime - *"looks as if you were right, Cath - there is a heart problem!"* BNP blood test result was 283, which indicates there is a probability of heart failure (accepted 'normal' level is under 100). Alan continued to decline even further during the remainder of the day - more breathless episodes and some chest pains. I put in a request to the surgery for Doc M to make a home visit the following day. *Now we know what this new problem is ... we have a new mountain to climb and conquer!* Suddenly it all becomes very clear why Alan has been feeling so unwell for months on end ... this heart problem has obviously been brewing all that time.

Doc M calls in the next day to carry out re-assessment of chest situation and concludes the chest infection requires more aggressive treatment and that angina symptoms can be dealt with when chest is cleared. Talking about the awaited X-ray results Doc also confirms it is inevitable that because Alan's cancer has already spread and there are confirmed bone mets via the lymph system, there will be mets in many or all other organs. They could be so small as not to be identified on scans/x-rays - but they will be there. No point in worrying then! They're here to stay and until they become a problem in their own right, why even give them a second thought? The monkey pole has been delivered and is now set up in the bedroom. This will make life a whole lot easier for Alan when he's in bed.

We made a follow-up trip to the surgery on 14th May. At rest, Alan's heart rate is now 125. Doc M will make an immediate urgent request for an echocardiogram to be carried out, but he is aware of quite a long waiting list. So now we just have to wait for an appointment. More steroids are prescribed to help the chest in the meantime.

Chapter 12: Diversions from the main event

As if we don't have enough to contend with, on 19th May Alan's front tooth has broken. We call in to see our local dentist who advises that the root must come out. We need to seek advice from the Oncologist in view of complications caused by the Zometa infusions and its effect on bones, and especially jaw bones. The Onco was happy to give permission for the extraction to be done, but a course of antibiotics must be in place before the work is done. Once Dentist Pete (affectionately known as 'Pete the Prod') gets the green light he is happy to carry on.

During the past few weeks we have been pulling together arrangements for Alan's second 'Bucket Party' ... this year we christened it "Alan's Jubilee Weekend Bucket Party – Revisited". The BBC was asking for people to write in and let them know how we, the public, would be celebrating the Queen's Diamond Jubilee weekend ... so I wrote in and told them! The next thing we knew was the local radio station was on the phone wanting to interview Alan – they had never heard of a 'Bucket Party'. A young lady arrived to carry out and record the interview, which was broadcast on the breakfast show on 23rd May. So many listeners phoned in to wish us luck – thought it was a very novel idea! For one day Alan was world famous In Hereford and Worcester!

The 24th May was the long anticipated arrival in the area of the Olympic Torch relay. We knew it was going to pass our front door. The local media had advertised the times and affected roads were duly closed. We had visitors that day and we decided to go down to the roadside to see the whole entourage go by. Alan didn't feel well enough to stand for any length of time and returned to the house. The staff from the nursing home opposite were also standing at their gate. A couple of police outriders glided through the village, lights ablaze and sirens blaring ... then ... nothing. We waited and waited. It must have been a full 10 minutes before the rest of the vehicle convoy appeared ... speeding through the village at 40 mph! If you blinked twice you missed it. How sad when folks have turned out to see the spectacle in outlying country districts that they could not have slowed down a bit and made more of an effort to wave and acknowledge our presence. We'd made more of it in fun in the garden last year!! Ah, well – we saw it and it was a once in a lifetime event … something to tell the great grandchildren about when you're 106! Not as exciting as the Titanic story, but it will have to do!

26th May: This is a massive day for our daughter, Givvi. For months she has been in training to undertake a marathon length walk from her house in Worcester to our home in South Shropshire. She has been out walking at least three times a week since the beginning of the year in all weathers … mostly cold and wet. She has been advertising "Givvi's Walk to Alan" to gain sponsorship with the aim of donating the cash to the Prostate Cancer UK Charity. Her line of thought had been that if Alan needed her at any time, she would walk here if that was her only option. She had a small team of close friends who were willing to help her and act as her support crew on the day. Leading the team was her husband, Percy. The route had been dissected and rest stops planned along the way.

On the hottest day of the year so far this became a gruelling marathon during which Giv was on the point of collapse at the half way stage. The day was re-paced and she arrived at our home after 13 hours! This was a mammoth task as in very general terms the route from Worcester to South Shropshire is all up hill. Our bungalow is at a height of 1200 feet above sea level! The last two miles of this walk are the most gruelling. The support crew had been armed with cash tins and had rattled their way through all the villages en route. A very tiring but thoroughly enjoyable day for everyone … except Givvi, but she was very proud to be able to send the charity some £1500 to show for her efforts. Alan was extremely touched by the sentiment of what she had done for him.

Alan's appointment for an echocardiogram came through for 29th May and therefore we made our way to Kidderminster. Doc M had asked us to get as much information from the technician whilst we were at the appointment as results were sometimes slow in reaching the GP. As the technician was carrying out the tests, we related to her what our Doc had requested. We were informed that she was not able to give any details to the patient! However, she would do her very best to get the results in the post by the next day. Although I didn't fully understand what I was seeing, I watched the machine's display screen with interest. I attempted to engage in any sort of conversation with the technician but responses were somewhat difficult to get. However she suddenly decided that she would do her very best to get this information out to the GP in today's post. The scanning continued. She then asked if our surgery had a fax machine as she could fax the results over before the end of the day. Alan's heart rate during the test was 114. Alarm bells starting ringing in my head. In a matter of minutes we had gone from an attitude of 'your doctor will get the results in a standard amount of time' to 'I'll fax them over today'. I knew all was not well.

We had made a dental appointment for Alan that would coincide with our journey home from Kidderminster. Pete the Prod carried out the two extractions and we were given instructions on how to best deal with the cavity and signs to look out for should problems start occurring. He explained that it would be a considerable time before the healing process would be complete and it would be at that time when we could have the discussion about a plate being fitted.

This had been a busy and totally exhausting day for Alan. Once we were back at home all he was able to do was fall asleep on the settee.

A couple of days later Doc called in for a home visit. Alan is most unwell. Doc confirms that Alan does have heart failure and that it is far worse than expected ... it is Left Ventricular heart failure with an efficiency of just 30%. He prescribed some new drugs in an effort to alleviate symptoms and problems until advice could be sought from a Cardiologist. We are concerned it may be difficult to find someone who will see Alan in view of his 'terminal' status. Doc took more blood for a new set of tests. Now the comments made back at the beginning of April start to make sense ... "All good results ... so why does Alan feel so unwell? Is this the price one has to pay for having satisfactory results on paper?" However, I don't have too much time to analyse what we have been told. We have a busy weekend ahead of us as it is Jubilee weekend and we have a Bucket Party to get underway. Alan is very tired and still feeling most unwell so is unable to contribute anything towards the arrangements. The weather is miserable and the forecast even worse. Oh joy!

Saturday 2nd June: The weather could not have been worse if it had tried! It was very difficult to get everything ready on time. Alan kept telling me to go and get my shower and get changed ... but I wasn't ready yet and continued back and forwards from house to marquee trying to get everything in place. Finally with about an hour to go before people would be arriving, I managed to get in the shower and attempt to make myself look presentable. When I emerged from the bedroom after I had done my best to get my hair to behave itself, I was told by my girlfriends that Alan had a bit of a surprise for me and that I should wait in the kitchen until he was ready. Eventually I was escorted out of the front door and down to the marquee. I was not prepared for what I saw there!

Alan and three of his army mates were lined up ... dressed in their regimental blazers and displaying all their medals. All of them looked so smart! Our family and friends are all standing around grinning like Cheshire cats. Alan told me that the arrangements for the day had been changed. This was no longer a bucket party. We were about to renew our marriage vows and a Vicar was due to arrive within minutes! Without my knowledge and with a huge amount of help from Givvi, Alan had arranged a Vicar, flowers, ribbons, bows and balloons, Orders of Service ... the works! I was so shocked I broke down into tears. This was such a huge gesture on Alan's part to make some very special memories for us both not knowing how much longer we would have together. We were both quite emotional – this was just so out of character for him!

As the rain was having a break for half an hour, we managed to conduct the ceremony with the Vicar in the open air ... well, in the

70

descending cloud ... with our family and friends around us. People commented 'oh, how romantic' ... but it was far, far more than that to the two of us. The Vicar was lovely considering that Givvi had prepared the wording for the ceremony and he had been told there would be no religion included! However, at the end of the ceremony we did allow him to bless us in his own way! There were beautiful certificates, which Givvi had made ready for signature in the dining room, and then it was time for the traditional photographs to be taken. As luck would have it we have what is sometimes referred to as a 'wedding gazebo' in the garden ... white metal – shabby chic! It was exactly the right place to have the photos taken. It suddenly occurred to me why Alan had been upset about having his front tooth out ... he didn't feel able to smile for the photos. I told him not to worry and I would make it look right before we had any prints done by doing a bit of photo manipulation on the computer!

I don't think we've ever experienced such an emotional and special day - a wonderful memory to hold forever ... however long that may be for us. Alan coped well for the ceremony but was then confined to the conservatory for most of the day as he felt very tired and unwell. Friends were still arriving and although everyone had a really good time, the weather put the dampers on proceedings to a very great degree. Civ's friends had brought all their music equipment and set up in a very damp marquee. They entertained us with live music for the best part of an hour. The day concluded far sooner than was anticipated ... even though we had prepared a huge curry for the evening meal, the weather was just too cold and wet to expect people to remain outside. Quite a few of them had squeezed themselves into the conservatory with Alan ... couldn't blame them really.

We ended the day with bodies scattered throughout the bungalow on the floor, inside, dry and warm rather than spending the night in tents as originally planned. Considering the time of year, the weather was just unbelievably bad!

Some of our friends were up and about early next morning and had already starting cooking breakfast for everyone. Plenty of bacon butties and cups of tea. During the morning we did our best to clear up from the previous day, but, if it was possible, I think the weather was even worse. It was pouring with rain and the wind speed was increasing by the hour! However, we did our best. Giv and Percy collected all the musical gear and eventually everybody was gone. Alan was exhausted but was comfy and warm on the settee, dozing for the afternoon.

The clear up operation had not included the marquee and the b'b'q gazebo. It was just too wet to deal with them. At around 5 o'clock I was sitting in the study – making a phone call to a friend who had been unable to attend yesterday's celebration. The rain was still thrashing down and the wind was strong. I could see the roof of the marquee billowing. Suddenly the whole thing lifted and took off in the wind and deposited itself on the top of one of the flagpoles!

There is no one living locally who I can call on to help in a situation such as this. I had no alternative but to phone Givvi and ask for help. They were both in bed and asleep trying to recover from the weekend! However, they would be straight over to help; but in any event, the journey would take the best part of an hour. I decided to do what I could. Alan wanted to help but was so breathless he virtually collapsed within 30 seconds. I gathered up all the bent and twisted metalwork and with a huge effort managed to pull the marquee roof and sides off the flagpole. All the chairs and tables had been left in the marquee so I did my best to stack them out of the wind. The smaller tent was still standing although the cloth cover was completely soaked. I did what I could but was becoming more and more upset as the time went by. When Givvi and Percy arrived, I was sitting in the garage, totally and utterly soaked to the skin, surrounded by chaos, crying my eyes out. I really was at the end of my tether. I was sent inside and told to get a hot shower whilst they carried on with the clearing up operation.

This may have been a very memorable weekend for the Queen celebrating her Diamond Jubilee ... and it's also a weekend we will never forget!!!

Life is not about waiting for the storm to pass …
It's about learning to dance in the rain!

What a great saying that is! It passes through my mind virtually every day

Chapter 13: Spanner in the works .. why me?

We realize that the heart medications Alan has been given are standard issue and will work for the majority of patients. However, it would appear that Alan is not responding in the same way! He is generally feeling very unwell and quite nauseous. I know that he got very tired over the Jubilee weekend with everything he had planned coming to fruition, but this seems to be something more. When Doc M phoned late in the day, he wasn't too happy with the situation and asked me to phone the out of hour's service and get a locum doctor in to have a look at Alan. This doctor doesn't seem to be unduly worried and will not change any of the treatments as we will be seeing our own doctor within a couple of days.

On 6th June the latest round of Zometa is due and also the Zoladex implant. These are done at the Cottage Hospital and yet again we have an excellent set of blood results ... PSA is 0.8 and ALP is 78. Doc makes minor adjustments to heart medications and we'll chat on the phone in a couple of days to see how things are going. At the time I made the phone call, Alan was quite bright and was fine. Therefore Doc is confident all will be fine over the weekend. However, during that evening Alan was in excruciating pain. It occurred to us that this may be urine retention and felt it best to call out a locum doctor again. He was unable to pinpoint the actual cause, but was able to confirm that urine retention was not the problem! Stay in bed, stay warm, drink plenty ... thank you and goodnight!! The pains continued and during the night Alan was violently sick and is now feeling very unwell.

The next day was spent in bed and mostly asleep. He managed to eat a small meal but is not getting enough to drink. His blood pressure is a little low but his heart rate is still up at 108. The following days run to a very similar pattern with periods of vomiting and sickness now a daily occurrence. Process of elimination led us to stop the antibiotics ... hey presto - no more sickness. Alan is now feeling much better in himself but the heart rate remains high and has peaked at over 140 this week. Doc M has called in to see Alan twice during the week ... and we managed to get an ECG done on 14th - which appeared OK. Doc has sent an urgent fax to the Cardiologist and is suggesting bi-ventricular pacing. We wonder if he will even consider it in view of the PCa? (We now have copy of Echocardiogram report that states left ventricular EF is just 30% and the right side is also 'impaired'). We can only hope that we get an appointment soon as this heart problem is now a much bigger concern than the cancer!

Doc M is now on holiday for a week – that's always a concern to us as we depend on him so heavily. Alan has continued to feel very unwell all week. His blood pressure remains low and his heart rate still over 100 and peaked at about 135. The practice senior partner made a home visit early in week and changed the particular diuretic tablet as Alan's potassium level had risen above an acceptable level. An appointment has arrived in the post for 4th July with the Cardiologist at Kidderminster Hospital, and hopefully there will be talk of a pacer. In the meantime the Cardiologist had written to the surgery making certain suggestions as to what drugs should be put into place prior to the hospital appointment. The senior partner again made a home visit on 21st to check out Cardiologists recommendations but after consideration he decided not to change anything! He did, however, prescribe a new inhaler. He will visit again on Monday 25th. I duly collected the inhaler from the surgery and read through the notes enclosed in the box. How can I justify giving a man with terminal prostate cancer medication which, within the instructions for use, contains a very plain warning that this medication should not be used if you suffer prostate problems. Confidence is not high!! As Alan's legs seem to be getting weaker and weaker, we decided to buy a walking frame for his own safety. So he has a new toy to play with as it was delivered today. Better safe than sorry!

Percy, our son-in-law, had planned a sponsored parachute jump in order to raise funds for the Prostate Cancer UK Charity. It was planned for this Sunday 24th June, but he has heard that it has been postponed in view of the bad weather. It is a disappointment, but Alan would not have been well enough to go, so hopefully he will be well enough to go to the re-scheduled event on 21st July. We had also planned a weekend away in Leicester for a social get-together at the end of the month, to meet up with some on-line friends, also PCa sufferers, but in view of how Alan feels, we have decided to cancel. Another disappointment!

25th June: Alan collapsed just after midnight. He had got up to go to the bathroom and had just crumpled in a heap in the hallway. His blood pressure is obviously far too low. I managed to get him off the floor and back into bed, but it was difficult. He broke a walking stick on the way down and smacked his elbow into a doorframe. I telephoned 999 and was given the third degree. I was told that a paramedic would phone me for a chat. After some to-ing and fro-ing the control room advised that an Ambulance wouldn't attend, and that if we wanted a doctor to call, there would be a minimum 3-hour wait before he could attend! During the telephone conversations they all seemed more concerned about his elbow than his heart! What is it going to take to get someone to monitor this situation? Three hours would take us through till about 5am and as I could contact our own surgery at 8am I told them not to bother. I find it of great concern that a cancer patient with a heart problem should be treated in this way. Our holiday cover GP phoned the following day after seeing a report of our overnight fiasco, to advise that Alan should attempt to be more mobile in order that his body gets used to functioning with a lower blood pressure! This can't be right, surely? I will have quite a list of questions for the Cardiologist next Wednesday, 4th July. We are frustrated that the recommendations made by the Cardio for medication changes have been totally ignored by covering GP … we see it as a lost opportunity to get the heart rate down and the blood pressure back up! Can't wait to get Doc M back in charge, as Alan is on the point of collapse at some point virtually every day.

26th June: Who's a clever girl then? I've been hedge trimming this afternoon! Well someone's got to attack it! I'd been slogging away at it for all of 5 minutes before I cut through the power lead! Bang! Oops! Ripped! The guys arrived to cut the grass, which takes about an hour and a half … and by the time they were ready to go I had finally managed to repair the lead and change every fuse I could find. I was spitting nails, I can tell you! Wonder how short the lead will be by the time I've finished the hedges?

During the early hours of **2nd July** I wake up with heartburn – something that happens to me from time to time! The usual remedy is to take antacid tablets, prop myself up in bed and try to get back to sleep in a more upright position. After an hour or so when the tablets had done nothing for me, I took more – that should do the job! Another hour went by and the discomfort is growing rather than abating. Final remedy for me to try is bicarbonate of soda mixed with a small amount of water. There are two possible outcomes to me taking this … 1 – it will shift the wind in a very loud manner and the pain will ease, or 2 – it will make me sick and that too would solve my problem. Nothing happened, other than an increase in pain that is now reaching a worrying severity. One last try with the bicarbonate also fails to produce results. As the pains continue to increase they soon reach a level comparable with being in childbirth labour. Earlier I had contacted a friend asking if she had any other bright ideas as to what I could try. After an hour or so she had phoned back and it was obvious to her that I was in real trouble. By now Alan was aware that I was most unwell and he was obviously concerned as to how we were going to deal with this. Our friends arrived unannounced as they had realized that I was going to need help today in looking after Alan. However, when she saw me she immediately phoned the doctors and insisted on a home visit … sooner rather than later! I didn't care who came to see me as I was in so much pain. I couldn't sit … stand … or lie down in any sort of comfort.

Luckily it was Doc M who turned up. He knew that we had certain medicines in the house and suggested that I tried one of those. He had another home visit to make and would come back here immediately after that to re-assess the situation … in about half an hour. There was no improvement during this time – in fact things were getting worse. When he returned, he immediately gave me a considerable dose of Alan's liquid morphine and telephoned for an ambulance. Alan and my friend managed to get a few essentials into a bag for me to take to hospital. Obviously he wouldn't be able to come with me, but thankfully there would be someone with him to make sure he would be OK. Within 20 minutes or so the morphine was taking effect. The paramedics arrived and got me into the ambulance. I was given another dose of morphine to help make the journey to hospital more comfortable … it would take about an hour to get there. By the time we got to Worcester, Givvi was there to greet every ambulance that arrived but she failed to recognize me on the trolley … jeepers I must be ill!

I was put onto a ward and assessed by a doctor who considered this was very likely to be a gallstone attack. They put me on an intravenous drip of antibiotics and gave me more pain relief. Being so drugged I was floating in and out of sleep. Arrangements would be made for me to have a scan the next day. I was allowed nothing to eat or drink other than sips of water. After several hours the pains had subsided but they continued to feed the antibiotic drip alternating with a saline drip. Giv and Percy came to see me that evening. I was worried about Alan but they told me our friends would be staying with him. What a relief.

By the next morning the situation was considerably better and I was taken for an ultrasound scan. There were no surprises … other than the size of the main gallstones that were identified. Apparently I have part of Stonehenge in residence in my gall bladder! The consultant advises me that as the gall bladder is very enflamed at the moment, then he would be unable to operate immediately. When everything had calmed down, I would go home and be sent an appointment for an MRI scan in a few weeks, and based on the results of that scan a decision would be made regarding surgery. He told me that I could go home that night provided I had managed to have something to eat and drink without incident. They gave me a sandwich and all seemed okay, so I was discharged. Givvi and Percy came to collect me and we headed back home.

By the time we were three quarters of the way back, I began to feel unwell again. I didn't say anything hoping the symptoms would calm down. They didn't! So by midnight I was on my way back to hospital in another ambulance! Other than dealing with the pain with painkillers, nothing can be done. I was allowed home on Wednesday afternoon. Givvi and our good friends have suddenly become 'carers', in rotation ... but hopefully this situation won't last too long. *We weren't expecting this* - and could certainly have done without it!

I was very upset not to have been able to go with Alan to the first Cardiologist appointment as there were so many questions to be asked. Our friend Lynn went with Alan and wrote notes for me. There is to be a new drugs regime implemented and the follow up to this appointment will be about 8 weeks. Hopefully there will be improvements to report by then, and the possibility of a pacer will be discussed. As Alan was due another Zometa infusion at the Cottage Hospital, Lynn and Mark took him there too. All went well apparently.

This is the sort of pacer we feel may be considered for Alan – information taken from my research into the subject!

Biventricular pacemakers are utilized in patients with congestive heart failure (CHF) to improve their functional capacity. These pacemakers are more advanced than the typical pacemaker used to treat a slow heartbeat. Biventricular pacemakers allow for cardiac resynchronization therapy (CRT), which paces the hearts ventricles, or pumping chambers. Many times, patients with CHF do not have all four chambers of the heart working together as they should. With CRT therapy, the four chambers can be optimized to contract at the most desirable time and increase the efficiency of each heartbeat. Getting the right and left heart chambers to contract in synchrony with the other can improve your cardiac function and reduce the symptoms of heart failure.

The generator for the biventricular pacemaker is typically implanted in the left chest through a small incision. The three leads are implanted into the heart, as compared with one or two for a regular pacemaker, and attach to the generator. The entire device can then be programmed and monitored without another incision. One night in the hospital is generally all that is needed for what is often considered "minor" surgery using local anaesthetic and sedation. Patients generally return to normal activities quickly.

Mark and Lynn were able to stay with us until Thursday when Givvi came over to continue the role of carer as neither Alan nor I were capable of looking after ourselves, let alone each other!

What a turn-around appears to have been achieved in such a few days. Four days since the introduction of the new medication regime, Alan's heart rate has dropped from the 125-140 region to somewhere in the high 70's or 80's. He feels so much better and is even talking about being able to think about doing a bit in the garden … totally unmentioned in some 18 months! I so hope that this improvement will continue. As for my own problems, I think everything has calmed down for now. Trying to stick with a diet of less than 2% fat and drinking plenty of apple juice. Hopefully I will be able to have the gall bladder and Stonehenge removed within a few months.

By **19**[th] **July** the improvements being seen last week fade away and Alan is again feeling most unwell. I have spoken to Doc M and he will send urgent fax to the Cardiologist for advice and an early appointment. The Cardiologist replies and immediately halts one of the new medications (Ivabradine) … also we have a new appointment made for 1st August.

Sunday 21st **July** was the new date for Percy's "Leap of Faith" for Alan … the charity fund raising parachute jump in other words! He had chosen this method of raising money as Alan was a member of the Parachute Regiment during his military career. Alan has been really touched that both Percy and Givvi felt the need to do something like this for him. It was quite a pleasant day and we made our way down to a small airfield just outside Cirencester. Alan needed to be in his wheelchair all day, which turned out to be longer than expected. There were so many people jumping that day and it just so happened that

Percy had been put on one of the last jumps of the day. Still we made the most of being out in the lovely weather and enjoyed the picnic we had taken.

Finally it was time for Percy to be instructed in the finer points of falling out of a plane, before being bundled into a van and taken to the plane. We all watched intently as the plane took off and its slow and steady climb to some 10,000 feet. We heard the engine being cut back and scoured the skies for the first signs of the free-fallers. We managed to identify dots in the sky but had no idea which dot was Percy! When the chutes opened identification was somewhat easier as we knew what colour we were looking for. The only problem with a jump like this is that it is all over so quickly. Before we knew it Percy was on his final swoop down and he was on the ground in seconds. Giv was delighted he had landed safely – as were we all, of course – and Percy swaggered off the airfield as if he was in a scene from "Top Gun"! What a great experience it had been for him and he would love to get straight back on the plane again.

With the job done and Alan getting increasingly tired, we decided to make a move and get on our way back home. It was going to take us a couple of hours to get home. The journey back was uneventful other than spotting a policeman almost buried in a garden hedge armed with a 'radar' gun in the middle of one of the little villages en route. We arrived home very tired but grateful that Alan had felt well enough to be part of the day. We had another set of blood results on 27th July which were still consistently good -PSA was the lowest ever at 0.3 and the ALP figure was 70.

29th July: Strange ol' day ... Alan daren't stand up for fear of falling down!! It has happened about 8 times today. Roll on Wednesday and the hurriedly brought-forward appointment with Cardio ... hopefully a decision will be made on the fitting of a pacer. My gallstones are kicking off again ... back aches and just under ribs so very tender ... but no full blown attack, thank goodness.

So who did I upset last week? Mr. "I've got a speed gun pointing at you"!! Why can't I have a fixed penalty like everyone else? You know the sort ... £60 + 3 points? No, not me .... I have to get the 'Notice of Intended Prosecution' letter! I was caught - banged to rights!! 38 mph in a 30 mph!! Oh, dear ... never mind! I've written to them including "my husband's not a well man" explanation for rushing home, told them we're broke and to be generous with their decision-making!! I was right out in the sticks, not a soul in sight apart from a bored bobby and his radar gun sat in a hedge. Oh well - tomorrow is another day – and hopefully a better one!

Although we could virtually write off the month of July through Alan feeling very unwell, which had mainly restricted us to staying at home, at least now, regardless of how well he felt or what the weather was doing we had the diversion of the Olympics to keep us entertained. Like so many of the British public we were not totally convinced that, as a nation, we could pull this off ... but having sat enthralled by the opening ceremony we felt that maybe ... just maybe ... we could actually do it.

Chapter 14: To Pace - or not to Pace? That is the question

1st August, 2012: Today could be life changing for us. We are hoping for a decision on whether or not Alan can be fitted with a pacer to help his heart condition ... but first he must have his 10th Zometa infusion at the Cottage Hospital. These are such a regular occurrence now; they are just taken in our stride! The Cardiologist has decided on yet another new regime of medication which is to be trialled for eight weeks, at which time he will see Alan again. Apparently Alan is not a classic subject to have a pacer fitted, although it has not yet been totally ruled out. The waiting game continues ... and Alan continues to feel unwell. Not as life changing as we had hoped!!

The next day I went to see Doc M to give him an immediate update on what the Cardio is planning. Digoxin will be re-introduced to heart drugs' mix and Furosemide dosage doubled. Eplerenone not available until 6th August so will be introduced then. Ivabradine is now out of the equation and Nebivovol is to be the beta-blocker of choice but will not be started immediately ... in about 3 weeks. We understand the reasoning for phased drug introduction ... but it is just so frustrating. Doc M is concerned this combination will only make matters worse as the drugs are likely to drop blood pressure even further, which will only add to the 'falling down' problem. We are of the opinion that our Doc is now between a rock and a hard place ... I think he feels as if his hands are tied and he cannot interfere in the Cardio's decisions. Frustrating ... and also somewhat worrying!

We have to make a decision ... and it has to be made now. This refers to whether or not we pursue our original GP through the Courts in an effort to get financial compensation for Alan. We have no idea which way the GMC is viewing our complaint and we can't get any information out of them at this time. We were told that any solicitor undertaking this task would need at least 18 months to complete all investigations and to be ready to lodge paperwork with the Courts by the latest date of 2nd March, 2014. We have thought about it long and hard and have talked to our family and friends. The consensus of opinion is that we have nothing to lose and provided we both feel strong enough, then yes, this doctor certainly has something to answer for. On the recommendation of a friend, we have instructed a firm of solicitors in Bristol who are specialists in the medical negligence field. The legal process will now begin.

It's **9th August**, the new medication regime has been in place just a week and Alan has collapsed again today. This is the 6th time since the end of June! This is frightening, but apparently considered acceptable, and expected, according to the Cardiologist. Alan must take extra care!

(Drunks who fall in the street are regularly taken to A & E by ambulance, but it seems that different rules apply for a terminally ill cancer patient with a serious heart problem, who through inappropriate medication or imbalance collapses on a regular basis. We were told that sending for an ambulance under these circumstances would be totally inappropriate – that's what the cardio advised us.)

This advice and attitude seems so wrong to me ... and so does it to many others to whom I've spoken. As yet, no broken bones - but the law of averages won't be on our side forever! We're on day 8 of the soaking wet beds ... profuse overnight sweating being the cause. I am having to deal with endless laundry. It may be summer but the weather is rubbish and the tumble dryer is working in overdrive. We have questioned this situation on so many occasions with so many different medical professionals ... nobody seems to have an answer, other than to tell us that it is a common situation for heart patients! Therefore all we can do is continue to add to the profits of Persil, Comfort and the utility companies!

After just four days on one of the new drugs, the overnight vomiting has reared its ugly head again. We really don't need this! *(My gallbladder MRI scan went well today.)*

As an ex-Paratrooper, Alan has been interested in the construction of a new Airborne Memorial which has been erected at the National Memorial Arboretum featuring the winged horse Pegasus. The memorial was dedicated earlier in the year but he was not well enough to make the trip on the day involved. As the weather forecast is quite good, we decided to make the trip to Staffordshire on 12h August. We would meet up with Mark and Lynn who would be bringing their grandsons along too.

Chapter 15: EMERGENCY!

Dictionary definition of Emergency: A serious, unexpected, and often dangerous situation requiring immediate action.

Who in the NHS redefined this word? When did that happen? Why wasn't I told about it? I am talking about *Emergency* Ambulance Services ... and Accident and *Emergency* Departments.

Sunday 12th August, 2012: The day started quite well in warm weather. Alan behaved and used his wheelchair. We were able to admire the wonderful Pegasus memorial and then make our way to the Army Dog Unit (Northern Ireland) memorial which holds a very special place in our hearts. Alan and I are totally responsible for the installation of this memorial. We planned it, designed it, sought the funding, physically put it in place and then organized a very special day back in August 2010 when the memorial was dedicated in a special service attended by over 200 people, including 100 ex-dog handlers of the Unit. We followed this up with a reunion party afterwards .... but that's a whole different long story!!

Alan's wellbeing declined very rapidly today, there being 5 or 6 episodes of him keeling over, and the only reason he didn't hit the floor was that there were enough of us around to catch him. However, when we returned home, for a short while there was no one to catch him ... he fell to the floor and was initially unresponsive when spoken to.

At 6.30pm a 999 call was placed requesting an ambulance in view of a heart patient having collapsed. The operator stayed on the line until Alan was responsive, help was close by ... open the door in readiness, start putting items into a bag to take to hospital and get any medications together to be available to paramedics. The local first response car arrived within 15 minutes ... maybe less. The paramedic was very efficient and had been advised that a full ambulance crew was on its way. However, shortly afterwards she was advised that a vehicle check of the ambulance was almost complete and there would be a short delay in the Kidderminster crew starting their journey to get to us. Time crept on! Eventually the paramedic received information the ambulance was on its way and was some 19 miles from our address. It was concluded this ambulance was not coming from Kidderminster, just 17 miles away.

The first response paramedic carried out tests and completed paperwork. Three separate ECG's were taken – each appearing to come from a different patient as the tracings were so different on each occasion! She commented that one looked to her like classic left ventricular bundle block (referring to an opposing comment made by Alan's cardiologist in a copy letter we had received – which she was reading). Finally the ambulance arrived at about 8.25 pm. This crew had been sent all the way from the other side of Worcester and it was questioned why a Kidderminster crew had not been sent ... or alternatively a crew from Bridgnorth, Tenbury, or Ludlow. The information this crew had been given from their control room was for a non-urgent fall ... they had not been informed this was a heart patient – a call which would have been rated as a higher priority with a quicker response. There were a few words exchanged before Alan was finally put into the ambulance which got on its way to Worcester at approx. 8.45 pm. What part of 2 hours and 15 minutes am I expected to assess as an emergency response?

The crew were quick to say they had no problem travelling this considerable distance but after their experience the previous evening they were beginning to question the efficiency of decisions being made in their control room. The day before they had been sent on a call which involved travelling from Worcester, to a patient just north of Birmingham city centre. The journey had taken them past the Ambulance Station on the Bristol Road, Birmingham ... some 5 miles or so from the patient. They had seen five ambulances parked up at that location. When the question was asked of the control room as to why one of these had not been asked to respond to this particular call-out, the crew were informed 'they are on their break'. This crew had been forced to work 10 hours into a 12 hour shift before they had been allowed their 20 minute break.

They are convinced the control room staff members are deliberately trying to make life difficult for some of the paramedics. It would seem there are many very upset paramedics driving around in ambulances at the moment!

Unfamiliar with this part of the county, the longest route imaginable was suggested by the crew's Sat Nav resulting in a prolonged journey to Worcester Royal Hospital. Arrival time approx. 10 pm. The hand-over to A & E staff was relatively quick considering the number of patients in evidence. A nurse duly carried out all the usual tests ... ECG, blood pressure, heart rate, oxygen saturation, temperature, BMI, etc. We told the nurse that Alan was due a set of meds at this time and it was agreed that if these were normally taken they would allow him to take them!! Half an hour later a drink arrived so that he could take his tablets!!! I would suggest that it was then a good hour before Alan was seen by a doctor who went over all the same ground and questions as the paramedics, and the nurse had previously documented. He would take advice from the 'medical team' and get back to us. He returned to inform us that Alan needed a chest X-ray and he would come back and see us after this was done. A porter duly arrived to take Alan to the X-ray unit and he was back in the cubicle within minutes really.

When Alan gets bored he plays up! I had been out for a cigarette and came back to find the cubicle 'decorated' with the little stickers used during an ECG test. Alan had been pulling them off his flesh and then flicking them everywhere. They were really sticky ones and had stuck to the walls really well ... so I had to spend the next five minutes removing them all before we got thrown out for misbehaving!!

When the doctor re-appeared we were told the X-ray was totally clear. He said it appeared that Alan was now stable and suggested that I should be able to cope with this situation at home. Oh, no ... absolutely no chance! He was told immediately that I would not be taking him home. I suggested to the doctor that as Alan had been lying on a trolley for some four hours at this point, and that all tests and observations were relative to him being in that position, and they had no idea what would happen when he got to his feet. I suggested/requested he should ask Alan to walk down the corridor and see for himself how long it took him to fall over - and until this had been done I was refusing to accept responsibility for him at home. The doctor declined to try this experiment but would re-check with the medical team instead. He came back to us a little later to advise that Alan was to be admitted and would be moved as soon as a bed was available.

Alan felt I could now return home. It was 1.30 am and there was really no need for me to stay. I was concerned about Alan's medication routine and felt I needed to explain this to someone before I left. Our A & E nurse told us that one of the doctors would prescribe the drugs which he felt appropriate for Alan's stay in hospital. …. Um, no … I don't think so! Although we appreciated that Alan's heart medications may be brought into question and revised, anything relating to his Prostate Cancer or PTSD were part of an essential, long established routine which should not be changed. I offer to put out the next day's tablets in a similar manner to the routine we have at home, which she agreed might be very helpful … and for this purpose she fetched 4 'denture' pots and lids all labelled with his name and marked up 'morning, noon, evening, night' to which I added the more appropriate actual times we used … 9am, 1pm, 6pm and 10pm. However, by now the porter had arrived to move Alan to the ward. During the walk to the ward/unit the nurse was trying to get to grips with the comprehensive drugs list I had given her. She commented that the hospital would be unable to administer the Zoladex (listed as 12-weekly) and the Zometa (listed as 4-weekly). I told her these were not required but were obviously included on the list as part of Alan's on-going PCa treatment. Each tablet is marked up clearly on this list as to what time of day it is taken … some on multiple occasions, others only single. Finally she grasped the significance of the list and how it was visually able to illustrate when, and in what quantity, any of Alan's medications was required. Success! … Not for long!

Alan was handed over to the care of the Acute Medical Unit … a different nurse, and a completely new team. There was no bed for Alan

... he was to remain on a trolley. We then experienced the onslaught of one of the most overloaded paperwork systems I have ever seen. Not only are there forms to complete ... but booklets! Now, I appreciate that detailed records are essential, but this was mammoth – total overkill. I think there were 8 or 9 booklets to be completed. Subjects covered by these booklets were very varied, including possessions brought into hospital (jewellery, watches, clothes, etc.) ... next of kin details ... dignity conformity! ... and much, much more! I asked if dignity conformity meant they would pull the curtains around Alan's bed before removing his pants. Unbelievable! By now it is almost 2.30 am ... Alan was asked his weight. When a patient tells you he weighs about 90kg, he's probably right. But 'about' is not accurate enough! 'You will have to be weighed' – scales duly fetched. 88.5kg. Well, we were very close then! Had Alan been due to be anaesthetised in the following few minutes I may have appreciated the urgent need for this figure to be so accurate – but obviously that was not the case! However when a patient is so visibly exhausted and falling asleep you have to ask the question whether it is totally necessary to get him off the trolley onto a set of scales ... especially when the figure given for his height was immediately accepted as correct rather than feeling the need to stand him up against a wall and get a tape measure out!!!

Finally, all boxes ticked and new set of stats taken, the paperwork was complete. Before leaving for home, I asked to go through the drugs with someone and related the suggestion by A & E that I should use the 4 pots to set up Alan's meds for the next day. Oh, dear! Wrong!! 'Totally out of the question! Unless a tablet is in its original packaging, it cannot be administered.' I was advised to leave them all on the Unit as there are some they did not have in stock. However, they could not accept any 'controlled' drugs and therefore the Zomorph and Oramorph must be taken home. Then came the request ... 'Actually, can you please leave us one of the Zomorph tablets as we don't have 100mg capsules in stock as it is a considerable dose.' As the nurse was checking through Alan's list of drugs she suddenly questioned what we had told her in relation to Alan having no allergies. That's right, no allergies. 'But it is noted here that you had an adverse reaction to one of your previous tablets .... That's an allergy.' Not in any sense we have ever understood ... that was an 'adverse reaction'. An allergy, to us, is likened to dust getting up your nose and you sneeze. Two very different things, but not according to the NHS definition!! Well slap your wrists, you naughty boy – you failed the test; you've incorrectly answered a question! Not only that, now has the form had to be altered so that this new information can be recorded. Now, in which of these 9 booklets am I going to find the original question? Oh ... please!!

As I was about to leave I explained to the nurse that as Alan was in a strange environment it was possible for him to suffer with a panic attack as he suffers from PTSD. "What is PTSD?" Oh, dear ... we're in trouble here!! With trepidation and guilt I had to leave Alan in the hands of the 'professionals'. It was 3am and I was facing a journey of over an hour to get home via daughter's house where things needed to be collected from. He was still on a trolley ... and totally exhausted.

Monday, 13th August, 2012. It's 9.30am. The phone is ringing. It's Alan. *"I can come home ... they are discharging me. They've juggled my heart drugs a bit ... it'll be fine. Can you come and pick me up?"*

"So someone from Cardiology has been to see you and made these changes?" – *Yes I think so not sure really, but it was a doctor who came to see me.*

"Why are they not keeping you to monitor the situation?" – *I don't know, but it'll be fine.*

Oh my god ... it's only 6 hours since I left him and miraculously this situation is resolved? I really don't think so! But I did tell Alan I would do my best to be there by 11am.

This cannot be right! This just cannot be right! After all we have gone through in the past few weeks and in particular the gruelling and frightening day we had had yesterday – this just cannot be right.

91

First line of attack ... get on the phone to Doc M's secretary and explain the situation. She will advise Doc between patients and get back to me. When she phones back, I am told that Alan is not to be discharged until AMU has received confirmation from Alan's cardiologist – Doc M has spoken with Cardio's secretary and this is the message which has been received back. I said I was happy to phone AMU to advise them of this development as I know how busy the practice secretaries can be, especially on a Monday morning.

First call ... put through to the wrong AMU! Apparently there is more than one and I need AMU 'A'.

Second call: Right department, ask to speak to Sister in charge, please hold ...... line goes dead, cut off!

Third call: Right department, same young man, will fetch Sister ... can you hold, she'll just be a couple of minutes. Like many phones these days, ours displays the length of the current call ... 5 minutes ...8 minutes ... 12 minutes ... I'm still waiting ... 15 minutes ... 22 minutes ... I'm still waiting ... 25 minutes .... and I'm not still waiting!! Ring off, start again!

Fourth call: right department, same young man .. "I was cut off my first call and I have waited 25 minutes on my second call for someone to come to the phone and speak to me. If I do not speak to someone within the next two minutes I am going to present myself in your unit in one hour and all hell is going to break loose" ...

"Morning, Sister speaking, how can I help?"

'Can you please confirm to me that it was a member of Alan's Cardio team who has made the changes to Alan's meds and that he is to be discharged?'

"No. This decision was made by our Unit Consultant."

I then relayed the message about GP's contact with Cardio's secretary, the required liaison between Cardio team and Unit Consultant, and that I would be unable to collect Alan until I had this confirmation.

'Please advise Alan to settle in for the day and I will see him at normal visiting at 3 pm … but if you get this confirmation in the meantime, Sister, no doubt someone will call me and I will come and collect him immediately.'

There was no phone call.

I arrived back on the unit just before 3pm, fully loaded up with sandwiches, crisps, cakes, flask of tea, etc., knowing full well Alan would be needing something.

"You're late – you told me 11am." Alan had been told that I had been on the phone, but had either not been told, or totally misunderstood, the fact that he was not going to be discharged just yet until Cardio had agreed to the change in his medications. He tells me that after I left at 3 am he was woken on three separate occasions to be asked details of how and why he had been falling. Sounds to me that he lost his temper somewhat in the end (not surprisingly) and he had asked the question 'how many times do I need to be asked the same question?' He had not been given a drink early morning and was offered no breakfast. His first drink arrived with medications at 11am. (Only a couple of hours late – his slow release morphine dose would have timed out by 10am). He had been told that he would be taken from the bed as it was needed and made comfortable in a seating area until he was collected! I need to speak with the Sister.

Well, on the basis that she is so busy that I was kept holding on the end of a phone for 25 minutes, after speaking to her, I am convinced that she is disappearing up her own exhaust pipe, and that she only transmitted part of the message to Alan. She did apologize for the lateness of the drugs round during the morning, but got tetchy when I mentioned that, right now, was actually the time for his second set of meds. She will deal with it! As no one is sure when Cardio will be in touch about the meds, I ask the question … "can you please confirm that Alan will not be turfed out of his bed and expected to sit and wait in a waiting room because you need his bed? This is what he has been told."

'No, no! That won't happen!'

"So he gets to keep his bed for as long as needed?"

'Yes.' She's talking through her teeth by now!! Actually, she was becoming slightly defensive.

Apparently someone with a clipboard came to see Alan just before visiting time asking him to rate his experience of the Unit and how he had been treated. Score 1 – 10 … 10 being the best high score. (Oh, had they ever chosen the wrong patient!) Alan related to this person that he had been woken three times after 3am to be asked the same question he had already answered so many times. He was not offered a drink during the early morning and had not been given any breakfast. His drugs, including timed morphine, were two hours late. As a new patient he'd not had a choice of lunch and the tuna pasta bake he had been given was best described as 'gopping'!! However, he had enjoyed the rice pudding. So in response to the rating question, his score would be a maximum of minus 1. The guy went to walk away. *Write it down then … you asked - and I've told you!* Apparently it didn't get written down … what a shock!

About 20 minutes before the end of visiting, a young blonde nurse bounced over … *"All ready to go home then, Alan?"*

'Pardon? Not yet! Has the authorisation for the drug changes been received from the Cardiologist?'

"Oh, I don't know anything about that!" came the response.

'Well could you go and ask as Alan's not going anywhere until we have that approval. If you're not able to get an answer by 4pm (end of visiting), don't worry, I'll go away and come back at 7pm.' After about 10 minutes she came back to advise that no such approval had been received, she had spoken to the Unit Consultant and he was quite happy to come down and speak to us ... in fact, he was on his way.

We were introduced to the Unit Consultant who told us that he had made every effort to contact the Cardiologist ... had left two messages ... but had heard absolutely nothing back. He explained his thought process for the changes he had made, and his decision to totally remove one of Alan's drugs which, he felt, was the major problem and the cause of the falls. The properties of the drug were fully described to us and its particular function and a full explanation of what it was actually doing to Alan. It was in his opinion a totally inappropriate drug for Alan and as it had been doubled within the past 2 weeks would be completely responsible for Alan's inability to remain upright! I asked him directly "Are you telling us that you are prepared to over-rule the Cardiologist's drug adjustments made just 2 weeks before?"

'Absolutely' was the word used in reply. He had done his best to liaise with Cardiologist but it hadn't happened. He was in charge of the Unit and Alan was currently his patient, so this was a decision he was prepared to take. He would like to see Alan in a couple of days to confirm that improvements are already in evidence. It was his opinion that a wait of 2 months between Cardio appointments was far too long (especially with the cancer lurking in the background) and significant changes/responses to drug changes can be observed or appreciated much sooner. It was his opinion that we were being 'fobbed off' by that particular department. (Food for thought!) We were all happy with the logic of his explanation and his 'executive' decision so we accepted that Alan could now be discharged. Definitely impressed by this guy.

I am still of the opinion that having been admitted to the Unit in the full knowledge that Alan was a current Cardio patient under the care of one of this hospital's Consultant Cardiologists, that one of the Cardio team should have been requested to visit Alan, to assess and report.

The Acute Medical Unit is a particularly busy and noisy place struggling with a lack of bed availability ... but from my observations it would also appear to be a place which is drowning under a mountain of paperwork leaving little time for anyone to practice their nursing or communication skills. It gives the impression of being a 'one rung up the ladder' A & E department but without the drunks and screamers. Quite frankly, it's a bloody awful place; shoddy too, considering it is in a new 'state of the art' hospital. We will avoid it like the plague after the one return visit we are required to attend. Certainly wouldn't be awarded anything in a star rating ... only the comment "Not Recommended".

Emergencies need to be dealt with speedily ... the quickest part of this whole experience was the speed at which a discharge was attempted!

15th August, 2012: appointment with Unit Consultant to update. We arrived on AMU in plenty of time for a 12.30 pm appointment with Unit Consultant. We were shown to a waiting room and told that he would be informed we had arrived. There were half a dozen other patients already waiting. We realized we had a problem when an orderly came into the waiting room and offered everyone some lunch ... so we're in for the long haul then! Quite a good choice on the menu ... Alan commented that it would have been nice to have been offered food when he was an in-patient!! No one accepted the lunch offer but it was an ice breaker and we started talking to the other patients. Their appointments were timed well, well, before ours and tempers were beginning to rise.

We had a previous appointment back in Ludlow at 2.30pm and in view of the horrendous weather conditions we would need to leave by 1.10pm. No sign of the consultant by 1.05 pm so we reported to the desk that unfortunately we would have to leave. The doctor's on his way and will only be a couple of minutes ... Is he actually on the Unit? No, but he is in the hospital though. (This hospital is the size of a village – he could be anywhere!)

We just had to leave ... ran out of time.

By the time we got home at 3.45pm there was a message from the Consultant waiting on the answering machine. When we finally spoke he confirmed that he had managed to speak with the Cardiologist who had 'whole heartedly' agreed with his alterations to the drugs!! He was delighted Alan was feeling so much better ... confirmed that steroids should be reduced slowly ... and if at any time we felt we wanted to see him again he would be only too pleased to see us and hoped that Alan would continue to improve. Nice man!

All's well that ends well!

Thirty-five tablets a day at the moment! Alan gets frustrated that all these are needed to keep him on an even keel and complains every day about taking them. I have a daily system whereby the tablets are divided into four shot glasses to be used at various times throughout the day. He would dearly love just one day off! Clever juggling may be required from time to time, but generally speaking this is how life is going to be for the foreseeable future. Within a few days Alan is a somewhat better man! He feels about 80% back to his old self. The Unit Consultant said this could well happen. So far we have had no more wet beds and certainly no more wobbles or falling over. We have called in to see Doc M today to bring him up to date on the events of the past few days.

Between us we decided to start the beta-blocker Nebivovol the next day and just take things very steadily. Doc admitted that we are actually no further forward than we were 4 months ago so I think all of us have our fingers crossed that the Beta-blocker will do a good job for Alan. Doc will also request a re-think on the bi-ventricular pacer sometime soon, but we must see how successful this new regime will be. The Unit Consultant on AMU is convinced we are being 'fobbed off' by the Cardio because of the prostate cancer - it was also his opinion that beta-blockers were not going to work. We need to find a way to convince the Cardiologist that Alan is worthy of treatment. That's a dreadful statement to make ... but is the truth of the matter.

I put in a request to Worcester A & E department for all the ECG traces taken last weekend to be copied to our GP. We were told these graphs were very confusing and showed several different problems. It may be that this is the sort of evidence required to convince someone that a pacer may be a good option. The scans duly arrived and we now have copies ourselves. I have also researched and found a new cardiac team in Shrewsbury, specifically set up for the provision of pacers – I'll speak to Doc M next week to see if it would be appropriate to ask for a referral in view of first cardiologist's reluctance. Alan continues to remain upright with no more falls … but is still very breathless and quite tired. There is no doubt that we are both feeling very stressed about this whole situation … the frustration is through lack of progress. Alan is suffering severe nightmares and I worry each morning about what I may find when I go to wake him. It really is a traumatic state of affairs to contend with every day but both of us continue to project a positive outlook. Just can't let the b*stards grind you down!

22nd August: Just when we thought we had the 'wet' bed problem solved, out of the blue it has happened again today … so we are back to the drawing board with that one! District Nurse came to take blood samples but had a great deal of difficulty in getting the blood saying she thought Alan was dehydrated!! Not surprised after that bed this morning! Alan is still having 3 or 4 severe sessions of breathlessness each and every day.

I had to visit the Royal Worcester Hospital today to get the results of the MRI scan taken with reference to the gall stones. To operate or not to operate? NOT!! Gallstones are encased within the gallbladder and the duct is clear, so there is no urgency to remove gallbladder. Situation will be re-assessed in 6 months which leaves me free to concentrate on making sure Alan gets the best treatment possible, as quickly as possible.

24th August: Blood results … PSA = 0.5: ALP = 58: still amazing results!

I'm waiting for incident No. 3! Everything happens in 3's, doesn't it?

1. The conservatory TV is being picked up tomorrow - just two years old and broken again!! £60 to have it looked at and produce an estimate. Have lodged official complaint with Sony - 'not of merchantable quality'!

2. Hot water system needs a replacement gizmo which looks as if it will knock a great big hole in £100. So what's the third thing going to be? Better be soon as the suspense is killing me! ... and it better be cheap as I don't have a money tree!

29th August: Zometa at the Cottage Hospital and Zoladex implant. All went well! We're so used to this routine now it becomes a social outing! Doc M has made the decision to increase the dose of Nebivovol (beta blocker) immediately as there have been no improvements during the first two weeks. He wants me to phone him in a week and let him know if there is any improvement.

6th September: There has been no discernible improvement in Alan's condition since full dose of beta blocker ... blood pressure is on the low side, heart rate remains over 100, still very breathless, extremely tired and still regularly producing a 'bed'!! Yet again, Doc M has sent an urgent, very assertive, fax to the Cardiologist requesting he ignores the terminal prognosis on the prostate cancer as it is well under control, and has suggested the fitting of a bi-ventricular pacer as soon as possible. We all know this might not work for Alan ... but then again, it might just be the answer we are looking for to restore a quality of life which would be more acceptable. Anything would be better than the way we have had to live for the past 5 months. If this Cardio is not going to help us then we will have to start looking elsewhere! Shrewsbury, perhaps!

11th September: Developments!! We have received a phone call from Cardiologist's secretary. Alan can be seen at 4pm tomorrow. He remains very breathless and has had some kind of fit today whilst he was dozing which has frightened him ... understandably! We think this is make or break time for us.

12th September: Cardiologist is not mincing any words! A bi-ventricular pacer is not an option at the moment! However, he feels that more changes in medications would be helpful. The beta-blocker is to be stopped immediately and substituted with Ivabradine twice a day. (I questioned this drug – Alan's had it before and been unwell on it! "No, he hasn't - this is a new drug!" In other words "shut up Catherine.") The Cardiologist is now prepared to get a second opinion on Alan's condition by re-examining the echocardiogram with the Cardiac team in Coventry. He will see us again in a month's time. Well yippee!!

I'm not sure we are even treading water any more ... I think we are either going backwards or in a circle as the change in meds reverts back to those being used unsuccessfully at the beginning of July – two and half months ago! I knew I was right about that drug!

17th September: It seems we may have another spanner in the works. Alan thinks he has a second hernia ... this time on the left hand side! So now he has a matching pair .... unbelievable! Just how much more are we expected to have to deal with? Good news is that it would seem his heart rate is trying to come down on the new medication, although at the moment it has not made much difference to the breathlessness. We will go and see Doc this week. We want to ask about 24 hour ECG monitoring to see if the 'body shocks' he suffers show something significant on the read-out. They now cause the occasional palpitations and pins and needles in the left arm ... so it really does need to be checked out.

20th September: Well, what a turn up for the books!! Seems Cardiologist has had a change of heart - excuse the pun!! We have received a personal letter from him and after seeking the opinion of his complete team and that of a colleague at the Walsgrave Hospital in Coventry, the conclusion has been reached that there is absolutely nothing to be lost in fitting a pacer should the new medication not improve matters enough, and if there is evidence in a new echocardiogram to support the decision. All we have ever wanted is to be given a chance at this ... so if the scan shows a need, then the pacer will be fitted. My suggestion of 24 hour ECG monitoring was thought not to be a helpful exercise! Oh, well ... it was just a thought!

21st September: Vampire nurse failed, miserably ... she tells us Alan is dehydrated and she will send someone else out on Monday.

24th September: Second District Nurse called today to collect blood samples. She also failed ... even more miserably! We ended up in surgery to have Doc M take the samples ... success! However, he was not impressed by the inefficiency of the girls – they have enough practice and should be more than capable of drawing blood under any circumstances. He told us to tell them just to pull the tourniquet tighter next time! The results were good – again ... PSA = 0.5: ALP = 64: Testosterone = <0.1: Still superb!!

**** *Alan and I have discussed the possibility of gradually reducing some of his 'comfort' drugs in an effort to improve his general wellbeing - this process will start today. Obviously we won't be interfering with his heart or prostate medications. He is on such a cocktail of drugs we really feel it is not helping the situation any more. We will monitor the situation closely.* ****

27th September: It never rains but it pours. I went off to the hairdressers – haven't been for ages and I need my low-lights done again. The girls had just about finished getting the foils into my hair when the phone went ... it was for me! Alan is unwell and distressed. He thinks he has had a heart attack. He wants me back home. I tell him I'm on my way. Picture this ... a white haired pensioner doing a great impression of a Christmas tree running through the village. If the locals didn't already know I was mad, they do now! One young man gave me such a quizzical look – "don't ask" I said. I drove back home as quickly as I could. Luckily it's only some 4 miles. I was worried sick as to what had brought this on and what state he was going to be in when I arrived home.

Alan was most upset and very distressed. He had been taken ill in the bathroom and had really struggled to get to the phone in the study where he was able to collapse into a chair. He was a dreadful colour and sweating profusely. He could hardly walk and the whole incident had very obviously frightened him. When he calmed enough to be able to tell me what had happened, it would seem that he tried to have a shower, had become very breathless, and had felt very poorly and thought he was going to keel over and not be able to get to the phone. Basically, he was telling me that I shouldn't have left him on his own. It had never been a problem in the past for me to be out for shopping, etc., but apparently now it was most definitely a problem. I phoned the Doc and he will call in later today. I made Alan comfortable on the settee, made him a drink and then had to leave him to get my hair sorted out. I don't think he was impressed by this ... but I couldn't leave the colour on the hair 'cooking' indefinitely! Yet again, the mad old woman of Cleobury Mortimer was spotted in the village doing her Christmas tree impression! The hairdressers cannot believe what I have just done .. they would never have the nerve! When needs must ...! Doc M arrived later in the afternoon to check all was OK. He asked that we attend the main surgery tomorrow morning so that a blood test could be done to confirm whether or not this 'event' had been a heart attack. The events of today have left Alan totally exhausted.

28th September: Alan underwent a TropTonins (TropT) blood test this morning which ascertains whether or not a heart attack has taken place within the past few hours. Delighted to say the test was negative. Such a relief! Not sure what happened, but certainly not a heart attack ... but again, he remains very tired. Ten years ago today Alan and I moved into "Everest". It's frightening how quickly these years have passed us by ... all the work that we have done ... events that have taken place. Luckily it is a home we both continue to love, which is a good job really, as we are now virtual prisoners within its four walls. We are lucky to have such lovely surroundings, but life is being particularly cruel at the moment.

Yet another month has gone by and still there doesn't appear to be any progress, in fact I wonder if we are actually going backwards!

6th October: For weeks I have had arrangements in place to travel to Ibstone, near Hemel Hempstead, for a social afternoon with other ladies whose men folk have prostate cancer. We are all members of a FaceBook support group called "Ladies On Line". About 25 of us are making the trip. In view of recent events at home, I cannot make this trip without someone covering for me at home. Givvi was due to come with me to Ibstone, but as it is so long since I've been out at all, she offers to come and sit with Alan and bring Percy with her to do any jobs which may need attention.

It's a long drive and about half way there I was beginning to wonder why I was bothering with this! I set the speed limiter to 74 m.p.h. whilst on the motorway – can't afford to get booked for speeding again. It took over 2 hours to complete the journey. However, it was well worth it, actually, as all the ladies I met that day were lovely – somehow not strangers as we talk every day on FaceBook and have seen photos of each other. We all enjoyed a meal together and a few drinks. Some of the ladies were staying at the hotel overnight, but this was far more than I could have expected to achieve! I left at about 6pm knowing that I could make the majority of the journey home in daylight and be on familiar roads before darkness fell. I was glad to be back ... the Lisa Tarbuck show on Radio 2 for most of the drive home was so bad it was almost brilliant! Listeners invite her into their homes, via the telephone, whilst they cook their Saturday night evening meal! How mundane is that?

9th October: This is the third day in a row when Alan has slept virtually all day - today he has been awake just 3 times for about 20 minutes each time. All he can tell me is that he just feels very unwell.

10th October: Alan is again much stressed and feeling most unwell ... trouble breathing and on the point of collapse yet again. As Doc M is on holiday, substitute GP, "The German Maid" called in to assess. Her feeling is that in view of pending Cardio appointment she will leave things as they are and tells Alan to just take it easy for a couple of days. Alan is still not eating ... this has been going on for 4 days now.

11th October: Alan was very late getting up today and looked absolutely dreadful. Within 10 minutes he was on the point of collapse yet again and went back to bed immediately. A different substitute GP was called out, "The Italian Belle". Alan's blood pressure is dangerously low. She would agree to have Alan admitted to hospital but feels it will sabotage tomorrow's Cardio appointment and suggests that heart medications are stopped for today in an effort to increase blood pressure enough to make the journey to appointment. Alan tells me that he has 'had enough' and feels he can't go on any longer. It's heart-breaking ... I can't bear to see him in such a dreadful state.

12th October: I cannot tell you how difficult it was to get Alan ready to go out today and to actually get him from the back door to the car, which I had moved to the closest point. Half way to Worcester Alan suggested that I stop the car and telephone for an ambulance .. that's how bad he feels! I press on with the journey and get us to Worcester as quickly as possible. I helped Alan into his wheelchair and into the waiting room hoping that the consultant is pretty much on time with his appointments today. Cardiologist was shocked to see how Alan had declined in just 4 weeks. He looks absolutely dreadful and can hardly support himself in the wheelchair. Cardio immediately admits him to the cardiac ward where he will be monitored for the weekend. He apologized that he had been unable to increase Alan's quality of life with medications but will carry out another echocardiogram under the supervision of a doctor and will then make final decision on pacer ... he only needs to feel there is a 20% chance of improvement to carry on. In the meantime, the Cardio will contact the Harefield Hospital with a view to asking if Alan may be considered for a ventricular pump ... but he is not hopeful for several reasons ... Alan's age ... his Prostate Cancer ... he is not a transplant patient ... and the pumps are only licensed for use on heart transplant patients. He advises us that at the end of the day, it may be that nothing more can be done for Alan, in which case all that can be offered is palliative care with low prospects. We are just devastated by this news. Admission to the ward was fairly quick on this occasion. All Alan wants to do is be in bed and sleep. In view of his bone mets the nurses organize a ripple air bed in the hopes that he will be more comfortable.

My next task is to return home and collect all his drugs and essentials that he will need for a few days in hospital, and get back to the hospital again. By the time I have made the second trip I can see that Alan is settled and comfortable. I spend some time with the staff explaining the drug regime and hand over a printed list of all the drugs in use, the dosages and timings to be taken. They tell me they fully understand the print out and everything will be fine. There is little point in my sitting by the bed with Alan asleep, so I leave him to rest and make my way back home again.

13th October: 13th by name ... 13th by nature! Nightmare scenario emerged! Hospital staff had totally misunderstood information on Alan's drugs regime and consequently had doubled all the medications which he takes twice a day. Therefore, they had handed Alan twice as much Morphine (160mg instead of 80mg), Cyprostat and Ivabradine than he was due to have. This happened Friday evening and Saturday morning. Luckily Alan realized something was wrong and had hidden all the tablets he had been given! When I arrived, he gave them all to me to sort through and I was able to give him the correct amounts. I had to demand to see a doctor in order to get all the notes corrected. The staff were very concerned they had overdosed him and therefore watched him like a hawk and wouldn't allow him off the ward. Alan is very tired and is not enjoying the hospital food. I asked Alan if he really wanted to put himself through an operation if a pacer was an option. He says this will be his last chance to buy a bit more time ... and he wants to take the opportunity if it is offered.

14th October: As Alan seemed a little brighter I have helped him shower and he has managed to shave. He feels refreshed and I was able to deal with his overgrown toe nails!! Wrapped up warm I was able to take him outside into the glorious sunshine and he was able to have just one cigarette before he felt totally exhausted and wanted to go back to his bed. We have subscribed to the TV services as he will be in bed for so many hours. He has a bed by the window and a great view of the helicopter pad where Air Ambulances have been landing several times today. He wanted me to leave early. He was just so tired. All he wanted to do was sleep. Hopefully tomorrow we will have some news about the scan. I decided this was the right time to phone his friends who live at long distances so that they are aware of the situation.

16th October: Repeat Echocardiogram undertaken.

17th October: To Pace or not to Pace? It took the Cardio until 3.30pm to come and talk to us! At 3pm I had said that we needed to know what was going on, so they asked him to come down. The answer to the question is an emphatic 'No'. The explanation we were given is that Alan's heart does exactly what it's meant to do, in the right order, and at the right time ... it is just a totally knackered heart. Therefore a pacer would not make things better and could even make things worse. It has been deliberated and discussed within 3 different heart teams at 3 different hospitals and this is the final, final answer. So now we start Plan Z ... the last one on the page. There may be a bit of tinkering between ACE inhibitors and Beta-Blocker ... but that's about it. Cardio wants Alan under the care of a specialist Heart Nurse - but unfortunately our GPs' surgery doesn't subscribe to this service locally. He has also been talking to us about needing to organize a care package with Social Services and he will pass on details. We will see him again in a month. He can give us little guidance as to how long Alan may be able to fight this ... 6 weeks, 6 months? ... who knows! Losing a little weight would help - but not a lot - and he has suggested that Alan gives up NONE of his current creature comforts (and that includes smoking!) He has been very straight with us when we have asked the awkward questions ... and the "Do not resuscitate" info will be put back in place tomorrow when we see Doc M. Not good news at all ... but we're used to that, and just have to face it head-on.

However, it is somewhat unsettling to realize that the Cardio's possible 6 month prognosis leads us to next April ... which is almost, to the month, the same timing as the original PCa prognosis of two years. We were previously told to accept any life extension past April as a bonus. We have to wonder if we are actually going to get that far!

Chapter 16: Matters of the Heart

We are just past the 18 month mark in dealing with Prostate Cancer, and unfortunately we have arrived at a new chapter in our battle against illness and disease. Whilst Prostate Cancer was the centre of our world for in excess of 12 months, it pales into virtual insignificance now that Alan has a new and more urgent battle for life. Having been given a terminal prognosis for his advanced cancer just 18 months ago, its response to treatment has been wonderful, but we now have to re-adjust to the fact that the Acute Left Ventricle Heart Failure, which is confirmed as 'severely life limiting' with low prospects, impacts dramatically on our daily lives, and the quality of life we now endure. How many people have to deal with being given this type of devastating news twice in just 18 short months? Not too many that we know! Once was bad enough! How can life be so unjust?

Home is where the heart is - no pun intended! So I have brought Alan out of hospital to be where he belongs … with me … at "Everest" – our hill-top home in South Shropshire. He is still very tired but at least it will be more peaceful here in our own beloved surroundings … and, of course, we are together. We are still mulling over everything we have been told.

18th October: Quiet, peaceful day … just a visit from Doc M and Lubna (his current medical student) - and even though the discussion was all about carers, community nurses, end of life drugs pack for the house, etc., etc., we have all managed to sit here laughing our heads off with tears rolling down our faces!! The hilarity was all about 'Mrs. Vicar' who called to see Alan when he was in dock! Alan had left her totally lost for words - she was sure the hospital would be able to 'put things right for him'! "Oh, good" he had said to her "all I have to do then is wait for the terminal cancer to get me!!" Doc M said to Alan "well, you won't mind if you go with a G & T in one hand and fag in the other, will you?" We all agreed … that would do nicely!! Doc agrees that Alan's life will now be bed or sofa … very little else.

19th October: We had been taken off the District Nurse's list for today - they thought Alan was still in hospital. Luckily I managed to catch her on her rounds so that she was able to visit to take blood samples - right in the middle of one of Alan's vomiting sessions ... lovely!! The PCa treatments will continue as before. Alan feels very unwell today and is spending his time in bed. He actually ends up sleeping for 17 hours straight, only being woken for bloods and cups of tea.

PSA=0.6/ALP=74: Results still extremely stable and heartening.

23rd October: Alan is to have a couple of broken teeth out today. We have sought permission from his Oncologist and this has been given provided that this week's Zometa infusion is cancelled and treatment is not restarted until the healing process has taken place. Actually getting Alan to the dentist in the village will be a challenge today! Mobility scooter delivery expected today after being let down yesterday.

25th October: Alan was a little more 'with it' today. He is having Zopiclone at night to ensure that night-time is the priority for sleeping, rather than the daytime. Our Mac Nurse, Jenny, arrived and was quite dismayed to see the change in him since she last visited. Anyway, she has managed to 'fast track' our request for assistance and has secured funding for 3 visits per week for showering, etc., and part funding for 1 x 3 hour respite session for me. The manager of the domiciliary care company is coming to visit on Monday to find out exactly what we need. Haven't a clue what I will do on my own as Alan and I have been joined at the hip for almost 20 years and have never done anything on our own! This arrangement will last for a minimum of 6 weeks initially and hopefully will be funded beyond that, but if we have to get our hands in our pockets, the cost will be in the approximate region of £17 per hour - at which point I will not be going out for 3 hours a week!

Doc M arrived about an hour before surgery ... kicked off his shoes, feet up on settee, coffee, shortbread biscuits and Maltesers! We just needed to have a good general chat with him ... talked about loads of things including his 'magic box of tricks' (end of life drugs to be kept in the house) but ended up talking about Alan's funeral and what would be happening to the ashes, etc. Was Alan frightened ... or me, come to that? What was it that troubled him most about dying? Alan told him it was the thought of having to leave me. Alan has already decided that it will be his heart that kills him now rather than the prostate cancer - (well, we've all known that since April!) ... but he feels it will be quick, which he sees as a bonus. Not eating well? ... not too much of a problem! If Alan fancies choc-ice and chips - so be it! And Doc said that he wouldn't be upset if he turned up on a visit and Alan was p*ssed as a newt! "Do whatever it is that makes you happy" - was the advice! Doc M's own grandfather (well into his 80's) went on for over a year in this sort of state, apparently!

I've been looking at Wiltshire Farm Foods and may get half a dozen in to see if Alan can be tempted into eating something a bit more substantial. The other interesting thing today is that Alan saw a mouse on top of the fire place!! Hallucinations! That's all we need! Shame last night's spider wasn't an hallucination!! He went skits ... hates spiders!!

26th October: Alan has slept the clock round to some 13 hours and was then awake for less than 2 hours before falling asleep again on the settee where he has remained until asking to go to bed at 9 pm. He couldn't even manage to stay awake for Giv and Perce's visit this afternoon and has only eaten half a piece of toast and attempted several cups of tea. He will be asleep by 10pm and the whole process will start again. So sad. He doesn't want to live like this.

27th October: Alan has slept 29 of the last 36 hours ... said he felt better this morning ... had cup of tea and tablets and within half an hour was vomiting again! Luckily he managed to hold on to the tablets!

Alan's not had a proper meal since 6th October and that seems to have been the pivotal date as since then he has slept most of the time, including his time in hospital. I'm so uncertain as to how long things will continue like this ... or is this the slow decline to the end? I just feel that without proper food it won't be too long before other organs start to malfunction. He is already very confused and his speech is even more difficult to understand since another two teeth came out this week. He's not been dressed for over a week and I just can't see where any improvement is going to come from. He's having nightmares and very strange dreams and last night was convinced he wasn't going to get up the stairs to bed ... we don't have any!! He was quite convinced he had seen a mouse on the mantelpiece the night before! I stay with him holding his hand most nights whilst he falls off to sleep as he seems so twitchy and troubled, and I find that I'm up two or three times in the night to stand at his door to make sure I can hear him breathing. I'm finding it hard to hold it all together and have many a tear when I'm on my own now. The thought of having to go on like this for weeks or months ... or more, is almost unbearable and so heart-breaking.

28th October: Spoke with Givvi on the phone today as it's her 38th birthday. She has a busy day ahead of her and a gig tonight with Wolfsbane in Derby ... the final night of their tour. Sammy came to visit with Jordan but Alan was incapable of staying awake more than 10 minutes of their visit. Jordan amused himself by creating a circuit around the bungalow that he could negotiate on the mobility scooter!! Kept him amused for an hour or so! He knows that Grandad is poorly and he seemed quite amused when he saw him asleep in bed in the middle of the day!

29th October: Flu jabs due today – wondering if we can actually get there. We had phone call from the local hospice to arrange some 'respite' cover for me to have a break - I can have 4 hours a week starting next week on Thursday ... not sure yet what I will be doing whilst a carer comes in to sit with Alan for the afternoon. The manager of the domiciliary care company, Gill, responsible for providing help to us visited to find out exactly what help we need. We have initially decided that two visits a week to help with showering would be appropriate and this will start on Friday of this week. Alan was not well enough to attend for the flu jab, so his favourite nurse sneaked out of the jabbing session in the village hall to come to the house and do the job! We are so lucky to have such lovely folks around us.

30th October: Alan is much brighter today! He woke at lunchtime and got up and washed. We had a quick visit from Brummie and Lynn this afternoon and Alan was awake and lucid the whole time. He's managed to eat a Wheetabix, a few flapjacks and have a milkshake, so quite an improvement there. He was very tired tonight but managed to stay up until almost 10pm. Alan is becoming more breathless by the day and I will ask the surgery to arrange for an assessment to be made with regard to having oxygen available in the house ... or the use of an oxygen concentrator.

2nd November: This is the first day of the new care system we have in place. I've had to phone and cancel as Alan is not well enough to get out of bed, let alone be showered by a stranger. At least I had the company of my old friend, Janet, for a couple of hours this afternoon which was a welcome diversion as Alan remained asleep in bed for the rest of the day.

3rd November: Another typical day. Alan up by 11am. He felt able to attempt his shower by noon, but exhausted and asleep by 1pm in the lounge. Slept till 6pm and was then ready for bed where he immediately continued to sleep. He got up at 10.30pm for tablets, tea and toast, then straight back in bed and asleep by 11.30pm. Can someone please explain to me how this equates to the 'improved quality of life' (for either of us!!) that the cardiologist was striving achieve? The fireworks on display down in the valley this evening were a very pretty sight and one of the few freebies we can enjoy from the top of this hill.

4th November: A somewhat better day! Alan was up by mid-day and has managed to eat considerably more than of late. He was able to stay awake all day before going to bed at 9pm. Hopefully we can build on this improvement.

5th November: Alan has woken up, finally at 3.10pm. He went to bed at 9pm last night so that I could watch Downton Abbey in peace!!

By the time he actually gets out of the bed it will be 4-ish ... now what exciting things can we do in the day's remaining daylight? Alan gets up and comes into the lounge ... but is asleep again by 4.15pm after having one cup of tea and taking his tablets. Obviously I am making life far too warm and comfy in front of the fire!!

6.30pm - I need to get to the shop!! I have written a huge note and put it on his lap ... what's the betting the phone rings and startles him whilst I am out? I was only gone 10 minutes! He was still asleep when I got home and finally woke up at 8.30pm. So that's our record so far ... 23.5 hours of continuous sleep! This can't be right, can it? And he's struggling to keep his eyes open by 9pm ... tea in one hand, cigarette in the other!

6th November: As at 11am today Alan had slept for 36 of the previous 39 hours. Gill came in to help with showering this morning which seemed very easy to her and Alan felt at ease ... but it still left him very tired. This evening I have checked his blood pressure and SATs only to find that they are all in his boots. At rest blood pressure was only 100/65 ... heart rate 75 ... and his SATs have suddenly dropped to 92%!! No wonder he can't keep awake! I shall be on the phone first thing in the morning for an emergency oxygen supply prescription.

7th November: La Bella Italiano made the house call – Doc M is away again. She examines Alan and looks at his list of medications. Silly me! Morphine over-dosing ... that's the problem - apparently! I should have known! This problem is nothing to do with oxygen! (Alan's morphine has been reduced over the last six weeks from 100mg twice a day to 60mg twice a day. So work that one out ... I can't!) She will make sure emergency oxygen is prescribed for use when he's struggling. As bloods are due to be done tomorrow a check will be made to see if Alan is Digoxin toxic (a problem if he is!) as well as everything else. Apparently I should be 'cattle prodding' him every day to get him up according to this doctor! Yeah, right!! That's a divorceable offence, I suspect!! I have been querying a drug called Ivabradine for the last six weeks or more as Alan has been declining rapidly since this was prescribed by Cardio about eight weeks ago ... but nobody is listening. I'm tempted to flush them down the loo. I got very upset when our Mac nurse, Jenny, was here and have cancelled the 'Alan sitter' for tomorrow ... I just don't feel comfortable leaving him - it doesn't seem right at the moment. I think we are going backwards as there is certainly no progress. Her opinion is that Alan is declining as the heart failure progresses and this is not drug related. Eating is still a major issue. It's just not happening - and has been this way since the beginning of October.

Alan and I have made an 'executive' decision this evening after having checked back on how he has been on this particular drug, Ivabradine. We are going to withdraw it from his regime. He's not having any more of it for now ... we'll take stock of the situation again on Monday. We should know by then if he feels any different, be that better or worse! It can always be re-instated and if I'm wrong, then I'll hold my hands up ... but we are both totally exasperated that no one has listened to our concerns about this particular drug. Surely, if all this sleeping was down to morphine overdosing, Alan would have been asleep for the past 21 months! Well, enough's enough. What can they do? Hang me? Bring it on! They're not the ones having to live with this lot! I sometimes think people have absolutely no idea what it's like to live with someone going through the 'big sleep'. Hopefully Doc M will be back at work next week.

8th/9th November: We've had a couple of comparatively quiet and uneventful days. The District Nurse called in on Thursday for bloods - she was gone very quickly!! Alan has been awake most of the time which is a vast improvement on what's been happening of late! We took delivery of the emergency oxygen supply and all the rules and regulations which go with it. Showering Gill came in on Friday to help Alan, which again left him extremely tired and consequently he was dozing on and off all afternoon.

10th November: Giv's house move today and we can't be of any assistance, unfortunately, but understand that it's gone mostly to plan but has been extremely tiring. She has had a good crew of helpers

114

around her today. I had to cancel Sammy's visit with the children as Alan has felt very unwell and was actually asleep all afternoon. He has managed a very small meal today, which is progress, and by this evening he was actually feeling much better in himself. Fingers crossed!

11th November: Remembrance Sunday.   It was such a beautiful day today, even the air balloons were taking advantage of the day ... but for Alan, who had another vomiting episode mid-morning, the day was lost to sleeping. He was not even able to watch the march past at the Cenotaph on TV. He was up by 5pm and actually enjoyed some soup and a cream cake a little later. Unfortunately he was back in bed and asleep by 9pm ... just so incredibly tired. He had been looking forward to the Celebrity Jungle starting on TV tonight ... but couldn't even stay awake that long.

12th November: As the experiment of withdrawing Ivabradine appears not to have worked in our favour, we have re-started the tablets again tonight. Alan really doesn't feel any better and his heart rate has increased to over 100 again, but at least we tried to improve the situation - it just didn't work. I weighed Alan today and he has lost 1st 4lbs in just three weeks. It's not surprising when you consider how little he has been eating. His sleeping routine is still much the same and his time awake over the past ten days averages out at four hours a day. Doc M is back at work so presumably he will call in this week.

13th November: 13th by name – 13th by nature! I've just had the worst day from hell in a very long time. Everything bubbled over today and I have cried and sobbed uncontrollably at times. Gill came in to do his shower and we had to put Alan on oxygen afterwards to help him recover from the exertion. There's nothing different going on here with Alan and he has managed 4 hours awake in the middle of the day, but has not eaten a thing. He's also had some knife sharp pains across his heart today ... something completely new. So, for whatever reason, today was the day it all got the better of me! I have emailed Doc M so that he will be up to date when he visits on Thursday.

14th November: I've had to write to our Phuket hotel to let them know we will never again be able to visit - so many memories spanning so many years - so many Thai friends never to be seen again. Nothing to look forward to anymore ... just something else to tear us apart.

15th November: Our life is truly a rollercoaster!! Yesterday it was in the depths of despair and yet today the news is much brighter. Doc M has spent an hour with us today going through all of Alan's drugs and looking for what may have caused Alan's decline over the past few weeks. He feels that the present combination of drugs, which includes morphine, has resulted in Alan becoming permanently 'stoned'! So morphine is to be reduced, again. Out with the beta-blocker; halve the Digoxin; introduce Dexamethasone, plus an anti-sickness type drug and hopefully this will improve matters. Obviously the cancer drugs will have to stay in place. All of these changes certainly can't make things any worse, so let's give it a whirl! Changes will be phased in over the next week ... we're starting with the morphine!

16th November: The District Nurse arrived about 10am to take bloods, just as I was out at the shops and fetching new medications from surgery. I had to cancel Gill coming in for Alan's shower as even though he got up feeling OK ... that soon changed. We have had a house full of visitors today ... Giv, Sam, Zoe and Rem ... and Janet this afternoon. Alan has tried to eat today but with little success. By this evening Mr. Grumpy Nasty Pants is in residence .. so least said, soonest mended. He was in bed by 10 pm and asleep very quickly.

Chapter 17: A brush with Norovirus!

17th November: Alan did not wake till 3pm ... had a cup of tea and went straight back to sleep until 5pm when he got up, but fell asleep within minutes on the settee until 9.30pm. He went off to the loo and then I heard him call out ... I found him in a crumpled heap at the end of his bed. I managed to get him into bed, eventually, and straight on oxygen until he had recovered. Poor sod has to be really p****d off with this lot! Doc M wants me to phone him Monday morning expecting great things ... oh well, he'll just have to learn to live with disappointment - like the rest of us!! Alan's had 2 Wheetabix and is already asleep again! Unbelievable!! Went to check on him later and he's a bit emotional about how ill he feels and doesn't know how much longer he can carry on feeling like this. He feels he would just like to turn over, go to sleep, and never wake up. I can't express in words how dreadful it is to see a loved one suffering in this way. Maybe tomorrow will be different for him ... please! He has three appointments next week and at this moment in time I don't have a clue as to how I'm going to get him to any of them!

18th November: Sunday morning kicks off with a vengeance! Alan makes a very urgent bathroom visit followed by vomiting. Finally I managed to settle him back in bed with tea and tablets. He then continued to sleep until mid-afternoon when he decides he would like to get up for a while. He feels unable to eat still, and now not able to drink - everything either tastes or smells 'wrong'. He was back in bed and asleep by 8pm ... he didn't wake again during the evening, so no medications given.

19th November: Alan has woken me three times during the night to help him. He is vomiting again. From 8am onwards he has been back and forth to the bathroom from his bed and also there has been intermittent vomiting. I spoke with Doc M before 9.30am who will call in to see him after morning surgery ... in the meantime give sickness tablets every 4 hours and keep in touch by phone. As everything smells 'wrong', I have had to change the bed and all Alan's clothes! How odd is that? Doc M arrived at 2.30pm and gave Alan an injection to halt the vomiting. I express concerns about dehydration. If vomiting stops then Doc M will administer a drip at home this evening, but as this is not the case, he organized an ambulance at 6.15pm after speaking to the hospital requesting Alan be admitted. He feels this is most likely the Norovirus. He later calls back to the house to deliver referral letter for the hospital.

It took the ambulance two hours to get here ... then an hour's journey to A & E. By 10.15pm Alan was in isolation in a side room in A & E and immediately set up on a drip which would take a couple of hours to administer. It is hoped that he will see a doctor within these two hours before he can be moved to a ward where a further drip can be administered over a longer period of time ... they are choc'a'block tonight. He has been getting weaker for weeks (has lost another half stone in 6 days) and the chances are that he has picked up the Norovirus (not confirmed, by suspected) from someone visiting the house just before the weekend. Doc M had tried anything and everything all day to stop the vomiting and diarrhoea (visited twice, phoned 4 times), and nothing has worked. Once he is stabilized Alan will be moved to the local Cottage Hospital where there should be a bed for him on Wednesday. Hopefully he will be able to regain some strength there before coming home. Really not sure how long this is going to take as he is so physically weak right now ... hopefully not too weak for him to be able to fight this. Giv picked me up at the hospital and after a tour of her new house, brought me home by 1.30am. (Sam has told me on the phone that he has been ill on Saturday and Sunday with very similar symptoms, so have to conclude he, or grandson Rem, was the source of all this misery.)

We got another set of blood results today: The PSA=0.3: (Brilliant) and his ALP=88: (Considerable increase but still within very acceptable limits, and think this is the least of our worries at the moment)

20th November: By 9.30am the hospital is telling me that Alan can be discharged to home. I immediately spoke with Doc M who speaks with the hospital. He is informed that Alan is much brighter, eating, drinking and using the loo normally and ready to be at home. I arrive at the hospital to find Alan in the same A & E room ... half a cup of tea and a couple of biscuits on his table. Even though they have all his drugs, a full list of what is taken in the morning and evening, it would appear that in their wisdom the hospital has randomly selected only four of the 10 tablets Alan should have each morning. I also learn that the original small bag of saline drip is the ONLY treatment he has received. What is the point of all this disruption if they are not going to give the required treatment that Doc M wanted for him? A porter brings Alan to the car in a wheelchair and we make the journey home. During the journey Alan is becoming queasy but we still have the sick bag from the ambulance, so I push on till we get home.

Once Alan is in bed, the vomiting starts again. This continues every 20 minutes or so. I immediately call the doctors' surgery and request a visit for Alan to have a repeat injection to bring this under control. The retching and vomiting continue on a very regular basis and Alan becomes weaker and weaker, and of course his heart rate is going through the roof with all the exertion. Nothing is staying down including the sickness pills. He looks dreadful. I sent a text to Doc M to advise things worse than previous day. Doc M has replied to my txt and still feels Alan may need to go into local Cottage Hospital tomorrow for more re-hydrating. Hopefully in an hour or so we can get some morphine into him so that he will be more comfortable and able to get some sleep .... he's been sipping on Oramorph but it keeps coming back! Even water is coming back at the moment! Can't start to tell you how Alan looks (he's the colour of calico and very black around the eyes) ... and I'm certainly not telling him! I also phoned the hospital to advise of the deterioration and to find out the name of the doctor who had signed Alan out on the discharge papers. (I am furious they have done this to him - this is the second occasion when Worcester hospital has discharged Alan too quickly.) Unfortunately Doc M is day off. Our lovely 'German Maid' doc has been to give Alan another 'anti-sick' injection. She is now off to do local surgery and I will liaise with her at about 6pm to make sure everything is OK for overnight. By 7.00pm he is sleeping peacefully at last - in the lounge, with me, in front of the fire. I took him down to bed at about 9pm and made sure he was settled. Hopefully we will have a quiet night. Undisturbed night ... Alan still asleep at 9am the next morning. Result!

No visitors will be allowed until we are well and truly over this setback. (Dentist - cancelled. Gill - cancelled. Breast screening - postponed.)

21st November: This has been a really rough few days. However, you would not believe the turnaround now. Double dosed with morphine last night (OK - so hang me!). Alan slept for 14 hours. The only meds today are 'comfort' type ... Prozac (oh, yes!!), morphine and Cyprostat. He is in no pain, no vomiting ... or the other! He's managed to have cups of tea all morning and 'hint of lemon' water ... plus biscuits and toast. Doc M and Lubna arrived lunchtime-ish and were delighted at his progress. His blood pressure and pulse rate are good. Therefore, Doc M has made the decision not to give any heart meds tonight or tomorrow morning. Effectively Alan's had none since Saturday evening! He will visit again tomorrow, early afternoon, and see how things are at that point before making any changes he thinks necessary.

Alan is bright, coherent and already abusing his mates on the phone – as well as the banter he has had with Doc M! He is still physically weak and can hardly walk, but we can work on that!! Mild symptoms returned during the evening, but hopefully the specific tablets for these will do the trick. Noticeably more breathless tonight so need to identify which heart drug will be most effective to deal with this. So it's very much happier on the hill today!! Told you he was a fighter!! We now have a new dress code for all visitors – "hospital scrubs"!

22nd November: Life on the hill was actually quite pleasant today ... it's a long time since I could say that! Alan had trouble getting to sleep last night, but a bit more morphine sorted that. He slept in a bit late, but hey ho, what the hell!! He has eaten better today than he has since the beginning of October ... and that seems like light years ago! His fluid intake has also increased quite dramatically. Doc M and Lubna arrived about 2pm and we sorted out the business end of the heart meds and how and when to re-introduce them. After that, it was all tea, coffee, biscuits, jokes, laughs ... quite a party. Lubna, in her final year as a medical student, is due to finish at the surgery within two weeks - don't think she will ever forget working with Doc M and her visits to us!! As there are some shortbread biscuits left, they will be back tomorrow - to check on Alan, of course, making sure he is going to be OK over the weekend as Doc M is heading to 'Geordie-land' for a family do. Must admit I feel like an 'on demand' TV station today and now totally cream crackered! We both feel that a corner has been turned today and hopefully improvements will continue. Alan is extremely breathless at the slightest physical exertion, but with the phased re-introduction of his heart medications hopefully this will ease in the days to come. It was good to see Giv for a couple of hours this evening.

23rd November: Cardio appointment cancelled – (rescheduled for 4th January). Today has been something quite special. At last I feel as if I am getting 'my man' back! He has improved so much again since yesterday - I really hope things will continue to improve. Perhaps, in a strange way, this virus and everything that went with it, has done us a bit of a favour. Alan was free of any medication other than anti-sickness drugs for about five days, giving us the chance to start again with a new drugs regime. We have started with the essential pain control and prostate drugs before a slow introduction of selected heart medications and it seems to be working. With the value of hindsight, we have worked closely with Doc M to identify which of the heart medications will be most beneficial to deal with Alan's symptoms, and it may be Alan will never take some of the others again. Since he became so unwell back in April with a 'chest infection' (ha!) it has been all downhill, getting progressively worse as the weeks and months have gone by, and has included three hospital admissions. Nearly seven months of hell and mental torture have now passed us by, hopefully! Now, his appetite is returning ... his sense of humour is bubbling ... he's been walking around and 'pottering' ... enjoyed his shower this morning ... and he's shouting at the TV again!!! Now that's more like it!!! The fighting spirit has returned ... Alan's even talking about a third 'bucket party' next year!! We know he will never be the physically capable man he used to be ... but it's looking as if we may have the opportunity to get some quality of life back for both of us ... and that would be a novelty ... and just a great bonus!

24th November: Today has been so, so .. ordinary! How wonderful is that?!

Chapter 18: Feeling vindicated

29th November: No wonder we are smiling like a pair of Cheshire cats today. We have had some very satisfying news. Our contact at the GMC telephoned, as she promised she would when, and if, she had any news for us. The GMC Case Examiners (one medical, one not) after having seen all the evidence, have upheld my complaint and ruled in my favour. What a relief! I now feel totally vindicated, and justified, in the action I took. Their legal department will now take over the case and will be formulating sanctions/restrictions under which Dodgy Doc will be instructed to comply in order that he is allowed to carry on in his career as a doctor. As the case is not finally closed, we are asked not to reveal the details to anyone until such time as we have final confirmation in writing. This could take another couple of months, in view of the approaching holidays at Christmas and New Year. When the whole matter is concluded, we will be able to apply for all the paperwork in relation to our case which will include a copy of the Expert Witness report.

Our understanding is that it is a rare event for a member of the public to achieve a result such as this without the intervention of solicitors. Obviously we are delighted and can't help wondering what sort of undertakings Dodgy Doc will have to agree to in order to continue practicing. There are example 'undertakings' listed on the GMC website which are far reaching and this is now a really serious situation for the doctor. We had almost come to the conclusion that he could well get away with a warning. We also suspect that a warning was what he was hoping to receive – and what his colleagues would have been hoping for, too.

The undertakings will be tailor-made by the GMC Legal Department and will directly relate to the circumstances and details of our case. We understand from the GMC website that it is usual for about a dozen undertakings to be put in place ... an example would be having to work under supervision. We will have to be patient a little while longer to see the final outcome of this, but in the meantime we have contacted our solicitor as this must have a positive bearing on the legal proceedings already in hand. She is delighted and will eagerly await the case's conclusion and the paperwork which will follow.

6th December: We were very much hoping that a corner had been turned and that improvements would follow. However, after 9 weeks without Zometa, the last infusion brought about quite severe bone pain which needed the use of extra morphine. Although much brighter in himself, Alan is still utterly fatigued and can sleep very easily. His blood pressure and heart rate have settled nicely on less medication but he gets very anxious when having to move around the bungalow. He is becoming even more unstable on his legs. His care nurse, Gill, comes in twice a week to shower him but this is leaving Alan extremely tired. Next Tuesday he is due for re-assessment to establish whether his "NHS Continuing Health Care" funding will be allowed to continue. It would be a real shame to lose this service after just six weeks! What is a little bit strange is that he actually looks quite well physically! Doc M called in for a chat and is pleased that less medication seems to be controlling the heart rate and blood pressure. He has confirmed that he feels the excessive fatigue is just natural progression of the decline in the heart and is to be expected. He has suggested that Zometa could be stopped altogether if the bone pain continues. Alan would not be happy with this as general bone pain was much worse without it during those nine weeks. He feels this reaction to the latest infusion is almost a kind of 'flare-up' which will subside quite quickly.

10th December: We had Brummie and Lynn arrive for a couple of hours on Saturday and Alan struggled to keep awake during their visit. He was back in bed shortly after they left. He was a little bit more 'lively' on Sunday when Giv and Perce called in to help us with a couple of jobs, including removal of all the broken TV's from the house! He was back in bed by 8pm.

Unfortunately the weekend ended on a somewhat sour note with a family problem – little spoken of here previously! We just feel we have enough on our plates to contend with, without 32 year olds behaving as if they had the "terrible 2's" ... and therefore, another chapter closes. Their lives, and ours, will be less complicated and fraught without each other.

We have had a long chat about the Zometa and Alan has decided that he wants to continue with this treatment as he feels that, overall, it has been a useful addition to his cancer medications.

11th December: NHS "Continuing Health Care" Assessment day! This is quite a lengthy process undertaken by our Mac nurse, Jenny, care nurse Gill, and ourselves in the first instance. It requires very detailed information about all aspects of Alan's care needs and covering areas, not necessarily what you would have thought about, in order to achieve two showers per week. Each point raised needs hard evidence to back it up. Full details of hospital admissions required, and a complete list of medications in use. Further risk assessments and nutritional reports have to be done plus further liaison with District Nurses and Doc M. Every piece of information from all parties involved will be laced into a report to accompany the application form. The decision could be many weeks away and therefore, for the time being, we will continue with the arrangements we have in place.

12th December: I had to cancel Alan's dental appointment today within an hour of the allotted time. Having spent time getting himself washed and shaved, the effort has caused him to have an 'event' which left him needing immediate sleep. Breathless, unstable, feeling very unwell – I don't like it when this sort of thing happens. Difficult to know how or when we'll ever get back to the dentist ... last two appointments have been cancelled. He has remained extremely tired for the rest of the day, snoozing on the settee and in bed by 7pm. He is becoming increasingly frustrated with this continuing state of affairs. Unfortunately, he now seems to be going down with a cough and cold. Could do without that!

13th December: Alan's cough developed quickly today and became quite 'chesty' so I have been to the surgery and picked up a course of steroids to ease the situation. He was in bed before 6pm. Spoke with Doc M and he is calling in to see us tomorrow after evening surgery. For three hours tonight we have had a very unpleasant and distressing time. I'm not going to be graphic other than to say that Alan was in the bathroom for all of the three hours and the Twilight nurses had to be called for assistance. However, they are based over 30 miles away and we were second on their list for a visit with travelling time of over an hour once the first job had been done - so we expected a two hour wait! Anyway the situation did resolve itself before they arrived. They were still about 10 miles away when I phoned them back. This isolated incident has left Alan exhausted and upset. Lesson learned by us both in respect of this unmentionable event!

14th December: District Nurse was early this morning and bloods were done before 10am. Alan spent the morning in bed recovering from last night's escapades. We have postponed his shower until tomorrow. The coughing bug has taken good hold of him today and is becoming troublesome … so much so Alan has needed to be on oxygen after going to bed early again. Ten to fifteen minutes seems to work well for him. Doc M called in this afternoon, more for a social type visit, I think - obviously needed a quick break for coffee and cakes! He knows where to come!

15th/16th December: Coughing bug has got to both of us now … but obviously far more of a nuisance to Alan than me, necessitating more use of the oxygen supply. However, I was bad enough to spend Sunday in bed and neither of us surfaced until 5.30pm. I just hope it's not going to last too long.

17th December: As we are both still suffering with this coughing bug and Alan is very unsteady on his feet, I have arranged for the Zometa infusion to be carried out at home on Wednesday. Doc M will call and do the infusion before surgery. I have a feeling this may become a regular occurrence.

PSA=0.6: ALP down to 71: Testosterone still below 0.1: Absolutely no worries here!

20th December: Doc M and new medical student, Sara, made a home visit to administer the Zometa infusion. Talk about 'field medicine'! It was quite comical to see a drip bag hanging off a walking stick, stuck down the side of the settee in the lounge. The infusion was left to Sara to organize, under the watchful eye of the Doc M, and she performed extremely well – very efficient. Doc M was concerned about us both and our chests. He suggests we both have the same infection. Antibiotics all round then!! I have to admit we are both feeling quite poorly with it which is especially unusual for me. Alan and I have been together almost 20 years and he has never known me to have a cold ... let alone a cough!

21st December: Doc M has been sent home from work suffering something akin to the Norovirus. We have everything crossed here that nothing was passed on yesterday. Alan still feeling very tired and was in bed by 7.30pm. Sleeping at night is a problem for us both with this cough, and I am planning a second night wrapped up in a chair!

22nd December: We are both struggling with this cough and Alan is again very tired, during this afternoon he has suddenly complained about feeling sick. Oh, no, please ... not again! Have started him on anti-sickness pills immediately and have Imodium waiting in the wings! Fingers crossed. The terrible weather is back causing floods and travel mayhem. Christmas just lost all its sparkle for many folks. We remain warm and dry within our own four walls and we are not even contemplating trying to attempt to get anywhere!! Thank you Mr. Tesco for the Christmas food delivery! We are no longer in fear of starving!

23rd December: I've put myself back in bed again after a third night in an armchair trying to overcome coughing. I got up, for a short time, solely to get the turkey out of the garage freezer. I've got elephant ankles and legs from sleeping in a chair ... I wouldn't mind but this is how I usually arrive in Thailand after 14 hours on a plane and with a long holiday ahead of me! Not so this time! Alan is as rough as an old dog and certainly won't be moving today. My voice sounds as if I've spent a life-time on brandy and fags ... well, not too far from the truth, I suppose!! Do my lungs really extend below my rib cage? Everything is hurting when I cough!! Exhaling is very tuneful and seems to be echoing through a very stuffed up head, and to top it all, I have the grandmother of all cold sores erupting on my bottom lip. On a lighter note … it's stopped raining.

24th December: As both of us continue to struggle with bronchitis (yes, that's what it's been confirmed as!) Doc M suggests that Alan may be better off in hospital - given the choice I would prefer to keep him at home, and that's where Alan wants to be. He is staying put! We have cancelled all visitors for fear of more viruses being brought into the house, but a germ-free Percy kindly called over for an hour with presents … but we'll wait till we can all be together before we open those.

Christmas Day: Our 20th Christmas together was spent very quietly at home together. We shared breakfast very early in the day … the traditional hot turkey sandwiches as the bird had been cooking all night! We later exchanged small gifts knowing they will probably be the last. Unable to cope with the idea of a full Christmas dinner we just picked at little bits we fancied, and spent the day cosy in front of the fire. Alan was very tired all day but managed to stay awake for several hours, finally asking for his bed at about 8 pm. Not what we had expected or wanted for this particular Christmas.

Boxing Day: Today is Alan's 64th birthday. We daren't have visitors, but in any event Alan was so tired he was only awake for a couple of hours. Enough time to open cards and personal gifts. We've had calls from family and several close friends but our traditional Boxing Day with Givvi and Perce had to be put on hold until she is germ-free! Alan was ready to go back to bed at 4pm.

What I find so upsetting and hurtful is that folks who know us, claim to be friends, know our circumstances and realize this may very well be his last birthday, can't spend two minutes of their precious time to phone him or even consider sending a card. Please don't let them come crying to me when it's all too late! I can honestly say this has

128

been the loneliest, worst Christmas I have ever had to endure – even worse than last year when Alan was again so poorly. I'm glad it's all over!

27th December: At last, we have managed to have visitors! Today was our late Christmas and birthday celebrations as Giv and Perce were able to come over. We took advantage of Percy and got him doing a couple of jobs which needed attention ... but it was nice to exchange presents and have a few laughs together. And the bonus was that Alan managed to be awake almost all of the 4 hours they were here! Doc M called in to see us during the afternoon to check the progress of us both. He feels, in the circumstances, we are doing OK!

28th December: Nothing too exciting about today other than Gill coming in to do Alan's shower and it wearing him out ... so he slept the majority of the afternoon and evening!!

31st December: The last day of a year – and it hasn't come a day too soon! I won't be sorry to see the back of 2012. Sadly, it would seem, we leave the year with four less friends than we had at the beginning ... perhaps some people just can't cope with other people's illness and what it can entail. Alan is fighting on for as long as his heart will support him, and, as a goal, is already planning a summer celebration in the form of Bucket Party Mk-III. Positive thinking!

2012 has been the very worst year of our lives together. We can but live in hopes of a little respite in 2013 and have already set several date goals for Alan to achieve ... but as is usual for us now, we'll have to take just one day at a time.

Life is not about waiting for the storms to pass ...
It's about learning to dance in the rain!

I think we are struggling at times to be able to achieve this! I have never experienced stress levels such as this in all my life, and have continued to refuse medication which may ease my thoughts and

129

fears ... because, at the end of the day, I may need a bit of help when life gets difficult! Ha!

Chapter 19: 2013 - How long is a piece of string?

1st January: Well, last night when off with a bang ... literally! After all the noise last night Alan has been having nightmares and was awake quite early this morning. The explosions put him straight back into Northern Ireland in the early 1970's – he was having a PTSD attack. What an excellent way to start the year ... not really!

We had a visit from one of my LOL Prostate Support ladies and it was great to have a couple of hours chatting away. This on-line FaceBook support group is really useful and the membership of about 130 is worldwide. Lynne originally came to see us with her Dad, who lives just a few miles down the road, and had never wanted to discuss his illness. Once he had been here and chatted to Alan, I really think he was able to cope a little better. Other ladies do the same sort of thing by linking up for coffee in their own areas. Yes, it's a pleasant group to be part of and friendships are being formed. By lunchtime, after all this chat, Alan was very tired and dozed for the rest of the day.

2nd-10th January: Generally speaking, Alan has felt unwell and has been extremely tired during this time. Visitors for a couple of hours one day left him totally exhausted and he spent the week going to bed anytime from 4pm to 8pm. Spoke with Doc M on 10th Jan and he has suggested doubling the Digoxin to 125mcg and to re-establish Predlisinone at 20mg per day to see if this will help with the tiredness.

3rd January: Today is the first day of a court case in which Givvi will be a witness tomorrow. It's a disturbing case involving sexual allegations and something which Giv has lived with for over 30 years. It is causing her distress and I wish there was more that I could do to relieve this for her. We chat on the phone daily as there is no way I can get down to Worcester to be with her.

11th January: Bloods done mid-morning followed by Gill for Alan's shower. It is immediately obvious that the extra steroids have made a difference to how Alan feels and he had a much better day.

PSA=0.6: ALP=72: Still what appear to be excellent results.

Our application for Continuing Health Care funding has been deferred on the basis that the panel needs more detailed information. Our MacMillan nurse is dealing with this so have left message for her to call and see us. We are having to jump through hoops to get funding for 2 x 1 hour sessions a week to help Alan with showering. I phoned the CHC Panel and asked what it was they needed and I was just asked to write down everything that I do for Alan. I told the lady on the phone that I didn't think I had enough paper ... and that she wouldn't have enough time to read it all!

12th-13th January: Quite good days from Alan's point of view as he has felt significantly better and has been able to 'potter' around the house rather than being in a chair all day. However, today he has mentioned, for the first time, possible problems emerging. Through feelings and sensations he is very concerned that the primary tumour may be enlarging again and he is also suffering significant discomfort in the area of his right kidney. This is already affecting his mental state as he does tend to worry about each and every little thing that happens.

14th January: Have spoken with Doc M and he will visit on Thursday afternoon.

(Having researched the possibilities of what is occurring here, it is evident that mature primary tumours can evolve to produce low PSA secreting cells which are hormone and chemo resistant and which will regenerate the growth of the tumour whilst the HT or chemo continue to deal with the shrinkage and destruction of the high PSA secreting cells. As the PCa cells become more virulent they stop making the antigen that is measured in the PSA test, to conserve energy and focus on replicating themselves. Seems there could be many Onco's unaware of this [from stories I have been told]. We may have to wait a little longer

before we actually know what is happening .. but a course of RT would probably be the only option available to deal with a rogue tumour. Time will tell. Have spoken with the Specialist Nurse at the QE hospital as they still have Alan's notes, and he advises not to leave things too long before investigation.)

Back at the end of November I expressed satisfaction and delight at some news we had received. What we have had confirmed today is the fact that after making an official complaint to the General Medical Council last February, about Dodgy Doc, the GMC has, after a full investigation, expert witness reports and legal advice, upheld my complaint and ruled in my favour. Sanctions on Dodgy Doc will now be put in place - what we had been waiting for was confirmation that Dodgy Doc had accepted these sanctions. At long last - he has! We should receive the final paperwork in about 4 weeks. At that time we will also be able to apply for copies of the expert witness reports and any other paperwork we are allowed under the Data Protection Act. It should make interesting reading! During the period 2005-2010 when Alan had presented him with classic symptoms during at least 18 separate appointments, he failed to carry out any tests or examinations whatsoever. Had he done so, and the Prostate Cancer been found several years earlier, Alan's treatment options would have been very different, and he may even have been totally rid of the cancer through surgery. Dodgy Doc will now have to work under quite obstructive sanctions for a period of at least 18 months and a GMC appointed 'trustee' (a qualified doctor) will be monitoring his work until it is of a satisfactory standard, whenever that may be after the 18 month period. This 'black mark' will remain on his public and internet file for a period of 5 years, but will remain on his 'closed' file for life - this being the file available to potential employers. Hopefully he will now not leave another patient in such dire straits. Litigation with specialist solicitors was instigated last August and the positive outcome of the GMC case obviously removes the 'burden of proof' aspect of a legal case.

15th January: Two soaking wet beds on the trot. I have a new theory about this. Stress/anxiety peaks. For the last couple of days

Alan's stress levels have been off the scale and we immediately return to the wet beds ... the sweating is very profuse! One extra Prozac given today!! Let's see if that works to eliminate the problem.

Mac nurse Jenny also called today to go through the forms again for NHS Continuing Health Care funding. Our original application had been deferred as the Panel wanted more information. It seems there is a query about the amount of 'clinical' things I do for Alan rather than having outside services coming in to look after what is required. There are 12 separate sections to the 'Care' component of this application. I was asked to comment in each of the 12 sections as to what it is I actually do for him. I typed the whole thing up in a professional manner ... took 6 hours to complete and I finished at 2am. They will be in no doubt now as to what 'clinical' involvement I have!!!

16th January: Zometa infusion is actually due today, but as there has been a 'bit of a do' as to who is now funding this (the local hospital or the surgery) it's not actually been ordered yet. Doc M's secretary emailed me to ask if I knew what the actual prescription was for the Zometa as she couldn't find any record of it in Alan's files!!! (... and the Continuing Health Care team wonder what 'clinical' involvement I have?) Having told her on the phone, it will now be ordered. I then confirmed the details by email ... and, naughtily, promptly printed off the email as evidence for the CHC Panel. MacMillan Jenny arrived at 3.30pm to collect my report - so we'll have to wait and see what happens now.

17th January: We are now on a snow warning for heavy falls tomorrow so have been out locally picking up supplies to last us a few days. Doc has phoned to say that Zometa has not arrived at the surgery, so he will do the infusion at home tomorrow providing it arrives early enough, and if he can get to us should the snow arrive! Managed to pick up supplies of all Alan's medications from the surgery so there is no fear of running out of anything. By 4.30pm the driveway is frozen and the snow has already started to fall!! Good job I got out and did some gritting on the path to the back door this morning!

18th January: We've had heavy snow overnight which continues all day. Got on the phone first thing to cancel Gill's visit - there's no way she would get here anyway!! Doc M has crashed his 4 x 4 and in any event the Zometa has still not been delivered. We'll try for it again on Monday. Still think our driveway will be impassable. Very eerie day here on the hill … so quiet … absolutely no traffic passing the house. Can only surmise abandoned vehicles are blocking both sides of the hill leaving us totally cut off from the world!! If we suddenly have an emergency it will be an air ambulance job!! Solicitors handing litigation against Dodgy Doc have been on the phone, desperate to get their hands on the GMC reports. Have checked and these will not be available till mid-February, so the matter is going to be somewhat delayed. In the meantime, she would like copies of the report I have done for the CHC funding. I suspect negotiations between legal teams will not even start till mid/late March.

19th-20th January: Comparatively quiet weekend in more ways than one! Very little traffic and Alan is very subdued on Saturday and not feeling great on Sunday!

21st January: I cancelled the car service due today - driveway still impassable. Having cleared the new snow on the pathway in readiness for doctor to call with Zometa infusion, we heard nothing all day. When I phoned I was advised Zometa had still not been delivered to the chemists, but hopefully it will be here for tomorrow. I just wish they could let us know! Alan has been most unwell today - insisted on getting up and dressed - and was then asleep on the settee all day. He has not eaten a meal and is in bed by 7pm. Breakthrough pain becoming a problem. He could have done with Doc seeing him like this!

22nd January: Alan is still sweating profusely overnight … I wonder if this is the Digoxin increase as his stress levels are not particularly high at the moment. It's the only thing we have changed recently. Doc M has suggested the dose should be halved, as from today, back to original level, and see where we are by Friday. I've had to cancel Gill this morning as Alan's had such a bad night. Alan didn't get up until after 2pm. Still trying to chase up Zometa, I have learned that it is on order with two chemists locally but not likely to be delivered until Thursday at the earliest. It will be 8 days late ... I will not let this happen again! More snow due tonight ... oh joy!!

23rd January: Today has been stupid! Have been close to tears myself! I have felt as if I'm hitting my head against a brick wall - apart from Alan, Giv and care nurse Gill, I sometimes feel I'm surrounded by idiotic inefficiency! Alan is still feeling unwell and very tired.

9.00am - Opened the back door ... we have another 4" of snow and icicles which could maim!

9.15am - Chemist no.1 has Zometa delivered. Where shall we deliver it? Docs' surgery is 25yds across the road ... we're uphill all the way, and 6 miles away! Tell you what; drop it in at the surgery as the snow is so bad! Doh! So difficult to work that one out!!

9.30am - Mac nurse Jenny on the phone ... she has secured 3 hours respite through local hospice - great – *"so it's not really worth continuing with CHC application!"*

"What? Just submit it, Jen, and if they want to throw it out, I'll go to appeal."

"Well ... but ... maybe ... I don't think you're going to get it and you'll think I'm letting you down!"

"Don't worry about it ... just get the bloody form re-submitted and we'll deal with things as they happen." Exasperating!

11.30am - Gill arrives to do Alan's shower - he's unwell but has it done anyway.

12.30pm - Front door bell rings even though I have put 'No Entry' sign on front gate - no snow cleared and very icy! He must be visually impaired! It's the washing machine engineer - a proper wimp!

He doesn't have a clue why the washing is not clean in this new machine ... so he fits a new mother board, as that must be the problem! Yeah, right!!

2.00pm - Giv's having a really bad day because of on-going court case ... such a difficult time for her.

2.05pm - Another visually impaired driver, from Chemist no.2, arrives at front door with Zometa no.2. "Did you not see sign?" Doh!

6.00pm - Nurse from docs' surgery phones. She has delivery driver there with Zometa. "Oh, good!"

Should she accept it?

"Yes! FFS .. just give it to Doc M!" As for the driver? Well ... 25 yards in 9 hours?!! Thank goodness I didn't suggest they delivered here!!!

7.00pm - Local weather forecast - Friday ... as much snow again as we've had already!

7.30pm - Alan back to bed, poor soul.

So I hope you will excuse me whilst I hoist myself up the second flag pole and scream till I've got no voice. I'll survive, I know (no other choice as hill dwellers!) but why do people have to make life so frustratingly difficult?

24th January: At last ... the Zometa is done!! (and I've got the spare in the safe!!) Alan wore his red trousers so the blood wouldn't show if we had a blow-back like last time! The Zometa was hanging off the pole hook we use for opening the loft doors! Sara did all the work today ... she tells us her final exams are in 9 weeks' time ... we're sure she's going to do fine. I managed to have a chat with Doc M in the kitchen and he gave me a very supportive hug ... he knows I'm well and truly stressed out at the moment.

Tesco is due to deliver tomorrow morning (before the next dumping of white stuff) ... well, it's the only way I can get the tobacco and cigarettes replenished! There will be a few other real essentials being delivered at the same time ... Tiramisu ... cream cakes ... chocolate ... oh, yes and a loaf! With any luck I think the driveway will be clear by Tuesday or Wednesday of next week if the promised thaw starts over the weekend. The icicles started to break off today ... frightened us to death ... sounded like gun shots!

Today has been a little bit more interesting!

25th January: For the first time in about 53 years, I have forgotten to send cards to two old school friends for their birthdays ... I feel quite guilty now! I think they will understand when I let them know we've been snowbound for over a week!

Alan took an extra Prozac last night to help him sleep and woke up with a 'hangover' ... but he had slept well. Gill came in to do his shower and the rest of the day has passed off peacefully. We are now awaiting another load of snow to go on top of the 12" we still have lying almost everywhere. Let's hope the promised thaw kicks in this weekend! Giv's court case is at the summing up stage ... thank goodness it will soon be over.

26th January: "Help the Aged" Day! Giv and Perce have given up their day and have been over to help us with the jobs which need to be done ... including replenishing the log shed, digging us out and general snow clearance! It's at times like this that I start to feel my age and can't get used to the fact that I am becoming reliant on others to help me with certain chores.

27th January: We can escape from the Hill ... all the snow has gone!! Yippee ... we've been snowbound for 11 days!

I'm speechless ... spitting feathers ... swearing under my breath ... why does this keep happening to me? CHC funding application ... deferred. I was personally asked by the CHC Panel Administrator to write down everything I did for Alan. I did this two weeks ago and handed it to the Mac Nurse who has been dealing with application. She had appointment today with CHC Admin at their office to go through the form again and re-submit it .. along with my report. She has been on the phone this afternoon telling me that all my evidence has been included on the form and it's now back in the system. "So they've got my report as well?"

"Well, no ... I've hung on to that and have got it in my file ... to keep everything together". Please help me someone! I had a feeling this was going to happen. I even offered to email my report to CHC Admin but was told there was no need as Mac Nurse was due in with it on Monday.

Anyway, by the end of our phone conversation she is going to return to the CHC Admin office either tomorrow or Wednesday and hand in my report. I've told her I will print off another copy for her precious file! Is it me? Do I expect too much of other people? I would have no expectations if I wasn't promised things ... and she told me she would deliver my work along with the form ... and she didn't! I rest my case!! ... and don't mention washing machines to me - that's a whole different story!!!

30th January: OMG ... I've just heard the weather forecast? I got out in the car for the first time just yesterday, and now they're telling us to expect snow again on Friday. Jeepers ... give me a break!! I've had no car all day as it was in for service ... so tomorrow I feel obliged to go anywhere and everywhere before we get snowed in again! However, will need to avoid the floods! The heating oil was delivered today – just in time by the looks of it, seeing the amount he got into the tank. I think we must have been running the heating on fumes! £750! It's a killer, isn't it?

CHC funding ... Mac nurse Jenny has not phoned to confirm she has delivered the paperwork and she is now off till Monday! CHC office not answering their phone this afternoon - will try again in morning. Mustn't forget to order the Zoladex tomorrow. Hotpoint are ignoring me ... dangerous, as I'm fast approaching 'aggressive assertive' mode with only 13 days of the washing machine's guarantee remaining.

The jury's out on Givvi's court case so hopefully we'll get a result on that tomorrow.

Alan's in pain but being unco-operative about pain relief ... so live with it, dear ... don't moan to me!! Doc M will be back next week ... he'll soon pull him back in line!! *"Have you made any cakes?"* ... yes, dear ... try looking in the tin!

Me? Oh yes, I'm fine, thanks ... I'm the one with a duster in one hand, iron in the other, phone lodged between chin and shoulder, pushing a shopping trolley full of logs ... and the broom stuck up my ****!

31st January: It has taken 24 hours for me to get anyone in CHC to answer the phone ... but finally, yes!! And they do have all the paperwork they should have. One less thing to worry about!

The jury is still out on Givvi's case - hope they come back today with result, but there are about 22 different charges to consider.

Sweaty soaking wet bed syndrome in full flow - again ... I think today's is no. 8, or is it no. 9? I'm past counting now as the routine of bed changing is the same every day!! This all started again on 14th January - have not had this for months!!

Alan had only been up a couple of hours or so before the dozing started. He is so tired he has slept all day on the settee, only waking long enough to have his evening meal ... and then to bed early again. Still nothing from Hotpoint ... but I did remember to order Zoladex?

2nd February: A day of memories, pain and hurt ... in more ways than one. 2nd Feb 1973 was one of the happiest days for me, ever! How things change. I hope my son had a happy 40th with his own family, including the two children I have never met.

5th February: Biggest 'non-event' of the year! I'm 64 today – wonder why I feel 94? A quiet, pleasant, but busy day. The sweaty wet beds are obviously here for a while and they also appear to be linked with extreme breathlessness at the same time. I'm not sure we will ever know for certain what causes them. Alan was too tired by the end of the day to venture out for my planned birthday meal - we'll have to try again another day!

6th February: Alan didn't feel able to get up until almost 3pm. We have managed a quick visit to the dentist to check that healing is complete after previous extraction. All is OK so we can now plan to get the part denture made. He was ready to go back to sleep by 5pm but I did my best to keep him awake till 9pm – and he was in bed and asleep by 10pm.

Boiler serviceman tells us we have potential fatal crack in heating oil tank and it should be replaced, plus there would need to be a new concrete pad laid underneath the new tank. This sounds quite expensive to me! Oh dear!

7th February: Doc M came to discuss stress levels, but has decided to leave Alan's medications as they are.

8th February: District Nurse has a complete failure trying to get blood today! Different nurse will call again on Monday! Sweaty wet beds still in evidence ... wonder if we will ever find out what this is really all about? Shower went well, except for extreme breathlessness.

9th February: Quite a red letter day! In fact, it's been a day to put the flags out, as Alan has joined me on a trip into Kidderminster to B&Q. It's really sad how such a mundane event has become something to celebrate. He has not been on this sort of outing since last summer! Although only away from home a couple of hours, Alan is totally exhausted and fell asleep on the settee after just one cup of tea!

11th February: The snow has arrived again and, as ever, the driveway is impassable without a 4x4 vehicle. District Nurse arrived mid-morning for second attempt at getting blood ... it's so easy for some of them!! Pain in area of right kidney is becoming a bit more troublesome.

It was very nice to have visitors today. Our friends Jo and Jason are both full time retail managers whose day's off are very precious to them. It was lovely to see them after so long and we all had a very enjoyable Chinese take-away meal at the end of the day. Alan has excelled himself, staying awake most of the time ... so all round it made a very nice change.

12th February: A day for shower and sleeping – nothing else!

13th February: PSA=0.5: ALP=69: These results complete 24 months of tests and results for Prostate Cancer. Alan has done so well in this respect and if only the heart medications could have dealt with the acute heart failure in the same way, things would have been very different! We needed to have PSA results under 4 (the lower the better) and ALP results anywhere between 30-130 (but preferably about half way between the two) - job done! We have to be delighted with this.

Today has been yet another sleeping day ... he is still just totally exhausted.

14th February: Valentine's Day – no time for niceties! Having taken a sleeping tablet last night - the sweaty wet bed was not in evidence this morning! Interesting! We'll have to wait and see if it continues! I know it seems odd to introduce sleeping tablets when it would appear that Alan does little else, but recently he has lain awake during the nights and we must try and establish a more normal sleeping pattern. It would be a pleasure for us both to be on the same 'shift'!

With the treatment schedule shot to pieces last month because of the late appointment for the Zometa infusion ... today would only need to be taken up with the Zoladex implant. Medical student Sara made an excellent first attempt at the job under the watchful eye of Doc M.

Alan has another chest infection so is back on anti-bio's and extra steroids. The time span between these problems seems to be getting shorter.

During a conversation with GMC today it was obvious to hear their frustration in the fact that Dodgy Doc appears to be stalling and has not yet signed the agreed undertakings. Final paperwork is still about a month away. I have told our contact at the GMC that Alan feels Dodgy Doc is hoping he will die before the conclusion of the case. She tells me his legal team repeatedly request minor alterations to the wordings of the undertakings. She will send out a letter today expressing their disdain for his actions, inform him that he has had more than enough time to comply with the GMC requests, and place a 7 day time limit on completion.

15th-17th February: Breathing space! A fairly quiet and uneventful few days but the sweating at night does seem to have gone away since the introduction of sleeping tablets! Only problem is that Alan wakes every morning with a dreadful headache! If it's not one thing, it's another!

18th February: At long last we have had a response from the Continuing Heath Care Panel. Our application has been approved, although they will want to re-assess in 12 weeks. This is a verbal message from our Mac nurse who has spoken with them on the phone. However, unless they know something we don't, what part of terminal cancer or acute heart failure did they fail to understand? The precedent has been set and I think it will be difficult for them to remove the funding now it has been granted. Apparently, they need to see a continuing steady decline in the applicant! In other words, the funded recipient must be dying at the correct speed, otherwise they won't qualify! I suggested we should tell them we have booked the hearse and vicar for week 13! Perhaps then they will leave us alone and stop asking us to jump through hoops! Should this funding be removed at the end of 12 weeks, I don't think we will bother to pursue it further. To us it really isn't worth all the heartache, and I'm sure there are deserving folk, far less capable or willing to put up a fight, who lose out on this funding every day.

I had another quick word with the GMC today explaining that we thought they were allowing Dodgy Doc to 'run the show' by his delaying tactics and how stressful this was becoming. Our GMC rep agreed and has confirmed she will try and sew up the whole matter within a week. That would be good!

19th February: Shower as usual this morning followed by Alan's appointment with dentist to have impressions made for denture now that gums have healed following the extraction. Plates hopefully ready in a week or so.

Quick trip into Kidderminster to see Sammy's daughter Mela on her 3rd birthday. Far too much for one day – especially as it involved boisterous children! Alan was shattered and fell asleep in the car, and again as soon as we got settled at home.

20th February: Even though Alan has been on antibiotics for his chest infection for almost a week, there is no improvement and he actually seems to be getting worse as the chest infection still seems to be developing. In bed by 4.30pm - just not fit for anything. Luckily Doc is due tomorrow. Pain in kidney area persists. No urine infection present.

21st February: Today was one for quiet celebration! Our GMC rep came on the phone late morning to confirm that our complaint procedure is now totally concluded and that 19 separate sanctions have been imposed on Dodgy Doc which will take effect from today. These sanctions are described in full public view on the GMC website against his registration. It has taken one year and three days ... but, although frustrating, it has been worth the wait to have gained this justice. No doubt Dodgy Doc's life will now be turned upside down as he attempts to further his career with this millstone around his neck. We expect to receive official confirmation in the mail tomorrow. We are surprised at the number of sanctions as a dozen would be more normal. We have asked ourselves just how close he was to being struck off! Formal application for copies of all documents has been submitted and these should arrive within 40 days. 40 days? Another seven weeks effectively! The waiting continues but it will make interesting reading, I'm sure!

Alan was much brighter today after receiving this news. Doc M called in to administer the Zometa infusion. Alan was tired enough to be in bed before 8pm again ... must have been all the excitement!

Alan's 3 month old flat screen bedroom TV is capput!! I've only just managed to get it onto a wall bracket – and now I have to dismantle the lot! Just something else to deal with when I could least do with it! Tesco have been very co-operative and the TV will be exchanged tomorrow by courier, without question. Thank you Mr. Tesco! As soon as it arrives I know I will be expected to get it installed on the wall bracket – no peace for the wicked!

22nd February: *GMC letter confirming conclusion of my complaint arrived this morning with some very enlightening précis notes from the expert witness, who formulated the report on our case. It would seem that this case came very close to Dodgy Doc having to appear in front of the 'Fitness to Practice' Panel when he could well have been struck off, as suggested by this extract - "The issues are serious with the potential to affect the doctor's registration". Another extract from the notes reads, "The expert concluded that the standard of care fell seriously below that expected of a reasonable GP and highlighted the following deficiencies ... 1. inadequate assessment; 2. poor record keeping; 3. inappropriate treatment; 4. lack of investigation. Of Dodgy Doc's response to allegations, the expert had said "his evidence is less than compelling"!!*

Alan has a very severely bruised left hand after yesterday's infusion ... well done, Doc M!! He's christened it 'Blism' (embolism!) I can see that each and every bruise he gets from now on will be a 'blism'! Gill's day for showering. A small fan heater arrived today so the two of them will be a little warmer in the bathroom! Alan's new TV arrived and was duly fitted to the wall. We have had a second day of quiet celebration deliberating the success of my complaint to the GMC. Yes, it is well satisfying. Hopefully future patients will not suffer as we have done.

26th February: After waiting since last May, Alan was able to have his new denture fitted today. At long last he has his smile back! When appointments have to be cancelled time after time, as we never know how well Alan is likely to be on any given day, it is really surprising just how long this particular job has taken. I could have produced a baby in this amount of time!

27th February: A valued visit from my oldest friend, Janet, as she is in full time employment and there is little spare time for visits. She never arrives empty handed – usually a couple of cream cakes for Alan and flowers for me. How lovely is that! She was here for a couple of hours which left Alan totally exhausted! We have known each other since primary school days, went to the same grammar school and college. She was my witness at my first marriage. 56 years we have known each other!

The past 12 months have been a particularly challenging time for our friendship – you see Janet is Dodgy Doc's secretary, but we made a pact at the time I made the formal complaint to the GMC, that the matter would never be discussed until everything connected with the case is concluded, or when she retires from the job – whichever comes first. She has been at the practice for the best part of 30 years and it has been difficult for her to deal with divided loyalties, but she has been professional in her job, and extremely supportive and helpful to both Alan and I. She is the same age as me and I wish she was without financial burdens which disallow her from retiring as yet. This is one friendship I would never want to lose. Janet is the one friend with whom I can truly laugh ... it's always been the same!

Just before tea, Alan suffered a very sharp and extremely distressing pain in the area of his heart. It was gone as quickly as it arrived but left a very noticeable ache in his mid-chest area and left him even more fatigued than earlier today. Completely knocked him for six. Early to bed and early to sleep.

Chapter 20: Two years on and still fighting!

3rd March: On this day two years ago we woke up without a care in the world ... on holiday in our beloved Phuket. Before lunchtime our lives had been changed forever. Well how time flies when you're enjoying yourself!!

Two years ago today we got the devastating news that Alan had Prostate Cancer, which was 'old' and inoperable. This is as far as the Thai diagnosis went. However, back in the UK and following more tests we were finally told the even more devastating news that Alan's cancer was so advanced it put him in the terminal camp with a prognosis of 18 months to 2 years. And what a 2 years it has been!

So today we will be celebrating by holding up two fingers to those pessimistic medics we first saw in the UK and who have wrecked Alan's head for all this time!!

Today is a huge mental milestone for Alan ... and hopefully he will view his 'bonus' time more optimistically. (Luckily, or not, the 12th of this month also covers the 2nd terminal prognosis in respect of his heart failure, when we were told 6 weeks to 6 months! Nine days away - I think he's going to make that date too!) Three times, so far, Doc M has been convinced he is 'on his way', only for Alan to take up the challenge and fight on! This won't always be the case, I realize that, and one heart attack will close the show! But at the moment our glasses are half full!

An odd date to celebrate? Maybe! But I'll get him out for a meal tonight come hell or high water, as the last time we had a meal out together was 3rd March, 2012! It will also give us a chance to start planning Bucket Party Mk-III. I wonder how many annual Bucket Parties we are going to achieve?

The carvery meal was lovely – we use a local pub some 8 miles away and it made a great change for both of us. Alan came home totally exhausted. We were only out for an hour and a half - and he went straight to bed as soon as we walked in the door.

5th March: We've decided on a date in July for the third Bucket Party - this year's will be known as Alan's "Against All Odds" Bucket Party Mk III - so today I have designed and ordered the invites. Positive thinking! On the previous two occasions the weather has let us down so badly. Basing our choice of date on past experience in August and June, then hopefully July will be a winner. We have had to replace both the marquee and gazebo – the marquee being lost to the weather and the gazebo being lost to mice in the garage! They had managed to chew holes in every single side panel leaving us no option other than to replace it. I laid traps and poison ... not sure how many of the family were lost altogether, but we had evidence of two!

8th March: Alan and Gill enjoyed a totally hilarious shower time today. The belly laughs were a delight to hear ... not going to divulge what it was all about, but wine gums came into it somewhere! The laughing knocked him out for the rest of the day!!

PSA=0.6: ALP=61: PCa blood results still continue to be excellent.

9th-17th March: Alan has been on a 'plateau' for several weeks but during the past two or three weeks there has been a noticeable deterioration again. He is suffering severe irregularities in heart function, especially during the nights. It's a worrying development but we're hoping that the situation may subside again. His physical ability is again reduced and his walking capability is down to 10 yards or less. He is spending considerably more hours in bed than he is able to spend up and dressed.

During the extra hours Alan has been sleeping and in bed, I have been researching matters concerning prostate cancer and heart failure in the hopes that I may come across something useful – especially matters relating to the profuse night sweats.

Well, I feel that I have found something truly significant. There was a research project undertaken in Sweden, in conjunction with one of the UK cancer charities, over a period of several years and involving 97% of all prostate cancer sufferers in Sweden at that time. The results were published in 2009.

The research had involved the use of hormone therapy in advanced prostate cancer and what effects the main two types of treatment had on the heart. Using the type of hormone therapy which Alan has been on since the beginning of his treatment, the increased risk of heart failure and mortality was put at over 40%, in patients with no previous heart problems, and apparently symptoms would appear within months of commencing treatment. Looking back it is apparent that Alan started to have minor problems (which can now be related to the heart) within 6 months of the first tablet taken! The situation had become progressively worse until diagnosis in early May, the following year. In all of Alan's medical records there is no mention whatsoever of any type of heart related problem. He did have an ECG and echo-cardiogram back in 2001, but all was pronounced 'normal'.

Having read the layman's version of the report several times I am only able to draw one conclusion ... and this may be considered a very simplistic viewpoint, but had Alan's prostate cancer been diagnosed in 2005 or 2006 there is every chance he would have been able to have his prostate removed and, therefore, would have been cancer free. However, in view of the lack of investigation by Dodgy Doc during the six years in question, and the actions taken against him by the GMC as they considered his actions to be very seriously below the standard of a reasonable GP, then Dodgy Doc is responsible for the *only* treatment Alan could be prescribed to fight his cancer. Effectively Dodgy Doc is totally responsible for Alan's heart failure too as there is a more than 40% increased incidence rate when using this particular type of hormone therapy.

Having sent a copy of the report to our solicitor, she feels this will be a very useful piece of armoury with which to fight the litigation case. She had previously felt the opposition would use the heart failure against us, claiming that the heart failure would cause Alan's death far sooner than the prostate cancer ever would and, therefore, our claim that Dodgy Doc's lack of diagnosis may have lost us 10 years together was no longer valid. Now we can use this extra information in rebuttal of any such suggestion. It can be challenged that the heart failure would not have materialized if it had not been for the hormone therapy. Nobody can prove either way how, or why, the heart failure happened, but there is compelling evidence to create enough doubt that this was not an incidence of naturally occurring heart failure.

I am hoping Dodgy Doc's legal team have not done as much research as I have done, and that this strong evidence will be a total surprise to them and knock the wind out of their sails. Perhaps the gods could smile on us for a change!

Awarding financial compensation in a case such as ours seems to be illogical at times. The figures can vary so dramatically. I have seen cases settled as low as £50,000 and yet another case was deemed worth well over £300,000. Both these figures involved late diagnosis of terminal cancer (not PCa) ... and yet a teacher whose arm was shut in a filing cabinet door by a pupil – not exactly life threatening – was awarded £308,000. My own opinion is that £1million would not make up for what Alan and I have been put through, but we have to be realistic and practical.

We have had to draw up an assessment of the financial impact on us through Alan's inability to continue to maintain our property. I would dearly love to continue to live here after Alan's death but my income would not be sufficient to support all the work required on a property of this size. Consideration also has to be made for the outlay necessary for the alterations we have had to make to bathrooms. When considering everything, it is quite frightening the amount which will be required. However, on the downside of any assessment, Alan is not of working age, does not have dependents and prior to diagnosis would have had a life expectancy of probably 10-15 years. The second element in the calculation will be for 'pain and suffering'. I have no idea how one person's pain and suffering can be deemed any more or less than any other.

The fact is that we have to come up with an acceptable figure upon which our solicitor can base her negotiations. Her knowledge of the Courts and awards is obviously far greater than ours and we will have to be guided by her advice. In my view negotiations should start at a considerably higher figure than that which is acceptable in order to achieve the acceptable.

This conversation is due to take place on 8th May.

18th March: We have gained approval for an extra shower session each week from the Continuing Health Care panel. We made the request in view of the profuse night sweats. The new plan will cover Monday, Wednesday and Friday each week, but Gill is very flexible should this need to be changed.

The establishment of a new specialist team to look after oxygen supplies will be of great help to us. We have been visited by the new Specialist Respiratory Nurse. She wanted to make a full assessment of Alan's needs and innocently asked if he had been to the Worcester Breathing Clinic where he would have been put on a treadmill to assess his heart and lung functions. Alan and I both laughed out loud! Oh dear! We can't even imagine the scenario!! The nurse then suggested she should walk with Alan from the lounge as far as his bedroom. She attached a SATS machine to his finger. At rest his heart rate was 90 – by the time he had walked the 10 yards to his bedroom it was 140! After a period of rest, we managed to get Alan back to the lounge and re-settled comfortably. The nurse immediately appreciates that the suggestion of a treadmill test was totally inappropriate! Not her fault – this was the first time we had met her. She will authorize a second large cylinder for use in the house and the new supply of 2 portable cylinders for use on outings, if we ever get out through the door! Considering that we applied for a portable cylinder at the beginning of January and the fact that I have been chasing the matter since then, I don't think another couple of days are going to make a great difference!

19th March: We've had some sad news today. We have heard that one of our 'Phuket' friends has died. We have known Bob and Sandra for about 10 years and have spent many a happy hour with them on the beach at Cape Panwa, and they have been our guests on both yacht trips we took from the hotel. Bob was taken ill after his last trip to Phuket, not even 12 months ago, and was being cared for in a nursing home. A sudden and totally unexpected heart attack was the cause of his death today. Such sad news and devastating for Sandra. At least we still have memories of happier times together. RIP Bob.

20th March: There's been some clerical hiccup in organizing the new oxygen supply. Tomorrow!

21st March: The oxygen supply didn't arrive today! I had a phone call from 'Roberto', the delivery driver, who was desperately trying to deliver our supplies to the house we left over 10 years ago! Tomorrow!

Field surgery on the hill planned again for today ... in other words Doc M and Sara (the med student) are due to visit to administer Alan's Zometa infusion. How is it this sort of operation never runs smoothly and ends up akin to a comedy sketch? Still, better that way than any other. The laughter does us all a bit of good!

First question ... *'have you got any needles, Cath?'*

"Well no!" Supplies fetched from Doc's car.

Second question ... *'have you got a tourniquet, Cath?'*

"Errr, no!" (note to self: buy a tourniquet!)

'Tie a rubber glove round his arm!' Sara obliges! The Zometa is hanging off the pole we use for opening the loft and the working area is in total disarray with wrappings, tubes everywhere, needles, plasters, dressings and tissues all over the place! Hilarity and laughter plus coffee and cakes adds a bit of interest to the day!

'Sharps, sharps! Make sure we've collected up all the sharps, Sara! Don't want any accidents!' Doc M can be untidy at times! You should see his bag!!!

We will be saying 'goodbye and good luck' to Sara as she completes her 3 months under Doc M's guidance ... and goes straight into her finals. She'll be fine, I'm sure ... a very competent young lady! The infusion went well although very rushed as Doc M was chasing his tail today!! We relayed the story of the Respiratory Nurse's visit and he has suggested Alan starts another heart medication (Ivabradine) in addition to those already in place in an effort to reduce his heart rate whilst walking ... the most physical that he gets! Hopefully, it may help reduce the breathlessness too. This is the third time for this drug! It's not going to work ... bet you!

22nd March: We woke to about 4" of snow this morning and it has continued all day. Housebound on The Hill, yet again!

Obviously the new medication has not yet had chance to take effect, but Alan has been exceptionally tired today. He was up by 11am for his shower ... lunch at 1pm ... asleep by 2pm ... back in bed by 2.30pm! Has slept on and off for the rest of the day and suspect he will sleep the night through as well. Not good!

Oxygen delivery driver, Roberto, phones to advise he has both 'condensers' on board and will be with us late morning. What two condensers? More clerical errors! I have told him that what he has on board is incorrect for us. I will phone the office to advise them of the mistake. I suggest that he does the same. However, he still turned up on the doorstep! I told him I was quite happy to accept the portable cylinders, but nothing else. He is not allowed to deliver 'part orders' and will have to return to base and start again! Bye, bye!

Several hours later, the doorbell goes again ... it's Roberto! This time he has all the correct cylinders for us – in all the right sizes and all the right colours! Finally we have all the supplies which the specialist nurse approved! Almost three months we have waited ... good job we weren't desperate and had managed with what we had!

23rd March: More overnight snow leaves us with about 10 inches. Our predicted period of being housebound suddenly increases! We had a short power cut at 7am ... let's hope there's no more today!

Alan was up and about by about by 1pm today having slept really well. However, by just after 4pm he was ready for bed again, only waking long enough to have some soup before falling asleep. He had to be woken for his evening tablets and is sleeping again. Snow has been falling very finely for the whole day and depending on drifting we have 8 or 9 inches in some places and 2 feet in others, but in general there is 12" of laying snow over most of the garden. Everything is looking particularly picturesque. I think this is possibly the worst snowfall we have had in the 10 years since we moved on top of this hill!!

24th March: The time has come when I have to make the effort to dig us out as both accesses to the bungalow are blocked! I'm certainly not used to this type of back-breaking work as, since the surgery on my own back, it is not recommended! I know I'm going to suffer for this even though I've only cleared a narrow pathway to the drive. Some local 'good Samaritans' have been clearing the driveway which is a great help for all of us. This is what Alan used to do when he was well and it would annoy us that the neighbours made little or no effort to contribute to the job. They will certainly need to give it more thought in the future! Now it's our turn to take a back seat. The automatic garage door decided to misbehave so I've had to lift it manually ... another little job to sort out when the snow has gone!

Alan was up for just a couple of hours before falling asleep again for the next couple of hours, and therefore he decided bed was the best place for him to be and was tucked up shortly after 4pm. Sadly, and I have no idea why, Alan has decided that he will not see September this year - where this has come from, I don't have a clue, but hate to think of the mental anguish he is obviously suffering without anyone being able to convince him otherwise.

25th March: No more snow ... but everything is frozen solid. Weather forecast is not good for the rest of the week.

Having waited since the very beginning of January, Givvi's court case will finally conclude today when sentencing is due to take place. Hopefully this will help bring some kind of closure to an incident which took place over 30 years ago and which has played a huge part in the formation of her character, personality, attitude and mental state. I hope they throw away the keys!

Givvi has phoned from the Court. This animal has been sentenced to 20 years plus 5 years on licence. Wonderful news for all those involved. The judge also thanked and congratulated Givvi, and another lady involved in the case, for their compelling accounts of events in which they were involved as children. Hopefully everyone will now be able to get on with their lives.

26th March: Another quiet day especially as I have crippled myself clearing the snow on Sunday. No improvements in Alan who was falling asleep by 2pm but forced himself to stay up until 5pm.

27th March: It's snowing again on the hill ... let it ... I'm not clearing up any more - my back just won't cope!!

A comparatively quiet day, seeing Alan back in bed by 5pm. He did emerge for a meal, but then was back in bed by just after 7pm. He can hardly summon up enough energy to comb his hair these days. So sad to see him like this.

28th March: The day we have been waiting for finally arrived! Since last November we have been attempting to get a copy of the GMC Expert Witness report on the complaint I made about our original GP, Dodgy Doc. All the papers have arrived today and it does make for interesting reading. The report is damning and there is not one good word to be said about Dodgy Doc ... not one! The expert's conclusion being "In my opinion, because of the multiple facets to the inadequate and inappropriate care provided, Dodgy Doc's care fell seriously below the standard to be expected of a reasonably competent GP." At last ... we have it in black and white!

Alan has felt considerably better today and has been awake for many more hours than he has been recently. Perhaps the Ivabradine is starting to make a difference. The recent run of heavy sweating during the night also seems to have stopped ... fingers crossed!

29th March: If Mother had been alive she would be 92 today! Strange what little facts come into your head from time to time!

Alan woke up feeling very rough. Gill came and he had his shower OK but only wanted to watch television afterwards ... not interested in any lunch until after 3pm and was ready for bed by 4pm. He slept through till almost 10pm before wanting something to eat and his end of day tablets. The thaw is underway ... but not fast enough!!

30th March: Must remember to put the clocks forward tonight. I don't think the lost hour will make a scrap of difference to us! The thaw continues at a slow pace. Alan has had yet another quiet and tired day and did not want any meals. We are both somewhat stir crazy with the monotony of our own four walls, but there seems to be little we can do about it at the moment!

31st March: Easter Sunday: A very quiet and uneventful day. However, I did manage to finally clear the car and get out for a Chinese takeaway Easter meal. Alan wouldn't have been well enough to go out, so this was the next best thing!! And as a treat, we have both had a Cadbury's Crème Egg! My goodness, we really know how to push the boat out!

3rd-4th April: Alan got up quite late today, about mid-day, but was asleep again shortly after 1pm and wanted to go back to bed by 3.30pm. And there he stayed .. all night ... all morning ... through Doc M's visit ... and beyond. I have never experienced someone being able to sleep for all these hours ... well, not until this heart failure took hold of him.

Doc M has decided there is little or no point in attempting to introduce extra heart medications as nothing is improving matters - and may even be making things worse. Therefore Alan will be weaned off the Ivabradine over the next couple of days ... told you it wouldn't work, didn't I? Doc M has also decided that this problem may be sleep apnoea which is causing the tiredness and will arrange for Respiratory Nurse to supply a sleeping mask to see if the situation can be improved that way. I'm not at all convinced with this suggestion as I regularly check him overnight and have never noticed that he stops breathing, and looking back on my diary of events, the same complaint about tiredness has never changed since the original diagnosis almost 12 months ago. Alan was awake just long enough at 10pm to take his tablets and have a cup of tea! Then ... sleep! Bloods tomorrow ... perhaps something may show up there.

5th April: Bloods taken today for next round of routine testing and whilst here the nurse checked Alan's elbow. For several weeks now it has been becoming increasingly sore ... it's obviously a bed sore. Unfortunately the skin has now broken in four places. She has left some great dressings to use! Gill has been keeping a check on it for weeks and it's such a shame it has had to split.

6th April: "Best day I've had for months and months" - that's the way Alan has described today after being out in the garden, in the sun, for just 10 minutes ... and managing to stay awake until 8pm before he decided he was ready for bed! Can't say fairer than that ... hopefully we can build on it tomorrow! He was quite amused to still see some snow in the garden!! Yes ... still!

8th April: I knew it was too good to last! Alan has been totally wrecked again today ... had his shower plus a lovely foot massage from the Hospice Helper - and was then back in bed and asleep before 4.30pm. On the plus side his blood results are all good ... again ... PSA=0.5; ALP=78; Testosterone=<0.1 ... so that's my silver lining for today! On a sad note, we hear that Margaret Thatcher has died. Very mixed emotions being aired by the public!

9th April: I left Alan in bed when I left home at 7.45am for a hospital appointment in Worcester. By the time I got home approaching lunch time, Alan was up and shaving! How he managed to stay awake long enough to visit the dentist today, I have no idea. By the time we got back home mid-afternoon, he was worn out and ready for sleep. Valiant efforts were made to stay up for the evening ... but it was a lost battle and he was in bed by 7pm.

10th April: I can feel myself nearing the point of melt-down! I am finding it so difficult to cope with life as it is. Today I woke Alan at 10am with a cup of tea and his tablets. He was up and about in time for his shower at 11.30am, which takes up most of the next hour. At this stage of the day he is awake and jovial, sharing jokes with Gill and I. We have a bit of lunch around 1pm, but then he falls asleep on the settee before 2pm. After a couple of hours he wakes long enough to have a cup of tea, watch a bit of TV, but is then asleep again well before 5pm. I had to wake him for a meal at 6.30pm, but he was not particularly interested, and asleep again by 6.45pm. At 7.15pm I suggest he might be more comfortable in bed ... but by now he is very unstable on his legs and slightly confused. Having undressed him and helped him into bed, Alan is immediately asleep again ... not waking until well after 11.30pm and promptly having a vomiting fit. He has tablets and medications to take - doesn't know what day it is, or where he is - and spends the next hour or so awake. In very general terms this is how life has been over the past 6 weeks or so. I have little or no motivation to do anything - just go through the motions of the essentials within the house. Seems there is nothing anyone can do to improve this situation and we just have to live with it. Heart breaking! On a lighter note ... I think all the snow has disappeared from the garden - finally!

11th April: Lack of steroids! I have had a lesson from Doc M on the adrenal glands and the production of steroids. If someone has been on steroids fairly long term (as Alan has) then the body becomes lazy and the adrenal glands are no longer efficient in supplying the body with enough. Are you keeping up with this so far? Alan came off steroids altogether three weeks ago. The three weeks prior to that he was being weaned off them on a weekly reducing regime. Therefore, it would appear that there is a high probability of a direct link between reducing Alan's steroid intake below 20mg per day, and the sleeping pattern we have seen over the same period of time. Could it possibly be as simple as that? Doc M has put him back on an increased steroid dose of 30 mg per day for the first week, which will then be reduced to a permanent 20mg per day. Alan's chest is also sounding somewhat wheezy so a course of antibiotics is prescribed. Hopefully, this will put us back on an even keel!! If this is right, he should be feeling much better by the weekend. Fingers crossed!

12th April: Surprisingly after a very restless night, Alan has managed to stay awake all day and not return to bed until a very respectable 9pm!! Even having a shower today didn't knock him out! Would be good if this lasts!

13th April: Big day for our daughter as her first album is released today – *"Givvi, Thieving From The Magpie's Nest"*. Alan had another poor night but was able to enjoy Giv's visit today. However, by 2pm he was already asleep on the settee where he remained until woken for a meal at 6pm. Having consumed that he returned to his previous state until 7pm when he decided this would be a good time for bed. He has continued to sleep all evening only waking to take tablets and seems to be settled again for the night. So, as yet, no improvements due to steroids. The launch party for Giv's album was due to kick off at 7pm but it seems the drinks were flowing well before that! I'm sure it will continue long into the night!

15th April: The 'big sleep' continues! We're well into our 7th week of this now and the steroids started last Thursday seem to be having little or no effect as yet, other than Alan's chest has eased somewhat. He managed to be up by 11am, had his shower followed by a snackette at 1pm. He was asleep by 1.30pm and in bed by 4pm. Am I p*ssed off? Totally! But I'll get over it!

16th April: We had a plan for today! Fatal! You note that I'm talking in the past tense here! The plan was for me to be up bright and early, showered and ready to wake the sleeping beauty (?) at about

9.30am, in the hopes that we could be out of the door by 11am. Well, the first bit went to plan! 9.30am wake Alan and deliver tea and tablets. 10.30am no movement from the bedroom - only a loud call for the 'sick bowl'. Although he had managed to get out of bed he hadn't even got as far as getting his socks on. After the inevitable use of the bowl, I told him to get back into bed for half an hour. We could always go out this afternoon. That was the last I heard from him and suspect I won't see anything of him at all until sometime this evening - if then. In view of showers, treatments and visits we don't get another opportunity this week - I'm not even going to bother to put it on next week's calendar ... what's the point?

17th April: Today I struck whilst the iron was hot! Alan had his shower this morning and seemed quite bright afterwards. So I told him to get his shoes on, gave him a jacket and his walking stick and got him out of the door! We escaped from the hill for 3 whole hours!! We called in at the day hospice to see what goes on down there. Alan has been invited to attend on a weekly basis every Tuesday from 10am till 3pm. This would give me the opportunity to have a few hours out and about – something I've been unable to do for over two years now. The hospice has qualified nursing staff and support personnel for different issues which may arise. The alternative therapy ladies are also on hand to carry out treatments. Everyone attending has a free lunch freshly cooked by the resident chef, and other refreshments throughout the day. They are obviously making supreme efforts to deal with their patients' whole well-being. All sounds very pleasant and Alan feels this is something he would like to take advantage of. I think it could do us both a bit of good!

We then went to one of the department stores where I did some 'silly' shopping ... pegs, table mats, copier paper, mugs and a rug. Absolute total non-essentials as you can see!! Didn't matter as it wasn't the point of the exercise. We had a cup of coffee in their café and made our way home. Alan was really upbeat and said how nice it was to be out together. Result! He's knackered now but strangely enough has stayed awake all evening. Now he's done it once, hopefully we'll do the same next week!

18th April: Today we have had a really productive meeting with Alan's new Mac nurse, Jo. He wanted to talk to her about what type of respite cover we may qualify for as I had not had a break in two years. We talked about the possibility of Alan staying in the Cottage Hospital, but in view of previous hospital experiences elsewhere, I wasn't too sure I would be happy or able to relax with that arrangement. We explained that when Alan wakes up from daytime sleeps, he never knows what day it is, where he is and sometimes is not sure who I am! Jo sees this as significant and confirms that Alan would not be able to be left on his own at any time. She is going to apply for extra hours from the Continuing Health Care panel on that basis, and the fact that there has been no respite cover in two years. I have a feeling she may well just pull it off!

Later in the day Doc M arrived to give Alan his Zometa infusion ... which would work a whole lot better had he remembered to bring the bag of saline solution with him! After he had set up the cannula, he disappeared back to the hospital to collect the saline. He would return after his local surgery. It was 6.30pm before he returned. The flow line wouldn't behave and had bubbles in it which took some shifting ... but finally the infusion got underway. He was delighted to hear that we had managed to get out and is convinced that Alan needs to stay on a certain amount of steroids permanently in order for him to feel at his best.

19th April: Opticians for me! Eye sight is changing somewhat where reading and computer are concerned. The quote I have is for £376 using my own frames for one pair of varifocals and one pair reading glasses. Who are they trying to kid? The reading glasses I can get changed for £15 on line with a company we've used before and the varifocals can wait until I track down a frame that I like ... but I'm sure I can do them for a better price than £360. I'm a 'poor' pensioner now, not 'Rockefeller'!

20th April: First day of the year back in the conservatory. What a difference that seems to make to Alan. He has been much brighter again today and has even taken his turn to make the drinks! Real bonus! As the sun was shining, we have managed to take a walk around the garden – and sit and watch the world go by for five minutes. The only downside of that is we can see just how much work needs to be done outside! Never mind ... it will have to wait!

22nd April: Bit of a hectic day! Gill came in for Alan's shower. Liz, the Alternative Therapist, had to cry off as she's not well, but Mark and Lynn called in for a few hours as they are off on holiday on Wednesday. New Mac nurse, Jo, phoned to say that she had been in touch with CHC panel to apply for extra hours, but that they wanted justification for the request! She had also spoken to Social Services. They have phoned this afternoon but there seems to be a bit of confusion about what help we actually need. I'll have to chat to Jo again for clarification. For some reason I am exhausted today and have had to have forty winks!

23rd April: What a beautiful morning! The sun is up early and I think we're in for a good day.

Local Day Hospice: I have to tell you - this is a lovely place we've been to. Alan will never be up in time to arrive at 10am, so we rolled in at about 11am. We have met most of the staff, including Mrs. Vicar and her sidekick, the Chaplain. Took Alan a couple of hours to find a 'mate' and I can see there will be troubles ahead!! Lunch was lovely (shepherd's pie followed by apple sponge) and we found ourselves chatting to a very nice guy sitting next to Alan - the new CEO as it happens. There was hair cutting going on, wig fittings, nails being manicured, massages, Communion for some, bread making and sampling, plus a bit of arty-crafty stuff. Everyone is allowed to wander in and out to access the lovely gardens with tables, chairs and ashtrays. Three patients arrive with oxygen packs (including Alan) – there's one stroke victim, a couple of COPD and three or four cancer patients. The girls were serving drinks all day including alcohol, if that's what was wanted! Stroke victim Barry was having a lovely day in the electric recliner - up and down, backwards and forwards, till he nearly launched himself! He had such a big smile when he was amused. He can hear and understand everything said to him – but cannot respond vocally. I could do with every Tuesday in there myself ... no pressures! Alan is definitely up for it and will be going back next week. Sainsbury's send down the out of date flowers every day and they are given to the patients - so we came home with flowers too!! Good day had by all! How can such a restful day end up being so exhausting?

26th April: Having increased Alan's morphine earlier in the week, his daytime breakthrough pain seems to have subsided somewhat. Gill came in to do his shower. New recliner chairs have been delivered today which hopefully will make his summer days in the conservatory more comfortable ... but now we need a big reorganization of the space and have ordered a bracket to put the TV on the wall which will open up a new big area in the corner - ready for me to fill!

27th April: Alan has felt well enough to make the trip to see the grand children in Kidderminster today ... we have been able to deliver the Easter Eggs at last!

28th April: Alan and I have both suffered overnight from nightmares and consequently didn't get to sleep till about 6am. By the time we both woke, we'd lost half the day!! Sleeping tablets tonight, me thinks!

29th April: Slept really well! Gill having a weekend break so not calling in today, but Liz, the Hospice helper, has been here to give us massages - makes a change to relax for an hour or so!

30th April: Alan has been at the local Hospice today - first time on his own. Dropped him off at 11am and didn't return to collect him until nearly 3pm. He seemed very chatty about how things had gone - he'd obviously enjoyed it. I carried on with my retail therapy which had started last week and also had a pleasant lunch! We were both somewhat tired by the time we got home! There has been talk today of there being a second day available at the hospice for Alan. I think we'll just have to see how things go for a while .. two days out may be too much for him. We did manage to sort out the complementary therapies which can be done for both of us on the days Alan attends. That will be nice!

1ˢᵗ May: Not a good start to the day! I was woken up by the doorbell ... it was 11.40am! Gill had arrived for showering duties. Oh, dear! I'm not going to take Zopiclone anymore ... they work too well - but I must have needed the sleep. Mac Nurse Jo was also soon at the door and was with us for about an hour. She has still not heard from the Continuing Heath Care Panel about the request to increase our allowance of hours, but she is confident she will have the answer in time for her next visit in three weeks' time. We have spent the afternoon getting the wall bracket in place ready for the TV to be put up when someone strong turns up to help!!

3rd May: District Nurse Toni called in this morning for the regular blood samples - we had to wake Alan! At least he was awake in plenty of time for his shower. Spent most of the day re-vamping the conservatory now that we have created a bit of space by getting the TV on the wall. All looking good!!

PHOTO GALLERY: IN PHUKET

THE FUEL DUMP FOLLOWED BY VIENNA AND KUWAIT! GREAT VIEWS, EH?

RESTING OUT OF THE SUN .. AND "OUR" BEACH AT CAPE PANWA

ALL ALONE AND CONTEMPLATING THE ENORMITY OF
WHAT HAS HAPPENED AND WHAT THE FUTURE HOLDS

LONG AWAITED TRIP OUT TO "CATH'S ISLAND" ('FLOWER ISLAND)
WHICH I WAITED 15 YEARS TO SEE UP CLOSE!

PHUKET'S BIG BUDDHA WHICH WE HAVE VISITED FOR SEVEN YEARS WHILST
UNDER CONSTRUCTION. WE HAVE SIGNED MARBLE TILES INCLUDED ON THE
LILY BASE - PART OF US WILL ALWAYS REMAIN HERE.
ARTIST'S IMPRESSION OF THE SITE WHEN COMPLETED

THE VIEW FROM OUR HOTEL BALCONY TO THE TOP OF THE MOUNTAIN
AND SOMETHING A BIT MORE UP CLOSE AND PERSONAL

JACUZZI FUN ON THE 'PANWA PRINCESS'

YOU CAN'T EXPECT AN ENGLISHMAN TO GO WITHOUT A CUP OF TEA ..
EVEN IF HE IS ON THE BEACH!

THE CAMERA NEVER LIES? OH, YES IT DOES.
THE SMILES ARE A MASK FOR THE OUTSIDE WORLD, COVERING OUR WORRIES

THE RIDE IN ONE OF THESE IS AWESOME - KNOWN AS A FOOD MIXER
BOAT WITH CHEVVI ENGINE AND EXTERNAL PROPELLER

173

JUST ONE OF THE MEMORABLE NIGHTS WE HAVE SPENT
WITH MIKE AND GERRY

WHICH USUALLY INVOLVED COPIOUS AMOUNTS OF COCKTAILS!

PHUKET OFFERS SUCH WONDERFUL SUNSETS

AND OCCASIONALLY THIS "END OF THE WORLD" TYPE STORM

Chapter 21: Mind games make reality unreal

4th May: Alan was in a bad mood today – ready to pick a fight! He'd taken his Prozac so I think it's pain which he's not saying too much about in case I threaten him with Doc M and more Zomorph. His coccyx is still very troublesome. On the original and only MRI, Alan's worst bone met is his right hip, ball and socket completely engulfed. He only ever suffered pain there once in November 2010 (four months before diagnosis) when he did the Veterans' March at the Cenotaph. It was so bad he almost passed out. Nothing since ... until this last week when it has resurfaced twice. I don't think they will repeat the MRI as his numbers are good and stable ... but I think I'll ask.

Second point, more worrying in a way, is his memory ... a known side effect of hormone therapy. Names have been a real problem for months, more recently he has become incapable of finishing sentences ... totally loses his thread. Very often, on waking, he has no idea where he is, what day it is, etc., but today he can't remember how to use a little computer program he has used for donkeys' years. It is very obvious to me that things are getting much worse in this department. He relates the same story repeatedly to people who have heard it before ... and I've had to start gently reminding him of this before he bores people too much. Where is the line between the onset of Alzheimer's and/or Dementia and severe side effects of HT? Of course he is frustrated by all this ... and possibly adding to his mind-set!!

I only appreciated this was all changing so quickly when my old friend Janet arrived and commented as she was leaving on how difficult he was becoming. She hasn't seen him for about a month.

5th May: Giv has been helping me clean windows today and Percy had a good fire to upset the neighbours!! Alan is very concerned about his memory thing so I will need to speak to Doc M and get him to call in ... will ask him about the vitamin B12 theory. Busy week ahead ... just hope I can stay awake (out like a light by 4.30pm this afternoon for an hour!!) Someone has suggested to me contacting Age Concern about getting help with the hedge cutting … will ring them tomorrow. The sunshine was quite late getting to us today, but what we had was very pleasant!!

6th May: Bank Holiday Monday and the sun is shining! We've not seen that for a long time! The only thing missing today was the camera! I could kick myself! After Alan's shower we went to the local garden centre for bedding plants - abandoned that! We'll do better getting them from B & Q - honestly!! However, we did find a lovely little pub down by the River Teme in Little Hereford where they were serving lunches in the gardens. We sat in the sun for an hour waiting for the meal to arrive (they were very busy) but it was worth the wait! Fabulous! Steady drive back home, into the conservatory for a little nap. No phone calls. No door bell. Just heaven! Alan actually slept from 4pm till 8pm and then went straight to bed – today's fresh air was obviously a shock to the system!

7th May: Mac nurse Jo was on the phone first thing this morning. Good news! CHC panel have approved my application for 4 hours respite per week … on top of the 3 hours Alan has for his showering! Bad news! We're due for re-assessment in 4 weeks! Will cross that bridge when we get to it … but for the time being I'm trying to work out how best to use these hours. I'll speak with care nurse Gill tomorrow about it as it will be her company covering the hours.

Alan has been at the hospice today and has been introduced to an ex-military nurse who was serving during the same years as he did. She's red hot on PTSD apparently, and matters of the head. He's willingly accepted an offer of sessions with her - phew! - on a weekly basis, and I'm so hoping she will be able to sort out the issues he holds in his mind with regard to Dodgy Doc. Now wouldn't that be a result?! Did I mention he wanted to buy a hearse? He found a lovely one for sale on-line priced at under 2k and seriously wondered why I wouldn't let him buy it! Or that he's been looking at coffins to buy on eBay? Does my head in!!! (As carers are also catered for at this hospice, I'm hoping I may even be offered the therapy service eventually, as one of the complementary therapies. I have a feeling that could be quite beneficial for me.)

Apparently during lunch when all the patients and staff sit together there was a bit of a comical incident. Dessert was strawberry Pavlova. Alan and one of the ladies had been given a second helping ... she commented *"Oh, these are to die for!"* Alan had retorted 'You can't say that in here!' There were shaking heads and titters all around the table – seems he has brought some humour into the place. Not sure if they had much before – but they've certainly got it on a Tuesday now!

The staff likes to be able to offer a small 'tot' to any of the patients who would like a special treat, but they have to buy these drinks out of petty cash and can only ever afford small bottles of spirits. I've been through our cupboard and have found at least a dozen bottles of different spirits which have been sitting there, doing nothing, for far too long. It is a very, very rare occasion when we have a 'drink' at home. We'll take these with us next week so that they'll have enough alcohol for quite a party if that's what they'd like to do!

I will have to find something more constructive to do other than wandering around shops whilst Alan is at the hospice. On his first visit, I found plenty to do and see as I'd not been to the shops in such a long time. However, it's obvious that this can't continue every week. It would be impractical to return home, in view of the distance, as it would leave little time to get much work done before returning to pick him up. However, if this time is intended to give me a break from everyday life then I must make the effort to find something relaxing to do during this time each week. My friends either work full time or live too far away to meet up, so I need to find something new to fill the hours otherwise I can see myself sitting in a car park somewhere killing time rather than enjoying it! I have to say, though, that whilst Alan was at the hospice this week, I found myself getting quite upset that we weren't together ... it just feels so strange being apart.

However, I did visit the local Age Concern UK office in Kidderminster as I had heard they could supply gardening services, at a price, and thought this may be the way forward in dealing with the hedge situation. At first they insisted we were far too far out into the country, but then realized that they advertised coverage of our postal code. A message was left for their gardening supervisor to phone me later in the day. It didn't happen!

8th May: Not sure whether or not I'm looking forward to tomorrow. Our Solicitor is due to visit from Bristol in respect of our case against Dodgy Doc. We have not seen her since last August ... how time flies! We have to get down to the 'nuts and bolts' as to what financial assistance will compensate for Dodgy Doc's treatment (or the lack of) over a 6 year period and what will be needed to maintain 'Everest' for the next 10 years or so, plus take into consideration the pain, suffering and mental torture we have both suffered. Millions wouldn't put it right for me ... but we have to be sensible and realistic ... so haven't a clue where to pitch in with a figure! It will be interesting to hear her thoughts now that we have a positive result from the GMC.

This month's blood results still all good ... PSA @ 0.6 and ALP @ 61! No irregularities in anything else tested. Every month when we still have these excellent results with regard to the prostate cancer, it really makes us reflect on the lifestyle we may have achieved if the heart problem hadn't presented itself. Obviously we don't know for certain, but we feel that Alan may well have been able to continue much as he did before diagnosis – tending the garden, which he loved to do in the summer months, and be able to come and go as we pleased. Even sitting on the tractor mower is now out of the question.

Yet again, no phone call from the Age Concern gardeners.

9th May: Solicitor arrived right on time at 11am. To us this matter of liability/responsibility is very black and white. As far as the law is concerned, then things are not quite so clearly defined! After a long chat with her about the GMC result and the additional research material we have to do with hormone therapy and the effects on the heart, we have come to an agreement with the solicitor as to the way forward. She still feels she must obtain three more independent reports ... one

Onco, one Cardio and one from a GP - but in the meantime, she is going to hit the other side with our statements plus the GMC findings and go for an immediate interim payment.

By taking this approach she feels it will send out a strong message to Dodgy Doc's legal team - they will understand that we are confident and up for the fight. By the time she gets a response to this, it is hoped the other 3 reports may be in. She is looking at a time frame of about two months. She wants her approach to the other side to be very detailed and I have now made copies of every receipt in connection with bathrooms' conversions and everything we've bought to make life a bit easier - wheelchair, mobility scooter, walking frame, etc. These are seen as expenses which would have been totally un-necessary, and therefore recoverable, had Alan not had such a late diagnosis. Frighteningly this already amounts to some £14,000. I have also been asked to get a detailed quotation for gardening services over the period of a year. Having two pieces of land totalling over one third of an acre, with trees, hedges, lawns, and borders, there is much work to be done.

I have contacted a local gardening contractor to visit and give it some serious thought as this will be a long term arrangement when we can find the right person. He will need to include some non-gardening work which is also essential – clearing guttering and maintenance of the patio and footpaths around the bungalow, for example. I would just like to find someone we can trust, who will bring our garden back to the beautiful condition it was in two years ago. Alan was always so proud of his efforts ... and it did look beautiful with pristine hedges and grass. It is the solicitor's intention to include all these costs in her claim. At the moment she still does not know what the final figure will be, but her gut feeling is that it will be a 6-figure sum.

With regard to Alan's showers, she feels it is 'against his human rights' not to be allowed a shower every day. She suggests we have this conversation with the Mac Nurse and attempt to get more days covered!

Guess what? Still no phone call from the Age Concern gardeners, so, to be honest, I've sent them a stroppy email along the lines of ... do you cover my post code – Yes or No? Do you supply a gardening service – Yes or No? If the answer is 'no' then please advise which office I have to contact. Let's see if that will get some action!!

10th May: Strange day. Alan seems OK but obviously isn't. I don't know whether it's pain, lack of sleep, or what's in his head ..but sarky comments and snide remarks have been order of the day. He was fine whilst Gill was here for his shower and talking about the extra hours we've been awarded ... but then his mood changed. The Continuing Heath Care panel phoned to confirm they have awarded me 4 hours per week 'sitting' time so that someone can be with Alan whilst I do whatever it is that I can do in 4 hours ... but this award is for 2 weeks only and then must be reassessed. It's an absolute joke to be honest. This means that I have a total of 8 hours over the 2 weeks in which to catch up on over 2 years 'me' time and to be able to relax. It's hardly going to allow me to get to that beach I so desperately need!

I had a phone call early this morning from Age Concern gardening supervisor apologizing for the delay but he had been given the wrong phone number!! Yeah, yeah ... yawn, yawn! Had I got his email and would it be OK to call up late morning? No to the first, yes to the second.

I then went to check the emails. Oh, was this man ever p*ssed off with me! He had cancelled three appointments on the instructions of his boss just to facilitate travelling all this way to assess the hedges. (Obviously not used to taking orders!!) He signed off the email ... Joe Bloggs, MBE. MBE? Doesn't break any ice with me, pal! It's a gardener I want, not an over-inflated ego!

When the Age Concern gardening supervisor, ... MBE, turned up, he was accompanied by three other bodies, all travelling in two cars! Just how many brain cells are needed to give a hedge cutting quote? At least 4 apparently! Why does it take two vehicles and four men to make the near 40 mile round trip? Two to drive, one to carry coat tails and one to carry the MBE! Not a pair of shears between them! Oh, please, give me strength! I can hear the three useless additions lurking behind the hedge *'my god, that's a big one – we can't do that'*. Mr. MBE informs me that they usually work in gardens the size of postage stamps, weeding borders, for £25 per hour (almost twice as much as local gardeners!) and couldn't possibly contemplate dealing with a tall hedge like ours! Even though he wasn't wearing it, he was at great pains to tell me he had been awarded this MBE for his services to one of the local towns, and obviously felt completely naked without it. Well, good for him! I felt like telling him that my husband had a CDM, but that we didn't brag about it! His parting shot was a suggestion that perhaps I should be thinking of moving house! Oh, go away you puffed-up condescending little man! My time is precious and I can't be wasting it with this sort of uninformed, mindless clap-trap. Bye, bye!! I devour things bigger than him for breakfast!

11th May: I've known better days! Ran out of cigarettes in the early wee hours of the morning, so was out the house just after 7am to get re-supplied!

The central heating had to go back on today! Where has all the sunshine gone?

Alan is not at all good today … he reports yet another rough night - he has had a couple of painful 'heart' events … not sure whether this is about his pain levels or what's going on in his head … he's very breathless, and his chest is becoming wheezy again … can hardly walk, and at times totally confused. His memory is getting worse by the day. Consequently he is grumpy and just wants to sleep in the chair for a while.

The local gardeners turn up late to make an assessment of all the work which will need to be done on a regular basis. (Everyone has trouble finding us the first time!) A father and son team with whom I am hoping to form a long term relationship as I would like to be able to stay here for at least another five years … but without this sort of service in place, I would have no chance with the up-keep. They will prepare a quote for the solicitors based on an annual figure for all the work involved - not just 'gardening', but which will also include gutter clearing and patio maintenance as well as fence painting. They are quoting a price, in general terms, of £15 per man hour, so hopefully their quote is going to be an affordable figure. At the end of the day we're going to have to bite the bullet ... the work has to be done however crippling the price may be. Our primary concern is just two of our six hedges ... these two have not been cut for 18 months and will be a very big job in the first instance. Once they are tidy again, then the maintenance shouldn't be too time consuming.

Alan's mood did improve during the day but he is very unwell in all honesty. He has tried to complete some bits of woodwork, but I have ended up trying to help him just so that they are finished and out of the way. As he is incapable of doing much, he is very much reliant on the TV for entertainment and the weekends are notoriously dreadful. However, we did manage to find two films to watch which certainly helped to pass the time for him. He hates being left in a room on his own during the day ... even if he has fallen asleep! Should he open his eyes and find me not there, he starts to sing that song "Lonely, I'm so lonely"! Therefore, I'm pretty tied myself! He really would be better off in the comfort of his bed, but he is fighting it all the time as he sees this as just 'giving in'. By 8pm he's had enough, and heads for the comfort he so needs.

Listening to his chest this evening we have decided to increase Alan's steroid input from tomorrow. We'll clear this with Doc M on Thursday when we see him, but he has always trusted our judgement when there is a need to increase or decrease pain relief medications or steroid intake – saves trying to track him down all the time to get his permission to make small changes.

Just when I think he is settled for a while, he calls for me. The bedsore on his elbow needs dressing! Job done he's happy for me to disappear for an hour when he expects me to return with yet another cup of tea.

12th May: Well, there was only half a day left by the time I managed to wake! Apparently Alan brought me a coffee about 10.30am which was stone cold by the time I found it! What a wonderful night's sleep!

Tesco were on the doorstep before I had even cleared up in the kitchen! Stripped the bed and set the machine going. Alan feels somewhat better today having rested up in bed this morning. Lunch consisted of some beautiful fresh rolls which came with the delivery this morning.

About an hour after lunch I am beginning to suffer pain ... it's not indigestion! This pain is under the ribs mainly on the right hand side and it travels through to the equivalent place on my back. It's those b*stard gallstones again! I have tried to ignore it hoping that it will go away but over the next hour or so this pain amplifies to the point where I can't sit comfortably any more. The best place for me is on the bed and hope the pains will subside. Apparently I was snoring my head off within minutes, but when I woke up about half an hour later, the pain had gone. So my tea consisted of rabbit food and raw mushrooms – what a delight!. I'll have to take it steady for a few days and hope that the whole situation calms down.

Yet again we have had a sad day on the LOL forum as another lovely lady's husband dies of Prostate Cancer. I think that is either 8 or 9 this year. Most people just don't comprehend that this is such a prevalent killer ... they see it as a 'good cancer'. They must be joking ... it's a hideous disease. A new lady joining us has a husband of 44 with advanced PCa – but, of course, the press will lead you to believe this is 'an old man's cancer' – yeah, right! What part of being 44 could possibly be considered 'old'?

How much longer is the wet weather going to hang around? It was just like November today up here on the hill – living in the clouds ... again!

Today has been the first time in a week we have been on our own! Our 'social calendar' is suddenly very full every week ...

Monday – shower and alternative therapies
Tuesday – Hospice
Wednesday – shower
Thursday – Doc's usual day
Friday – shower

Doesn't sound too exhausting ... but you'd be surprised how much it takes out of both of us.

13th May: Even though we've had some huge showers today, I have finally managed to get the washing dry! Getting it ironed will be a different matter!

Our massage lady, Liz, has seen a bit of Alan's 'other side' today and she was quite shocked. Whilst he had his massage I left them alone and quiet so that he could enjoy the full benefit of it. I didn't go into the room once. I prepared Alan some lunch and left this for him on the kitchen table. However, when it was my turn for a massage, and I'm relaxed with closed eyes, there was no way he was going to let the calm continue like that! Liz threw him such a telling look – the sort which left him in no doubt that he was being somewhat selfish! This, for once, was not about him and was not 'his time'! He got the message, but I do wonder if he feels that I shouldn't be having this quiet half hour. Tomorrow is hospice day and I have absolutely nothing to do in Kidderminster. We have been offered transport to the hospice, and I had suggested that perhaps it would be useful for one of the two journeys so that I could get some work done at home. Well, that suggestion when down like a lead balloon! He decided he would drive himself (even though he's not been behind the wheel for well over 2 years!) So it would seem I have little choice other than to kill time for 4 hours whilst he has his cosy day out in the company of others. This placement at the hospice is supposed to be for the benefit of us both, but if we have to carry on like this, then it's all looking a little one sided. I must live my life for his convenience ... that's my job as his 'carer'! Is there a little bit of jealousy coming to the surface as people are now concerned about my wellbeing too? Will have to get this dealt with PDQ I think!

After being showered this morning followed by the massage, Alan is totally exhausted and has no trouble falling asleep in the chair when massage Liz has gone.

So did you hear me swearing? You should have! Our meal tonight was planned to be gallstone friendly ... baked fish, new potatoes and peas. I left everything simmering nicely, made a cup of tea and took it into the conservatory. We'll eat at 6pm and watch the news, as usual. No – not today! Next thing I know it's gone 6.20pm. I've woken up with a jolt, and I've shot out of the conservatory swearing like a trooper, to find the potatoes well and truly fused to the bottom of the saucepan, the peas just about to go the same way, and the fish as dry as a witch's you know what! Sh*t, bugga, sh*t! How I managed to scoop enough 'innards' out of these once beautiful tiny potatoes, now impersonating lumps of charcoal, to give to Alan, I have no idea! He got the best bits of fish too - not that any of the pieces had any life left in them. *"You only just saved that in time!"*

'I know (under my breath!) Don't worry, I'll find you a great big cream cake to fill you up after!' Poor sod ... the things Alan has to put up with sometimes!! Oh dear ... never mind!!

I seem to be able to fall asleep at the drop of a hat these days ... really must try and get more sleep ... meaningful sleep.

And just to complete this 13th day of the month, my beloved little Dyson has a problem! Luckily less than 12 months old, Dyson will supply a new battery free of charge ... they seem to think this is the problem. Hopefully they know best!

14th May: Strange ol' day. I overslept this morning which made me angry and upset as it was Alan's day at the hospice and should have been more organized. Actually managed to drop him off only a few minutes late ... but as we were armed with a donation of a dozen bottles of spirits for their stock, no-one was very upset!

I had little or nothing to do today – quick trip to B&Q for a couple of bits and that was it really. So I took myself off to Sammy's house where Zoe was entertaining her Dad and his partner. The children seemed really pleased to see me, so stayed for a cuppa and then wandered aimlessly back into town. Picked up some lunch from Tesco and then parked up in a side street just to kill time until I needed to fetch Alan.

Quiet time on my own just to think about everything going on in our lives. Gets far too upsetting so decided to ring Giv and have a chat. We think Alan's appointment with the psychiatric nurse will be really helpful if she's good at her job. As any terminal patient, Alan is frightened. He has lived beyond the expectations of the medics, given to him as a prognosis on both health issues, and the thought of death is with him daily.

It has occurred to me that the dreadful state of confusion he feels on waking is due to the fact that he actually doesn't know, in that instant, if he's dead ... and it's not until he sees or hears me that he knows he is still alive. If this is a possibility of what goes on in his head, then it's not surprising he gets upset. But I too suffer similar mental issues – my problem is the fact that I have to go into his bedroom every morning not knowing what I am going to find. I don't want to find him dead. I want to be given the chance to say 'good bye'. I just hate living like this.

However, back to today! It is ludicrous to think I can spend my Tuesdays sitting in side streets killing time. There is no respite in that! There has to be a more constructive approach to these hospice days. I have been told by the hospice head nurse that there are volunteer drivers in this area who could collect Alan for the morning journey. This way I could make an impression on the work which always needs to be done in the house and not leave until it's time to go and collect him. Alternatively, I could catch up on sleep if this is what is required. I've now spoken to Alan about this and as the transport is direct rather than a collection service, he will consider using it. Next week I'll get it organized! Strike whilst the iron is hot!

It was hectic when I arrived back at the hospice as many more patients had attended today. Alan is obviously tired and falls asleep in the car before we get out of Kidderminster and repeated this when he got to his chair at home. He didn't even manage to drink a cup of tea. He was in bed by 7pm.

The most disappointing part about today, not just for Alan, but for me too, is that the psychiatric nurse arrived too late to have a session with him, and so this has now been postponed until 1st June. Could really have done with getting these sessions underway today. C'est la vie! He took up the offer of another foot and leg massage though!

Rain, rain and more rain ... with the promise of snow overnight. Oh, joy!! It's the middle of May FCS – so when do we get the sunshine?

15th May: An even stranger day! Givvi came over today just to visit and for a bit of company. During her visit Gill arrived to do Alan's shower. He is extremely tired this morning and tells me he has been having dreadful nightmares, but never enlarges on these. Actually we are both exhausted!

Once Givvi and Gill have gone Alan makes himself comfortable in the conservatory and immediately goes to sleep. I make some lunch, eat mine, and leave Alan's in the kitchen, then join him in the conservatory. I too fall asleep.

When I awake, not only am I on my own in the conservatory ... but in the whole house. The weather is not good and I cannot imagine Alan is sitting out in the garden, but I will go and check. The first thing I realize is that the car is missing! Panic! Alan has not been behind the wheel for over two and a half years, so why now. Doc M has said a couple of times in the past that Alan should not be driving, but has never made this official. I have no idea where he has gone or how long he has been gone.

As it happens, he arrives back home within minutes and to be honest, I shouted at him. "Don't ever do that to me again ... leave me a note somewhere to tell me what you're doing or where you have gone". I was so upset and crying. My imagination had run wild in those few minutes he was missing.

'Well, if this has upset you ... then what I've done is going to upset you even more' is what I was told.

"What have you done?"

'I've just bought a car from Harold (local garage owner about half a mile away) *... a little MG sports so I can go out when the sun shines and be windswept and interesting. My DLA will cover the car tax. I don't know how much the insurance will be and Doc M has never told ME I can't drive. We'll ask him tomorrow. It needs a bit of work and two tyres which Harold will sort out, but a bargain at £1600 and I'll put it on my credit card. But now I'll be able to drive myself to the hospice as it is obviously such an inconvenience to you.'*

I went straight down to the garage and told Harold to hold fire on the car until we had spoken to the doctor ... apologized and left.

Talk about being slapped in the face. I felt gutted that he would do something like this without even talking about it. I decided not to say anymore on the subject. I went and collected pie and chips from the local shop and let the evening ride.

However, before he was ready to go to bed I thought I must make an effort to sort out the 'whys and what's' as to what had gone on, and deal with it in the way I thought best ... just jump in with both feet and see what happens!

"I'm sorry if I have totally misunderstood or misread what it is that you want in the way of care. I thought I was doing what was best for you, but obviously not. I need you to tell me exactly what you would like to happen and what you want organized in the way of care." I've laid no blame or criticism in his direction so hopefully he will tell me the truth.

'I only agreed to go to the hospice so that you could get some time out, but I am totally bo**ocks and it all too much', I am told.

The discussion goes on and I just sit there calmly and write down exactly what he wants so that I can relate this to Jo, our palliative nurse, when I can get her on the phone tomorrow. The list goes like this:-

1. Increase showers from 3 to 5 a week, on weekdays only.
2. Only attend the Hospice once a fortnight.
3. Have appointments with the Psychiatric Nurse on the days he is attending the hospice.
4. Have a complementary therapy at the hospice every other week and one at home every other week, thus achieving one per week.
5. If I need to go out, then I should go ... he does not need a baby-sitter. I shouldn't make such a fuss!

After being in bed a couple of hours Alan would like another drink and suddenly becomes quite talkative. He tells me that for some time now he has been having trouble controlling his bowels. He feels he has almost lost all control and is very concerned and upset about becoming incontinent. We have a chat about this and about the help we can get to minimize this, but I have to assure him that things will be OK and we will manage.

Suddenly, the mood swings and aggravation of the past few weeks becomes understandable. It would be so much easier if he could tell me about these problems when they first start to worry him, which may save both of us some of the upsets which occur, but I suppose as long as I've now been told, we can work towards getting the problem dealt with the best we can.

Also, he thinks he is becoming allergic to poly-cotton bedding ... is convinced this is not helping with the sweating he suffers. I have promised to get some plain cotton bedding ... eBay, here I come!! I love the internet. It's 1am but I can find, order and pay for everything we need tonight, and it will all be in the post tomorrow and could even be here as soon as Friday. Brilliant!

16th May: Having found the bedding and ordering it the time had rolled on to 2.30am. I have had a somewhat unsettled and sleepless night with my head in turmoil after yesterday. So I start the day just wanting to go back to sleep! However, things to do ... places to be. The house has a layer of dust you could stuff pillows with and I have to be ready for Doc M and Gill this afternoon for Alan's treatments – Zoladex and Zometa today. Cobwebs are in abundance so must find my feather 'tickling stick' to deal with those. There is wet washing in the machine, half dry stuff in the dryer and a pile of ironing trying to hide from me in a basket under the kitchen table. Spoilt for choice on where to start!!

I suppose just going back to bed and sleeping is not on the option list, then? No ... I didn't think so!

My first phone call was to care nurse, Gill, to attempt to change the arrangements in place for Alan's showers. I will give up two of my respite hours so that he can have two extra showers per week. I wanted her to be able to change the arrangements with Fay ... the lady who was due to help me out for those 4 hours a week.

Second phone call was to palliative care nurse, Jo, who was so shocked to hear what had gone on, she came to the house immediately! We sat and discussed the situation whilst Alan remained in bed. She, too, agrees this current outburst is an attempt by Alan to regain control of his life, but he has to understand there are limitations on what he can do now. He must not drive! She has suggested Alan is admitted to a hospice/nursing home/Cottage Hospital for a week just to give me a break ... but this will need to be discussed with him. I went through the list of requests he had given me yesterday, reference more showers, less visits to hospice, etc. As re-assessment for Continuing Health Care is due next week she will be requesting more time for his showers so that my hours can be replaced.

The message I have tried to get across is that I find Alan's demands on my time somewhat challenging. Once he is up and dressed, then he likes us to be together ... apart from the odd few minutes here and there. In the past he has been critical of me should I spend half an hour on the computer in the study, complaining of being lonely. Even if he falls asleep, he wants me to stay in the room. If he wakes and I'm not there, he will wander round the house looking for me singing 'lonely, I'm so lonely' ... it's all added pressure. I have even contemplated taking up knitting or embroidery to keep me occupied in the same room. All of this means that 'my' time does not begin until he is happily settled in bed at night. At that point my time is my own!

I like to keep in daily touch with the ladies in the support group and I have tried to keep my diary website updated regularly during the past two years ... but I can't even start on this until nearly 11pm and it may be that I'm still involved with it at 2am ... so yes, I am tired ... but need this bit of time to myself to remain sane. Life has been like this for over two years now.

Alan got himself up and came and joined the discussion. She mentioned the respite time away and we have agreed to give this some thought and talk about it together. I don't really want Alan to have to be admitted anywhere ... I just want him to let me have an hour here and there to quietly do my own thing within the house! There have been times in the past when I have felt little more than an 'on demand servant'. Of course, when Alan has been poorly, then I will devote every waking second to caring for him ... but when he is stable and comfortable, then I do need a bit of space ... how else can I write this book?

192

Jo will complete her paperwork for the CHC assessment and will be back next week, with Gill, to complete the task. In the meantime, she is going to phone Doc M.

Doc M and Gill arrived mid-afternoon to administer the Zoladex implant and the Zometa infusion. Jo has already spoken to Doc M on the phone to put him in the picture and therefore, the conversation immediately centres on what has happened. He also confirms Alan is not to drive and that respite as an in-patient is available as and when required. He also 'demands' that I visit him in surgery tomorrow morning ... he can see I am clinically depressed and identified it months ago (... and I know I'm depressed, but have refused medication up until this point!) ... but perhaps now the time has come to succumb to accepting this type of help. He knows how difficult life is and has been but can see that Alan's way of coping and mine are totally different. Alan uses the blackest of black humour to cope ... whereas, unfortunately, I become very emotional and distressed. The two do not mix together well!

17th May: I woke up at 3.30am and decided to make myself a drink. However, Alan's bedroom light is on and it is obvious that as yet he has had no sleep. He tells me he is pain ... his back is playing up. I duly make us both a cup of tea and make sure he has Oramorph by the side of the bed. There is no need for him to be in pain but the choice as to whether he takes the medication is his. I leave him to it and go back to bed remembering to set the alarm ... just in case.

I presented myself at the surgery as instructed at 9.30am. However, the waiting room is busy, so put myself on the doctor's list and returned home. They will ring me when I need to make my way back. Alan is awake but still in bed when the call comes ... Giv will be here soon, so I disappear off to see Doc M.

He is shocked and perturbed at what Alan has done in respect of the car and talks to me in very general terms about how life is and how Alan behaves. It is useless me hiding things from him. He needs to know exactly how I feel otherwise he can't help me. He says that he feels he knows us well now ... but I have to tell him that actually he only knows the tip of the iceberg! There are many issues which don't present themselves during his home visits and things which he is totally unaware of ... mostly more recent incidents than historic, and mostly things which have come to the surface since we have been offered respite type help. He listens and comments and then tells me his feelings on the whole situation.

He knows that we are both living in a very difficult situation. He knows that we love each other dearly but some things are going to have to change before Alan's health goes further into decline and the whole situation becomes more difficult to handle.

He used words such as ... emotional blackmail, mental abuse, bullying, manipulation, stupidity, childish, disrespectful ... all of these adding up to unacceptable behaviour.

As Alan's carer it would seem I have been too lenient over a long period of time and the time was coming for some 'tough love' to be brought into effect. I would have to stand up to his demands more effectively for the sake of my own well-being.

However, Doc M needs to get me onto an even keel before implementing any plan and prescribes me anti-depressants to help me become less tearful and stronger in myself and asks to see me again in about 3 weeks to see how things are. As for Alan, he has prescribed him Diazepam to try and ease his anxiety. He admits there are parts of Alan's make-up which we can do nothing about – his PTSD - and we will have to accept these. He suggests that no amount of therapy would make any impression on this problem.

I get back home to a house full! Giv has arrived. Gill has arrived to do Alan's shower and has brought a young lady along called Fay who will be coming to help me for a couple of hours every week with housework.

First job … give Alan his first dose of Diazepam before he gets in the shower. Giv spends most of the day ironing for me whilst I sort out a query from the solicitor. Alan falls asleep! So the rest of the day is quiet and by the time Alan has had his third new tablet, I'm hoping he will have a good night's sleep.

Let's hope my new tablet will do the same for me!

18th May: I slept really well … and so did Alan. He tells me he actually feels 'rested' and had no nightmares. So far, so good.

We had a pre-arranged visit from Sam, Zoe, Mela and Rem during which total mayhem reigns. Much as it is lovely to see them all, both of us find it totally exhausting and we always draw the conclusion it is far easier to see them in their own home environment! So after the 2 hour visit, I quickly clear up the trail of crisps and grated cheese which seems to spread itself throughout the house, and then settle down for a quiet hour.

Alan falls asleep and although I woke him for his tea he was hardly able to stay awake to eat it.

By 8pm I really feel as if I've had enough for today and decide to go to bed. Alan throws up no objection as he will just move his sleeping from chair to bed.

I'm not sure why I feel so emotional tonight, but as soon as I'm settled in bed I'm just overwhelmed with tears. Are these guilt tears … should I have spoken so frankly to Doc M yesterday? I really don't know but have an overwhelming need for sleep. Hopefully this is a first step in re-building myself to deal with everything the future holds for Alan and me.

19th May: Although Alan has slept well and feels rested, he is still very tired. I planted the pots outside the front door and hope they will survive! After lunch we sat in the conservatory and Janet arrived with cream cakes and flowers in hand. During her visit Alan is due to take one of his new tablets but tries to hide it rather than take it! I don't want to stand over him whilst he takes his medications, but I will if needs be! We can both see that he is tired. Conversation comes round to his episode with the car and he still sees this as a bit of a prank ... does not seem to be able to comprehend why everyone but himself is frowning on the whole thing. He's outnumbered so decides to go and play on the computer in the study.

When Jan has left, he picks up his power screw driver ... there's a couple of screws in the gate need re-doing and I haven't got round to it since we spoke about it yesterday. He comments that it's obviously far too much trouble for me to do. Next thing I know he's taken the gate off ... all but one screw which he asks me to remove. What the hell are we doing this for?

Anyway, the gate has to be brought up to the patio, scrubbed and washed both sides, hosed down, in readiness for painting. Apparently it will not be re-fitted today. Oh, yes it will ... how are we meant to keep the sheep out?

Unfortunately, we've had 'words' again. I'm just not sure what he is trying to prove or what the agenda is. One minute he's comatose and the next he's striding round like something possessed.

I hope my new medications kick in fast because I'm really not sure how to handle all of this. Will see how the week goes on and if need be will call in Doc M for Thursday. This is all very unsettling.

20th May: I was woken up at 10am by the front door bell. Janet thought she would come and help out getting done whatever I needed help with. I really don't want to take up others' time but she is insistent so I leave her to attack the ironing. Even in the short time she is here, Janet feels there is a tension between Alan and myself today.

Gill arrived to give Alan his shower. She is over the moon at the arrival of her first grandchild over the weekend – a 7lb 9oz boy called Harvey.

Having made an early call to the gardeners and being told they would arrive on Wednesday, it came as a bit of surprise to hear the strimmer being started up. I need to get to the post office to withdraw money to be able to pay them and I also have a lot of paperwork to send to our solicitor. The gardener's quote has still not arrived for me to include in this paperwork!

Before the gardeners have finished their work, the front door is going again, and this time it's Liz, our complementary therapist – here to give us both a foot massage. I've only just handed Alan his lunch! Having paid the gardeners, we decide I'll have my massage first. I'm totally relieved to be able to sit down for 20 minutes or so. Alan has his massage whilst I grab a bite to eat and by 3.15pm the house is clear and we can sit and relax in the conservatory.

The gardener with the quote arrives at 5pm and the figures are twice as much as what Alan and I expected. This may only be an outline quote for the solicitors but in reality there is no way we can afford to be paying in the region of £4,000 per annum for the upkeep of the garden. However, in the first instance we have agreed to have all the hedges brought up to spec for £500. He reckons that with his son the job can be done in two working days. This I can't wait to see!

There has been a noticeable tense atmosphere between Alan and myself today and I'm beginning to wonder if this is all my fault and that I've had a sense of humour 'blockage' – but there is a lot of serious stuff going on around us at the moment and I'm finding it difficult to see the funny side of anything.

I'm on my fourth tablet tonight and although I am sleeping better I'm not feeling any different in myself at the moment ... hopefully soon!

21st May: Alan was up first this morning and brought me a cup of coffee in bed. It would seem that he is pain free this morning ... something he has not been able to say for a long time. I manage to finish off all the ironing before Gill arrives for shower time. We have decided to cancel having the hedges cut, so I have to come up with an excuse for the contractor ... and I found such a good one!

By law you cannot disturb the habitat, nest or eggs of any wild bird as they are all protected species. Their nesting and breeding time is deemed to be 1st March until 31st August – so, therefore, the hedges cannot be cut during that time. Sorted! The contractor is not best pleased, but will have to learn to live with disappointment like the rest of us! I have contacted two other gardeners to give quotes on the work. I phoned our solicitors and told them to work on a figure of £3,000 per annum ... that's £60 a week over the year and should be more than enough. In truth we want to get all this work done for less than £2,000 a year.

Anyway by the end of his shower 'Mr. Sweetness and Light' has returned to our midst. I'm sure this behaviour has been a PTSD attack which was kicked off by the over-crowding at the hospice last week. However, five days' worth of Diazepam has returned him to an even keel and he is much happier in himself today. It's a real relief as I find these episodes very upsetting. Alan has asked me to contact Doc M and get him to visit on Thursday. No problem!

The babies from the nest under the ridge tiles have had their first outing today spending most of the time sitting on the roof guttering calling for food! Flying appears to be a bit tricky but they've made it as far as the first tree about 15 feet away. The next few days will see them grow in confidence.

During this afternoon Alan has again become very tired and has slept most of the time. He is also complaining of quite severe, sudden pains in his chest and pins and needles down his right arm and fingers. Obviously worrying, but we just have to accept this sort of thing from time to time.

We have chatted today about our plans for a 3rd Bucket Party and both feel that we are too tired to go ahead with it this year. Official invites have not yet been sent out, so our decision won't cause too much bother.

So again, we are both in bed early and hoping for a good sleep again tonight. Another big day ahead tomorrow ....

22nd May: Today I'm getting some help so have decided to spring clean Alan's room. Help is due at 10.45am. The curtains come down and into the machine. The windows and frame are cleaned inside and out. Alan's new bedding arrives and although I would prefer to wash it first, his instruction is to just get it on the bed ... but I can't without ironing it first! That done, I make a start on the bedroom getting the cobwebs off the coving and walls. My help should be here ... but isn't!

Our beds are extremely heavy and I find it difficult to shift it on my own ... but I've started ... so I'll finish! There are cigarette lighters, packets of tobacco, cigarette paper packets, dog ends ... you name it, and it's down behind the bed! The skirting boards look very fluffy but very quickly they are all clean again. The little vacuum clears up nicely behind the bed and with everything wiped down it's time for the bed to be put back in place. My help still hasn't arrived. I reckon I'm 75% through what needs to be done!

Gill arrives a little early to do Alan's shower ... time for a coffee and a ciggie.

Help finally arrives – communication breakdown! Never mind! All that is left to be done is one small corner of the room and the top of Alan's chest of drawers which is covered in all sorts of Buddha bits. That part all clean, the two of us can now remake the bed with all new Egyptian cotton bedding. Looks lovely.

Gill is not leaving as we are expecting Mac Nurse Jo to go through the assessment forms for the Continuing Healthcare Panel. Just as Jo arrives and I get her a drink, there is another visitor ... a local gardener who is going to give us a quote for hedge cutting and dealing with the grass. This involves me taking him on a tour of 'the estate' so that he knows what we need. Wasn't here 5 minutes in total! He will phone me with a price. OK ... bye!

We had gone through most of the details with Jo last week when she called and Gill only had a few bits to add. Doc M is doing a report apparently and the forms will be submitted by the end of the week. We then have to wait 28 days for the result. The request we are making is for Alan to have showers 5 times a week and for me to have 4 hours respite. We have said we will be happy with a compromise of 5 showers and only 2 hours respite. We can work with that.

Jo talks to Alan about how the Diazepam is working for him and it is decided that the dosage actually needs to be increased. Will speak to Doc M tomorrow.

We are clear of all visitors by 2pm and are able to have

lunch. Alan and I go for a walk around the garden in the sunshine and generally potter about for half an hour. By this time Alan is exhausted and gets comfy in the conservatory and falls asleep ... till almost 8pm when he decides to go to bed. He's had no tea, but a tin of rice pudding fills the gap for now. I too head for bed early ... seems to be the only way I can cope!

There has been a terrible terrorist murder in Woolwich this afternoon ... they think the victim is a serving soldier. He has been run over and then hacked to death by two assailants. What is this world coming to?

23rd May: So the victim of the horrendous attack was a serving soldier ... a young man called Lee Ripley, only 25, with a 2 year old son. How sad is all of this. May he rest in peace.

I'm paying the price for yesterday's escapades in the bedroom ... everything hurts and my legs don't want to work. I'm going to have an easy day!

Gill arrived for Alan's shower and Doc M phoned to say there was no need for him to call in if the only query was about increasing the Diazepam dose. He has told us to double the dose for now and see how things go during the next week or so. Consequently Alan has been in a lovely place all day! He slept most of the afternoon.

We've had a letter from our solicitor saying that it will probably take another 3-4 months before she will be in receipt of new expert opinions in respect of our case, but in the meantime she will go ahead with her plan to get an interim payment organized. Seems we will be extremely lucky to have this whole situation concluded by the end of the year ... but if there are problems then papers will be placed in court before our deadline of March 2014.

I have explained to Alan that our home no longer feels like our home with this vast array of folks who have to call on us on a virtually daily basis. We have vowed that Sundays must be kept free to have to ourselves ... I may even disconnect the phone, too!

The gardening guy phoned back with a really good quote. £29 to cut the grass ... £385 to cut all the hedges. I think this will be our man!

Early night again for us both ... another busy day ahead tomorrow!

24th May: Even though Alan was still awake at 4am he is up and ready to leave for the hospice by 10.30. Although I have felt fine on my new tablets, perhaps a little more tired, I have found their effects quite noticeable whilst driving ... I just don't feel quite 'with it'.

Having spoken with Kate at the hospice, she will arrange a volunteer driver as from next week to pick up Alan at 10.30am so that I can have a few hours at home to get some essential work done. This way I won't have to leave home until 2pm.

I've arranged to meet up with Giv at noon in Tesco's coffee shop and also take the opportunity to get a few extras for the weekend.

Alan has enjoyed his day far more in the quieter environment, but is still extremely tired when I pick him up. Once settled back at home all he can do is fall asleep needing to be woken for something to eat before he sleeps away the rest of the day. He dozes in bed for a couple of hours and is then awake. Unfortunately I find him still awake at 3am, so his time clock is shot to pieces yet again. I really don't want to get back into the routine again of him sleeping all day and awake most of the night. Life becomes too lonely for us both when this happens.

Another guy came up today to give a quote on the gardening. Seems he is not interested in cutting grass ... only hedges for which is quoting a ball-park figure of £500 ... so yesterday's man is our man for the job!

25th May: After Gill came for Alan's shower, we were able to spend the rest of the day basking in beautiful sunshine in the garden. This is all that Alan has wanted to do for such a long time ... enjoy his garden in some lovely weather. He enjoyed it so much he fell asleep at around 6pm and was in bed for 8pm! Nice day!

26th May: A beautiful day ... bright sunshine all day – exactly the same as it was last year on this day when Givvi did her 'Walk to Alan'. However, this year the 'big sleep' has returned. Alan got up convinced we were expecting Gill and when he realized she was not coming promptly fell asleep again in the conservatory. He woke for some lunch and spent a little time outside in the garden, but by mid-afternoon he was in the land of nod again. I had to wake him for some tea at about 6pm but he fell asleep immediately afterwards and didn't move until he finally went to bed at 9pm. He's very unsteady on his feet when he wakes and is bumping into things. Will have to keep an eye on this.

27th May: Today has been all about remembering Dad. Had he still been alive he would have been 92 today. Alan and I have been to Malvern to his grave and laid flowers for him as we always do on his birthday. Eleven years on and I still can't stand at that graveside without tears.

This is only about an 80 mile round trip and by the time we get home we are both tired out. Had a quick bite to eat for lunch and then both fell asleep. I had about an hour but Alan didn't budge really until he was ready for bed at 8.30pm. He's needed oxygen tonight as his chest is very rapidly getting worse ... and so is his cough. Need to speak with Doc M tomorrow.

28th May: Alan woke in a right state this morning, buzzing me at 7.30am. He was already on oxygen. His cough has developed quite quickly and he has needed a fair amount of Oramorph today to help deal with it. He didn't recover fully until after his shower and lunch. The rain has not given up all day and consequently we had to give up on the conservatory and move back into the lounge to be able to hear ourselves speak. During heavy rain the conservatory is akin to an old fashioned metal caravan and the noise becomes deafening.

Managed to change all Alan's 'blood' dates from Fridays to Tuesdays ... had to do this as he now goes to hospice on a Friday. Have arranged early showers with Gill on Fridays as well ... thus keeping away from her having to work weekends.

All in all, not a bad day! But must organize Doc M for a home visit on Thursday.

29th May: The 'big sleep' has returned. Alan's chest is getting progressively worse. Doc M is unwell and not at work. I've arranged for the 'German Maid' to visit tomorrow. I'm thinking a belting dose of antibiotics will be needed to improve matters. He's been on oxygen and taken extra Oramorph which has certainly helped relax the chest. Alan did manage to eat some tea, but he was falling asleep at the same time – would be comical if it wasn't so serious!

30th May: Well we didn't get a visit from the doctor today ... one on holiday, one sick, 20 patients in the waiting room ... absolutely no chance!   However, I explained that Alan needed antibiotics – a big dose – so a prescription was done immediately and I was able to collect the tablets just after 4pm.   He was quite good when he first got up but then slides down this slippery slope during the rest of the day to the point of almost total collapse.   He has been on oxygen a couple of times and taken extra Oramorph which also eases his chest, but by late evening he is 'proper poorly' again.

At 11pm I've had to help him back from the bathroom and go through the oxygen and Oramorph routine again ... and then the phone rings!   Never good news this late at night.   It's Percy ... Givvi has collapsed during the first night of three of the concert she is involved with at the Swan Theatre in Worcester.   He is not sure the air conditioning was working and it was very hot in the auditorium.   Giv has been checked over by Paramedics and they assess she is totally exhausted ... she's had a really rough and busy five months so far this year.   Now at home and in bed, hopefully she will be able to recover enough to continue with the show tomorrow.   I do hope so ... we have front row tickets!

We have an early start tomorrow and it's going to be a big day ... have set the alarm ... let's hope it all goes to plan!

31st May: The day's plan did start off well!   Gill arrived early to help Alan with his shower before leaving for his day at the hospice.   Between us we decided that Alan was not well enough to go and cancelled all those arrangements.   Fay arrived to spend some time helping me with housework and we managed to get most of the work done in the time she was here ... but yet again, I've upset my back and I'm going to suffer!

Lynn and Brummie arrive mid-afternoon, but Alan and I have already decided that he is not well enough to make the trip to Worcester to see Givvi in concert.   Brummie will stay at home with Alan and get a

Chinese meal in for supper. Lynn and I end up at a '2 for 1' pub on the outskirts of Worcester before going to the concert at the Swan Theatre.

Giv looks very unwell as she walks on stage but pulls off a belting performance during the first half of the show. The second half has been re-jigged so that she is only on stage for the final number. It's the only way she thinks she can survive the night. She gets out of the theatre very quickly so that she can get some more well deserved rest.

Lynn and I arrive back at about 11pm to find Alan in bed and Brummie watching TV. The evening has gone well ... the two lads have enjoyed some 'quality' time together. As they have an hour's run back home they are gone by 11.30pm.

The day turned out to be a good one ... even if it hadn't gone to plan!

1st June: The sunshine was lovely but even so Alan was feeling chilly - hence a jacket and blanket were needed so that he could sit in the garden. He wanted me by his side all day whether he was awake or not ... have got absolutely nothing done. Whilst sitting with him, listening to his chest and laboured breathing, it suddenly swept over me that he could be in his final days ... horrible feeling and I hope I'm wrong. He has not an ounce of strength and is very unsteady on his legs. He wants to see Doc M on Monday, but I don't feel there is anything he can do and therefore may be seen as time wasting ... will see how tomorrow goes. His mind is all over the place and he's very confused, and his speech is very slurred at times making it very difficult for me to understand what he's saying. I just have bad vibes about today and feel really sad.

Givvi's final show tonight and I'm just waiting to hear if she has managed to get through it.

Alan was in bed quite early and I've heard that Givvi did well tonight and is at home tucked up in bed ... and resting. Thank goodness for that.

2nd June: Well, twelve months have gone by since Alan and I renewed our marriage vows. I thought he was unwell then ... but nothing like he is now!

We are trying to keep Sundays to ourselves these days as there is so much going on during the week. Alan has felt somewhat better today and wanted to do bits and pieces of work which he has been working on. Unfortunately he used the souvenir programme from Givvi's concert for mixing up some 'plastic padding' type stuff and I pretty much lost my temper with him. Just thoughtlessness on his part but he really can't understand why I'm upset! For one, I like to keep things like that in pristine condition and two, I'd not even had chance to read it all as yet. Hopefully Givvi will be able to get another one for me.

Rather than have a full blown row about it, I decided to disappear and get some ironing done ... give him a chance to think about what he's done.

The rest of the day has passed off quietly enough and I do think he is much better than he was yesterday. Doc M is due to phone in the morning and it will be his decision whether or not he makes a home visit. During one of Alan's moments of confusion he asked what month we were in ... June, I told him. "Yes, I was right" he said "definitely don't think I'll get past September". This is weighing so heavily on his mind ... how the hell does anyone know how long they are going to last. I know we are both having to live with the knowledge that, in fact, he could have a heart attack any day ... but then, so could I, I suppose.

I would like him to enjoy life a bit more ... and not behave as if he was already dead – hard to explain, but I'm sure you know what I mean!

You should see the dust in that conservatory ... must get in there first thing tomorrow with a duster, and also upset the spider population!

3rd June: Alan was feeling really rough when he woke and we decided to cancel his shower for this morning and also double check we were on Doc M's list for a phone call ... top of his list apparently. However, after Alan had finished in the bathroom he called out for me. He could hardly stand, couldn't catch his breath. He literally held on to me round my neck as I walked backwards back into his bedroom and then managed to get him into bed. He had to have oxygen and I also gave him some Oramorph to ease his chest. Made second call to Doc M's secretary and said we could really do with a visit. However, Doc M has a long surgery this morning, but another doctor, 'The German Maid', would visit immediately after her surgery.

Alan went to sleep and continued like that all morning. I managed to get loads of work done and was sweating like a pig when the German Maid arrived at about 1.30pm. Blood pressure, SATS, temperature all fine ... but the right side of his chest is very noisy. She hopes the antibiotics will be helping within the next 24 hours and all the other measures we have put in place – increasing the steroids and using extra Oramorph – were the right things to do. However, she has suggested that Alan should use an inhaler he used to use for asthma as this may help with the wheezing. If he has not improved by morning, she wants me to phone and she will call in again. She has suggested that he stays in bed and that we arrange to have a commode delivered so that he doesn't have to walk to the bathroom.

I've made arrangements for a commode to be delivered tomorrow – not sure I'll be in or not, but no doubt they will leave it outside for us. Alan is not keen on having a 'loan' item like this, so I have found a folding commode on eBay which should be delivered by Thursday. We can then return the loan item. He'll be happier using something which is our own.

Alan had a cup of tea and a couple of buns before falling asleep again ... for the rest of the afternoon! Three times I called in to check on him and every time he had attempted to roll a cigarette ... and three times he had dropped the tobacco in the bed! During the afternoon our complimentary therapist arrived for our weekly session. So today I did really well and stole Alan's slot as well as having my own! She will see Alan at the hospice on Friday and will be able to give him a session then.

I've spoken with our new 'lawnmower man' and he will be coming to cut the grass for the first time on Wednesday or Thursday. I want to be here for the first visit just so he knows exactly what we need from him. I feel better now we have found someone who can be responsible for the grass and all the hedges at an affordable price.

When Alan woke late afternoon he was feeling much better. He decided he wanted to get up for his tea and was actually much more stable on his feet. I took this opportunity to vacuum out his bed!! He was up till about 9pm and was then ready for bed again. I've had to stop him carrying drinks around. His hands are shaking so badly he is spilling drinks everywhere – there are spots on the carpets all over the place. He's also spilling drinks when he's in bed and of course this all singing, all dancing washing machine that we have is still not dealing with the stains. I've had to throw sheets and pillow cases back in the machine today ... trouble is I don't spot the problems until I come to iron the things. It really is an absolute pest. Remember the name – Hotpoint Aquatic – don't buy one!

So tomorrow's plans are very 'liquid' and will totally depend on how Alan feels first thing in the morning ... but he will have no choice about the vampire nurse who is due before 10.15am!!

It has been such a busy day that I'd not had chance to realize until I went to bed that it was the anniversary of Dad's death – 11 years. How quickly that time has gone. He's still in my thoughts at some point most days ... just a bit late today.

4th June: The day didn't start too well with Alan struggling for breath as he woke up. I cancelled his trip to the hospice to see the psychiatrist and phoned Gill to see if she could do a shower and cover for me whilst I nipped out to the shops.

The Queen is on TV this morning for a service in Westminster Abbey to celebrate the 60 years since the Coronation. Unfortunately I am old enough to remember watching the ceremony on TV at the tender age of just 4 when Dad had invested in the television set especially for the occasion. The sun is shining today ... shame it couldn't have done that 60 years ago!

District nurse was here for 10am to take bloods and Gill arrived at 11.30am giving me just an hour to get to Tesco some 8 miles away, get the shopping and be back for 12.30pm. Made it with just a couple of minutes to spare!! Alan is actually somewhat better in himself than yesterday.

During the afternoon Alan has spent time out in the glorious sunshine and expects me to be his 'goffer', which stresses me out beyond words. Why can he not get everything around him he needs to do a job before he starts? Why should it be frowned upon that I would rather be doing something else? Again we have a few 'words', so I end up doing exactly as he wants in an effort to keep the peace. When he has had enough sun he comes back into the conservatory and falls asleep, only waking for his tea before falling asleep again until 9pm.

Having helped him to bed and sorted out pills and drinks, I am finally able to sort out a few things of my own. However, I find it somewhat annoying that I am ready for bed at about 10pm only to find him wide awake in bed ... and still awake at midnight. So why do I have to spend so many hours on my own during the day whilst he sleeps? And yet, if I make a move to leave the room to do something else rather than just sitting beside him, his eyes will open!

If the tablets I have been taking for nearly three weeks are meant to be calming me ... then I would suggest they are not working, although they have enabled me to sleep better. Will have a chat to Doc M about it next time I see him!

5th **June:** Well, we're now the proud owners of a folding commode chair and clever liners! Aren't we just the lucky ones! The delivery man was on the doorstep before 9.30am – quite unusual this far out in the sticks!

Giv arrived with a signed copy of her new album ... she's very proud of it. She has every reason to be so! She's still not looking well after her collapse during the show almost a week ago now, but she has been resting in preparation for a big show in London tomorrow evening. After that she knows she must take a couple of weeks off work and concentrate on herself for a while.

Gill came to help with Alan's shower and we reclaimed the house for ourselves by lunchtime.

Alan tried his hand at gilding this afternoon which resulted in a resounding failure, followed by a cleaning off session in a bucket of water!! Gold paint is far easier to deal with! So I got lumbered with the job! Asleep by 4.30pm only waking for his meal which was again followed by sleep in the chair until 9pm when I helped him to bed. His breathing is still pretty rubbish and the antibiotics will finish tomorrow. His confusion on waking is still very worrying and his hands are shaking so badly now that he is incapable of carrying a cup of tea or rolling a cigarette. I will have to buy one of those little rolling machines as it is a talent I have never developed.

I can't believe that I have forgotten to phone the doctor's secretary today to get the results of Alan's blood tests. Don't think I've ever done that before! Tomorrow morning 9am!

6th June: PSA = 0.6 and ALP @ 61. Brilliant. Can't ask for better than that.

It was just like November first thing this morning. Low cloud and very thick ... summer? What summer? Gill is almost shivering as she arrives to help Alan with his shower. However, by lunchtime the sun has burned back the clouds and it is the most beautiful of days. We have been able to sit out in the garden and enjoy the warmth. We've had our first ever 'garden' consultation with Doc M as we were included in his rounds today. He wants Alan to continue on antibiotics for another week as his chest still sounds like a symphony orchestra!

As the afternoon progresses and the heat gets to Alan he retreats into the conservatory and settles down into a lovely sleep only waking for a short while to be fed! By 8pm he is ready to be in bed and falls asleep almost immediately.

All in all a very pleasant day!

7th June: Hot. Hospice. Housework. In that order! It's a beautiful morning and Alan is picked up by a voluntary driver to take him to the Hospice for the day. The plan is that I will be able to get a good deal of work done with the help of young Fay who will be with me for a couple of hours. We managed to clean all the windows not in direct sunlight, make the beds, and clean the bathrooms and kitchen floor. Washing load done too and out on line. That'll do for today. Drove down to the hospice for 2.30pm and we were back home just after 3pm. Alan has enjoyed his day but is worn out. He manages to stay awake until 5pm .. had to be woken for his tea ... and into bed by 7pm.

By this time the clouds have over-run the sky and as the temperature drops I retreat inside. Pleasant day!

We have had a 'bit of a do' overnight with Alan having a coughing fit which resulted in him fighting for breathe. It's frightening for both of us when this happens. All I can do is give him oxygen, followed by inhaler, followed by angina spray and finally Oramorph to calm his chest. Luckily there was only one such episode ... but as the chest becomes looser after the infection, then I suspect it won't be the last episode in the coming week.

8th June: Today has been quiet and uneventful in the beautiful sunshine. After having to vacuum the bed yet again as it was full of tobacco, I have decided it will be easier and cleaner for me to roll Alan's cigarettes so I have bought a little machine to help me! Just another skill to hone.

9th June: ..... and today was even more uneventful than yesterday. Alan slept the whole glorious day away and awoke at about 8.30pm and was back in bed before 11pm.

10th June: Today would have been Mum and Dad's 69th Wedding Anniversary ... just another piece of useless family info!

Alan still very tired. He was up at 9am and back in bed by 10am! It was at this point that I can see that what looks like a whole mug of tea has been spilled all over the brand new bedding! I just wish he could tell me so I had a chance to get the stains out before the bedding has dried.

I phoned Gill to cancel his shower. I emailed Doc M to let him know how the weekend had been. He phoned late morning and feels that Alan has probably overdone things by going to the hospice on Friday, and spending much of Saturday in the sun ... and that this was 'pay back' time. He will visit on Thursday for the Zometa infusion but I am to phone if I need him beforehand. Liz, the complimentary therapist phoned and I said we would cancel this week as Alan was in no fit state. The Tesco delivery arrived on time with the usual errors and strange substitutions ... and folks wonder why I get upset!!

I forgot that Jo, the MacMillan nurse, was due ... and she turned up at 1.30pm only to find Alan still in bed eating a fresh cream cake, with tea and ciggies on the side cabinet! Oh, well ... never mind! She feels it may be as well to reduce by half Alan's Diazepam intake during the afternoon ... hopefully this would make a difference to him being able to stay awake. We'll see!

Alan finally decided to get up by about 3pm which at least gave me a chance to strip off the bed and get the stains in soak. Washing the duvet itself will have to wait for the next session of good weather ... or perhaps it's time to replace it!

The new grass man has failed to turn up yet again, but on the phone has told me the grass will be cut by Thursday afternoon at the latest. Not a great start to a new contract!

After being up and about for just 4 hours, Alan was ready for bed by 7.30pm and spent the evening watching TV.

Hoping for a little more normality tomorrow!

11th June: Normality? Not a lot of chance here although the day did start off in quite a normal way for us with Gill arriving to give Alan his shower. We watched the Prostate Cancer awareness interviews on the TV as an acquaintance was appearing. We had lunch as normal and Alan was titivating with one of his Buddha's which needed repair. I had a few phone calls to make and Alan fell asleep in the chair late in the afternoon and I had to wake him for his tea ... and then he fell asleep again. So far, so good ... all fairly 'normal' for us!

Alan woke up at 9pm and needed the loo. He struggled to get out of his chair and for all intents and purposes appeared to be totally drunk! He was unsteady on his feet and wobbled about like a bent over old man. He has even commented that if he continues like this he will have to start using his walking frame more often. He has no idea where he is. I settle him into bed and made a cuppa.

The phone rang and I had a short conversation with the friend who was calling. Alan had got up to find out who was ringing. By now he seems to be completely 'compos mentis' and is walking OK ... he'd been in bed about half an hour. Back in bed and looking at the clock he tells me there is no point in going back to sleep and Gill will be here soon. It's 10pm and he is totally convinced that he has slept through the night!

Alan's also been dreaming! Apparently he has just knocked out Cliff Richard for making some derogatory remark about me! Makes you wonder where dreams come from ... he can't stand Cliff Richard!!

This is all very odd and has to be something to do with a conflict in his medications. His pupils are very small. Everything points to an overdose of morphine and yet he is still struggling with pain, but I think we need to explore the possibility that the morphine should be reduced and an anti-inflammatory introduced as this may be nerve pain rather than bone pain.

Apart from morphine, Alan takes two different tablets to help with his depression and anxiety, two heart medications, steroids and others, then it should not be surprising if there is a conflict in there somewhere. Doc M is due on Thursday and we will need to talk at length about the best way forward, but for the time being will have to continue with the tablets as they are.

Normal? Perhaps that is asking a bit much!!

12th June: We've had another session of Alan not knowing where he is after waking and having difficulty in walking. Gill saw a bit of it this morning and agrees that something is not right! Later in the day Alan has even forgotten how to use the phone in the house!

Giv came over for a couple of hours which broke up the day nicely. The weather is dreadful again ... more like November than June!

Alan has managed to stay awake more today but wanted to be in bed by 8pm ... and he was asleep by 10pm. Hopefully we'll have a quiet night!

13th June: Yet again ... 13th by name and 13th by nature!! Strange how often this happens to me!

Alan is due his Zometa infusion today. Doc M would normally come to the house during the afternoon. However, today he is not available to visit, but could visit tomorrow morning. That's no good as Alan is due to go to the hospice and has an appointment with the psychiatric nurse. It is suggested that perhaps the Hospice staff could do the infusion but after a short conversation with the nursing lead we find out this will not be possible.

I telephone the nurse at the local Cottage Hospital who has administered these infusions in the past ... would she be available to do it today? Yes, provided all the necessary paperwork is faxed across to her. Next phone call back to Doc M's secretary who then deals with all the necessary paperwork and makes the arrangements for us to go to the hospital.

Gill comes to do Alan's shower and shortly after she leaves, we get the phone call letting us know that the hospital is ready for us. We took a very leisurely ride down to the hospital and our nurse, Tara, is delighted to see us again. The infusion is carried out most professionally and we even get tea and coffee!

Back at home the afternoon goes along nicely until I take a phone call from an ex-Army Dog handler who has phoned regularly for two years to find out how things are going. Alan went into 'hurt the one you love' mode which ended up with me shouting at him and walking out, leaving him on his own for a couple of hours. The whole time I'm away I'm actually fretting about how he is and what he may be doing.

When I returned home you could have cut the atmosphere with a knife. I just reiterated that I wasn't prepared to be spoken to in that way ... all I have ever tried to do is look after him. However, I was told that I wouldn't have to worry much longer as he would be leaving before the end of the next week. All I could do was reassure him that I do love him and I don't want him to go. At that, he breaks down and tells me that he has heard whispers that I intend to send him away to a hospital or a home – not for the suggested respite break – but for a long time ... and obviously he didn't want to go. Where do these thoughts come from? I have no idea ... only respite has ever been spoken of. I have told him that I don't want him to go anywhere and that I'm the one looking after him and that is how it will stay.

We have both shed a fair few tears tonight but by the time Alan is in bed, he apologizes to me, and the matter is closed.

I have concerns. I have mentioned many strange things that happen to Alan to Doc M but have always been told that we must expect the unexpected when a person is on as much medication as Alan. However, I'm not totally convinced. I think we should be making an effort to eliminate other possibilities for Alan's behaviour and feelings. My worry is that the metastases attached to his bones may now have entered his brain ... which would account for the strange things which happen. I found a list of symptoms ...

The ones marked * are things which happen to Alan on a daily basis and I feel justified asking for investigations.

Headaches
Seizures
Loss of balance *
Nausea and vomiting
Difficulty walking *
Loss of coordination *
Speech problems *
Vision changes, such as loss of vision or double vision
Weakness * ... on one side of the body
Memory loss *
Personality changes *
Fatigue *

I will see how the weekend goes and get Doc M to come out and see us on Monday if I'm not happy with things. It's two years since Alan had a scan of any sort, so it's not unreasonable to request these, I don't think.

14th June: Alan's day for the hospice. Driver turned up 15 minutes early which resulted in Alan disappearing for the day without cigarettes and without glasses ... neither of which I realized until I picked him up!! So his day could have been better!

Giv arrived unannounced and helped me have a quick run through the housework ... Fay also arrived, but I sent her away as I really wasn't in the mood for outside help today and I'd not arranged anything with her boss, Gill.

Alan's laptop has suffered recently from a couple of falls off the bed ... the screen was shot and corners were damaged. However, after my disappearing act yesterday, it had suffered even more having been kicked around the room .... apparently! It has now certainly died. We had talked earlier in the week about getting a new one, so that was my mission for today. Have ordered one through Tesco and have managed to save about £50 by way of promotions, coupons, vouchers and staff discount! It'll be here on Monday.

Alan slept most of the time after getting back from the hospice and when he woke ready to go to bed, we have had unexplained tears again. It's heart-breaking to see.

Hoping for a better weekend!

15th June: Alan felt quite good when he got up today and Gill came in to do his shower. Sammy arrived mid-afternoon and was able to spend a quiet couple of hours with us without the children. Seems he was desperate for a break from them and the mayhem at home.

Alan is very tired by the time Sam leaves and sleeps until he is ready to get into bed at 8pm. He then sleeps through until 10pm.

We've had quite a chat tonight about how Alan is feeling and he is describing it as being on a bad 'trip' ... very strange thoughts and feelings - odd dreams too. He tells me he is uncertain about what is reality and what is a dream or thought. In fact, he says he has no reality. The big concern to us both is that the dreams are sometimes violent ... but is it a dream or is it reality? He has no way of knowing, but obviously he doesn't want to cause any damage or injury. Come hell or high water we will have to see Doc M on Monday because this is all getting very weird.

16th June: Father's Day. A very lazy day! Neither of us woke up until mid-morning and both of us decided to stay in bed with a drink. Giv had delivered a huge Father's Day card for Alan on Friday which I gave him this morning. He has always been very touched by the fact that she felt this was something she wanted to do and would be devastated if she ever gave up the habit! Alan had been given a card by Sam yesterday but I only looked at it this morning ... it's caused much amusement today. "To a wonderful Father" – so far so good! – "from your loving Daughter"! Was there something Sammy hadn't told us? We called him on the phone and his disbelief was so deep, I had to scan the card and send him a photo by email. He was having a bad day without his son, Jordan, but seeing what he had done caused much laughter!

Alan is still extremely tired even though he's had a lie-in and during the afternoon we decide that it is essential to see Doc M tomorrow, even if that means us travelling down to the main surgery – just can't allow the current situation to continue.

Early to bed, alarm set ... ready for tomorrow's onslaught!

17th June: Up bright and early to make phone calls! Gill came in and helped Alan with his shower and then Liz turned up for our complementary therapy.

I managed to get an appointment to see Doc M this afternoon ... he was duty doctor today and couldn't leave the building. All three of us have had a long chat and the bottom line is this ... there is nothing more he can do. All we can do is a bit of juggling with the drugs we already have and try to achieve stability for Alan's mental state. The PCa is looking after itself for the time being ... the heart valve is still flapping around like a worn out Tesco bag - so for both of these we will have to leave well alone.

I asked about a brain scan. "OK ... we'll do the brain scan - what if the results show us a couple of tumours? Do you want radiotherapy to your head, Alan?"

Alan gave an emphatic 'No' to that question! "Then there is little point in doing the scan"! I do understand his logic! So the palliative care will continue with the team we have around us now, but if things start to get 'out of hand' then Doc M is quite prepared to admit Alan to the Cottage Hospital and give me some respite.

It's not a great outcome, but we sort of felt we were at the end of the road where heart and mind were concerned. Same old story then ... one day at a time!

18th June: Alan has seemed fairly well today. Shower with Gill went OK. I had a phone call from an occupational therapist who wants to come and see Alan to talk about 'fatigue management'! Should be interesting! As she only works one day a week we will have to wait until next Tuesday to be enlightened ..... can't wait!

My delightful neighbour saw me coming back from our garage today. She was sort of hidden behind her trees. Just as I was coming in through the gate to the back door I heard her shout ... Don't try hiding you filthy dirty thieving f...... c...! Worse than any council estate!! And she's over sixty! Unbelievable!

They built a 9' fence behind our garage ... Alan asked them to take it down to suitable height and they refused so I reported them to the council who came out and inspected it and ordered them to lower it. That's 4 or 5 years ago now. Her husband had a massive stroke last October and has only just got back on his feet. You'd think she'd have more to worry about than being abusive to me. She has a go at every opportunity and it must be winding her up that I don't react and don't reply. Sad, stupid woman.

Brummie and Lynn came this afternoon and spent a few hours with us. It was nice to see them and have a chat. We told them about yesterday's appointment with Doc M and it seems today that Alan is more accepting of the situation. Let's hope the more positive attitude can stay with him.

Alan managed to stay awake until 10pm tonight and tells me he wants to be up and about by 8am! I'll believe that when I see it! Not even sure I'll be awake at that time!

We are expecting one good day of nice weather tomorrow. Alan obviously wants to make the most of it ... and I've got all the washing ready to go on the line first thing! Just hope the forecasters have got it right for once!

19th June: Managed to get a bit of housework done whilst Alan was being showered. Due to be the hottest day of the year so far ... got the washing out onto the line whilst the going's good! Had a bite of lunch during which time Alan fell asleep mid sandwich!

The rest of Alan's day was occupied by sleeping ... that's all!

20th June: Well, today started off the way yesterday finished! Alan was so tired this morning, although he did attempt to get up for his shower, he soon put himself back to bed. Unfortunately far too late to stop Gill arriving, but she was able to have a coffee and update her notes.

Well, I have a bit of news on Continuing Health Care funding! What? That old chestnut again?!! Alan has to be assessed every 12 weeks now for this funding to continue. Originally we had funding for 3 showers a week (3 hours). We then got offered 4 hours per week 'respite' for me to be able to get out to shops, etc. Alan decided he wanted 5 showers a week .. so I gave up 2 of my 4 hours to enable this to happen. Now - in the latest round of talks we have been offered a definite 5 showers + 2 hours for me .. and they are quite willing to extend this to 7 showers + 2 hours for me. Actually, we think 7 showers would be counter-productive as it does make him so tired and he needs to be awake on hospice day and we like to have Sunday's to ourselves.

Our new McMillan nurse, Jo, has done all the work on this - not like the original application which was a total nightmare for me. So this is a significant result ... well pleased!

Alan managed to surface by about 2pm but still extremely tired but he has managed to stay up until 9pm before heading for bed. Hopefully he will be awake enough to make his hospice day tomorrow.

21st June: Longest day of the year! Alan seems to have had a good night and is up and ready for his trip to the hospice in plenty of time, and his new driver also arrived right on time.

I managed to get some of the housework done and Fay has done all the ironing!! Called in at Tesco for a few weekend essentials before collecting Alan at 2.30pm. Last week he forgot to take his cigarettes ... this week he had forgotten a lighter! Hopefully we'll get it right next week!

Back at home, Alan is again very tired and happy to relax in the conservatory but soon falling asleep. The heat today is very oppressive, but we shouldn't complain.

I have raging toothache tonight ... will have to find some good painkillers!

22nd June: The good weather has gone ... again ... back to the predictable rain and wind this weekend! Gill came in to help Alan showering and Giv and Percy visited during the afternoon. Alan very sleepy but managed to stay awake until our visitors had gone.

Toothache is here again ... more painkillers.

23rd June: The only day of the week to ourselves. We both take advantage of a morning in bed ... Alan sleeps through till almost 1pm. He did manage to get dressed but came into the conservatory and promptly fell asleep until 9pm ... and in bed again by 10pm. His walking seems particularly bad today, but have to assume that it's because he's half asleep!

The expected 'Super Moon' has remained hidden behind clouds. Perhaps I'll catch a glimpse of it if and when I'm up during the night finding yet more painkillers for this damn tooth!

24th June: Just another Monday! I was on the phone to the dentist at 9am to beg an appointment for this morning. Luckily Pete the Prod had a 5 minute slot late morning. However, he then took 10 minutes to tell me all about how his Mum had died recently and the strange events surrounding that, which allowed him about 30 seconds to pack the hole in my tooth with a 'we'll see how long that lasts' remark followed by 'when it plays up again it will have to come out and we'll have to see about a partial plate'. Oh, great ... really looking forward to that one!!

Alan has felt quite good today and we finally managed to get the Chinese meal for tea we had promised ourselves about four days ago!

25th June: Fatigue Management!! The long awaited visit of the specialist in fatigue management happened today. She arrived at 2pm and Alan was already out for the count! We chatted for quite a while before Alan woke up almost choking ... something I had described to her earlier.

Apparently we all need good 'sleep hygiene' ... where does all this **** come from?!! Common sense I think. She tells us the more you sleep ... the more you need. I think we've all known that for donkey's years. Too much sleep is never 'good' sleep, she tells us, and you will never feel refreshed.

Then she got to 'the plan'!! Oh, yippee, a plan – I can hardly wait!! It's all about pacing ourselves!

I must wake Alan earlier than I do ... she suggests 9am. His shower time should be brought forward much earlier. He must then carry out activities until he feels he needs to rest. Then rest ... not sleep. When rested do another activity - something small like peeling potatoes for me! (Have you stopped laughing yet?) ... then rest. We should have an activity to look forward to, which we can do together after lunch, before a period of rest and relaxation ... not sleep. We should have a meal together and then perhaps watch an hour of television together before starting to make plans to go to bed ... to sleep! If not asleep within 20 minutes ... get up and go to another room and do something boring until you feel tired, and then return to bed!! She has left us with an 'Activity, Rest, Sleep' diary to be filled in using 3 different colours, broken down into hourly slots. We can use two colours in one slot if needs be!! Pretty!! (I bet you're still bloody laughing, aren't you?!) I can see this diary thing ending up in at least 3 pieces in a bin before the end of tomorrow!

What planet do some of these folks come from? She has never met us before - only has an overview of Alan's conditions - needs to live here for at least a week before suggesting anything but comes in here with the best divorce plan I've heard in years! Don't you just love it?! And she wants to come back!! Oh, sh*t!! I have a feeling Alan will be having a chat with the hospice on Friday ... not impressed!! But it's given us a smile today!!

Our next laughter comes much later in the evening when I have a game to play. Hunt the TV controller! In the bedroom! I'm sure you've all played this at some time or another, but I will have to find a permanent solution as I'm getting tired of the game.

With Alan in the bed I have virtually stripped the bed to make sure it's not in there with him or inside a pillow case. I find that last night's bar of chocolate has melted all over the one side of one of his six pillows, so that has to be changed! On my hands and knees I've gone around the circumference of the bed at floor level ... only to find the odd sock I've been looking for and half a biscuit and accompanying crumbs. I've checked every surface in the room and decided it could even be in the kitchen or bathroom ... but no! Back on hands and knees again, I start to double check ... and then look under the radiator cover. Bingo!!

The pesky thing has hidden itself behind the centre slat which just happens to be the exact length of the controller.

Tomorrow I will put my Blue Peter training to good effect ... it will not get lost again!

26th June: Once Alan had been showered and had his lunch, today was mostly about sleep for him!

However, he is having a computer nightmare with his brand new laptop which is formatted with Windows 8. We make the decision that I will part with my virtually new Windows 7 laptop, reformulated for him, and I will have to learn all about Windows 8!! This is not a computer I would have chosen for myself but seems I'm stuck with it now! It seems to take forever to reformat the whole machine and start loading up the programs which I like to use. Got through basics today ... will aim at refinements tomorrow!

27th June: Alan's day has been completely about sleeping with the exception of eating his lunch and tea! I have done a bit more work on the new computer but it's far from where I need it to be. It wants to do all sorts of updates and takes an age to do it ... can't believe how bad our download speed seems to be!!

He was not a happy bunny! I have had to give up my newish laptop and re-formulate it for him to use and by default I'm now working my way through Windows 8!! I've spent quite a bit of the last couple of days trying to familiarize myself with the new machine (which had I known was going to be for me, I would have chosen something different).

Alan is not particularly 'on form' - extra aches and pains at the moment and has slept the majority of the last few days which I always find somewhat depressing, spending so many hours on my own, especially as it's been raining all day. It's hospice day tomorrow and I'd almost put money on the fact he will be awake, up and dressed in time for the driver! I've had a colour run in the washing and pillow cases are now sort of tie died pink ... soaked in Vanish followed by bleach – but still there! I've also been trying to track down an affordable ripple air mattress for him to replace the existing mattress – could do with a double sized one though and I'm having trouble finding any. When I do I know that's going to cost and arm and a leg!! Single size is about £600 and I'm struggling to find a double sized one. The hunt continues!

28th June: Hospice day ... and as I predicted Alan is awake in plenty of time to get ready for his lift arriving at 10.30am. Giv arrived after having taken Percy to work ready to help me de-frag the airing cupboard which is overflowing. Fay, my little helper, also arrives just after 10.30 ready to attack the ironing.

My tooth decides to kick off big time so a phone call to the dentist gets me an appointment for Monday morning ... just have to get through the weekend!

After a productive morning I got down to the hospice at 2.30 to be told that Alan is involved with a session with Beth – the trick cyclist – which continues till almost 3pm. He seems happier about today's session and plans to continue them.

29th June: How can one tooth cause so much trouble?!! Pete the Prod packed the offending tooth on Monday and was quite confident it would last a considerable time ... Thursday! Friday it was 'fragile' and by lunchtime today I started on the CoCodamol ... followed by Tramadol ... and finally Oramorph. Took 15ml in all to deal with the tooth pain ... but it has made me feel very sick. In bed and asleep by 8.30pm!

Alan has stayed up trying to finish off his 'bits' of brassware and the ebony walking stick which is undergoing transformation. Even through my drugged stupor I'm aware of Alan pottering around, and using electric drills ... or something!

30th June: Sunday – day of rest? Not here!! One of 'those' days! I have got through it screaming, crying, frustrated, and bloody angry.

225

Not impressed by the layer of dust which has been left all over the conservatory and dining room due to Alan's antics whilst I was in bed last night. Sanding of wooden items really should be done outside. When asked, is he bothered? – not one bit! Unbelievable – nothing like making more work for me! ... and this was the rest of the day -

> Toothache - goes without saying!
> Upset stomach.
> Blocked loo.
> Fuse blows on extension whilst ironing.
> Whole plug has to be changed.
> Water spray bottle breaks (used for ironing).
> Washing done and out to dry.
> Tesco delivery - no sliced turkey ... again.
> Alan has slept all this time.
> He manages 10 minutes work on his 'bits'.
> Cup of tea, cake ... asleep.
> Roll him some cigarettes (he shakes too much now)
> Get the tea, wake Alan.
> He falls asleep eating!
> He says he'll go to bed, it's 7pm.
> I get moaned at as blanket is not on.
> Do you think tomorrow could be just a bit better?

Forgot to mention that the new computer and Windows 8 are being sent back tomorrow - so I had to uninstall all my programs and reformat it back to factory settings first thing this morning!! I shall be glad to see the back of it, piece of plastic ****!

1st July: Alan feels most unwell this morning and as Gill is not coming to do a shower today, he decides to stay in bed until lunchtime.

Pete the Prod didn't want to take my tooth out this morning ... he would paint it with some magic gunge to calm it and we would talk about crowning it - but if it kicks off again he would take it out tomorrow! I hadn't even got home (4 miles) before it started kicking off again. Got on the phone - gone to lunch! Phoned back just after 2pm and got appointment for 4.30. I had 4 injections and after 10 or so minutes he tried to get it out... "Uh, um, um!" ... in other words ... Stop! This thing is still live". So he gave me two more 'horse' type injections and waited another 10 minutes. This time we had pain-free pulling!! I'm now £49 lighter in my pocket ... 5 grms off my body weight and have a crater which could be compared with Vesuvius ... somewhere for the peas and sweetcorn to hide for a few days!!

I had a foot massage in between appointments ... that was my last one at home. Computer has gone back and Alan has had a 'reasonable' half day that he's been up. Mouth just about awake by 10pm so hopefully no more coffee dribbling out the side! Should feel human by tomorrow!!

2nd July: Not sure why, but stressed out today. District nurse came to take bloods and talk about the ripple bed Alan would like to have. Apparently he doesn't qualify ... what a shock. So I have spent the day looking for an affordable way to deal with the problem. Most companies want £1500+ for a replacement dynamic air mattress, so I've been trying to attack it from a different angle. I think we could solve the problem for about £600.

We were both awake early and had toast for breakfast ... almost unheard of. However, once Alan had been showered and spent an hour chatting with Jo, his palliative care nurse, he was asleep by 2pm. Just before Jo's arrival I was trying to clear up the conservatory as the layer of dust was still in evidence ... knocked over a cup of tea into a tool box containing gold leaf and collapsed in a heap on the floor crying my eyes out ... and that's how Jo found me today!

Alan went to bed before 10pm but for some reason I can't find his tablets which I prepare every morning. After much head scratching, I suddenly realize that I just hadn't prepared ANY tablets this morning – that's a first for me in nearly 2½ years of caring for Alan! So he's had nothing so far today ... no morphine, Prozac, Diazepam, heart medications, plus many others! I've certainly not been on form today!

Just as I am ready to settle down for the night – midnight – Alan buzzes me, needs help to the loo, would like a fresh cup of tea, takes his tablets and tells me he is unlikely to go on the hospice boat trip tomorrow. I'm now working the night shift as the bathroom floor needed cleaning after a bit of an 'accident' and I'm just waiting for him to decide he's hungry, not having had a thing since lunch time!

I'm going to sneak back to bed and hope for the best!!

3rd July: Quite unbelievably, Alan was awake before 7.30am and decided he would be going on the boat trip! He still had to be reminded of the time a few times before actually getting out of bed ... but we did manage to get on our way to the hospice on time.

I came straight back home and spent a couple of hours with Fay working right through the house to get it back into shape ... well sort of!! I still feel very upset that I'm getting the thin end of the wedge with Alan and having to spend so much time on my own whilst he sleeps the days away. How does he manage to program himself to stay awake on hospice or outing days? And if he can do it for them, why not for me?

Doc M telephoned this morning wanting to know how things are going ... and quite frankly, I told him that I am absolutely pissed off – Alan still doesn't know night from day, is getting progressively more angry, and I'm finding it very difficult to cope. He immediately tells me he will call in and see us tomorrow but that increasing the Diazepam is probably a good idea ... and not seeing the 'trick cyclist' lady again would probably be another good idea. Anger which had calmed has been re-ignited by her treatment and we can well do without that.

Collected Alan at 4.15pm. He is very tired – had enjoyed the day – and sleeps all the way home. However, once back at home he did manage to stay awake until a little before 9pm. We have had quite a long chat about several issues and I actually feel somewhat better in myself tonight. All my research into ripple mattresses can be 'filed' for a later date. He is still convinced that he doesn't have much longer to live – he says he just knows. In the past, I have to admit, that he has been right about other things which have happened ... and that's the worrying bit. I try to dismiss it but there are times when he has this sixth sense. Only time will tell!

4th July: If I felt slightly better last night, that feeling was well and truly shattered again today. Doc M came and although he can see we are both stressed and angry he sees it as a relationship issue rather than health issue and suggested perhaps we should seek advice from 'Relate'. Alan and I have never rowed in the 20 years we've been together until the rigours of this hideous situation started to take their toll. Two years ago I was offered 'happy pills' but said I would prefer to wait and ask for them when I needed them. I think now is the time and although I asked today, none were forthcoming. So I have resolved tonight that I won't allow myself to feel a failure in my care for Alan ... I'm not going to get a break as Alan doesn't want to go into respite – so I must just continue to work through this in the best way that I can. Both of us know this is not a relationship problem and would be totally lost without each other, so I think I will try and find a hotel for a weekend break.

The weather is particularly good at the moment and I think we must just take advantage of it all and get out as much as we can. Think positive ... we can get through this blip. Time is too precious to waste.

5th July: Better day today. Weather is brilliant at the moment. Dropped Alan off at the hospice at 11am and then hit the shops with Givvi. Took her to a departmental store she'd not seen before ... we could have bought something off every shelf. Percy will soon learn of this Aladdin's cave and be expected to take his wallet!! Just so much of everything!!

Enjoyed a pleasant lunch together, bought Alan the slippers he wanted from M & S and got myself back to the hospice before 3pm.

He's very tired after today and falls asleep at 5pm and not awake again until 9.30 when he wants to be fed! We watched the last set of Andy Murray's semi at Wimbledon which had continued under cover and lights. Great win for him again. We'll definitely be watching the final on Sunday.

The weather forecast tells us we are in for good weather for several more days to come. Must make the most of this rare English summer! We've waited long enough ... 2006 was the last time we had any weather like this! Hope we don't have to wait till 2020 for the next good spell ... I'll be 71 by then – if I live that long!

6th July: Brilliant weather again. Very sad day for Givvi. Her cat Ginger has been poorly for several days now and has been to the vets a couple of times. She stayed up with Ginger all last night and by this morning the poor cat was gasping for every breath. At an emergency vet visit she was admitted for blood tests and X-rays. Seems she has extensive tumours in her lungs and also has spread to other parts. The kindest thing, of course, was to have her put down. Giv is understandably very upset ... Ginger has been her constant companion for about 14 years. She has asked if she can bury Ginger in our garden as it is such a lovely spot – it'll be done on Monday.

Gill came in to shower Alan and then we made our way straight up to Coalbrookdale to see Brummie and Lynn. Don't think we've been up there since last year ... I know it's ages. We all took a trip down to Ironbridge and enjoyed a pastie and ice cream in the sunshine. After the drive home, Alan was very tired and fell asleep. Early to bed. Good day – sad day ... but it did make a nice change to get out.

7th July: Another beautiful day ... no visitors ... no phone calls ... do just what we want for just one day!! Wimbledon Men's Final kept me amused for well over 3 hours. Well done Andy Murray ... first British winner in 77 years! I've got a bit of washing done and dried and started on the pillows whilst the weather is so good. Only have four to do this year! I've also decided it's time for new duvets and have ordered them today ... the others are well past their sell by dates and it will be good to have all new stuff on the beds.

Alan has felt very tired most of the day .. didn't want to go to the pub for a meal (as planned) so we have ended up with a Chinese takeaway. Lovely quiet day!

8th July: Today has been a day for sleeping ... apart from a shower! Not me, you understand!

Givvi and Percy came over this morning to bury Ginger in the garden. Such a shame for them – both obviously very upset.

Janet called in for an hour this afternoon. She has absolutely no idea how I'm coping with this tedious situation which just seems to be never ending.

Apparently Doc M will be on day off this Thursday so we will have to make alternative arrangements for Alan's Zometa to be done. I suspect we will end up at the hospital seeing Tara. Will know more on that tomorrow.

9th July: OK .. so who nicked the Immodium? I've searched high and low for them! Oops ... too late ... again! We're in all sorts of a pickle here today - the washing machine hasn't stopped ... the bathroom has been cleaned top to bottom - twice. The bed has escaped so far! Very laboured breathing - shouting in his sleep - In bed with windows open and fan on - cancelled shower - cancelled dentist!! I've called out the doctor. The German Maid called after lunch and feels that he is over the worst of whatever has upset his stomach. Plenty of fluids and rest as his blood pressure is a bit low.

However, after she had gone he started crying ... tells me to get an appointment with Doc M tomorrow. Can't get one for a week so he asked me to text him and ask for phone call. He's cried for an hour - won't tell me what's up, says it's private – but it cracks me up to see him like this - and then I wonder if he is going to accuse me of something again. I find it all very unsettling. It's like rejection and no trust. How can he turn so quickly after what I've had to clean up this morning - including him. What have I done so wrong to be treated like this?

Alan's in bed asleep again now, but it's been like walking on eggshells this afternoon. Very 'anti'. Brummie, his mate, is wondering if his PTSD is coming to the fore again ... I have no idea - all I know is that things are bloody uncomfortable at the moment. He cannot seem to understand or accept that he is not the centre of everyone's world and is not everyone's no. 1 priority. He is sounding so selfish and it doesn't sit very well with me. Really don't know which way to turn. Perhaps he ought to be sedated for a week - I just don't know. What I do know is that I don't have a clue from one hour to the next what sort of a man I'm going to have to deal with and I'm going to need help to deal with this. The mental instability has increased since he saw the trick cyclist at the hospice and these 'outbursts' are getting closer together - he's so full of anger - and I think she has opened up a whole new can of worms and not sure that anyone is going to know the best way to deal with it.

10th July: I didn't like today! Gill was unwell and cancelled coming to do his shower. Alan was hardly speaking to me and told me he didn't want to sit with me all day and told me to go out. I asked why we couldn't go out together for a ride to which he responded that he would probably shoot himself. I spent the whole morning, in the raging heat, ironing! Anything to keep out of his way.

Anyway, by this afternoon he wants my help with one of his projects and things start to get back to a slightly tense normality.

After waiting all day for Doc M to respond to my text, I was very disappointed that he didn't phone. However, Alan did seem to want to get his bits and pieces cleared away today.

By the time he went to bed he was back to his normal self and wanted to read through the GMC file again. He's asked me to phone the solicitors for an update in the morning as it's been 2 months since her last visit here.

11th July: On Tuesday we were told Doc M was day off today and therefore wouldn't be available to give Alan his infusion of Zometa.

It had been arranged for us to have it done at the local hospital. However, when I phoned the surgery this morning to find out who would be in the Clee Hill surgery today and tomorrow, I was told it would be Doc M. So I decided we could strike whilst the iron was hot. Alan would have his Zometa at 2.30pm and it would take about an hour which would put us back up at Clee Hill by 4pm, just as surgery is starting, and he could see Doc M on his own.

The plan worked! After seeing Doc M for over half an hour, we picked up pie and chips from the local chippy, had our tea and then Alan fell asleep. During one waking moment he said "I'll tell you what I wanted to see Doc M for ... I'm going into the Cottage Hospital on Monday for a week" – and then he promptly fell asleep again for another hour.

Well, you could have knocked me down with a feather as it's only a week since he emphatically refused to even think about it. I'm not quite sure how I feel about this at the moment ... but I'm not going to put a spanner in the works and say I don't want him to go. So I am going to get a break ... the first in 28 months. I don't think it's even occurred to him that it's our wedding anniversary on Monday and I was planning on trying to get him out for a meal ... but we can do that when he comes out.

He's obviously been mulling this over for some time ... but of course the difference now is that he has controlled the situation. It's important that he still feels that he has some control over his fate.

12th July: Hospice day. As usual Alan is up and ready in time for his driver at 10.30am. All I manage to do is make the beds and a quick clear up before heading into town. Four circuits of the town looking for a parking space are enough for anyone to bear ... so I headed out of town to the supermarket for weekend essentials. Back home in time for a very quick bite to eat before heading off to Kidderminster to collect Alan from the hospice.

He had forgotten that we had arranged to go and see the grandchildren for an hour! They were delighted to see us and we managed to wind them up like coiled springs to the point of hysteria and decided that was the time to leave!! Don't you just love being a grandparent?

Back at home we are both tired but plan what needs to be done at the weekend in preparation for Alan going into respite on Monday. I was expecting an email from Doc M's secretary giving us more details but nothing has been forthcoming!

Weather forecast is still brilliant for the weekend, so we must make the most of it.

13th July: Hot, hot, hot! Made sure the ironing was done in a cool room before the heat of the day got too much. Have done very little today except charge Alan's iPod!! Alan has spent many hours sleeping ... very difficult to keep awake in this heat! Sunday tomorrow ... lie in!!

14th July: Hot, hot, hot ... again!! Not much work done today .. just making a pile of things Alan will need to take with him to the hospital. Rest and more rest! Givvi phoned to let me know that she's been out to see two kittens and has come home with them! What a shock!! They will have a very loving home and will be spoilt rotten!!

15th July: Today is our Wedding Anniversary. I had so hoped it would be a lovely day, but instead it has been somewhat 'tetchy' as Alan was in one of his confrontational moods. No, we haven't been married 18 years ... it's 15! Would you like to see the certificate? It's 18! Then he totally misread one of my personal emails and accused me of planning an outing without him. In the end I printed it off and made him read it properly. No apology! Went out for lunch, at the pub by the river. We ate in virtual silence, and then finally went down to the hospital by 5.15pm. Alan insisted on taking his mobility scooter which I have never had to load into the car on my own before - not sure where he's planning on escaping to, especially as he only has a tenner with him!! I left at 7.30 after Doc M had called in to prescribe his drugs. So, he's not a happy chappy ... but at the end of the day, this was his decision. But ... I am not convinced that he will stick it out for a week. I'll deal with his bedroom tomorrow ... just in case! Apart from that lot it's been a lovely day! Ha!

16th July: I was called down before 1pm as cleaner had cleared away fags and lighter, never to be seen again! Delivered new supplies and a pillow - but ended up being there an hour and a half. Took other supplies tonight. When I arrived he was outside but had just had a fall - knocked up one elbow. They haven't given him is mid-afternoon Diazepam (be it on their own heads!) and he's bored! I have achieved nothing today ... not even a rest! He is not happy that I've told him I'll see him tomorrow evening (rather than afternoon too!). This is going to be an uphill struggle I can see!! ... and he has mentioned that he wondered how far up the hill he would be able to get on his scooter!!! Oh dear, never mind!!

17th July: Fay, my little helper, was with me for a couple of hours today so the whole house got a 'lick and a promise' – but looks a whole lot better. The new window cleaners came and took them about an hour to do all the windows.

I got down to see Alan at the hospital at 6pm. He was in the garden having a cigarette and had a face like thunder. I had hoped that Brummie's visit this afternoon would have cheered him up ... but apparently not. He was extremely upset and in tears, and it took some time to calm him. In his confusion he thought he was coming home tomorrow (Thursday) instead of Friday – I had been led to believe it was next Monday!! He was so unhappy I told him I would take him home there and then, but he refused.

We sat in the car and he suddenly told me that I had a decision to make. What decision is that? Whether or not you want a divorce. Where the hell is this coming from? I am stunned ... I have absolutely no idea what this is all about. He seems to have it in his head that I'm having an affair! I can't believe that I'm having such preposterous accusations hurled at me without any cause whatsoever. I am totally devastated.

He looks dishevelled and he told me no-one had offered to help him shower ... so he hadn't had one. It's so hot and he really appreciates Gill coming in every day, he is missing his shower sessions. I left at the end of visiting time, but was so upset when I got home that I sat and cried my eyes out for an hour. This respite time is not working. If he is that unhappy there is no point in him being there, and I can't relax knowing that things are not going well. Why the hell did he suggest it in the first place?

I went back to the hospital in an effort to reassure him ... I will bring him home in the morning and I'll be there to collect him at 11am I will just have to cancel my planned day out tomorrow to have a Thai massage, and the plans I had for Friday. His welfare is far more important.

18th July: Today has been OK. Alan is certainly very confused about certain things, but we have ironed out a couple of problems and he has been much better since we got home. He had come to the conclusion they were giving him hallucinatory drugs. Things they were telling me were very different from what he was telling me. Personally, I don't think they had been briefed sufficiently as to why he was there and they were just leaving him to his own devices and to struggle on his own. Therefore, nothing was being done to help him with showers, getting to the loo (one accident whilst I was there!). If nothing else, it has made him appreciate home ... he said it felt as if he'd been away for a month - 2 days, that's all he was gone!! All I can do is hope that things will improve from hereon in!

19th July: Alan left the house in a happy mood today with his driver to take him to the Hospice for the day. He does seem to enjoy the company and camaraderie. I always pack an extra t-shirt in his bag as he is very good at dropping food down his front. Needless to say he came home in the spare again today!

He tells me that he has requested an extra day at the hospice and will now also attend every Tuesday until the situation is re-assessed in October. He feels this will help me have a little more time to myself.

As always after these visits, he was very tired when we got home although he did attempt to finish off the brass pieces he has been working on. He didn't get too far ... but there's always tomorrow.

The heat wave continues and the temperature got to 30C here today. We are being promised even higher temperatures next week! There is talk of 35C+!!

20th & 21st July: Alan woke up on Saturday morning gasping for breath and was straight on oxygen, followed by his spray and inhaler. I had to cancel the expected visitors and even though Gill arrived to help with his shower, he was already asleep to the point of being comatose! He was asleep for the rest of the day ... and night. On Sunday he didn't wake till almost 1pm – got up and dressed – and then fell asleep again in the chair until late evening. Quite a lonely weekend.

22nd July: After a disturbed night Alan was up in time for his shower with Gill ... and luckily today feels much better. The hottest day of the year so far and Kate, Duchess of Cambridge, chooses today, the day of a full moon too, to go into labour! We have spent a pleasant day just pottering and doing little jobs and being constantly bombarded with chatter from journalists awaiting the Royal birth. By 8.30pm we all know that an 8lb 6oz prince was born at 4.24pm. The next question everyone is asking is what will the new Royal be named? We'll have to wait and see. .....and if he lives to be 87 he will see the arrival of the 22nd century! Did we all really need to know all that today?

Can't see us sleeping well tonight as the temperature is not due to fall below 20C ... but the thunder storms are coming.

23rd July: The night was dreadful ... finally managed to get off to sleep at 4am only to be woken by the grandmother of thunder storms at about 5am! Alan was just about up early enough for his 9.30am shower and lift to the hospice which arrived at 10.15am. I did very little today other than essentials ... beds and bathrooms! It was soon time to leave to pick Alan up from the hospice and then, by arrangement, we went to see Sammy and the children. However, no children! This has happened a few times and it's really too much to expect Alan to make the trip to see the grandchildren and then for them not to be there. We were home by 5pm and Alan was very tired. We both need an early night!

24th July: Today has passed by virtually without incident! Managed to get my hair cut at the 3rd attempt and Alan has been happily 'pottering' and 'doing' – don't ask me what!!!

25th July: Another day when tiredness has overwhelmed Alan – after his shower, he slept all the afternoon, and hardly stirred when the grass was being cut. However he did rally somewhat during the evening. At one point he did wake up coughing and choking ... this is what happens when you fall asleep with half a biscuit still in your mouth!

26th July: Early start today on the new regime we are trying out on Tuesdays and Fridays so that Alan has a shower before going off to the hospice.

27th July: Last Thursday afternoon! Where's my wallet? Where you left it! Have you moved it? No ... When did you last use it? Don't know! Did you take it on the boat trip? I brought it back from there. Did you have it with you in hospital? Can't remember .. could have done. Well perhaps it's gone to the same land fill as your tin of cigarettes and your lighter! No, no, it must be here somewhere.

Move on 24 hours and after a complete search of the bungalow by both Givvi and myself we all come to the conclusion it's gone to land fill. I even checked the fridge! Two bank cards, one credit card, one disability card, driving license and a £100 crocodile skin wallet now presumed lost. It took me over 2 hours on the phone to get the cards cancelled - the sweat was pouring off me reminiscent of a waterfall and there was steam coming out of my ears. Anyway, job done ... new cards on the way!

Move on a further 36 hours ... it's 1am and I can hear the sound of footsteps approaching my room. Alan sticks his head round the door with one of those silly, little boyish grins on his face ... guess what I've got? ... and then held up the wallet. Where the hell was that? In my sock drawer! Unbelievable! This HT and memory loss has a lot to answer for!! Have I got to go to school today? Shouting for his Dad in his sleep! I swear to you all that the men in white jackets will be taking me off to the funny farm quite soon, I suspect!

28th July: Sleep ... to be honest, almost comatose! Very late tonight I've had a message letting us know that Brummie is being taken to hospital suffering a heart attack. I've told Alan and he is so very upset – this is his best mate and he's very worried.

29th July: Early start today ... dentist for Alan by 9.30am. One 10 minute appointment which ran on for 40 minutes! Two fillings done – no charge! Many thanks. Gill comes for Alan's shower and then we spend the rest of the day having a general clear up. Thunder storms of some magnitude this afternoon ... totally deafening in the conservatory.

The news on Brummie is quite encouraging. The problem is with his left ventricle which has timing issues but it is planned to fit a pacemaker on Wednesday which should solve the problem.

Alan so very tired again and in bed by 8pm. Another early start tomorrow!

30th July: Early start! Up at 8am to make sure Alan was awake ... Gill arrived at 9.30am and whilst she was showering Alan so two District Nurses turned up to take blood samples. I was happily watching 'Heir Hunters', but they wanted to know why I'd not got the Jeremy Kyle Show on! What riff-raff they have on that programme ... can't stand it!

Driver arrived on time to take Alan to the day hospice, and

then I relaxed, did little, until it was time for me to get to the shops and then collect him from Kidderminster.

I phoned the solicitors for an update and find out if Dodgy Doc's insurance company had responded to the claim which has sent to them. Nothing as yet.

He always comes home very tired ... and there was nothing different about today. He did try to do some work on a special stand he wanted to put some Buddha's heads on ... but he broke it, swore, sat in the chair and went to sleep. Seems that's the end of that bright idea!

31st July: Gill arrived to give Alan his shower with a new young pair of helping hands for me .. Georgie. We didn't get as much done in the house as I had hoped, but the essentials were done – changing Alan's bed and cleaning up the conservatory. Good job really as after his shower Alan made himself comfortable in the conservatory and that was the last I heard of him till after 7pm this evening ... sleep, sleep and more sleep!

The rain has been pretty continual today ... but tomorrow they are forecasting the complete opposite ... possibly going to be the hottest day of the year. We must make the most of it if possible.

Lynn has phoned to let us know that Brummie has had the pacemaker fitted, and feels as if someone has kicked him in the shoulder! His spirits are high and he should be discharged tomorrow. We plan to see him Saturday. His consultant has told him he must not drive for at least 6 months so I envisage quite a few trips to Telford in the future! Just so pleased he has got through this OK.

1st August: August? Heaven's above ... where does the time go? A pretty normal day today ... spent some time outside in the beautiful weather. Alan finished polishing all his brass bits and pieces. Can't say I'm sorry to see the end of that job which has been going on spasmodically for about six months!! Brummie has phoned ... he is home and all things considered is feeling fairly well. We'll go and see him at the weekend!

2ⁿᵈ August: Early shower today and driver on time to take Alan to the Hospice. For me, a little time to relax and have a quiet shower before going to collect Alan again. The place has flooded again in the bad weather. They really have their work cut out trying to clear up this mess ... and, of course, the insurance company is trying to wriggle out of their responsibilities. No doubt this story will continue for some time!

3ʳᵈ August: Trip out to Telford today to see Brummie and Lynn to make sure he is OK after his pacemaker fitting. He looks quite well considering all that has gone on. He's not allowed to drive for 6 months now so we will have to make this trip on a more regular basis. Back at home the weather moves in and we have a huge storm, plenty of thunder and lightning ... and a particularly beautiful double rainbow. I could see both ends of it, so spoiled for choice as to which end to run to for the pot of gold. By the time I had made up my mind it had gone! Just my luck!

4ᵗʰ August: Sunday ... day of rest ... day for a lie in – that is until I realize that my Tesco shopping order is due! And they were right on time! Alan got up sometime well after 12 noon and even though the weather was very miserable we still decided to use the conservatory today. He was not long awake and by 4.30pm had put himself back to bed. He only wanted a cake for his tea and at some time soon after he came to tell me that he had spilled his tea in the bed ... again! This is all past a joke really! So he went and got into my bed whilst I changed his and got the washing machine going. I am now looking to find a spill proof mug ... look out eBay, here I come!

5ᵗʰ August: Yet another day of confusion for Alan. First problem today was that he thought he was due to go to the hospice ... no not till tomorrow. He was fine for his shower followed by a bit of lunch and then he fell asleep in the conservatory. The rain was hammering down but he wasn't hearing it. When he woke up, he said "we may as well go home – it's not worth being here in this weather" – thought he was on holiday and didn't recognize his own home. At this point he needed the loo ... but his legs would hardly support him, and as I guided him to the bathroom you would have thought he was well into his 90's. He returned to his chair and to his slumbers!

After our meal and two or three phone calls, I was happy to settle down to an evening of soaps on the TV. No chance! 'I'm awake now!' ... and don't I know it! Alan has decided this is the time he wants to drill things ... lose things so I have to go on a house search ... then wanting me to fetch this that and the other; knock over a bottle of meths, then send me looking for white spirit. I could

I have decided to attack the carpet tomorrow whilst he's out – at least I'll be uninterrupted!

6th August: Early to rise ... early to shower ... and out the door by 10.30am on his way to the hospice.

Got stuck into the carpet cleaning straight away and didn't finish till almost 1pm. Just time for a quick sandwich, quick shower and out the door to fetch Alan. He's had a good day talking to a young helper who is about to take her first holiday to Thailand, but comes home totally exhausted and was asleep by 4pm!! Was incapable of eating his tea but did manage a few strawberries and cheesecake.

The evenings are drawing in quite quickly and the temperature is dropping off by 9pm so Alan is insisting on having his electric blanket on for at least half an hour before he'll get into bed! Lucky that I put it on before 8.30 this evening!! He's just so tired ... so very tired.

8th-12th August: These last few days seems to have run into each other. I remember I didn't get any help on Wednesday as Fay, my little helper, had collapsed and ended up in hospital!

Thursday was pretty uneventful other than things going pear-shaped within the Prostate Cancer ladies' support group on FaceBook –

"Ladies On Line". I have been 'caretaker' for 5 months but the main administrator has threatened, yet again, to close the group. I have set up a new group and ready now to invite the ladies who also want a change. I have called it "WAGS United" (wives, girlfriends, sisters and daughters included!) all united by Prostate Cancer.

Friday I announced "WAGS" was in operation and 70 of the 96 ladies have immediately joined! Hopefully this will work out OK. Saturday I spent doing little jobs for Alan which seemed to take all day. He doesn't feel well and has slept a lot of the time.

Sunday was wonderfully quiet ... Alan has been very tired all day. I have written to the administrator of "Ladies On Line" and have left the group. "WAGS" is ticking along nicely. It's an international group of ladies and we will continue to support each other on a daily basis as we have been doing for the past two years or so. Shame it all ended with the original group but I refuse to give time and effort into something which is under threat of closure all the time. Job's done ... onwards and forwards!

12th August: Well the feathers have been flying in all directions in my cyber life today. The administrator of "LOL" has demanded that ladies involved with the new "WAGS" group must leave her group. The ladies don't take kindly to this sort of instruction and have made it clear to her that they won't comply, so in true dictatorial fashion she has booted them out herself!! Oh dear, never mind!

Alan has been very chirpy today ... up and about early – pottering around the house doing his 'bits and pieces'. Unfortunately he didn't sleep well and was early hours feasting on scones and 3 yoghurts!

13th August: Unsurprisingly Alan is absolutely shattered this morning. Early start, early shower and off to the Hospice with the driver who arrived early at 10.15am.

I have done essential housework and attempted to sort out a bit more of my cyber group "WAGS". The ladies all seem to have a new home for their support group and I'm sure things will run along nicely.

I've invested in a couple of small white boards ... I have one on the side of a kitchen cupboard close to Alan's chair. I intend to write on it daily – what day it is – what time his shower is happening – any plans we have for outings, etc. His memory is so bad we need to do something to help him sort out what he's doing.

I'm also on my third kettle in three weeks. The first one developed a spout leak after about 18 months. The replacement I got last week was well under powered ... and Alan didn't like it anyway. Today I have bought a high speed jug kettle and I'm sure this one will be just fine.

After collecting Alan from the hospice he fell asleep in the car, could not manage to eat his tea without falling asleep and stayed in the chair until about 10pm. It was only then that he realized the helpers at the hospice had painted his nails today ... he must have fallen asleep there too!

14th August: During daylight hours there was little to report other than the fact Gill was early to do Alan's shower as she had a meeting to attend. Fay still off sick and Georgie not well today ... so no 'little helper' for me this week!

As a carer, I have been invited to the Hospice this evening to meet other carers. Alan has been to stay with Sammy and I'm under instruction not to leave him there for more than an hour. I was last to arrive and walked in to an extremely quiet room full of people who don't know each other. Oh, this looks like fun!! "I've come for the support meeting of Valium and Diazepam users. Is this the right room?" Giggles and laughter break the ice for the evening! Liz, the complementary therapist, was on duty and gave me a very quick 20 minute foot massage once the beef burgers and strawberries had been devoured.

Made a nice change and I did manage to leave on time as I had promised Alan!

However, once we had gone to bed and I had fallen asleep, I was woken by being able to hear Alan wandering around. Problem? He has dropped off to sleep whilst holding a full mug of tea and the bed is soaking! So I crawl out of bed and drag the duvet and cover from the spare bed and settle him down again. Shame the weather forecast wasn't a bit better!

15th August: Washing underway first thing as there is a message from Gill that she will be somewhat late today. It's after 1pm when she arrives so by the time the showering is all finished we're well over half way through the day, so not much to be done in the time left today!

16th August: Friday mornings, like Tuesdays, are always a bit of a rush now. Gill arrives at 9.30am and gives Alan his shower. She is just about out of the door when Alan's driver arrives to take him to the hospice. Once he's out the door at 10.30am I can sit with a coffee for half an hour enjoying the quiet!

After doing some essential bits and pieces around the house, I get on my way into Kidderminster quite early so that I can look at washing machines. The one we have is the bane of my life. Nothing is ever clean and tea stains are a particular problem! Seems it is going to cost in the region of £500 again, so must be really careful with my choice.

Called in at Sainsbury's for a few bits and pieces of shopping – I felt really disloyal. Haven't been anywhere but Tesco for the past 25 years! First impression? Quite nice, but definitely more expensive. I don't think it will be a regular visit.

Guess who spilled another mug of tea in the bed within the first hour of him getting into it? I give up! He won't use the travel cup which would be less devastating if he used it. I haven't changed it ... it can wait till morning. If he has to sleep in a wet bed then perhaps he will learn to actually drink his tea.

17th August: We've had long standing plans to visit a friend today. She is the lady who, 20 odd years ago, removed the tattoos from Alan's hands. We've not seen her for a year. I got up, did some ironing and then jumped in the shower. Alan asks for help getting dressed and makes himself comfy in the conservatory ... but his breathing is not good. Anyway, we had to call off the visit ... he's just not well enough. He manages to sleep the afternoon away till about 5pm when he feels somewhat better.

This seems to be a pattern which we follow every weekend. I suspect that with everything which goes on during the week his body goes into rebellious mood every Saturday.

Unable to do very much today other than watch Harry Potter ... yawn! We did have a heated discussion about cups of tea in the bedroom, but I'm accused of treating him like a child. So I've told him I won't be changing beds in the middle of the night any more if cups of tea are the source of the problem!

18th August: Even though Alan has slept for most of the day, it's certainly been different!! While I was hanging out the washing (again) Alan called me back into the conservatory. *"A little bird's just flown in and is behind that chair!"* OK ... so I start moving things away from the chair, quite slowly so as not to frighten it, and finally pulled the chair out of the corner. Nothing!

Second thing ... later on ... I'd been out to fetch the washing in and stood in the kitchen folding it all up ready for ironing. When I went back into the conservatory, he said *"Who was that?"* ... I said I hadn't heard the phone ring. *"Not on the phone ... out there"*, pointing to the garden. *"A man in a suit"*. I've checked all around the garden, driveway - in case there was a car there ... Nothing! So ... what's going on now? I don't have a clue!!!

19th August: Well ... The Hill has been transformed today. I had to set the alarm for 7am to make sure I was up and ready for our new hedge man to arrive. All the hedges have been cut in one day! He had a short break for half hour lunch and finally left here at 6.30pm. Everything was taken away and he cleared up really well before he left. What a relief it is to get them done ... the hedges have been a real worry to me, and finding someone to do them at an acceptable price has not been the easiest of tasks. The last two summers have been a bit hotch-potch ... but I'm delighted with what this lad has done. I've already booked him for next year!!

Alan managed a slow walk around the top of the garden to inspect the work which had gone on with the roadside hedge. It must be a relief to him too that we have found someone who tackles the job with such 'gusto'. After that exertion he was dozing most of the afternoon.

20th August: Another early start today to get Alan showered and ready for his driver at 10.30am. I've not done much other than get to the shops for a few bits and pieces. When we arrive back from the hospice our friendly mower lads are busy cutting the grass ... and they thought they were going to miss their cup of tea as we were out when they arrived!

So the garden actually looks more like it used to when Alan was looking after it ... absolutely lovely. He still feels very strange about someone else doing the work.

I've had my instructions again. I have to find out the cost of pre-paid funerals so that all arrangements are made before it's too late. I don't like him talking like this ... it's almost as if he's giving up. He really isn't very well and so utterly confused when he wakes up. I heard him get up and went to help him ... even though there is a small light on in the hallway, he is trying to use a cigarette lighter to find his way back to the bedroom. At times like this he doesn't even recognize his own home. It's a very sad state of affairs.

21ˢᵗ August: Gill rescheduled Alan's shower so we had to be up early again today! Fay, my little helper, also arrived ... so put her in the lounge in front of the TV with a huge basket of ironing! Didn't get very much more than that done today.

We've had some really good news in the post today with reference to the litigation case against Dodgy Doc. Our solicitors instigated another independent specialist report on Dodgy Doc's treatment of Alan and he has summarized to say that "this report will show that the GP care fell below an acceptable and reasonable standard for the first time on 30th March, 2005". This early a date has always been denied by Dodgy Doc ... but now two independents have come to the same conclusion - one report instigated by GMC and now this one. We are both well satisfied with the report.

As an ex-Para you would think Alan would remember how to fall properly, but apparently not!! He always landed like a bag of sh*t then ... and he still does today! He missed his footing going out of the patio doors and has ended up falling headlong onto the patio ... with half a bucket of water in his hand! The water's gone everywhere, he's lying there in a big puddle soaking wet and in the flash of a millisecond, I imagined everything being broken! However, looks like the worst of it is a scuffed knee, hurt pride and being really shaken up. Perhaps this Zometa is really that good for the bones!!! He's managed to eat a small meal and has now gone to bed with chocolate! Doc M will be out to see him tomorrow - arranged through my friend, Janet, who is one of the secretaries there. His BP hasn't been dropping so it must be wobbly leg syndrome. Bet he'll know about it tomorrow when the bruising becomes evident!! Never a dull moment!!

22ⁿᵈ August: After all of yesterday's excitement, we have had a very ordinary, quiet day! Doc M phoned to check how things were going but being rushed off his feet today he will not be calling in. We had a chat about Alan's blood pressure and medications – nothing to be changed, but he adds that occasionally Alan will trip and be unstable on his feet. It is to be expected. Alan has decided that we'll not bother him again unless a matter is really serious – like heart attack or broken bones. Personally, I miss Doc M's 'palliative care' visits, but perhaps he is just too busy these days. Having said that, if Alan feels he needs Doc M's care and support, then he is no less important than the next patient - so why should we feel guilty about asking him to call when something goes wrong, like yesterday's fall.

23rd August: Early start ... shower on time ... driver arrived on time – so Alan went off to the hospice ... and I bee-lined it down to the hairdressers for a long overdue session getting my purple stripes back in. Time to relax for a couple of hours!

When we got back from the hospice we made a start on repairing the footstool which Alan broke when he fell off it the other day. Should be finished by tomorrow.

As per his now 'norm', he was asleep in the chair by 7.30pm but I didn't take him to bed until 9pm. He is so ridiculously tired, poor thing. Tomorrow he can have a lie in!

24th August: Didn't get the expected lie in and therefore I didn't really get enough time to do the housework I wanted before Alan wanted to be in a comfy chair .. so I just had to work around him. Givvi came over to see us .. first time she has seen Alan since 8th July because of the fact that he was upset that she had spoken to Doc M about how low I had become and trying to get the point across that I needed a break. However, it all went spectacularly wrong and Alan has been making snide remarks about her for weeks. He won't accept the truth of the matter and Giv and I are both fed up with arguing ... so agree with him just to keep the peace. Anyway, they are fine with each other again.

As I am trying to get things ready for Mike and Gerry's visit tomorrow I would have appreciated it if Alan had agreed not to do any work on his bits and pieces today ... but no, and assortment of cleaning wheels, gloves, buckets of water, etc., etc., had to be set up on the patio along with the bar stool chair which I had only cleaned this morning from the last showering of T-Cut! As the afternoon progresses he becomes more tired and abandons everything out on the patio to fall asleep in the chair. I have to wake him for his tea and within an hour he wants to go to bed. It won't take you three guesses as to who has had to clear up the whole lot.... yet again.

Tonight we have had the most upsetting episode relating to his memory loss. He woke up at 9pm and went to the loo so I made him another cup of tea and prepared all his medications. The conversation went something like this ....

"There's only one bulb out there!" ... 'No, love, there are three'.

"Well the light switch outside the door is not working" ... I duly went to the offending light switch, and of course it is working!

"You must have pressed a button on the meter to make it work" ... 'No, my love, I've not pressed any buttons. The light switch just works'.

"You'll have to put some coins in the meter" ... 'What coins?'

"I don't know. You'll have to ask them at the shop which coins you need". 'We don't need any coins .. we don't have a meter like that'.

"Oh, it's this bloody chalet". 'What chalet is that?' *"This holiday chalet"*. 'This isn't a holiday chalet ... it's our house. Well it's not a house, it's a bungalow ... we don't have any stairs'. Very quizzical look on his face. *"Our house?"* 'Yes'.

"So we haven't got to move out in the morning?" 'No, this is our home'.

"Well, I'll show you tomorrow that that light switch doesn't work!" 'OK we'll look at it tomorrow'.

And with that he has taken all his tablets and I'm sure he will be asleep again quite soon. I told him I thought perhaps he was dreaming, but he consistently tells me that he thinks he's in a chalet .. not in his own home.

I'm sure I don't know what is happening to his mind, but I just find it so upsetting seeing him trying to work things out. The Alan I once knew doesn't seem to make many appearances these days ... and that makes me really sad.

About an hour after all of this, I become aware of a lot of nose blowing noises coming from Alan's room so I went in to him and found him in a dreadful emotional state – so upset and crying his eyes out. Oh how my heart goes out to him ... I hate to see him upset like this. He manages to explain to me that he feels such a fool ... he has realized that he was dreaming before and the whole experience has knocked him for six.

I had to stay and talk to him for almost 2 hours having several cups of tea and cigarettes before he was ready to settle down and go to sleep. It's dreadful to see him like this ... the strapping man who has cared and looked after me for all those years, now reduced to an emotional wreck with everything that plagues his mind.

25th August: I was hoping to be really organized this morning so that I would have time to call on Janet as it is her 64th birthday today – but sometimes the best laid plans don't work!! Her card and present will have to wait ... but I did manage to give her a ring!

Visitors arriving lunchtime today who will stay overnight. We've not seen Gerry and Mike (our Phuket beach buddies) for just over a year.

What an eye opener it has been for them ... they had absolutely no idea as to what it is really like here on a day to day basis as they've not seen us for a year and just couldn't believe the changes in him. After only a few hours they have no idea how I've managed to keep going ... there was yet another bed to deal with - Giv and I only changed it Saturday, so Gerry and I set to and did the whole job again! Good job the weather is fine here at the moment. Although worn out couldn't sleep properly last night and up at stupid o'clock this morning!

Mike was kind enough to sort out the guttering and down pipe issue which had been causing water to run down the wall of the conservatory which I had only found on Saturday morning. The down pipe was full of rubbish and I'm very grateful that we have managed to get the problem sorted before winter arrives. I'm sure the piece of wall will dry out now in a few days and I will be able to repaint the area.

After taking an hour to decide what Chinese takeaway to order, when I phoned the local restaurant there was an answering machine message telling customers they were closed till Wednesday!! The only answer was to get in the car and drive to the nearest Chinese in Ludlow and hoped that they had the same menu!! However, this was not the quality we are used to ... shame!

Alan went to bed early having eaten very little and the rest of us followed before 10.30pm.

26th August: Mike and Gerry were up by about 8am. We had a leisurely breakfast before they gathered up all their bits and pieces before heading back home. I'm sorry to see them go as I miss the time we used to spend with them on holidays in Phuket, but no doubt they will visit again. They have been here four times now and have still not seen the view! Previous bad weather and today's heat haze have prevented them from seeing more than about half a mile! It's a real shame as on a really good day we can see 50 miles and more.

Bank holiday or not Gill arrived for Alan's shower and he felt somewhat better in himself after that. He managed to start off a job in the garden on a couple of his bronze statues ... cleaning and using nasty fluid stuff – but again got too tired to finish the job, came in and sat down and promptly fell asleep. These statues have been hanging around for months being worked on so I decided to get out there and clean them off myself once and for all! Job done and all the messy stuff deposited in the bin. I also managed to get the two sets of bedding ironed and into the airing cupboard.

Alan was not interested in a proper meal today but was happy to accept the cheesecake and strawberries with cream. Ah, well, a little of what you fancy does you good! Actually ... no! He asked to go to bed at 6.45pm so obviously not feeling good at all.

27th August: Early start today as I was expecting to have to get Alan ready for a day at the hospice. But that was not to be today and both his shower and trip out had to be cancelled. Alan is complaining of an upset stomach. His breathing is also very laboured. He was not awake for long.

One of the District Nurses arrived before 10am to take the regular blood samples – I had forgotten they were due today! She took the samples whilst Alan was asleep and he never even flinched. She thought I should be calling in Doc M to see him as she was somewhat concerned about him.

I spent the morning on the internet and phone trying to sort out the best place to buy a pre-paid funeral. Alan has asked me to get all of this organized and paid for so that we don't have to think about it again. I find it upsetting as I don't feel he should be worrying about these arrangements ... but he is adamant, it has to be done. I need a Humanist Celebrant, some Buddhist Monks and a good funeral director! Work in progress!

Alan was up and about by early afternoon, complaining that he was bored and would I fetch some 'Brasso' from the shop so that he could polish his lion statues. By the time I returned with this he was in the garage desperately searching for something which has been put somewhere safe ... never to be found again. Consequently he was getting very upset and moody as the afternoon progressed.

We had a phone call from Jo, our MacMillan nurse, who had been speaking to the District Nurse and feels that she must visit us tomorrow in view of what she has been told.

Alan managed to stay up until 9pm tonight but when I called in to see him for a second time at 10.30 he was in a very emotional state again. Jeepers my heart just goes out to him when he's like this and all I can do is hold him until he gets over the worst of it. We've had a cup of tea and cigarette together and now he's going to settle down for the night ... hopefully. Not exactly sure what brought this on but his mind is obviously in turmoil still and I think we may have to contemplate being prescribed some 'knock out' pills to get him off to sleep before his mind goes into overdrive. I am still struggling to work out how it can be considered that we have any 'quality of life' and why is someone allowed to have to bear all of this. I just feel so sad for him.

28th August: The day started off quite well ... Fay arrived and started on the ironing. Then Gill arrived for the showering. Jo our MacMillan nurse arrived just after 12.30pm.

Alan had the most lucid conversation I've heard him have with anyone in a long time. We talked about his time in the Cottage Hospital and the fact that I had brought him home early. I also said how nice it had been of the hospice to offer him a second day as he enjoyed going there.

Then it emerged in conversation that Jo had been to see Alan whilst he was in the Cottage Hospital and knew how unhappy he was and it was she who had got on the phone to the hospice to ask for him to be given a second day each week. She and Alan had discussed this at the time.

I can't tell you how betrayed I felt by this ... I had no idea Jo had seen him or that she was responsible for the change in the hospice arrangements. Why had he needed to give me such a bad time, making me so upset, trying to make me feel guilty about him being in the hospital and pushing me into making what I thought was the best decision to bring him home. Why couldn't I have been told the truth? We have always done everything together, including all the medical stuff, so why is he now going behind my back?

After Jo left I felt I needed to say something about all of this – but Alan then turns everything around, saying that I don't tell him everything and all of a sudden Mr. Grumpy Nasty Pants arrives in our midst again. I am upset and absolutely furious. I feel upset, used, manipulated, and betrayed all at the same time.

So the rest of the day is actually quite tense. He didn't like the tea I cooked so left it all ... typical. Then on the TV something was mentioned about anniversaries. "Well there's no more of that here" he said. "I went to all that trouble to arrange our renewal of vows and didn't even get a card this year". I will say just two things ... 1. I didn't get a card either ... and 2. checking back in this diary it would seem that for the seven or more days leading up to this anniversary I had not left his side as he was quite poorly and therefore I had not been to the shops in order to get a card. Can't win! Seems there is not that much wrong with his memory after all! It's like Doc M said to me once ... we have no idea how much of his symptoms are real, put on for effect, or imaginary.

I get angry at the thought that I may have been manipulated in this way, but I know that as and when other things happen, I will do my best to make things right for him .... the way I've always done – I'm either a fool or a saint!

29th August: Janet called in to collect her birthday present and have an hour with me whilst Alan was with Gill showering. I explained everything that had been going on and that I didn't really know which way to turn.

Alan wanted to go up to Coalbrookdale to see Brummie as we've not seen him for a couple of weeks and wanted to see how he was coping with the pacemaker. He and Alan are good for each other, both being PTSD sufferers, and it would seem that they counsel each other as they both feel better after a session on their own.

During the journey up to Coalbrookdale he started to get agitated about something imaginary ... This was today's scenario ... Mrs. Vicar who is the spiritual guidance person at the hospice suddenly left. During the week before this happened she had said to Alan that anything discussed would go no further. She then asked Alan if he knew she was the wife of one of our surgery of GP's (he hadn't known until that point).

He is now pondering if she has left because of a 'conflict of interest'. He quite irrationally feels there is a conspiracy going on! "Between who?" I ask. His reply ... the doctors (including Dodgy Doc), the secretaries (including my best mate) and the hospice!!

The lay preacher also left the following week and I think it is something to do with the new management ... but he's having none of it. Says he will find out tomorrow when he goes to the hospice.

Dealing with reality is somewhat easier than the imaginary, and personally I think his mental state is running wild.

Lynn and I disappeared to the shops for half an hour ... long enough for me to tell her all the news. She too is at a loss to know the best way to go about dealing with the matter, but feels I should be talking with Doc M.

We had a quiet evening back home and Alan was in bed by 8.30pm.

30th August: Givvi arrived unannounced before Alan had left for the hospice and she felt his mood was 'spikey'. Gill and his driver were on time so Giv and I were able to talk about the whole situation and try to formulate a plan which would be best for all of us. The plan we formulated was ... see how the weekend goes and if there's more problems, contact Doc M and get Alan temporarily sedated. OK ... so far, so good.

However, when I picked Alan up from hospice he's a different man! It's been a good day, nice dinner, etc. etc. Relaxed in conservatory back at home, he starts to talk about this, that and the other and finally admits to me that his head is f*****d - (he's already told the post lady - so she reports, and he has told staff at hospice). For weeks now he has been trying to say that the 'trick cyclist' wasn't addressing the problem which needed to be addressed .. she was trying to probe right back to the 70's and Northern Ireland .. and sure enough she has managed to cause more damage than she could ever repair. I know counselling is not the answer for Alan and we will have to deal with this on a medication route which can hopefully be a temporary measure whilst he comes to terms with things again

I said 'how about if we ask Doc M to give you something on a temporary basis to help you close this 40 year old bag of worms which has been re-opened?" He said he thought that might be a good idea. Hallelujah!! So for whatever reason Mr. Happy Chappy is back in our midst and I'm hoping we can keep him here until Doc M is in the area again next Thursday and sort out the meds ... but, if I need to call him sooner, I will.

I don't know why this turn-around of events has happened ... and to be honest I don't particularly care. It is most likely as a result of talking with Brummie yesterday, but whatever the reason I feel quite big strides have been taken today, and hope we can keep things like this.

The arrival of the fly invasion at the weekend has continued all week but the mosquito net that I had ordered for Alan arrived today. It's up and doing its job tonight ... there's no flies on Alan!! Me? I still have to suffer!

So the weekend is upon us again ... no commitments, no visitors, and hopefully a pleasant time together after what has been a somewhat unsettling week.

31st August/1st September: What a warm, sunny, harmonious weekend we've had. No visitors and only a couple of phone calls. We have been able to sit outside, and take a stroll around the garden which allows Alan to see the maturity of the garden he planted. We've collected our first ever decent crop of apples ... all 7 of them! Edible, but a bit tart!!

Alan has slept in much later both mornings and continued to sleep in the conservatory until about 2pm each day, but is still always ready for bed by 9pm at the latest. He's not eating well either.

We sat outside on the patio for the whole of Sunday afternoon, cleaning brasses. At least they are all finished at last. The whole process with these brasses has taken the best part of eight months. Originally intended for auction, Alan has now decided to keep them all and this is why I had to buy shelves from B & Q on Friday. No doubt they will have to be put up sometime this week.

I find it strange that Alan is still convinced he is not going to see September out ... a feeling that is no doubt playing mischief with his mind.

The whole weekend rounded off nicely with a beautiful sunset, which Alan didn't see as he was already asleep. His mobility has been dreadful and his memory just as bad ... but you can't have everything, can you?!!

2nd September: Well, today has been one of those experiences you don't expect to have ... for us and for our visitor. We had invited the local Humanist Celebrant to visit to meet Alan and to make notes on his life in readiness for Alan's funeral. He had never been offered the opportunity to get a life story from the 'horse's mouth'. He was with us for 2 hours, and wrote reams of notes. In his words, he said he had never met anyone brave enough to contemplate doing things in this way and was quite moved by the whole experience. Alan is pleased that it's done, and will feel even better once we've seen the funeral directors on Thursday! What a strange week this is going to be!

Chapter 22: Nightmare of Biblical proportions

3rd September: As Alan was still up and dosing himself up on Oramorph at 3am, he got up early this morning in a very tired state, but was happy to have his shower and get on his way to the hospice.

I had a pre-arranged session of Reiki ... a first for me and I wasn't at all sure what, if anything, it would do for me. Perhaps it may calm the emotions, who knows? I did find it very relaxing and experienced intense heat from the practitioner's hands. Time will tell.

Alan tells me that a lady from Social Services came to chat to him today as he had been referred to her. He tells me that I must come off FaceBook as I'm being watched. Questioning one of the managers at the hospice the word 'safeguarding' is used. She thinks it's to do with an inappropriate web blog. I have no idea what all this is about really so will have to make some enquiries. In any event Alan asks me to remove my personal website from the internet which I have used as a diary for well over two years. It hasn't been updated for six months since I started compiling the diary for use in this book, so without question I have removed it.

His mobility has been very bad today as if his whole body was refusing to work. The short distance from the garage to the back door was very difficult and once he was comfy in his chair he immediately fell asleep from 4pm till 9pm when I woke him. Getting him to bed was just as difficult.

Doc M phoned at tea time, and sounds somewhat agitated. He had been hoping to arrange for Alan's infusion to be done at the hospice on Friday. We have already had this conversation in the past ... the hospice does not have the facilities to undertake the job!! We had a general chat about Alan and I have told him that things are deteriorating, especially the mobility aspect of things. We talked about his PTSD and he suggested we increase the Diazepam dose until Alan is more settled in his mind. He will be coming to see us on Thursday afternoon to administer the Zometa infusion ... and will most likely have a new student with him. I will lay money on it being a very pretty young lady!!

4th September: I telephoned and left a message for the lady who had been to see Alan at hospice yesterday ... had to leave a voice mail. Alan and I spent the afternoon finishing off the polishing of some of his bronzes.

5th September: Another strange experience today when the Funeral Director called by appointment to arrange the details for Alan's funeral. To cap costs we have decided to organize both funerals at the same time then neither of us will have anything to worry about. He was a very pleasant man ... obviously ... and the standard funeral costs will be capped at about £2,200 each. Worth getting it out of the way.

Doc M arrived comparatively early to set up Alan's planned infusion. He seemed somewhat agitated explaining yet again that there is little or nothing he can do for Alan as his cancer is behaving and his heart is not showing particular signs of decline. It is his opinion that Alan is somewhat better than he was 12 months ago. I have no idea how this opinion is formed and would question its validity. I think he may feel we contact him too much, and that he feels Alan is not currently 'sick' enough to warrant his attention ... he must prioritize. I understand that, but when Alan tells me he feels he needs to see Doc M, then what else am I supposed to do.

Nothing else new going on today except that the lady who interviewed Alan phoned during the afternoon and arranged to come and see me tomorrow. Apparently there has been a referral to the 'at risk adults' team of Social Services and we are under investigation! She will come to the house tomorrow at 11am to interview me, but she does confirm that the matter in question is an inappropriate FaceBook web blog.

I explain to Alan, yet again, this can be nothing to do with FaceBook as my Timeline can only be seen by friends, and any groups I am involved with are totally 'private'. I also tell him that at this point I am not prepared to leave FaceBook as I have this newly established ladies' support group to look after. I will wait and see what information is forthcoming tomorrow.

6th September: Alan gets off to hospice on time and Social Services lady arrives late.

Their position is this. They have received a phone call very recently advising them that I have published totally inappropriate details about Alan on a web blog. Their duty is to investigate, and immediately Alan's name has been 'flagged' as an 'at risk adult' with me as the person responsible for this need to investigate.

I am dumbfounded, and truly very upset. This website is personal ... very few people know that it exists or how to access it ... and it has been my way of recording what has happened to us since Alan's original diagnosis. It's been extremely useful to check back on events when some details have gone hazy. There are pictures of our parties and trips to the NMA maintaining the stone ... just the ordinary things we have done. How on earth can this be considered inappropriate? I told her that Alan had asked me to remove it from the internet, and although I didn't agree with this happening, I had complied immediately. However, I was able to show her the pages as constructed on the computer.

I don't have a clue who is trying to make mischief for me but my first thought is that it must be the original administrator of the ladies group on FaceBook – other than that, I don't know. All I know is that I'm devastated that this has been considered 'abuse' and I am judged to be 'the abuser'. What a stigma to have attached to your name when there has been no wrongdoing ... I am devastated.

When the interview was concluded the Social Services lady pronounced that she felt the allegations were not substantiated and would recommend closure of the case.

7th September: Sam arrived with Rem and Mila and we had a chaotic couple of hours. Alan managed to drop two drinks on the kitchen floor! The children were able to play in the garden, but Sam was hardly able to sit down!

Later in the day Alan managed to drop another drink in the dining room, which went everywhere – up the wall, furniture, door, out onto the hall carpet ... and then just before I was going to bed, I did exactly the same in his bedroom! The carpet shampooer will have to make an outing tomorrow!

A letter has arrived from Social Services confirming what I was told yesterday. The easiest way to explain what happened during the interview yesterday is to reproduce the complaint letter I have written and which will be in the post on Monday.

"Dear Sirs

TELEPHONE ALERT – ADULT AT RISK - ALAN E. SHINTON and CATHERINE SHINTON

With reference to the above and the subsequent investigation of allegations made in said phone call, please accept this letter as my official and formal complaint into the manner in which this matter was handled by your department.

Alan, nor myself, receive any services from your department although there was brief contact with an occupational therapist over 2 years ago with regard to possible equipment needs. Therefore you have little or no knowledge of us and really have absolutely no idea of our current situation.

I first became aware of the possibility of a problem when I collected my husband, Alan, from (******) Hospice last Tuesday, 3rd September. I was informed by a manager that Alan had been interviewed with regard to 'safeguarding'. All Alan was able to tell me was that 'I was being *watched' on FaceBook. He had a telephone number for a lady called H.R.*

On Wednesday 4th September I telephoned this number and left a voice message for H.R..

On Thursday 5th September, my call was returned and an appointment made for the next day at 11am.

My understanding of the situation gleaned from H.R. during her visit to my home is that certain allegations had been made against me regarding inappropriate details relating to Alan which were available on a web blog. I was advised that every suspected incident has to be investigated. I was advised that this particular phone call had been received very recently and within minutes I was able to establish in my own mind the perpetrator of the call, who I believe to be someone who was considered a friend until 2-3 weeks ago, and who has made this call out of malice and mischief rather than any genuine concern. To say that I was angry and upset is a total understatement.

I explained to H.R that this was a personal website using web space provided by my ISP. It was not traceable through any search engines and had been an on-line diary of events including photos of the journey we had been on since Alan's diagnosis of Prostate Cancer in the Far East in March 2011. The website address was known to family members, a few friends, and a few acquaintances of an on-line ladies' support group relating to Prostate Cancer. This is not a regular www address as in .co.uk or .com and under normal circumstances would not be found.

I asked H.R. if she had seen the website. Her reply was 'no'. I asked H.R. if her line manager had seen the website. Her reply was 'I don't think so'. I asked if other 'agencies' would be advised that Alan was a suspected 'adult at risk'. Her reply was 'yes'. I asked if any agencies had already been advised ... her reply was 'yes ... (*****) Hospice knew and also Jo M' – Alan's Palliative Care Nurse. I asked if our doctor *would be advised of this .. her reply was 'yes' ... but that had not happened as yet.*

By this time, I am almost beside myself with anger, stress and very upset. I found this information totally stunning and unbelievable. I consider that you have acted as judge and jury, having sentenced and broadcast incorrect information before you have heard more than half the evidence. It is a total disgrace.

At this point, I showed H.R. the direct link to the website so that she could see that it no longer existed on the internet, but I was able to show her the type of content and layout of the site as I still hold this as a diary on my computer. As I informed her, this has been extremely useful to look back on when certain dates needed to be confirmed. I also showed her a Google search for 'prostate cancer wife's story' ... there are literally 1000's of results including hundreds of personal blog stories. I doubt if every one of those authors has been investigated.

How can it be right that 'agencies' connected with Alan's care be informed of this 'at risk adult' status ... and for me to be branded some kind of 'abuser' BEFORE full facts have been established? This is nothing short of defamation of character for me and has totally compromised my position as Alan's primary carer. How can I possibly be considered a credible carer by any of the informed agencies? ... as we all know, there is no smoke without fire and even professionals will admit to thinking like that at times. I can no longer sit in a room with Jo M and Alan in case she feels there are things he may be wishing to say without my being present. I can't walk into (******) Hospice without the manager and staff thinking there is a problem between Alan and I. What use am I to him as a carer in this situation where his name could be 'flagged' on every piece of NHS paperwork? I find this whole scenario totally grotesque. I have done nothing wrong.*

Since March 2011 I have done nothing but devote myself to my husband, whom I love dearly, 'fighting the world' when necessary – I have put our original GP through the GMC who have ruled in our favour, and we are now going through litigation on a medical negligence claim.

I have researched, stood my ground and done everything in my power to make Alan's life as bearable as possible during the time he has left. He is dealing with two terminal prognosis – firstly the prostate cancer prognosis, and then within months we were then faced with a severely life limiting heart failure diagnosis. Neither condition is curable by any type of intervention. He was already suffering from PTSD. Putting all three conditions together makes for a heady cocktail of care needs.

Then, on the strength of one phone call .. possibly anonymous, I don't know and I really don't care at this stage, I am branded some kind of abuser and Alan as an 'at risk adult'.

I have a letter telling me this matter is being recommended as 'not substantiated' for which I am grateful to have in writing, but it isn't enough!

I would like a formal written apology for being wrongly 'accused', the order of events in which this investigation was conducted and the inappropriate timing of advices broadcast to other 'agencies'. I would also like a copy of the letters which you send to these agencies rescinding the 'flagging' order which has no doubt taken place on all of Alan's records, and my own, making it absolutely clear that Alan is not 'an at risk adult' and I am not an 'abuser'.

I have had a totally unblemished character since the time I was considered old enough to have a character, and on the strength of one, malicious and unsubstantiated phone call, your department has managed to destroy that in an instant. Your actions are unforgivable.

I will await your apology and advices as quickly as possible, please, as I live a life of continual stress without the need of any extra anxiety caused by the short-sighted and thoughtless manner in which you conduct your investigations.

Yours faithfully,"

Hopefully they will understand my logic and deal with my requests.

8th September: Things here this weekend have become increasingly heart breaking and frightening. Alan's eye/hand co-ordination has almost totally gone ... can't light a cigarette, keeps putting cups down on the edge of tables ... consequently they fall onto the floor and tonight he's asked me again when we are going home. Apparently we are in a holiday caravan and have been here for weeks and he wants to go home.

He can't remember days of the week, people's names. His mobility the majority of the time is rubbish, he can't get up out of his chair without help, and when I get him to his bed, he can't even lift a foot for me to take his slippers off or socks and trousers. He keeps getting annoyed because he can't get his iPad to work in the bedroom .. and it's working perfectly. He's getting well upset and I'm struggling to deal with this lot.

It took us five hours to get a shelf up today - he wanted to help but was so confused about everything. Took him an hour to decide where it would be put! How can you not show upset in these situations especially when tea can been dropped on the floor twice in a matter of 20 minutes or so? I'm only human, not a saint. I will have to go and see Doc M on Tuesday and ask for a brain scan. I know his cancer is considered to be in remission, but ALP figures only deal with bones .. not soft tissues, and I think it's time they checked whether or not it's got to his brain. I feel absolutely wretched tonight and can't stop crying.

The most upsetting thing for me tonight was I had to sit with a photo album of the bungalow ... showing Alan what it was like when we moved in and all the work we have done - trying to convince him that he is at home and this is our house. He thinks it belongs to our old neighbours in Worcester from 11 years ago. I asked him where home is .. Birchen Coppice - the estate he lived on as a child!

Hopefully tomorrow will be better ... I'm not sure how long I can go on like this. The recorded delivery letter to Social Services is ready to go and will be in the post tomorrow morning.

9th September: Gill came to help Alan shower and the rest of the day was spent quite quietly. Alan is still terribly confused and somehow seems to be missing our 20 years together from his memory. We've talked and I've had to repeat details of the years prior to us meeting ... his marriage to Diane and the arrival of his two children, the illness and death of his father eventually leading to his split with his wife and then on to the time when we met. He knows the names of different people and different addresses but he just can't pull them together as to how they are significant to us.

It's so very sad to see him like this as you can almost see the cogs turning over in his brain desperately trying to make sense of everything.

He happily went to bed with a cup of tea and a cake ... but when I went to check on him just after 10pm his bedroom floor was awash with crumbs, so I had no choice but to hoover up! Then I went to straighten his bed ... and that was the same! It's so difficult to hoover up a bed with a person in it. Finally the bed was 95% clear and I decided to leave it at that.

10th September: Today turned out to be one I would rather have not experienced or had to deal with.

As Alan was due at the hospice, it means an early start to get him ready on time. I went into him just after 8am. He was already awake, had been up and made a cup of tea. The look on his face was one of anger and upset.

"I think it's time you told me all about the lies and deceit you've been telling me for the last 11 years. This marriage is a sham and you did it without me knowing". He continued with a tirade of accusations from affairs, friendships and culminating with the most strange comment about how little I thought of him if I was able to wave to someone I knew from the back of a bus, just two days after his cancer diagnosis when we were on holiday in Phuket! At one point we met face to face outside the bathroom when he put his face within an inch of mine and growled some vile allegation at me.

I got Brummie on the phone and asked him to talk to him in an effort to try and persuade him that he was being irrational and totally incorrect in what he was saying. Well, that was a waste of time ... poor Brummie.

After a previous incident, Doc M told me that if it happened again I must contact him and he would consider changing Alan's medications to sedate him. I made the phone call and spoke to Doc M's secretary who could ascertain from my voice the seriousness of the situation. She would pass on the message.

By the time Alan came out of the shower, he was a much changed person and even followed me up the hall in order to become all 'kissy, kissy'. He has absolutely no idea of the hurt he causes. I keep trying to tell myself it's not him and try to walk away from the situation ... but it's nie on impossible.

His driver arrived and he went off to hospice leaving Gill and I to talk about the morning's events. She said she would speak to Mac Nurse Jo to discuss a better place than the local hospital for a respite session.

I think I spent most of the morning in tears and was quite incapable of doing anything. Givvi arrived on a pre-arranged visit and was distraught to find me in this state. I went for a shower whilst she went to clear up Alan's bedroom. When I came out of the shower, she came into the bedroom holding a carving knife. "Did you know Alan had this tucked down the side of his bed?" OMG ... I only sharpened all the knives on Sunday before I was going to slice the joint! Obviously I had absolutely no idea he had it.

Everything rushed through my mind .. he will have to be taken away .. will he have to be committed .. will he have to go into a mental unit .. is he having a breakdown?

The surgery phoned to confirm that Doc M would be calling before afternoon surgery so I have to get him back from hospice before 3pm. Not exactly sure how I managed to drive us to Kidderminster to fetch Alan back and to behave quite normally other than we would have to miss our shopping trip as the doc was coming to see him. He was pleased to see Givvi, but managed to sleep most of the way home.

Doc M arrived on time with a student in tow ... I ushered him straight into the study and explained the knife situation. He was horrified and agreed that things had moved to another level. He questioned Alan about the knife but could not get any sensible answer out of him as to why he would need it in his bedroom. He asked Alan if he would agree to having a brain scan done ... he would. Doc M said that we would need to wean Alan off one of his drugs and this would need to be done under controlled conditions in hospital. He immediately phoned to book a side room at the local hospital. I was to take him down to be admitted around 6pm.

At last Doc M has taken on board every detail I gave him in the email he received just yesterday.

Alan seems to accept that he is very unwell and admission to hospital was comparatively easy even though Giv and I were there over 2 hours.

Back at home we had a curry and I had a very large brandy. What a day! I was grateful of Giv's company today ... she really does shine through during a crisis. I sent her on her way home as soon as I could ... she needs her rest too! I was glad to get to bed!

11th September: Alan was on the phone in tears by 4pm. I got in the car and went straight to the hospital by which time he was in a right state, wouldn't speak to me, other than it was obvious I had no time for him. I just explained that the hospital didn't want me there all day, Sammy had visited him and I was due at tea time anyway.

He wouldn't speak to me so I told him I was leaving ... and walked out. I spoke to the staff, who don't have a clue about his problems ... still ... and that I would be back in half an hour or so.

I returned to a very tearful and very apologetic Alan ... and then we had a lovely couple of hours together. I shouldn't have to keep explaining things to the staff and I've told them we all need to be singing from the same hymn book - in that they don't want me there all day and I will join him at teatime. I think the penny has now dropped.

Brain scan will be Friday and he has told them he attends all appointments on his own!! OMG he remembers nothing! He tells me he's not had a pee for a week ... can you imagine that?!! He was well asleep before I left at 7.30pm - called in to see my friend and got home just after 9pm.

The ladies in my new support group are sending messages of support to both Givvi and I. They are a group of lovely ladies, each with their own Prostate Cancer problems, but who still have time on a daily basis to support the other members of the group. It's a lifeline to many of us.

In a flash of genius, I have contacted Tim in Phuket ... he is one of the managers at the hotel where we have stayed and we've known him since the first year he arrived there in 2000. His wife is Thai and he has a Buddhist Monk contact and is going to acquire for me a set of monk's orange apparel which is what Alan wants to be dressed in for his funeral. Tim has also offered to organize a service at the local temple for Alan when the time comes. Alan was so touched when I told him tonight, but I'm not sure he will remember it by tomorrow.

So much for a good night's sleep ... have been awake since 3.40am so it has been easy to 'chat' with Tim as he must be having his elevensies at work at the moment!

13th September: I went to the hospital for 9.30am in time for the ambulance to take both of us to Kidderminster Hospital for Alan to have a CT scan. As Alan's morphine has been reduced he finds that he is in pain more often and we could have done with some Oramorph with us on the journey. There was not too much waiting around at the hospital and Alan was duly called in for his scan.

During the scan he had to have an injection of something similar to that used by the Nuclear Medicine Department at the QE Hospital. We then had to wait about 20 minutes before the cannula could be removed. Unfortunately this meant that we missed our lift back to the Cottage Hospital. Another ambulance would be arranged! Before we left the department we were advised that a consultant was already checking the pictures and would report to Doc M by email.

We decided to have some lunch in the café whilst we waited for transport. After about an hour, I spoke to one of the drivers who was waiting at the front of the hospital. After a couple of phone calls he told us he would be able to take us back.

It was mid-afternoon when Doc M came to see us in the small garden outside Alan's room. There was absolutely nothing to worry about ... no mets ... no tumours ... no evidence of a stroke ... no evidence of dementia. A huge relief to us both ... but now we will have a prolonged period trying to sort out which drugs are working in opposition with each other. Alan will continue to be weaned off Diazepam.

14th/15th September: Alan continues to improve and has visits from Sammy, Givvi and Percy. I have stuck to my arrangement whereby I arrive in time to have tea with him and stay for a couple of hours. Alan asked me to take in some of his brasses so that he would have something to do cleaning them. He's also asked for a quilt as he's getting tied up in the hospital sheets and blankets!

He continues to be tired and to need Oramorph for pain relief. Although he is on an air mattress, I don't think his nights are too comfortable and he complains of being woken by different noises several times a night … and, of course, he is being woken at 7am which is a complete culture shock!

I've sent an email to Doc M as Alan would like to be able to attend the Hospice on Tuesday – day release!! Hopefully he will agree to this.

Have broken the frame of my glasses … luckily I do have a spare pair but I can see that I'm going to have to get some new ones. Alan ought to have his eyes tested too.

16th September: Even though Alan has been moved to the main ward to make way for a really poorly patient to move into the Grosvenor Suite, he is far brighter and his 'naughty boy' sparkle is coming back. He is starting to torment staff with jokes and banter and managed to flood the ward floor today. Oh dear! He was upset that I will have to change my visiting arrangements to fit in with normal ward regulations, but we can work around that.

He has been given permission to have 'day release' tomorrow and I have arranged a driver to pick him up to take him to the Hospice. I went armed with a set of day clothes and his 'dinner money'. I'm sure the outing will do him a lot of good.

During my visit he said to me "now I know what it's like to have a nervous breakdown" … that's what he feels has happened to him. The balance of his mind is obviously quite delicate and he says not to keep raking over the details of what he was struggling to remember, otherwise he feels the whole episode will repeat itself. We agreed to put it all behind us and concentrate on the future.

17th September: I managed to get some more washing and ironing done before the Tesco delivery arrived and the day was gone so quickly as I had to leave home at 2pm to collect Alan from Hospice. He seemed so very tired when I arrived and our planned visit to a coffee shop was cancelled in preference to coming home and having a decent cup of tea and a cake.

Alan saw the German Maid duty doctor in the hospital this morning who told him he could come home tomorrow. Apparently he asked her outright what had happened to him ... he is still confused and forgetful. She told him he had had a mental breakdown! He was happy with that explanation as he just wanted to put a name to what he had suffered. He is completely weaned off the Diazepam tablets and all we can do is take one day at a time and see how he copes with being at home ... and with me. They tell me he has been a model patient, even though he jokes about with the staff. I have given him a tin of Roses chocolates and about 6 boxes of mini bite brownies and snowball biscuits for him to give to the 'girlies'. They have looked after him well.

Tonight I must set the alarm ... can't afford to be late tomorrow morning. He is also very much looking forward to seeing Gill again who I have arranged to come in tomorrow afternoon and give him a shower.

It will be lovely to have Alan back home, but I can't deny that lack of responsibility for the past few days has been a welcome break after 2 and a half years without a significant break. Let's hope I don't have to wait that long again for the next respite!

18th September: I arrived at the hospital a few minutes early and Alan was already sitting in the reception area. He was angry and upset ... all I needed! Apparently there had been words with the night staff ... several issues, I think, but not completely certain! Something to do with him being outside at 10.30pm having a cigarette with a member of staff ... he says he was in bed asleep! Earlier in the evening he had called for attention needing Oramorph and had been ignored three or four times. When a nurse finally arrived he was told they were 'out of stock' ... sounds very strange to me. Finally, he tells me the night staff were 'having a party' at about 1am and he had walked up to the office and told them in no uncertain terms to shut the f**k up. Sure that went down well .. but as I say, not sure how much of this is totally accurate.

Anyway, I finally collected everything together and was able to get all his drugs so we could get home. Alan was very tired today and Gill came in this afternoon to give him a shower. He's eaten well today and disappeared off to bed at 8.30pm. However, even after I've said goodnight and told him I'm going to bed ... he still wants me to get up and make a drink because the last one has gone cold. Re-training required! I will get up any time of night for an 'emergency' type thing ... but cups of tea through the night have got to stop. He's going to have to learn that once I'm in bed ... I'm in bed!

19th September: Alan tells me he didn't sleep too well ... probably something to do with yet another mug of tea spilt in the bed .. and down the valance ... and on the carpet. First night at home! Give me strength.

We've brought forward the time of his showers, but as he was so tired today he made himself comfy in the lounge. Today he has told me he feels unwell and has basically slept away the day. I really don't have a clue what is going on. The hospital reported his mobility was good and he hadn't been breathless and they thought all things considered he was fine. Get him home - fell out of his chair yesterday, has wobbled when up and about today, sleeping and generally feeling unwell, breathless this morning and tonight he had to have oxygen.

Hopefully Alan will have a better night as he has an early start to get ready for his trip to the Hospice tomorrow. He has suggested tonight that perhaps the two visits a week are a bit too much for him. He is due to be re-assessed in October, so maybe it would be better to continue with the two visits until they decide differently. Will see how he gets on tomorrow and how it affects the weekend. He may be right!

20th September: Today turned into a total nightmare ... something of the kind I have never experienced in all my years. It's been one of the worst days of my life.

The day had started well with Alan up and ready for Gill to arrive for his shower. They chatted and laughed about the fact that Alan still hadn't had his hair cut but I think he may have decided to have it trimmed. His driver arrived on time and off he went in a really good frame of mind.

I spent the morning working around the house just catching up on some bits and pieces.

Then the bombshell dropped.

At 1.45pm the phone rang. When I picked up the phone it was Rebecca, Alan's estranged daughter. She told me not to bother to go to the hospice to collect Alan, he wouldn't be there. I was told not to go to her house or to Sammy's house, otherwise the police would be called and an injunction taken out. They were taking Alan out of the Hospice for his own protection. She told me that I had been over-medicating Alan putting him at risk ... and I was not to deny it as, apparently, I had already admitted this to the police. The phone went down.

I can't actually describe how I felt other than stunned rigid. I have absolutely no idea what the hell is going on.

I phoned the doctors, the police, the doctors again, the Hospice, the doctors ... I was getting nowhere. I eventually asked the doctors if I could get Alan back from Kidderminster, could he have an emergency appointment. One was booked for 5.10pm.

I finally rang Sammy's mobile and managed to speak to Alan. He was in a terrible state, could hardly talk to me, but he told me that he had been told that the police had taken blood samples when he was in the care of the Cottage Hospital and things were showing up that shouldn't be there (obviously sinister) and that I must have been giving him 'stuff'. The phone call was cut off. Eventually I spoke to Sammy and said I wanted to come down and pick up Alan and take him to the doctors. He agreed to this as long as I agreed not to touch any of Alan's medications again and to get someone else to give him his tablets.

I telephoned Gill, Alan's shower nurse, and asked to employ her to deal with Alan's medications that evening, and over the weekend. In total shock and disbelief she did agree to come. We also talked about getting the local pharmacy to blister pack a month's supply as an arse covering exercise. I truly can't believe this is happening.

I drove down to Kidderminster with 101 things rushing through my mind! I couldn't understand how a couple of weeks earlier when Social Services had spoken to me about a website, had sent me a letter saying all allegations were unsubstantiated ... that this could now be happening. During the whole of that previous episode the matter of drugs had never been mentioned by the Social Worker who had interviewed me. However, Jo the Mac nurse had been asked, so I later learned, but I still have no idea where this is all coming from.

I parked outside Sammy's house, walked to the front door and knocked it loudly, immediately turning around and getting back into the car. Alan looked a really sad figure struggling along the shale driveway and, as usual, had difficulty getting into the car. It was obvious that he was very upset and angry.

I asked him if he was OK to which he replied "What do you think? How do you think I feel when you learn that your wife has been buying drugs off the internet and trying to kill me?"

Trying to stay calm even though I am absolutely fuming inside, I said to him that no money had gone from our cards or credit cards that we didn't know about and in any event there were clever IT people who could find a trail on the computer – no matter what may have been deleted. He told me that the police had already tracked it all. He then went on to mention again the blood tests the police had taken and the strange results they had found. He tells me that Rebecca has a friend who works at Shrewsbury Police Station and has told her about it, and in fact, she had told him I was actually in custody! I said to him that he had been having regular 4-weekly blood tests for over 2 years and if there was anything untoward it would have been spotted straight away. He also wanted to know when I had spoken to the police. I told him my only conversation with the police had been earlier in the day when I was trying to establish whether Sammy or Rebecca had placed an official call, and had been told by the controller that no calls relating to any of the names mentioned had been made.

My stomach is in knots. I am so very upset and angry, I have to ask him the question "Do you truly feel in your heart of hearts that I could possibly have done anything like this to you?" His reply was something along the lines of 'well, the police know all about it because they've been investigating you'. In other words, at this point, he doesn't believe me!

The majority of the rest of the journey was in stony silence apart from another mention of the blood tests. I just said that Doc M would be able to tell him about blood tests, but that I had been told on the day he left hospital that his bloods were fine and urine tests were fine.

I cannot describe the devastation I felt at that time when the man I have been with and loved for over 20 years could doubt me. However, I keep telling myself that for months and months Alan has had memory problems and confusion. He's not himself. I know he's not 100%, but even so, the hurt is totally raw.

We arrived at the doctors' surgery and only had to wait about 5 minutes before Alan was called. I had asked him if he wanted to see the doctor on his own, but was told that this concerned me as well and we would go in together.

Doc M was already aware of a problem as both Alan and Sammy had spoken to him earlier in the day. I explained the best I could the garbled information I had, and referred to the supposed internet purchases. I just shrugged my shoulders – "I have no idea where this information is coming from". Doc M confirmed to Alan that all his blood tests were perfectly normal and that there had been no request from the police for blood samples or tests. I suggested that if Doc M felt Alan was at risk .. and Alan felt he was at risk, then perhaps Alan should be somewhere else to be looked after. Doc M said that if he felt there was any sort of problem with the administration of drugs, he would only ever have prescribed one week at a time – and this had never happened. He explained again to Alan that his blood results historically had always been normal, and if the police were looking for opiates, then of course they would be there as they are part of his medication. He also confirmed that he had not been contacted by the police and was really hoping that he wouldn't be.

Back in the car, Alan apologized for doubting me. At last, he finally believes that I have done nothing wrong. I said to him that all I would ask is that he would phone Sammy and Rebecca and tell them what Doc M had told us.

No one gets over this sort of shock in an instant ... not Alan, and certainly not me. Our journey home is still somewhat uncomfortable as Alan continues to digest what we have been told.

Finally home, I find out that Sammy has not offered him any food all day, so I immediately started to get some tea ready as it was now 6pm. I have no stomach for food and have nothing. As Gill will be giving Alan his drugs tonight, I throw down the sink the tablets I had prepared this morning.

We then have a discussion about the administration of his drugs and it is Alan's opinion that to involve Gill is allowing the person who has made these malicious accusations to win. His decision. We leave a message for Gill to phone ... which she does, and Alan explains his feelings, so her visit is cancelled.

During the evening Sammy phoned and it is blatantly obvious that he doesn't want to speak to me ... I don't want to speak to him either, quite frankly. Alan speaks to him and tells him that the story about the police and blood tests is 'bullshit' and explains what the doctor has told us. The phone call is brief.

Alan falls asleep on the settee for about an hour then tells me he wants to go to bed. So the usual nightly routine has to take place whereby I must help him stand up, support him whilst he walks to the bathroom and then to the bedroom where I undress him and help get him into bed – even though I am still thoroughly upset. I take him his tablets and a cup of tea. Still mulling over the day's events he tells me that he will no longer be attending the Hospice. He said *'I've done*

nothing wrong and you've done nothing wrong ... that's all that matters.'
We decide to get out of the house tomorrow and visit Brummie and
Lynn.

Having had enough of the day, I decided to go straight to bed,
too. Neither of us slept particularly well. Not surprising really and got
up in the night to make drinks a couple of times.

Nights are really long when the speed of your mind doesn't
allow for sleep resulting in feeling totally wretched the next day.

21st September: We're up and on our way to Brummie's by
11am and did extremely well for time getting to the outskirts of Telford
by 11.40am. However, some huge festival at Ironbridge had
necessitated the closure of many roads. We ended up spending the
next hour driving through country lanes in the hills trying to
circumnavigate all the closures. My phone was dead so unable to let
them know why we are late. Alan was ready to head back home, but
finally we made it.

Obviously we relayed the story of the previous day and they sat
there in total disbelief, both getting really angry at the suggestion I would
do anything to harm him. They are both very upset and tell Alan a few
home truths about his children ... which he totally accepts from them.
However, eventually the mood lifted and Alan was able to share a few
laughs with Brummie. They all had a bite to eat for lunch ... I still can't
face anything. After much discussion the general consensus is that if I
was under investigation by the police in relation to drugs offences, then I
would have been arrested a couple of weeks ago and Alan would have
been placed in either a hospice or care home. They suggest that I
should phone the police and specifically ask if I am under investigation
as word has reached Alan's daughter from a serving police officer that
this is the case. They are both very concerned for us and cannot
believe that someone can be so evil as to inflict this sort of pain on a
dying man and the person who cares for him. Nor can we!

The journey home is far less eventful and Alan sleeps most of the way. Once home he feels well enough to complete the polishing of his brasses ready for them to be lacquered tomorrow. He ate a good tea, fell asleep and was ready for bed by 8pm. Once I had him settled in bed I decide that it's the best place for me too.

Surely life is difficult enough ... and has been for nearly three years ... without this sort of cr*p being thrown at us. We've said it before and find ourselves saying it again .. just how much more can they throw at us? I can quite understand why people walk away from situations or contemplate suicide. Alan doesn't deserve this upset ... and neither do I. Is it worth hoping for a better day tomorrow?

22nd September: Quite miraculously we both slept well last night and had a late start to our Sunday. Finally I managed to get through to the Police this morning in an effort to find out whether or not I was under investigation for the allegations made against me on Friday. A very pleasant female officer took my details and checked the system thoroughly, checking she was spelling my surname correctly, and carried out searches in my Christian name. She confirmed that there is absolutely nothing recorded anywhere of any type of investigation involving me. She asked what the allegation had been and when I told her, almost laughing, she said that if that type of allegation had been made then be assured you would have been 'picked up' on the day!

Even though Alan and I knew there was no foundation in the misinformation he had been fed on Friday, there was a certain relief and an 'I told you so' moment!

Alan had not been up and about till almost 1pm - he was asleep in the chair again by 2pm! He obviously just needed that extra couple of hours. Once he woke up properly at 4pm he was on fine form and we've enjoyed a few laughs and jokes together.

Sammy phoned and immediately asked to speak to his father. Alan was very near to losing his temper with him and after a few minutes passed the phone across to me. For the first time ever I have read Sammy the riot act and really laid into him. He has absolutely no idea what he is talking about ... and neither does Rebecca. I can't say that there wasn't any satisfaction in this because there was, actually. I handed the phone back to Alan when my five minutes was done. He finished off the phone call. He said Sammy was now gutted that he had caused so much upset involving so many people. Hopefully he will have learned a lesson ... don't stick your nose in where it's not needed .. make sure you have your facts straight before you act ... don't believe street gossip rather than members of your extended family ... and if you have a problem, speak to the people concerned first before barging into other peoples' lives without a thought for what damage you may be causing unnecessarily.

We have been estranged from Rebecca for many years, apart from a short time in the past year or so, and therefore I am under no illusion that I will ever get an apology from her. As for Sammy, until he has made amends with me, then I want nothing to do with him or any of his family.

The rest of the day has passed off very peacefully .. thank goodness.

You can't appreciate the good times if there are no bad times to compare them with!

23rd September: I received a letter from Social Services in response to my complaint, saying that the investigation had been correct procedurally. The case was closed. The allegations were unfounded and unsubstantiated. The letter commented that my care of Alan had been the total opposite of that alleged. Copies of the letter to the hospice and Mac nurse Jo were enclosed as requested.

Alan was in no mood for his shower and decided to go back to bed immediately afterwards. He was very tired and just wanted to sleep. MacMillan nurse Jo arrived for our appointment but had no idea of the details relating to last Friday, so it took time to explain everything. Finally she went into Alan's bedroom to have a chat with him. When she came back into the kitchen, I explained that in view of Sammy's phone calls to the police and social services, it had occurred to me that this might spark off yet another investigation, so I had left a message for the social worker to ring me as a matter of urgency. Jo agreed that a second investigation was certainly a probability.

As we talked, I think I joked about the fact that Alan thought every car he heard coming up the drive was the police coming to take me away. With that we heard two vehicles on the drive and I went to look. A red car and a white van had arrived.

OMG ... it's C.I.D. and Social Services. All I can do is shake my head in disbelief, ask them to come in and offer to put the kettle on.

The social worker, who I knew from the previous interview, apologized profusely saying that she knew nothing about this until she got to work that morning.

The two officers, from the Vulnerable Adults Protection Squad, explained that they had not come to investigate me, in fact just the opposite. They had come in person to assure both Alan and I that they had no concerns about allegations which had been made against me with regard to over-medicating. They felt it only right and proper that this information was brought to us personally, and that they were here to help us. There would have been an investigation had the subject not been already covered during the first investigation. All enquiries had confirmed to them that my treatment of Alan and co-operation with Doc M and nurses had been exemplary and on that score I had nothing to worry about. Mac nurse Jo explained to them how particularly complicated Alan's care had been and the amount of drugs which had been involved would have been a challenge to a nursing professional, let alone a wife/carer. They had been made fully aware of that. However, they did need to speak to Alan. I took them into Alan's bedroom.

In the meantime, Jo, H.R. (social worker) and I continued to chat in the kitchen about the total nightmare Alan and I were being put through, especially as Jo commented that he was already in a vulnerable mental state before the onset of all this turmoil.

The two officers returned to the kitchen and told me that it was Alan's wish that he wanted no further contact with Sam and Rebecca, and then I was asked if we had made Wills. I confirmed that we had and they were kept in a locked safe in the study. I was asked to produce them. These Wills were drawn up just before our last trip to Phuket in 2011. I was told to keep these very safe and that Alan's solicitor would be contacting us, would come to the house with an independent witness with certain forms to be completed and that they should verify these Wills and keep a copy at their office. I was told that Alan's Will, as it stood, would be challenged. I told them Alan didn't have a solicitor other than the Bristol firm dealing with our litigation case. The phrase was repeated that "Alan's solicitor" would be in touch.

The female officer leant towards me and said that they were offering good advice. Client confidentiality meant they could say no more. Therefore, I suddenly realize Alan had told them something of which they now know I am totally unaware. Oh f**k, but thank them for their advice. Much food for thought. I have no idea what this is all about. The officers confirm they will be speaking to Sammy and Rebecca this afternoon to tell them Alan's wishes.

Finally everyone is ready to leave. I am told if there is a phone call from either Sammy or Rebecca that the phone must be given straight to Alan for him to explain his wishes. I am not to get into conversation with either of them and if further calls are made, we are to contact either one of the officers, who will deal with the situation.

I am shell-shocked and more than a little concerned about the Wills.

The advice is that these must be witnessed by a solicitor rather than friends in order to secure their validity in the case of a challenge in the future.

Alan continues to sleep until I wake him as Sammy is on the phone. I've had no conversation with him. Alan takes the phone and I can hear Sammy talking, but not the actual words. Alan's temper rises and he tells him about the police, that Sam has completely blown it, and it would be better if there is no further contact. He handed me the phone saying that Sam wanted to apologize to me, which he did. Sammy is totally distraught, but I'm not prepared to get into any sort of conversation, remind him of what the police have advised him, and ring off. Alan now decides to get up. However, in no time at all he is asleep again on the   settee.

Givvi and Percy arrived and sat open mouthed as the sorry story unfolded.   Shock, horror, devastation, being just some of the emotions they felt.

Alan woke up, not in the best of moods, took himself off to the kitchen and then to bed. Givvi wanted to say goodnight as she left so I went to check, only to find him in floods of tears. Giv and Percy disappeared and I went back into Alan. He had had enough. He wanted to die. Were all the tablets still in the safe? This is a twisted house and he's caught up in the middle of it. He just wants to be out ... in fact he will be gone by lunchtime tomorrow. *"No I'll wait till after the solicitor phones and then I'll be gone. Who the hell was that guy with Givvi? How dare she bring strangers here."* It was very difficult to convince him that Givvi had been here with Percy.

I find these outbursts so upsetting and really have no idea how to deal with them. All I want to do is hold him and comfort him but he rebuffs me. After about an hour or so, he is calmer and I leave him to go to sleep again.

Who do you talk to when your husband wants to kill himself and it's approaching midnight? Yourself! I clear out the little kitchen safe of all drugs as Alan knows the combination, and relocate them in the key combo safe in the study, which he has never mastered. The remaining Oramorph is poured down the sink and new bottles hidden. The car keys are hidden. I decide that I will have to sit up all night ... just in case.

Some two hours later, the buzzer sounds. I go straight to Alan's room where, yet again, I find him in tears ... but this time he is so very apologetic for the previous outburst. Telling him not to worry, I make us another drink and fetch a chair to sit in the room with him for a while.

Talking about the day's events, I told him I had phoned one of the executors of our Wills as she had moved house and we must have the new address put in place. He said *"My Will is dated yesterday"*.

'No', I said, 'we made them in 2011 before we went to Phuket'

.   *"No, my Will is dated yesterday. I've changed it. The Hospice had an offer on to make a Will for £30 and I did it Friday, but I haven't signed anything"*.

OMG ... yet again I am stunned into total silence with brain in overdrive. The words of the police officers suddenly returned to me and I now fully understood their concerns and why they were adamant that the 2011 Will would be challenged as both children would think this new Will had been completed.

Do not lose your temper, Cath ... do not lose your temper. Do not cry. Do not react. Three days he has kept this vital piece of information from me. Three days since Doc M confirmed to him in no uncertain terms that I was not trying to kill him. I now know this is all sounding very suspicious with the sudden appearance of both Sammy and Rebecca at the Hospice on Friday, and with this revelation about a new Will. I smell a huge rat, as did the police when I was asked if I had any thoughts on the children's motives. At the time I had said something like 'well, you only need to look at this place, plus the compensation Alan is likely to receive, and you have a perfect motive.' The existence of this new Will was the piece of information that they had been unable to give me.

Alan said *"We can go to T*****d's tomorrow in Kidderminster and tell them I'm not going ahead with it".* I just said a telephone call would suffice and, yes, we can deal with it in the morning.

Now, how am I meant to sleep? With great difficulty. When will this nightmare end?

24th September: I manage about three hours sleep before waking. I make a coffee and go back to bed. I can hear Alan stirring and coughing, so get up and offer to make him a cup of tea. When I took this to his room he asked me outright *"Do you think I've been manipulated?"*

'You've asked me a very direct question and I will give you a very straight answer. Yes, I feel you have been coerced by Sammy and Rebecca whilst in a very vulnerable mental state. So, yes, I do think you've been manipulated.'

I am so disappointed in the care the hospice have taken of Alan through Friday when it should have been plainly obvious that things were not right. I now realize that they blatantly lied to me when I asked the specific question as to whether anyone from an 'outside agency' had seen Alan that day ... and had been told 'no'. As this solicitor is not a member of their staff ... then surely they qualify as an 'outside agent'. I am now convinced that the hospice is not a safe environment in which to leave Alan as his mental instabilities leave him wide open to questionable suggestions. I feel so angry and let down.

Alan suggests that I should email the police and advise them of Sammy's call and that we have done as they suggested.

They responded to the email asking us to phone. When I phoned back I was advised that they had been in touch with T*****d's and they knew nothing of Alan ... Alan doesn't even know who he has spoken with about this new Will! They then spoke to the Hospice questioning their ethics in allowing outside companies to tout for business within a hospice environment and informed them they could well have been complicit in a possible attempted serious fraud. They immediately gave the police the name of the company of solicitors involved. A similar phone call had then been made to the solicitor involved, T******'s who operate locally, and the same scenario explained. On the thought of possible coercion and fraud, the solicitor tends to agree with the police!

I get the impression that both establishments may be 'shitting bricks' for want of a better phrase!

I am told that the solicitor will be in touch today and all Alan need do is tell them he is not going ahead with this will and for all documents relating to it should be destroyed. That will be the end of the matter. Having done all of this, the police now feel they have completed their work for us and hope that the future is somewhat more peaceful. Alan wanted to speak with the officer and was on the phone for some time. He is told that both the police and the solicitor thought that he was being coerced but this had now been put right. They spoke about Sammy and his conversation with a police officer about his concerns and they agree that he made this move out of total ignorance and not through malice. Alan suggests that he needs to have counselling and he would never consider being back in touch with Sam until this has been successfully completed. He would certainly never even contemplate getting in touch with Rebecca again. The phone call ends on a lighter note with both of them joking with each other ... but still with the offer that if we have any concerns then to get back in touch.

My feelings are that I never want to clap eyes again on anyone who holds me in such low esteem as to consider I would be capable of 'attempted murder' of a loved one. For me, they can 'go forth and multiply'. At this point in time, those are my feelings and I can't envisage a time when I will ever forgive either of them.

Doc M arrived about 3.30pm and he advises that the police have also been in touch with him wanting to know the likely state of Alan's mind on the previous Friday. He has advised them that Alan is very vulnerable mentally at the moment and it would be his opinion that

Alan had been coerced into making decisions which would not have been made by someone of sound mind. He has suggested Alan goes back on to a small dose of Diazepam as there is really nothing else which will comfortably mix with all his other drugs. Doc M is at his caring best today, knowing that both of us have been through the wringer during the past few days. He considers that Sammy needs serious help and we have told him that Alan has suggested he gets counselling. We thank him for coming as we really do appreciate his time is precious and I apologize to him yet again for us becoming the 'patients from hell'.

The rest of the day is ours and we spend it quietly in front of the TV until we are both ready for bed.

Enough, enough, enough!

25th September: I awake with a start and look at the clock. It's 10.20am and Gill is due at 10.30am ... as is Georgie to help with the housework. I quickly throw on some clothes, get the kettle on and wake Alan.

Suddenly I find myself breaking down and crying quite uncontrollably. Everything has caught up with me and this is the first time after five days of a living nightmare that this has happened. I suppose I was going to react at some time – just glad I was at home really.

Alan has his shower and Georgie gets done what she can in her couple of hours, and then finally we can relax on our own. After having a bit of lunch, Alan falls asleep in the chair and I must admit to having half an hour myself.

So today has been quieter ... well at least this afternoon! The weather's not good and the washing is limp on the line ... but does it really matter? I have washed all Alan's clothes ... along with an incontinence pad he had worn one day and left in his pants when throwing them into the wash bin, so I have a machine full of clothes covered in white lint. A re-wash does nothing to improve things. Hope the tumble dryer will eliminate it all! The oil delivery arrives and the price is a full 10p per litre cheaper than I was quoted last week ... one bit of good news!

Alan is in bed early and I have the first opportunity to speak to Jan on the phone to bring her up to date. She is stunned into silence wondering how on earth I have coped .. all I could say is that you just have to – what else can anyone do? She cannot believe that anyone could put us through all this and she too wonders when it will all end.

Time for bed, I think. I am so tired but as Gill is not coming tomorrow, there are no time pressures for either of us to get up. I very much hope the dustmen do a quiet job in the morning!

26th September: Unfortunately, sleep came in short bursts as I've been up almost all night with a very violent upset stomach. Again, I think this is a reaction to the past few days rather than a bug or having eaten something dodgy! I'll stay in bed until Alan stirs ... hopefully not before 11am!!

We had a late start but didn't see any problems in that. I phoned in to the doctors to chase up one of Alan's prescriptions and to get the results of his blood test taken on Tuesday. The figures are still brilliant. PSA 0.9 and ALP 76. Nothing to worry about there.

However, it was a different story when the firm of solicitors phoned. This conversation supposedly to talk about unsigned paperwork which was prepared after his visit to the hospice last Friday. Alan said to the lady on the phone that he would put the phone on speaker so that I could hear what was going on.

New bombshell about to fall.

"Are you saying, Mr. Shinton, that you wish to make changes to your Will dated 19th July, 2013?" July 2013? Yet again I'm stunned into silence. "You have a copy of this Will, don't you? The Will drafted

289

on 19th July and signed on 23rd July, 2013. The copy was sent to (*****) Hospice."

I immediately interrupted and said that we did not have a copy of this Will. Alan confirmed that amendments needed to be made. She will arrange for us to be contacted on Tuesday for an appointment to be made when the alterations can be carried out.

Alan is denying any knowledge of a copy of this Will and is devastated by what he has done. He tells me he doesn't have a clue what the Will contains or the changes he asked to be prepared on Friday of last week. All he can do is apologize if he has hurt me. Well, that's all tickety-boo, then! Is it hell! At this point I am wondering who exactly is the vulnerable adult?

How am I supposed to feel knowing that he may have signed away monies we don't have, and property of which he owns half. The scenario of the possibility of this not coming to light until after his death has left me feeling very unstable, hurt and totally betrayed, even though I keep telling myself these actions were not taken by the real Alan. Yet again, I can't eat today.

Trying to stay calm in myself we have a conversation whereby we agree that we will go back to the original format of 'mirror Wills' which has stood us in good stead since we married ... or so I had thought!

As Alan has gone to bed this evening, he is saying he cannot even recall the contents of this afternoon's phone call. This is obviously what he does ... blocks things out when he can't face the truth.

I will feel happier in myself when new Wills have been prepared and signed, but really don't feel inclined to use this solicitor who I feel has been complicit in taking instructions from a man of questionable mental state at the time. I may need to take advice on this.

Sammy phoned, still trying to say that the police told him they had it in black and white about me, and insists Alan also heard this phone call during Friday. Alan repeats that, as per what the police have told him, he (Sammy) needs to get successful bereavement counselling before he will consider speaking to him again. I am not including myself in this possibility.

27th September: Awake early again after another disturbed night, I feel very vulnerable not knowing the contents of this Will Alan has made in July. It is just possible that I wouldn't be able to stay in my own home after he dies, if he has Willed his half of the property to his children. Everest would have to be sold to satisfy their demands for money. Yet again my anger is directed at the Hospice as, having checked back on the dates given, it would seem that this was all round about the time when Alan agreed to buy a car, was admitted to the Cottage Hospital for respite, and managed to stay there just two days before breaking down blaming me for trying to get rid of him, and I took him home the next morning. It was in this frame of mind that staff at the hospice, with full knowledge of where he had been and the fact that he had talked his way out and back home early, felt he was mentally stable enough to give instructions on a new Will.

We had a discussion about this Will and as I have checked the legalities of destruction, Alan is at liberty to destroy the Will either by ripping it up or burning it, and then we can start again. But as I have said to him, I'm not happy to use this firm of solicitors again, and we will choose a local firm together and have new 'mirror Wills' made. These new solicitors will hold the originals. Until that is done I don't think I will be able to relax or eat properly.

We are expecting a call on Tuesday next week to arrange for the solicitor to come out and she will be told to have with her the original Will. She is under the impression alterations are going to be made. Once she is here, and I can get the Will into Alan's hands he can destroy it in front of her. She can then be told that's where our business ends and show her the door. I will suggest to her that the circumstances under which these instructions were taken were so dubious that it would not be sensible for her to invoice us for her time.

Alan just about managed to have his shower this morning and quickly fell asleep in the chair not really stirring till late afternoon when I was beginning to nod! So he managed to stay awake for a couple of hours and was pottering about with his Dremel until it was time for tea. He ate most of it but was very soon asleep again. He had taken two Diazepam last night and has decided that's probably a bit much for him at the moment!

Luckily I've managed to get most of the ironing done which has been in the basket some time and have also got all today's laundry washed and dried. Plenty more ironing to attack tomorrow! It's taken me until now to catch up with everything from his hospital stay!

We're hoping to go out tomorrow .. wonder if either of us will wake up early enough to make it worthwhile?

28th September: I was awake before 6am but was not in the mood for getting up at that time. I watched some TV for about an hour before making a drink and some porridge and taking both back to bed. Before I knew what day of the week it was, it was noon and I'm just waking up again! Alan had not stirred either!

We both get up and deal with all the morning pills. Alan is shattered ... don't have a clue what time he got off to sleep, but must have been the early hours of the morning. Consequently he makes his way to his usual spot in the conservatory and sleeps for the rest of the day.

Being in a 'can't be arsed' sort of mood, I suggested we have a Chinese takeaway this evening. Good plan. Still tired Alan is in bed before 9pm and to be honest, I wasn't far behind him! The weather is promising to be brilliant tomorrow ... probably the last good day of the season, so must make the most of it.

29th September: Alan still not feeling up to having a trip out and stayed in bed most of the morning. I took advantage of the time to start 'spotting' the carpets where there have been a few accidents. Once up Alan managed to do a little work on one of his walking sticks but then fell asleep in the chair.

Janet called in unannounced just to make sure that we were OK and she seems saddened to see how Alan is and to learn that, actually, he is now like this most of the time.

Although he managed to be awake for his tea and seemed to enjoy it for a change ... he soon wanted to go to bed and was asleep before 8.30pm.

As a devout Downton Abbey fan, I was grateful to be able to watch this episode without interruptions!

I have the mother of all cold sores erupting on my top lip ... a sure sign that I'm under the weather! I wonder why that might be?!!

We have a busy week ahead with all sorts of appointments ... Gill every day ... Jo the MacMillan nurse, Vajra Gupta (a Buddhist mentor), Steve from the funeral directors and Doc M – to name but a few! ... and expecting a call from the firm of solicitors who took instructions from a man who was mentally unstable and allowed him to completely change his Will. I'll play it by ear, but there is so much I would like to tell them and feel like reporting them to their governing body.

30th September: The day started off well and Gill was on time for Alan's shower which left us plenty of time before our Mac nurse's due visit. However when she was half an hour late I phoned her, and it seems I had totally misunderstood what she had told me last Monday when I was surrounded by police officers and social worker. It had been her intention just to phone today. Anyway, she is going to call in on Thursday. Interestingly she tells us that she has been invited by the Social Services Department to a meeting concerning our case. She wanted to know if we had an invite ... not as yet! I don't think for one minute we'll get one!

Next appointment today was with an ordained Buddhist who was coming chat with Alan about his funeral and what part he would be prepared to play in it. He was a very nice gentleman, Vajra Gupta by name. He was able to reassure Alan that he would be very happy to conduct part of the funeral service and include chants and readings. He is going to send some suggested readings for Alan to make a choice. He is also going to send us an instructional DVD on meditation ... he feels both of us would benefit.

When he had left, Alan told me that he felt quite calm and at peace about everything now he had all that he wanted in place. It's taken a long time for him to feel like that.

There was a definite change in the weather today and I wonder how much longer we will be able to stay in the conservatory as it has seemed 'chilly' all day and I even had to put the central heating on for a time. Autumn is definitely here!!

1st October: Neither of us has slept well and it's an effort for Alan to have his shower. Once he is dressed he is immediately ready to make himself comfy in the conservatory and is soon asleep again. But he did ask me to make an appointment for him to have his hair cut! Miracle! He has been looking very rough and ready for many weeks as he felt it was some sort of game to play knowing that I hate him to look that untidy .. but as he said 'I can do what I like, when I like'. Perhaps he is coming to his senses!

He has a late lunch and then we have to be ready for the Funeral Director to arrive with the paperwork for the two pre-paid funerals we have arranged. Paperwork signed and cheques handed over, this is another major step in getting everything sorted out once and for all. The price we have paid is very competitive in today's marketplace and is a secure investment with the Funeral Planning Authority.

As the solicitors have not phoned, I telephoned their office and asked for an appointment for us both tomorrow and for Alan's Will, which they have in store, to be made available during our visit. I tell them it is our intention to create two new 'mirror' Wills. We have an appointment at 2.30pm. Could be quite interesting. They, along with the hospice, have created this situation for us both and I'm interested to see how much they think they are going to charge us for the privilege!

I have contacted our friend Jason this evening just to confirm he would be prepared to be an executor on Alan's new Will I will leave my executors the same as they are already.

Alan has slept all evening and is in bed by 9pm. I'm hoping he may be a bit brighter once we have this last hurdle out of the way tomorrow.

2nd October: The only thing we need to concentrate on today is the appointment with the solicitor. Both Gill and Georgie arrive late, but we are clear of them by 12.30pm giving Alan time enough to have some lunch and a rest before we must leave at 1.45pm.

Earlier I phoned the Hospice as the copy of Alan's Will was sent there. I was phoning to ask them to send it on to him. However, they advise that Alan asked for this copy two or three weeks ago and they have a feeling that he has burnt it as they found ashes in the garden, which had initially puzzled them ... but this was their conclusion.

Arriving in Kidderminster in plenty of time as parking can be a problem, we were relieved to find a space almost directly opposite the solicitors' office. We had to wait a few minutes before the lady was ready for us. Of course, she knew Alan as they had met before at the hospice ... at least twice!   I have to admit to being a little hostile in my inter-reaction with her as I feel she has been complicit in this whole affair. She was instructed to formulate two 'mirror' Wills showing the minor alterations from our original Wills made together in 2011. She confirmed from the copy she was shown that the 2011 Wills were perfectly legal. In essence we could have saved £330 if Alan's July Will had just been destroyed! But following the advice of the police, these new Wills, drawn up and signed and witnessed in the solicitors' office, will halt any challenge which is likely in the future. Sod the money! Let's have it water-tight. She was trying to point out bequests Alan had made previously and I told her it was irrelevant as these were two totally new Wills. I don't want to know the details of the July Will ... why would I? Do it or don't do it! We can easily take our business elsewhere. I was close to spitting feathers. She confirmed we should receive draft copies tomorrow morning and we can return on Friday to sign off everything. These new originals will remain at the solicitors and will be registered with the Will bank. Thank god for that! Let's just get it done.

Back at home Alan again apologizes for f***ing things up and I have to tell him not to worry as it is all sorted now. My gut feeling is that a large proportion of his expected compensation money had been ear-marked for his two children. No doubt they will kick off when the time comes. Tough. They will have to learn to live with disappointment – like the rest of us!

Worn out by the day's events, Alan manages to eat a bit of tea and is asleep by 6.30pm and ready for bed by 7pm. Tomorrow should be somewhat less stressful!

3rd October: I woke up absolutely starving at 5.30am so I went and made myself a bowl of porridge and a cup of coffee. Next thing I know it's 10am and definitely time to get up! Gill was late, but, no worries, Alan didn't feel like getting up anyway!

Shower done, next visitor through the door was Mac nurse Jo. We had a very productive chat with her discussing morphine tinkering and possibly the Diazepam as well until we can get Alan to his best. She will fax Doc M with her suggestions. We also chatted about the events of the past couple of weeks and she is still finding it hard to believe all that happened. We discussed the hospice and the fact that Alan will not be returning .. he doesn't like their interference and I have no trust in them whatsoever any more.

I had always understood that for a few hours a week I was handing over my 24/7 care to the hospice and if there were any problems they would be straight on the phone. But no, any problems and a brick wall goes up and they hide behind 'patient confidentiality'. This is the only place I have been 'excluded' from his care ... with everyone else involved in his long history of care and treatment, I have always been there to help Alan understand what's going on. I don't like the hospice's work ethic and some of their decisions regarding Alan have been somewhat dangerous ... i.e. allowing him to leave the hospice with Sammy on the strength of Sammy's word that he will 'look after him'. What a joke that is! As far as I'm concerned, they've cooked their goose and I want nothing more to do with them. I feel sorry for Alan not having the outlet and company he shared there, but he really wants to be left alone now for us to do our own thing together ... and enjoy it!

Jo also suggested that in an effort to stop Alan's nightmares we should try using oxygen all night. It's about the only think we haven't tried. So this has been set up and put into use tonight ... not sure how long the tubing will stay in place, but he seems quite still and relaxed as I have come to bed. Fingers' crossed that this will work.

Early start tomorrow ... meant to be at The Cottage Hospital by 9am! I hate being woken up by alarms!

4th October: Very early start and it took a bit of effort to get us out of the door in time to be at the hospital for 9am ... but we managed it. Doc M set up the Zometa infusion within minutes of us arriving. Alan was in the mood to play up and shot a rubber tourniquet straight up the back of Doc M's head ... great shot. The nurses stood by in amazement at his antics as they treat Doc M with such reverence! It's wonderful to have a doctor with such a great sense of humour ... it really makes the medicine taste sweeter!

We were home shortly after 10am and in plenty of time to have a cup of tea before Gill arrived at 11am to do Alan's shower. We then had a quick snack and sat down for half an hour.

Finally the post arrived with the drafts of the new Wills which I had just about enough time to read and correct before we were on our way again to get to Kidderminster for 2pm appointment. The solicitor went through both Wills, had the corrections made and then wanted to see Alan on his own to check that he was sure this was what he wanted to do and that no pressure had been applied to get him to make a new Will ... again! However, he was able to assure the solicitor that this was what he wanted and making the July Will had been a huge error on his part. I was then invited back into the room and we both went ahead with signing the new Wills. The documents were witnessed by the solicitor and one of the admin assistants. Copies will be sent to us in the post. We handed over a cheque for £330 ... job done! Expensive, but at least my mind is back at rest and Alan is totally aware of the problems he caused.

A letter has arrived from Social Services inviting me to a 'case conference' on 10th October. This should be interesting. Not quite sure who else will be present other than Mac Nurse Jo who told us a week ago that she had been invited. I'm hoping I will be able to have my say about the hospice's part in this entire travesty, hiding behind 'patient confidentiality' and blatantly lying to me on the phone. Wiser from the experience, neither of us is keen for Alan to get involved with another such establishment.

Hopefully tonight I will sleep a little easier.

5th October: The oxygen supply is running out! Alan didn't have a great night and when he managed to get up he was still very tired. Doc M has agreed that the morphine can be put up by 10mg which takes us back to where we were before the hospitalization and before all the pain started to return. Hopefully within a few days Alan will feel the benefit and have less pain in his back.

Basically we've had a quiet day. I managed to get two loads of washing out on the line and best part dried before the dew started rising. Will soon finish it all off in tumbler. Tesco delivered all our goodies, so we won't be going hungry for a few days.

One small oxygen cylinder left for tonight and then there will be nothing until new delivery on Tuesday. Hopefully the Mac nurse will be able to organize a condenser quickly and then we won't have to bother with any cylinder supplies apart from a couple of back-up small ones.

We listened to the meditation CD sent to us by Vajra. Certainly very restful. I've put it onto our iPods ... think I'll have another listen in bed tonight!

How nice it's been to have a 'normal' day. With everything that has gone on I don't think we've had one for about five weeks! Long may it continue ....

6th October: The only thing to interrupt a lovely quiet day was a phone call from Sammy. Alan totally refused to speak to him, even though Sammy had been said if Alan spoke to him today, he wouldn't bother us again. So yet again Sammy has not taken on board the message given to him by the police, and if he phones again, then they will need to be informed as every time this happens, it just brings back all the hurt and upset.

7th October: Another comparatively quiet day! I was on the phone at 9am to the Respiratory Nurse, followed by the Oxygen suppliers, followed by the Mac Nurse. All have promised action, so by tomorrow we'll probably have enough oxygen to run a hospital for a week!! Concentrator unit also on order.

Gill came along to do Alan's shower, but tells us she will be unable to come tomorrow.

I managed to fix the lights in the conservatory which 'blew' last night ... just needed a new fuse and one bulb. To be on the safe side I have changed all the bulbs as they've been in use for some 10 years now. Didn't they do well?!! My other job for today was scrubbing the carpet next to Alan's bed again. It is getting badly stained now from drinks being dropped ... always in the same area. I think the Movecol mixed with Coca-Cola is the main culprit as the marks are quite orange! I'll just have to keep working at it.

Alan tells me tonight that he has a raging sore throat and is starting to cough. Please let him fight it off otherwise it will knock him out completely for a good couple of weeks.

I was so tired tonight I was in bed for 9pm and was just about dropping off when Alan appeared at the door wanting a cup of tea! I've listened to a meditation piece and then some relaxing spar music ... do you think I can get back to sleep? It's now after 3am so I think I'll get my head down and have another go at it! Come back, sleep, all is forgiven!

8th October: Well sleep did come at about 5am and luckily I was just about awake by the time Giv arrived at 11am!! Lovely to have a couple of hours with her. Alan managed to join us by about 12.30pm!

The oxygen supplies arrived this afternoon. No concentrator! Phone calls here. Phone calls there. It hasn't even been ordered!! *******! Respiratory nurse will not put order through until she has seen Alan on Friday ... even though she promised to fax the order off yesterday! So we now have to be available all day Thursday for a double order of cylinders to get us through next weekend. At least the cylinders did arrive here ... last time the respiratory nurse was involved she gave the driver our address from over 10 years ago!! Inefficient NHS? Too regularly!!!

Here's hoping "Mr. Sandman" will come for me early tonight ... just need a few good hours of undisturbed sleep!!

9th October: Full morning of housework with Georgie and yet again I'm doing a great impression of a waterfall! Not sure what has brought about all this sweating from my head but it really is getting past a joke. There is nothing worse than feeling the beads of water running across the scalp and then   making their way down the face and into ears or dripping off your nose. I seem to have a towel around my neck permanently and constantly having to rub my hair trying to dry it out.

We both have an appointment for a haircut early this afternoon but at the last minute Alan pulls out of the deal. He's not had his hair cut this year and he looks as rough as a tramp. Not quite sure what he is trying to prove but he looks dreadful. It's not that I want him to have it cut short ... just layered and reshaped would be enough for a start. He seems to think that it's very clever to wind me up like this, but to be honest I'm getting bored with it now and if he wants to look like a vagrant, then why should I worry. I like my hair to look fairly decent and this is why I am finding these sweating sessions so annoying.

Our friends Jo and Jason came to visit this afternoon. We always have a good time with them as we're not able to see them too often because of their work commitments. We had a beautiful Chinese takeaway and Alan managed to stay awake until 9pm. He was nearly on his knees though and couldn't wait to get to bed once they had gone.

The social worker phoned this afternoon as I wanted to know the format of the 'case conference' tomorrow. She tells me the meeting has been called by the police and a representative from the hospice should be there along with our McMillan nurse, the social worker and myself. Should be interesting! The hospice is the target of my wrath tomorrow ... the way they handled this whole affair was, in my opinion, totally unethical. It will be interesting to see how they feel they handled things! Hope they're not expecting a pat on the back, otherwise they're in for a shock! Meeting is at the social services offices in Craven Arms at 10.30am and it's going to take about half an hour to get there so at least I don't have to be up at some stupid hour. It is thought the meeting will take about an hour ... my bit will probably take about an hour so perhaps they ought to re-think that bit!!!

10th October: First things first! Respiratory nurse phones to change appointment from tomorrow to today ... between 10am and 2pm. We agreed as close to 2pm as possible as I have meeting to attend. OK! Just about to leave the house when Sovereign phone ... Gill has migraine and has been sent home. Great, that's all I need. No chance to re-organize so I ask Alan to stay in bed as long as possible and I'll get home as quickly as I can.

Only a short drive up to Craven Arms and luckily drop straight into a car parking space right outside the offices. The 'Case Conference' is late starting ... I had already been sat there on my own for 15 minutes!

Police officer, McMillan Nurse, Social Worker, Chairman, note writer and myself sat cosily around a table. The hospice had sent a letter of apology as no-one would be attending. Such a shame! However, I was able to get all my points across with reference to their behaviour on the day in question.

I had handed over my care of Alan to them. Why did they not inform me of a problem, in preference to allowing him to leave with 'anyone who walks in off the street'? How can it be right for them to hide behind 'patient confidentiality' when dealing with the wife and next of kin of the patient? How could they pass the buck of responsibility to advise me of the situation to Sammy and Rebecca? Why did they blatantly lie to me on the phone?

The hospice has no staff qualified to ascertain Alan's capacity and understanding on the day ... but they allowed two members of staff to check that they thought he was compos mentis. Just not good enough.

As this was such a serious problem, why had they not called in a Social Worker or police welfare officer (huge police station 50 yards across the road) to evaluate Alan's capacity on that day?

Why had they not checked the accommodation they were allowing him to be removed to? Why did they not check what facilities were available and whether or not all the equipment that Alan needed was in place?

Do they have policies and procedures in place which should have been followed in this type of event with a vulnerable adult?

Should they be encouraging outside firms, such as solicitors to enter the premises offering cut-price services to end of life vulnerable patients? The ethics of this are very questionable.

Were full discharge papers completed on the day as Alan was not being returned to his normal carer and home environment? ... this should have been included, and that they had checked on accommodation, medications, equipment, etc.

The Chairman of the meeting was very concerned as these issues were unknown to him until today. He was furiously writing notes about how these issues should be addressed.

I learned from the police officer that the complaint to them was made by Sammy and was worded "My Dad's wife is trying to kill him". No doubts about the attempted murder allegation, then! This was the first time that I'd actually had it confirmed whom it was to have made the complaint phone calls.

Everyone there was most apologetic about the anguish, stress, and problems this had caused me ... and Alan. It was concluded that all the allegations against me were totally unsubstantiated and the case is now closed.

However, I did make the point that I felt this had been a dreadful waste of tax payers' money with full investigations being made by Social Services and the Police over a number of weeks. No doubt there were far better ways in which this money could have been spent. I also made the point that both Alan and I were now stigmatized as everyone we deal with in connection with his health is aware of what has happened – they won't forget the allegations ... but may well forget, in time, that they were all unsubstantiated. You can imagine it, can't you ... 'oh look, there's that woman who tried to do her husband in'. It happens! We all know it does.

There is nothing more I can do and have to judge this as a good result …. but the events of the past few weeks will stay with Alan and me for life.

Back at home, well before 1pm, I thought I would be in plenty of time for the respiratory nurse's visit. Wrong! She had arrived before 12 noon and had got Alan out of bed … he could hardly manage to get to the front door! Having checked his oxygen levels, etc., she determined that Alan does not need a concentrator. However, in view of his complex situation, she has bent the rules and is going to allow one to be provided. Should we all get down on our knees in thanks? Alan's GP says he needs one. The Mac nurse suggested that he needs one and the District Nurses are in agreement. With all due respect, lady, you've not seen him in the past six months, so what makes you the expert on the subject of Alan? I know how useful oxygen is to him at times and it has certainly made a difference allowing peaceful, nightmare free nights. She had angered Alan … and as a by-product of that, she has annoyed me! When she phoned later in the afternoon, I made my feelings perfectly clear! She wanted to know where the equipment was to be delivered! She said *'I know I visited Alan at "Everest" but would you like the equipment sent to your holiday home in Worcester?'*

"Holiday home in Worcester?"

'Yes .. the Kilbury Drive address'.

"We left that address over 10 years ago and have no idea why it should still be showing on your records. I did tell you about this issue six months ago when you tried to deliver cylinders to that address."

'Oh, right … I just wanted to check. Your delivery will be tomorrow.'

How inefficient certain parts of the NHS can be!

The rest of the day is our own … peaceful, quiet, and undisturbed! Both early to bed … it's been a stressful day … again.

11th October: Gill arrived this morning feeling much better after her migraine. At least Alan feels clean again.

Oxygen engineer arrived with Alan's new machine. It only took him about 10 minutes to set it up in the bedroom and set the pipe to the right length. As Alan has been using a slightly higher flow rate than that prescribed, the engineer tweaked the works on the inside of the machine so that the dial on the outside reads as accurate to prescription, but is actually running a little higher!! Nice one! He has taken away most of the cylinders we had in the house. We are just left with one large and two small cylinders for emergencies and outings.

The temperature has dropped so much I had to put on warmer clothes by lunchtime. As soon as I had warmed up, I fell asleep. Stresses and strains catching up with me, I think. We will have to move out of the conservatory if this continues as it's actually no pleasure to be in there when it's cold. The heating has been on, but it's never been enough in the conservatory.

After dozing in the chair tonight, Alan has once again woken up thinking he is in a caravan and asking if we can go home tomorrow. All I can do is go along with him on this until he is fully awake and realizes that he's been talking nonsense again. He tells me it is almost a kind of 'out of body' experience. Very odd … but at least now he understands what is happening with these strange thoughts, it has eliminated the nastiness which could surround them in weeks gone by.

Having set Alan up on the concentrator tonight he was buzzing me within minutes. "Can you find me some earplugs?" Have to admit it is a little bit noisy but I'm sure he will get used to it – especially with earplugs. When he got up a couple of hours later he switched the machine off at the mains … wrong!!! All the alarms sound to wake you in the event of a power cut ... switching off at the mains = power cut! I wonder how many times that is going to happen? We are very much hoping this is going to reduce the amount of nightmares and the strange dream state every time he wakes. Only time will tell.

12th October: Well the first night on the machine went quite well. However the pipe work was abandoned on the floor this morning when I went to wake Alan and I have no idea how long the machine has been running unnecessarily. I had checked the electric meter at tea time yesterday so did the same today. I know that we use on average about 11.5-12 units per day. Today's reading was a bit of a shock ... we used 17 units in the 24 hour period. This would effectively put up our usage by 50%. However, the engineer will be back in 3 months' time to read the concentrator units used and some clever person with a formula will calculate how much electricity we have used on the machine and a refund will be paid into the bank. I shall be doing my own calculations as well ... let's hope we agree on a figure at the end of each quarter!

We have had another session of cleaning these damn brasses again today. Just how many times do they have to be cleaned? The plan is to lacquer them and wonder why it couldn't have been done outside during one of those lovely days in July! Apart from that we have done very little today.

As Alan went to bed quite early and the TV was very uninspiring, I took the time to compose a letter to the Hospice asking for a full explanation of their line of thought when dealing with this dreadful situation that occurred on 20th September. I will be interested to hear their response. I will check with Social Services before I send it as I don't want to breach their confidentiality clause from Thursday's meeting ... but, the points I want to raise with the hospice are the points which I raised myself at the meeting, so I can't really see a problem as, had the hospice sent a representative, I would have asked the questions directly.

13th October: A quiet, peaceful and lazy day! Alan not feeling great and has slept most of the time. I have taken advantage of some quiet time to complete the complaint letter to the Hospice and have spared no punches!

14th October: The weather is really miserable today but after Gill's shower we decided to get out to B & Q to change a couple of shelf units I bought 44 days ago and they have a 45 day refund policy! That done we came home in the pouring rain.

The letter to the hospice has gone off - Recorded Delivery! Wonder how long we will have to wait for a reply ... if we get one!

Alan's still not feeling great and his stomach is giving him quite a bit of trouble. During the evening there was a rush to the loo and within an hour or so he was suffering a rigor ... visible shaking with cold whilst he was wrapped up in bed! His chest is sounding like a full orchestra, he's coughing, his breathing is laboured and his nose has started to run. Classic man flu!

15th October: When I went into Alan this morning he has obviously suffered quite a fever during the night ... he is wringing wet and so is the bedding! He tells me he feels as rough as old boots and wants his shower cancelled ... and today's long awaited dental appointment!

So today has been particularly quiet for me as Alan has slept all day other than waking on a couple of occasions for a drink.

I spoke with Doc. M on the phone who is organizing some antibiotics to be ready for me to pick up this afternoon – the instructions being to give Alan a double dose today and tomorrow to see if we can nip this in the bud. Fingers' crossed! Doc M will review the situation tomorrow.

By early evening, Alan's awake and manages to get up for a couple of hours. He was ready for bed again by 10pm. Hopefully he will have a good night and be improved in the morning.

16th October: Alan seems to have had a good night and manages to get up for his shower, but he was very wobbly on his feet as he went to the bathroom. He went back to bed immediately afterwards and slept until nearly tea time.

I didn't feel the need to contact Doc M today, but will drop him an email tomorrow when I know how things are. It's his day at the village surgery tomorrow, so if we have a problem he will be able to call in.

Most of the housework and ironing got done this morning as I had the help of my little angel, Georgie, who can whip through this place in no time at all! Made for a pleasant, restful and quiet afternoon!

Alan wanted me to find him a SAD Syndrome lamp – found a decent one on Amazon, so didn't feel guilty about ordering myself a pair of cheap bi-focal glasses to replace the ones which I broke about a month ago!

17th October: Alan is much brighter today, thankfully! It's been a quiet and uneventful day, but at least he has felt able to stay awake all day and even enjoyed watching some television tonight until 10pm!

18th October: Up one day and down the next! Alan got up in a grumpy mood and by the time he'd showered he was feeling most unwell again. He put himself onto the settee where he slept for the rest of the day. Luckily Giv came over for a couple of hours which broke up the monotony!

I have had a response to my letter from the Hospice. How they can so easily justify the actions they took is quite upsetting – it's a total whitewash! For example ... I asked the question as to why they had not contacted me on that fateful day to let me know there was a problem. Response ... they asked Rebecca to put her mobile on speaker whilst she phoned me so that they could hear the conversation and, therefore, they knew I had been told! Unbelievable! They state they were never informed about Alan's PTSD issues. Absolute rubbish ... they've known since day one. If they knew nothing about it, why did they suggest to him seeing the psychiatric nurse who was going to be working there? They also claim they were not aware that Alan's recent hospital admission had anything to do with a mental issue! How strange, when you consider I had to phone them twice that week to let them know he wouldn't be attending as he was in hospital ... and told them why!

In response to my question as to how they would make amends for the debacle, they offered us both complementary therapies at home! Talk about adding insult to injury! They've closed ranks and feel everything they did that day was correct. How can these people sleep at night. They obviously have no conception of the collateral damaged that day caused ... and, quite frankly, they obviously don't give a sh*t.

I would like to reply to their letter, but Alan has asked me to drop it now ... but I'm not sure that I can, to be honest. It has really made me very angry!

PHOTO GALLERY - AT HOME

"EVEREST" .., CLOSE TO THE TOP OF THE CLEE HILLS
IN SOUTH SHROPSHIRE

HAPPIER TIMES WHEN ALAN WAS ABLE TO TEND THE BEAUTIFUL GARDEN HE HAD CREATED. IT WAS ONE OF HIS VALUED PLEASURES.

A SMALL SNAPSHOT OF THE WONDERFUL VIEWS WE ENJOY

THE BEST AND WORST OF LIVING ON THE HILL

APRIL 2011

HOW QUICKLY THE FACE CHANGES AS THE DISEASE PROGRESSES

MAY 2013

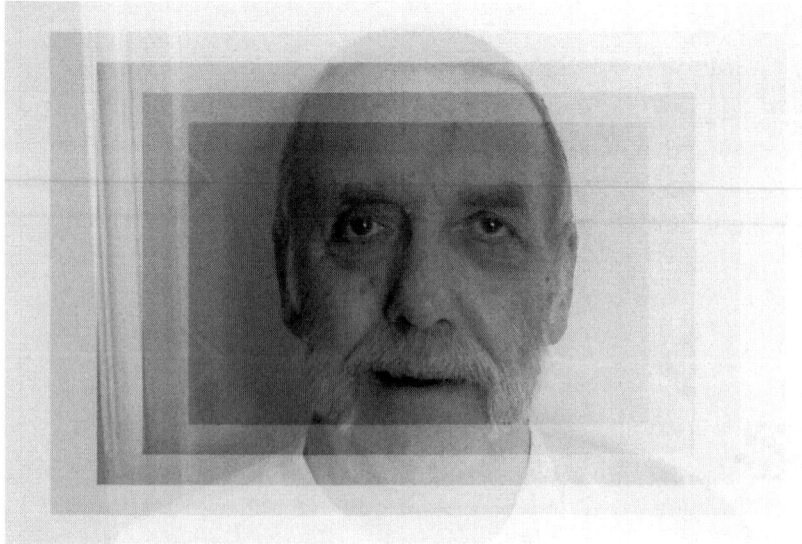

THE USUAL SLAPSTICK WHEN BRUMMIE IS ABOUT! REMEMBRANCE SUNDAY 2011
NATIONAL MEMORIAL ARBORETUM, ALREWAS. HOW UNWELL ALAN LOOKS JUST SEVEN
MONTHS AFTER DIAGNOSIS.

A DAY AT THE NATIONAL MEMORIAL ARBORETUM WHICH STARTED SO WELL
VISITING THE AIRBORNE FORCES MEMORIAL BUT ENDED UP WITH ALAN BEING
ADMITTED TO HOSPITAL. HE HAD COLLAPSED SEVERAL TIMES THAT DAY.

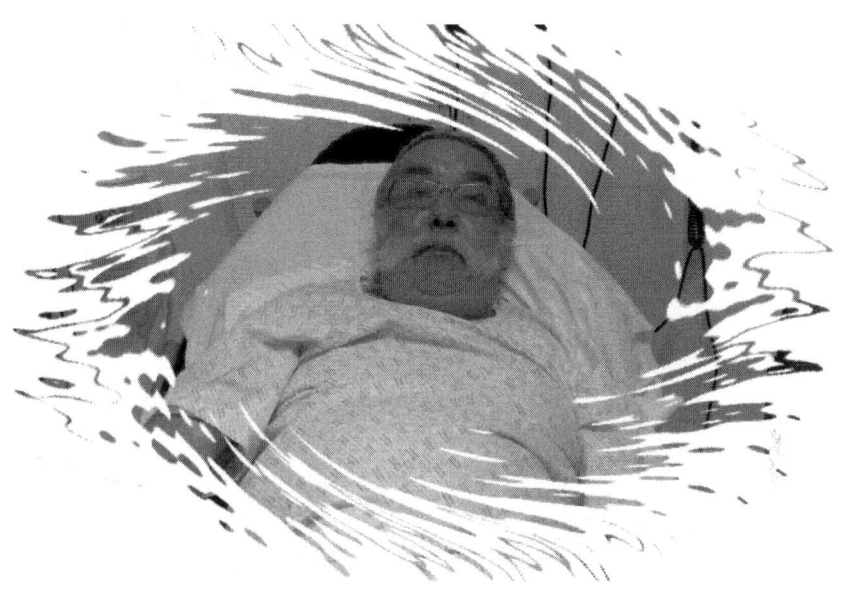

SO A FEW DAYS IN HOSPITAL WERE CALLED FOR WHILST MEDICATIONS WERE
ADJUSTED TO MAKE ALAN'S LIFE A LITTLE MORE STABLE

PERCY'S 'LEAP OF FAITH' FOR ALAN, CHARITY PARACHUTE JUMP

THE FINAL STEPS OF GIV'S "WALK TO ALAN" CHARITY EVENT
26 GRUELLING MILES ON THE HOTTEST DAY OF THE YEAR!

2nd JUNE 2012 - OUR RENEWAL OF VOWS .. IN DREADFUL WEATHER

GIVVI PROVIDING THE ENTERTAINMENT IN A VERY SOGGY MARQUEE
WHICH ENDED UP DRAPED OVER THE FLAG POLE

ALAN'S MOBILITY HAS DECLINED MORE AND MORE BUT AN ELECTRIC
WHEELCHAIR IS THE ANSWER TO INDEPENDENCE!

PARTY NO.1 - AUGUST 2011

Chapter 23: See you in Court ... maybe!

19th/20th October: For most of each day Alan has been no good at all and chose to stay in bed until late afternoon.

Had a pleasant surprise visit from Janet on Sunday afternoon! She came armed with cream cakes for Alan and a lovely pot plant for me. She is very much hoping to have her house sold by the end of the week and will be moving in with her son until she finds something she likes. We chatted about the hospice's response and it's also her opinion that I should write again to confirm that I don't agree with what they've told me ... and then that will be the end of it - but at least it will be on record that I've not accepted their version of events.

All in all a quiet weekend with dreadful weather!

21st October: Managed to sleep from 1am till 2.45am. Thought I would lull myself back off with a boring film ... but no! Not a hope in hell.

Alan woke about 10.30am and was immediately gasping for breath. By the time he got to the kitchen I was having to run round getting oxygen to keep him going. His chest is very tight and he feels awful ... just wants to curl up in a ball somewhere.

Phoned Doc M's secretary who asked the duty doctor to phone. It was decided it would be more beneficial for Alan to see Doc M tomorrow when he is in the area. Could be a case of even more antibiotics.

22nd October: One of the District Nurses was on the doorstep by 9.30am ready to take blood and give us flu jabs. As Alan has only just come off antibiotics she decided to leave his for a few days. She had three attempts to get blood out of him ... failed every time. She got on the phone to our favourite DN who arrived within half an hour to do the job properly!

Giv gave us a quick ring from the airport just as they were ready to take off for their short trip to Amsterdam. Managed to watch her flight all the way on one of the apps on my iPad!

By the time Alan had had his shower he was feeling so much better than yesterday, so just after lunch I phoned Doc M's secretary to cancel his visit for today ... really don't want to waste his time.

A letter has arrived from our litigation solicitor advising that she is intending to approach a Urologist for his opinion on the current situation and prognosis. Not sure this is going to be helpful to our case unless he also believes that the hormone therapy is the culprit in causing the heart failure issues as the cancer itself would currently be classed as 'in remission' (although this term is not generally used in Prostate Cancer). There has been no hint of the cancer advancing for almost 2 years now, but, of course, we had no idea this would be the case when we initiated the litigation. The other end of the spectrum is that Alan could have been dead two years ago. Will just have to wait and see what happens.

After some 18 months, it was today that Alan decided he was really fed up with his hair which he has been refusing to have cut. I have already made two appointments which have been cancelled due to him 'not feeling well'. So once he opened his mouth today and said I could cut it, the scissors were out and the job was done within 10 minutes. What a difference it has made! No more the vagrant who was looking very uncared for ... which I felt was an insult to me really! Hopefully he will allow me to continue to give it the occasional trim.

Weather has been dreadful and much more rain and winds expected overnight ... possibly with hefty thunderstorms thrown in for good measure.

23rd October: I've been awake since 3.30am! Seems Alan didn't sleep too well overnight either. When he finally woke this morning he had no "puff" at all. He was wobbly in his shower and just didn't have the energy for Gill to dress him. We had to get him on oxygen as soon as he sat down and then the two of us got him into bed with a constant oxygen supply from the concentrator. He was very quickly asleep and remained that way until mid-afternoon. I managed to grab a cat nap just after lunch.

I phoned through to the surgery to get the results of yesterday's blood tests. All is still good. PSA is 0.8 and the ALP 68. Shame about the heart!

I will have to phone again in the morning and see if I can organize Doc M for a visit. Alan is obviously suffering but I'm not convinced that there is a chest infection so not too sure that another course of antibiotics would be appropriate.

Jo, our palliative care nurse (used to be known as MacMillan nurses) is also due tomorrow. Hopefully she will have Alan's flu jab with her.

All in all a very quiet day but I did manage to get a fair bit of washing done and almost dry. Can easily finish that off in the tumbler.

The hall carpet which I scrubbed the other day is now drying out and it would seem all the marks are still there! I'll just have to get the machine out and do the whole hallway in the end ... unless I can find somebody locally who can do it for a reasonable price.

It's going to be Giv's 39th birthday on Monday and I don't have a clue what to get for her – have been looking through eBay for ideas, but as yet I've not found anything apart from a cover and keyboard for her new iPad Mini.

24th October: It's been a busy day on The Hill. Usual shower @ 11am and then Jo, palliative care nurse, arrived before Gill left. Alan still can't have flu jab. Jo has been in job since April and announced today that she's pregnant and goes onto maternity leave mid-December and will be off 6 months! As yet, no replacement. What a shock ... we weren't expecting that!

Doc M arrived @ 3pm and feels Alan must go straight back on antibiotics and increase the steroids. He was on good form today - asking if Alan's kids had visited with their cameras just so they were sure what was in the house!!! He took a well-deserved 'flick' with the tea towel which I had in my hand! Then he started talking about Oramorph, which Alan is always reluctant to take, turned to me and said 'try to resist giving it to him in half pint glasses!' B*stard! I'm obviously going to take some stick about all this drug business for some time to come!! They are both referring to me as the 'Black Witch' ... good job my back's broad!! Good visit with a bit of banter!

I've given up worrying about the drugs issue now because everything people were told was total fabrication, and they know that now ... including the Hospice who have yet another letter winging its way to them right now. I also sent copies of these letters, including Hospice response, to Social Services as their investigations are still on-going and they will be interested in the Hospice's comments. I'm past caring if I'm sh*t stirring where they are concerned!

25th October: Been another very quiet day here and Alan has slept most of it again. He has no strength in his arms or legs and just at the moment is incapable to doing anything. Let's see what tomorrow brings!

26th October: Awake again at 3.30am ... wonder what it is about that time in the morning that my body is so fascinated with? Couldn't get back to sleep but it was probably a good job as Alan was buzzing me at 5.30am absolutely gasping for breath. It took a good 10 minutes to calm him and get him breathing comfortably on oxygen. Luckily he has gone off to sleep now, but still connected up to the oxygen concentrator. Probably won't see him till mid-afternoon now!

As the Joey Witnesses decided to knock the door at 10.30am and put an end to the 3 hours' sleep I had managed, they got sent away with a flea in their ear! Unfortunately it woke Alan as well.

He didn't feel he had the energy to get dressed so has been wrapped up in a blanket all day and slept most of the afternoon. When he woke up he had another 'rigor' ... the same as last week – couldn't stop shaking and felt very cold. Put the fire on and got another blanket and he was soon warm again. Not sure where all this is heading, but all we can do is take one day at a time and see how things go.

End of British Summer time tonight ... and the mega storm of biblical proportions is making its way across the Atlantic and is due to hit in about 24 hours. Could be interesting!

I'm looking forward to the extra hour in bed!

27th October: Very much enjoyed my extra hour in bed! Unfortunately, Alan's sweats have returned and his bed was soaking this morning. What a shame ... that makes two of us having the same problem now. Mine started when Doc M put me on 'happy pills' back in July and are continuing night and day. The sweat pours out of my head and trickles down my ears! I have a permanent new fixture of a tea towel around my neck to catch the worst of it. Luckily Alan doesn't suffer in the same way during the day.

Alan very tired again today ... has slept most of it. More chest pains today and more confusion .. i.e. have we been out today? Have we been to church? Us - in church? The place would burn down!! He is thoroughly fed up of feeling so tired and sleeping so much. He says he could just sit and cry.

I have cleared up all the chairs in the garden, trying to make everything secure, in case the predicted storm arrives. The news is full of the details and there has already been one death ... a teenager being swept out to sea on the south coast. Managed to get some washing done and best part dried before I had to bring it in. So I will have the joys of ironing tomorrow.

Another quiet day .. not even one phone call!

28th October: Monday 28th October, 1974, 8.09pm. A baby girl comes into the world at great speed - kicking and screaming! I know this because I was there at the time! I was that Mum giving birth to a Little Miss Dynamite ... and she has never changed! We called her Cordelia ... but within weeks she was known as Givvi - and has always been known as such in her personal and professional life. So Giv is 39 today ... quickest way to make me feel old! She's been out all day with Percy and we hope to see her later in the week. As long as she's had a good time, that's all that matters

The 'beds' are back! Two days running now ... wondering if it's the increase in steroids? If so, this will hopefully be short lived as they are going to be reduced again. Could it be the antibios? Don't know! Just want it to stop!

I had the minutes of the 'Safeguarding' meeting come today. Alan read what the police officer said in the meeting and how his son had reported to the police that "his wife is trying to kill him". It's the first time he's seen it in black and white and he may have thought previous spoken accounts were embellished. For the first time in his life, so he tells me, the shock (of seeing it on paper) literally made him physically sick ... he just about managed to get to the sink in time! It really has knocked him about today. It's dreadful to feel that betrayed - but we live to fight another day ... as always! We're getting used to it now!

Suddenly had a thought today that we've heard nothing about Alan's State Pension which is due to start in a couple of months. I phoned through to Work and Pension who tell me he should have had a letter a couple of months ago. They will send the claim form through in the post as Alan failed the security test on the phone!! He couldn't even remember our phone number let alone our wedding anniversary! Still, no problem really ... we still have plenty of time to fill in the form!

He's been a little livelier today and has managed to stay up until 9pm which is a good hour longer than usual. He feels he would like to see the Cardiologist again and have another echocardiogram to find out if, or how much, his heart has deteriorated. He's thinking like this because of the extra chest pains he is feeling and a quite sudden need to use the oxygen more often. We'll have a chat with Doc M later in the week.

I have also asked for the engineer to call to assess whether or not the airing cupboard would be a suitable place to house the concentrator as it is disturbing Alan's sleep. He should be with us later in the week.

30th October: ... and the day started off so well! Georgie arrived on time and we set to cleaning windows in the conservatory whilst Alan lounged in bed for the morning. She managed to get round quite a few of the other rooms before her time was up. Alan was up in time for Gill to arrive for his shower and enjoyed cheese on toast for his lunch.

We spent the afternoon in the conservatory ... quietly watching television. Out of nowhere just before 4pm Alan suddenly went into some sort of fit. His body went straight and rigid so he was sliding down the chair. His breathing was extremely noisy. It lasted about 40 seconds before he started to 'come round'. I put him on oxygen whilst he calmed down. At the end of it he is a dreadful colour and totally wiped out. Says he had strange sensation in chest, no pain, which seemed to move up into his head. He thought he was fainting. He can talk OK and his vision seems all right ... just looks awful. His hands have been visibly shaking for a few days (more than usual) and he has had pins and needles in left arm, and evening chest pains. I have managed to get him into bed even though his legs and arms don't want to work. He's gone straight to sleep. Will have to cancel my bone density scan tomorrow - couldn't possibly leave him until we've established what this was. Doesn't sound great, does it?!!

At the moment this is an unexplained seizure and emergency blood tests will be done tomorrow morning - DN's will come. Doc M will be here tomorrow pm. Doc M feels A is probably having mini heart attacks - will ask him for echocardiogram as not had one for a year. If there is another problem tonight then 999 as seizures are treatable and he'll be whisked off to A & E. Obviously this is not a great development! But – his sense of humour remains! Sorry about this - but Alan said - 'that's the first stiffy I've had in well over two years!' What is he like, eh?!! He has eaten but still very tired.

Givvi is very poorly with flu so we won't be seeing her for a week or two. She must have picked it up in Amsterdam or on the plane going over there. She sounds absolutely dreadful.

Not sure what sort of night we are going to have and it has crossed my mind that I should be sitting up with Alan all night ... but I know I will be no good at all if I don't try and get some sleep. Fingers crossed that nothing goes wrong overnight.

31st October: Seems to have been a long busy day on The Hill. Having been awake since 4am I was up early expecting District Nurses to be on the doorstep at 8.30am. I got a courier driver instead with two huge parcels. Then the phone rang - it was the 'oxygen' engineer coming to assess re-siting the concentrator ... so he arrived within 20 minutes! Can't put it where we want it, so I have requested a quieter one which should be with us by Tuesday at the latest. Alan got up about 11am - still no sign of the DN's. Finally I got on the phone trying to chase them up - seems they had not had any instructions from the surgery! Surgery insists request was sent! I really don't care whose 'cock-up' this is, just get someone here to take his blood as the samples are collected at 1pm from the hospital. The senior DN arrived 12.45pm, was a bit of a butcher really, and went rushing off to make sure the bloods were on time. Gill was late arriving so we had a hurried lunch before waiting for Doc M. He arrived with an entourage - his niece (14 and wanting to be a doctor) and his final year student. Long and short of it is that none of us has a clue what caused yesterday's seizure and will probably never know. It could be a one off ... or not! I now have full instructions should it happen again. Student took great pleasure in giving Alan his Zoladex! Doc M was talking about the Safeguarding meeting minutes he had been sent and really how badly the whole thing was handled. He currently has grave concerns about recommending anyone to the Hospice! So all's well that ends well, and we live to fight another day!! Alan asleep by 6pm and I have to sleep walk him to the bedroom so he is in bed at 8pm - head hits the pillow and he's gone again! Poor sod, he's just so tired and quite truthfully, he's had enough now!

1st November: Bloody hell! November already ... doesn't time fly when you're having such a good time ... not!

Today's plan to be at the hospital for 12noon went out the window when they phoned and asked us to be there for 3pm instead. Alan was not bothered as he was able to stay in bed a bit longer!

Gill was a bit late and by the time the shower was finished and we'd had a bit of lunch it was time to head off to the hospital. We arrived on time ... but everyone else is running late. Doc M arrived about 3.30pm to canulate in readiness for the infusion. The sister assigned to do the job doesn't do these often and she was a chatterbox! The Zometa infusion usually takes about 15 minutes to run and the whole job can be over and done with easily within half an hour. Not so today! By the time we got out of the hospital it was well on its way to 5pm. Too long for Alan ... he's says he's not doing it again, the job will have to be done at home.

He just about managed to stay awake for his tea and then fell asleep for a couple of hours before I managed to get him to bed. Saturday tomorrow ... no showers, no visitors ... lie in – yippee!!

2nd November: When I said we could have a lie in today I wasn't exactly expecting what I got!! I had to wake Alan at 12.30pm to tell him I needed to go to the shops and suggested he stayed in bed until I got home. I was actually only gone for an hour and he was still asleep when I got home. So I waited and waited to get us some lunch thinking he would be awake any minute.

I spent half an hour on the computer and then half an hour in front of the TV having coffee. Feeling guilty I went into the kitchen to iron all the bedding which had accumulated this week. Still no sign of movement from the bedroom! It was 4.15pm when he woke! He stayed in bed for a cup of tea and get tablets down and decided to get up and dressed at 5pm. Ten minutes later he was asleep on the settee and there he has stayed until 10pm! Not sure how well he will sleep tonight but says he is still very tired. He feels his body is 'closing down' and is convinced he's on the downward slope.

If he's awake tomorrow and the weather is anything like half decent I will have to try and get him out for a ride in the car.

5th November: Well, we've had "job's worth" Roberto here today. Oxygen man! Oh, joy! I think he needs oxygen more than most - he doesn't stop his Italian chatter! He is delivering the new concentrator (quieter version) and 3 face masks. It's on his job sheet as 2 jobs so he turns up at the door with the 3 masks! He gets into his stride by carrying out a risk assessment ... just for the masks!! Ticks all the boxes on his hand PDA and gets me to sign. Back to the van, pick up concentrator ... doesn't take old one with him! Back in the house, he then proceeds to do another risk assessment (same as first one!) before he can plug the machine in! Then, as a knob needs twiddling, he wants to phone his supervisor to check it's OK to do! No signal in the bungalow so he's striding round the garden holding the phone as high as he can, praying for one bar to come up!! For whatever reason Alan has been reduced from 28% to 24% oxygen so a little gizmo has to be changed on concentrator, big cylinder and small cylinder. Apparently I have put wrong tube on small cylinder! In an emergency, as long as it has a tube, does it really matter? PDA out again, all boxes ticked and I've signed it. A 10 minute job turned into an hour ... all going on in Alan's bedroom. He is hiding under the bed covers as he can't contain himself! I preferred it last time we had a visit when Roberto was on holiday!!! I hope we don't run out of anything any time soon!!!

Alan's sweats seemed to have stopped for the time being but he is not feeling well at all. He is so utterly tired that for the past two nights he has been ready for bed by 6.30pm. What sort of life is this for anyone ... it's so sad.

6th November: I was awake at 4am so had a session with 'Billy Elliott'. Alan woke at 6am and I had to be up getting drinks organized. He decided to stay up for a while before returning to bed. Then neither of us was awake properly when Georgie arrived at 10.30! We were meant to be seeing Jo and Jason today but Jason messaged to say he had been called into work. I phoned Jo to call off the visit, but what I had forgotten was that we were meant to be going to their house! There would have been no chance today. We'll try again next week – but I think they will have to come to us!

I think we have a new problem. I think Alan has developed Tachycardia. Why no-one thought of this when he had the seizure last week, I'm not sure ... but it all fits. Lack of oxygen to every muscle in his body and his brain would account for all the symptoms over the past week. His heart rate today was 145 which is over 50% higher than his norm of about 90. His BP was only 90/70 rather than his regular 130/80 and his SATS have been up and down like a yo-yo between 91 and 96. He's been on and off oxygen today until we brought the SATS back up. And there's been another minor seizure today. Doc M is not at work so I will be asking for the German Maid to visit tomorrow. Alan got upset about it tonight ... not because we realized what it may be - but the fact that it's me who has to work everything out methodically and then present the evidence to the doctors. There again, I could be wrong ... but it does appear to be 'text book'. Will know more tomorrow ... I hope! I've sent an email request to Doc M's secretary to arrange for someone to call tomorrow (Doc M has all week off – selfish b*stard!)

Alan was asleep again on the settee by just after 6pm so wasn't ready to go to bed till 9pm. Must admit to having at least an hour's sleep myself.

7th November: Once again was awake very early and in attempting to get back to sleep ended up tossing and turning for an hour or more. Found a film to watch and then Sky News and at some point fell asleep. I was woken up by someone trying to knock down the back door! It was 11am and the Tesco man was at the door with the grocery delivery.

Unfortunately being woken like that has affected my whole day and to be honest I've been a bit spikey! Having put all the shopping away, I desperately wanted to have a quick shower, but Alan was impatient for me to dispense his tablets. Why can't he give me just 10 minutes to get dry? So that wound me up even more and I am beginning to feel quite hostile.

Before I know it Gill arrives for Alan's shower. He reminds me yet again to pay for an item he has bought on eBay. Give me strength! So he goes into the shower and I pay for the item! Then I need to get cleared up as quickly as possible to be ready for doctor's visit this afternoon. As he comes out of the bathroom he says not to forget his bed as he might need to be in it sooner rather than later. Would you like me to stick a broom up my arse as well? Bed done I return to the kitchen to find out what he would like for lunch. Nothing at the moment!

Doctor is due between 3pm and 4pm so at 3.10 pm Alan decides this is the time for lunch!

8th November: District Nurse was on the doorstep at 9.30am to give Alan his flu jab. Neither of us was up!! Oh dear, never mind! Alan stayed in bed all morning until a few minutes before Gill was due.

He has been a little quiet and subdued today wanting to run over the details of his funeral again and sort out the Buddhist readings to be included. Actually we found them quite quickly and seem to be very appropriate. We also sorted out what music he wanted as the choice has changed somewhat ... but now he's made his final decision.

Ride of the Valkyries

Paint it Black
Don't worry, be happy
Endless Love
Nimrod

He wanted me to design the service leaflet today, but I refused. I'll do that when I have to as I don't want to keep being upset about all of this.

Quite stubbornly he has made himself stay up and awake until 9pm and has gone to bed totally shattered. Not quite sure in the point of that, as he would have been far more comfortable in bed a good two hours before he went.

Hopefully we will have a better night than the past few which have been somewhat disrupted.

9th November: What a good day! Our visitors arrived nearly two hours early and Alan was still in bed. Brummie, Lynn, Pip and Maz are always welcome visitors here as we have such a laugh together. The lads start talking about the old Army days and the laughter starts and just gets louder and louder. The tales they talk about we've heard hundreds of times before, but it doesn't matter as they enjoy themselves so much. Not being prepared to get everyone lunch, we wives took a trip over to the local chippy for supplies.

Lynn and Maz helped me to change Alan's bed for the second time in two days! The washing is stacking up again, but tomorrow's weather forecast is good so perhaps I can get it all dried outside.

After four hours, both Alan and Brummie are feeling very tired, so it was time to break up the party atmosphere and get them on their way home. We had a quiet tea and spent the early evening in front of the television until Alan was ready for bed by about 8pm.

10th November: Remembrance Sunday and we have arranged to make a trip across to Givvi's, but Alan's not feeling up to it.

He stayed in bed and watched the Veterans' Parade at the Cenotaph, thinking back to the two occasions he had been able to take part himself in 2009 and 2010 – just before we took that last holiday and the diagnosis of Prostate Cancer. We had all enjoyed those two occasions and it's a memory no-one can take away from us. After all, it was the two of us who had set up the Army Dog Unit Northern Ireland Association in 2008 and made all the arrangements for them to march at the Cenotaph ... and all the other things we achieved in such a short time.

Givvi and Percy came to visit as we couldn't get to them but actually spent a couple of hours outside burning all the cardboard and papers which have been building up for weeks. Good job done though! We hadn't been able to see Giv on her birthday, so it wasn't until today that we could give her a birthday present!

Alan has seemed quite a bit better today. His heart rate has come down from around 145 to about 100 and his blood pressure has risen to something a bit more acceptable. I have to email the doctors in the morning with an update as he has been on extra medication since last Thursday.

As I had overslept this morning, I've spent the day trying to get washing dry indoors! Towels hanging on an airer and the sheets in the tumbler. Three lots of bedding to be ironed tomorrow! Never mind ... keeps me busy!!

11th November: Today must have been payback for Saturday! I didn't wake Alan this morning as Gill is unwell and won't be coming to do his shower. He slept through until 2.30pm and managed to get up by 4pm ... not dressed - dressing gown day! He dozed through till tea time, fell asleep again until 8.30 then went to bed. All his numbers were good today apart from SATS down at 94, but he felt dreadful! He's still feeling rough tonight ... sore throat, aches and pains, etc. ... I can feel 'man flu' coming to visit!!

12th November: Alan hasn't slept as much today but tells me he feels really rough. Probably a good job that Gill was unable to come again today. Another day without getting dressed - and dozing on the settee!

13th November: Gill's back and Alan enjoyed his shower today. We had been invited out to Jo and Jason's for the first time and it made a real change to get out of the house together for a while. First time out in almost eight weeks (apart from a couple of doc's appointments). What it is to have a hectic social diary!! They have just moved from Hereford to Leominster into a lovely 3-storey 4-bedroom house. Hopefully they will be able to settle there long term.

We commented that it is only just over three months until our case against Dodgy Doc is due in court. Must get on to the solicitors tomorrow and start pushing. She requested an interim payment at the end of May and nearly six months on nothing has been forthcoming. Time to get assertive, I think, as it would seem that Dodgy Doc's team are playing delaying tactics. Alan's condition has worsened in recent weeks and they ought to be made aware of this.

Also must check up on the 24 hour ECG monitoring that last week's substitute doctor thought would be appropriate.

14th November: Angry! Frustrated! Have just been on phone with solicitor for half an hour. She wants Alan to have appointment with Urologist in Nottingham for an up to date report. 120 miles one way - 2.5 hours - HOW?!!! Snow is due, and we only managed 19 miles yesterday after eight weeks! Time is running out fast as we'll lose two weeks over Christmas and New Year. She has Onco report and it's not quite what she would have liked ... so things are stacking up. Defendants are not co-operating in the hopes that Alan won't still be here by beginning of March. Bloody dreadful ... I could scream. If this goes pear shaped after all this time, I can see someone suffering real serious injuries!

I have a plan! I have found three eminent urologists who work out of a choice of at least three private hospitals within 30 miles of here ... one in particular is very prostate orientated. I will suggest them to solicitor tomorrow. However, if she insists on Nottingham then I'm not driving that far and back in one day. I'll hire something comfortable and its driver for the day. During research this evening have found some useful information about untreated prostate cancer, PSA and doubling times which would put into question what the oncologist has just reported ... so that's another bit of info to tell solicitor about.

Why is it only me who challenges every bit of information and manages to find facts which fit our situation so neatly.

Alan's had quite a good day after he gave in and had a dose of Oramorph for the pain in his back. Managed to stay up and awake until 10pm.

15th November: Alan has been much brighter today. Needed one dose of Oramorph for his back pain and he's been pain free all day again!

I spoke with the solicitor first thing this morning and she will check the credentials of the two Urologists I have suggested, and will use one of them if she can ... if not, we'll be off to Nottingham!

I did outline to her the PSA research I had done and she asked me to send her the paperwork.

I have spent much of the day playing around with the numbers as concluded by this research. What it is saying is that in untreated prostate cancer the rate of growth of the tumour is directly related to the increase in PSA number, i.e. if PSA has increased by 10% then the volume of the tumour will have increased by the same amount. The research also concludes that the 'doubling time' of the PSA number remains constant throughout a period of time.

Based on the fact that we know Alan's PSA was 2.4 in 2000 and 310 at diagnosis in 2011 the calculations can be done which result in some interesting conclusions. Working backwards from the 310 and halving the number each time we arrive at 2001 with a figure of 2.42 ... 0.02 higher than in 2000. I also conclude that the doubling time over the years has been 17 months which points to 2005 being the pivotal year when Alan's PSA would have been almost 20 and very worthy of investigation, being five times the acceptable level. This, of course, is the year that he was first troubled by his symptoms and therefore mentioned them to Dodgy Doc. It is quite likely that this cancer started way back in early 2002! Below is a chart which could show what happened ... age ... date ... PSA value

51		52		53		54		55		57		59		61		62
2000	-	2001	-	2002	-	2004	-	2005	-	2007	-	2008	-	2009		2011
2.4	-	2.42		4.84	-	9.68	-	19.37	-	38.75	-	77.50	-	155	-	310

All I need to do is have the opportunity to discuss this with the chosen Urologist and/or have the same opportunity with the Oncologist. This is far more than some chance co-incidence ... this is accepted research in both America and China, and if an expert witness would give it credence, then this would be very helpful evidence about the likelihood that Alan's cancer was established by the time of the first symptoms in 2005. Had he been offered the Government recommended 'over 50's' annual PSA test, then I have absolutely no doubt in my mind that our lives would have ended up being very different. Yet again I have to remain patient until I get a chance to discuss this with one of the expert witnesses and make them understand how relevant to our case this research information will be.

16th November: Alan's not been so clever today. He's back on Ivabradine which, in the past, he has only tolerated for about two weeks. I think this is the third attempt at using them and I'm quite expecting him to be feeling quite ill by mid-week if he continues with them and they are not bringing the heart rate down enough ... they want his heart rate at 80 and he's still hovering around 100. The aim was to get his heart rate down quickly, but I think he will have to stop this beta blocker and increase the   Digoxin which he already takes. Hopefully that will work - but will take longer. It's unfortunate that Alan has never tolerated heart medications well, but I think that maybe the heart is so badly damaged nothing is going to make an appreciable difference. Can you imagine gasping for breath trying to comb your hair? If he needs to use the loo for a sit down job then almost certainly he has to go on oxygen afterwards! He feels very angry and frustrated as what little strength he has is sapping away.

He was very wobbly and dizzy and yet his BP was OK. He's been wrapped up in a blanket on the settee all afternoon. He also has a troubling ache in the area of his right kidney ... says he's had it months, but feels he doesn't want to mention yet another complaint! Don't think it can be an infection as it hasn't disappeared through two rounds of antibios. Will speak with doc next week.

The more you dig, the bigger the hole! I found another scenario today with the PSA figures which has made me understand where this particular specialist Onco may be coming from ... but I think my scenario has as much merit as hers - trouble is, she is the 'expert'. The crux of the matter is what the growth rate is most generally accepted of prostate tumours. All evidence points to a doubling time of between two and four years ... somewhat faster if it is a 'high grade' tumour. However, it would seem the Onco's theory is based on this doubling time being less than 6 months. However, it would appear from all my research and reading that this would be totally out of character for this type of tumour. Her timeline would infer that Alan was having symptoms and problems a full 4 years before this tumour started? Sounds a bit unlikely to me!

'Scuse me while I go and find a bigger spade for tomorrow!!

We had a new little gizmo delivered today ... a Now TV box. Only cost £9.99 so worth a try. We can get access to some programs from the Sky stables without subscription. We have a 30 day free trial of Sky Movies and will probably continue this for a couple of months so that we have a better choice of what we can watch over Christmas and New Year. For that price I have ordered two more so that I can set them up in the bedrooms. All you need is wireless access and it seems to be working well!

17th November: Have to say we had a pig of a morning! Alan went off to the bathroom. When he came back he collapsed on the bed fighting for breath. His eyes were scared and looking like organ stops. Oxygen, of course - must have taken him a full 15 minutes to recover ... probably the worst he's been without losing consciousness. ... and the bed!! Without a word of a lie, I could have wrung out the bottom sheet by hand ... top to bottom, side to side, king-size bed, four out of six pillows, and the duvet. Luckily all water protected these days! Anyway, the afternoon was peaceful enough, but getting him to bed tonight was a bit of a trial - wobbly, breathless and stressed. I have no idea how much longer his heart can take the strain like this.

18th November: As I predicted Alan continues to feel worse and worse ... it has to be the Ivabradine. He's been on in 12 days. The first time he took it in July 2012 he lasted 14 days and on the second time of trying after 30 days he was seen by his Cardio who immediately admitted him to hospital as he was so near the point of collapse. So here we are some 16 months later, going round in the same bloody circle of drugs which are making him feel just as bad now as they did then. From this diary I have looked back and found that Alan became more breathless and wobbly on this tablet – exactly as he has been getting in the past few days. His heart rate is not down ... still hovering around 100 in general but when I checked his BP and heart rate when he had been in bed for 15 minutes tonight ... it was 133 and his blood pressure is all over the place .. 123/108 tonight.

Alan has told me not to add Ivabradine to his tablets tomorrow ... enough is enough. I have to phone the surgery tomorrow to make arrangements for the 24 hour ECG monitoring so I will try to get appointment to see one of the doctors at the same time.

19th November: Alan's made an executive decision! He is going to stop taking Ivabradine as from today. He feels dreadful ... more breathless, more wobbles and generally unwell. Last time he took these we made no progress with medications in five months ... well you can add another 16 months to that now! Ring-a-ring a roses ...

20th November: Day two off the beta-blocker and Alan's been great! He feels so much better in himself. His BP and pulse rate are rubbish, but you can't have everything, can you? Long chat with palliative care nurse today - her last visit before maternity leave. She'll be back in September! September? He's got to live that long first! Re-assessment for CHC completed so hopefully that will all go through OK again - can't see how they can refuse it as Alan just gets worse and worse. So wobbly today the walking frame has had to come out again. ... and I had a new toy arrive – a stethoscope! Alan said he wanted me in uniform now so I told him I'd buy a bell tent and paint a red cross on it!!

21st November: Busy day with a very bad start - had just got into shower when Alan banged on door on the point of collapse That took a good half hour to sort out. Then little helper came, then Gill, then out to dental appointment and a trip to B&Q where I had to lift Alan's motorized scooter out of the boot and have done my back in. Obviously had to reload it after shopping then unload it again back at home as it was running out of charge. Trip to the chip shop for tea and falling asleep all evening. I'm just knick-knacked ... in bed to watch 'the jungle' and now I just want to lie flat and settle this back pain. I'm just wondering if I will be able to move tomorrow!

We are both concerned that there has been no response to the email sent to the doctors on Tuesday ... seems odd that nothing has been said.

22nd November: A challenge a day (or two or three) keeps breakdowns away!! Haven't got time for one of those! Managed about three hours sleep so have been entertaining myself with new Downton Abbey box set! The back problem is historic - 20 years on from surgery now, but just sometimes it comes back to haunt me. Last time I had a hot bath I spent the following week on my hands and knees ... good enough reason to have the bath removed when we did! I'll take it easy today, then I'll be fine - I'm sure!

Bad start for Alan ... only went to loo and again gasping for breath. So back to bed with oxygen and then fell asleep.

Two firemen arrived to do risk assessment because of our oxygen supplies ... all OK there apart from suggestion of carbon monoxide detector in kitchen (because of boiler). Alan slept through the whole visit even when we were all in his room. Have to fit a smoke detector in there which the fire service give out like sweets, so it's all ready to stick to the ceiling and I'll do that later when he's awake. Cancelled Gill and shower.

As I'd had no response to email to doc on Tuesday, I phoned for doc to call. She did, said she would visit, but very 'off' with me. This is La Bella Italiano, lovely lady as a rule! Within minutes the receptionist phoned, said there had been a mix up, and doc would be with us in a few minutes. Strange one! Doc arrived all apologetic (she doesn't know us well and I don't think the penny dropped during the phone call who we were - the Dodgy Doc thing - and then she realized she would have to come out with a smile!!) I asked her if she had received my email sent on Tuesday. Absolutely not! Bottom line is she feels what is going on today is more COPD related and wants him to have a nebulizer. I could borrow one from the surgery for a couple of days. We rushed over there to pick it up and some supplies plus a prescription for the actual stuff she wants him to use in it. Got home to phone chemist to check if stuff is in stock ... she hasn't signed the prescription! 10 ... 9 ... 8 ... Phoned secretary, organized duplicate to be faxed to local chemist for them to supply and deliver asap. She also confirmed that my email was passed on to the doctor's email address, and, actually, she had printed off a copy and put it on her desk! Not quite sure what conclusions I'm meant to draw from that!

Bought a nebulizer from Amazon and it will be here tomorrow. Fell asleep for an hour as Alan was still sleeping. He buzzed from bedroom ... bedside lamp has gone 'bang'. I managed to find a replacement light, took the first one to pieces, kicked it round the kitchen, changed fuse and bulb ... bingo!

Alan feels he would like some tea and quite fancies mince and mash. However, by the time I have it ready he is already asleep again – so best left, I think.

Alan has just woken at 10pm and needed loo. He was straight back to the same state he was this morning. Put Oxygen on whilst I got nebulizer ready, which runs for about 20 minutes. Sadly, he has just said to me 'you know this is the end of the road, don't you?' He obviously feels so poorly that's what he thinks, and he's just had one of those rigor type cold shaky incidents lasting about 5 minutes. Hasn't eaten, doesn't want to, and is already falling back to sleep after a few sips of tea. I think everything that can be done for him has now been done and I just have to hope he's strong enough to fight it yet again. Not looking forward to tonight.

23rd November: Only managed to get three or four hours sleep again. Alan had me running around until after 2am when he decided that he was hungry! I ended up getting him a large tin of rice pudding and yet another cup of tea. I woke up well before 6am and decided to have an early run to Tesco to pick up some bits for the weekend.

Alan also stirred early and I let him know that I would be out for an hour or so. He wasn't bothered ... still feeling unwell and wanting more sleep. The bed was soaking wet, again ... wish we knew what it was that caused these huge sweating bouts.

I was only out for an hour and yes, Alan was still asleep when I returned. The post had arrived and there were interesting parcels waiting on the front door step! The nebulizer from Amazon had arrived and the two Now TV boxes for us to have in the bedrooms. All I managed to do was quiet things ... daren't make a noise when he's sleeping so well! I got my head into bank accounts and the budget!

Some people hate this sort of thing, but I happen to thrive on it. Love to see everything balanced and know our heads are still above water!

Difficult to understand how quickly things have turned around in just 24 hours. Thankfully he doesn't feel at death's door any more. I'm sure it will take a few days for him to regain any strength - I'm still having to hold him up whilst he walks - but the doctor should see an appreciable improvement by the time she calls again on Wednesday. Here's to a peaceful and uneventful Sunday!

24th November: Well, I had a very rude awakening on this planned peaceful Sunday. After two nights with little sleep, I was doing really well last night. Then the buzzer went. It felt like 5am but in reality it was 8.30am and Alan was ready for a drink! Just felt that I could have done with an extra couple of hours!

Yet another mega bed this morning, but as Givvi was coming to visit I decided to wait until she arrived before attacking it. Whilst we were at it we decided to turn the mattresses before changing every bit of bedding. Always nice to have a bit of help as these mattresses are far too heavy for one person to handle.

Alan's not eaten particularly well today, but has been picking on 'nicies' since he went to bed! He's gone tachy again - low BP

and high pulse rate so I've emailed the doctor in case she wants to tinker with his meds. I'm a bit concerned about tomorrow's trip to the surgery to have the ECG monitor fitted. Lying in bed this evening he has wound himself up about Dodgy Doc and the possibility we may run into him tomorrow ... he is threatening all sorts. I said to him he would lose Doc M if he caused trouble in the surgery and that would be dreadful at this stage in the game. I'll just have to get between them if Dodgy Doc appears. I'd love to smack him one too ... but it would have to be off the premises!!

Janet has phoned and she has finally moved out of her cottage. It's taken since about August to get this organized. She is moving in with her son for a while until she can find somewhere else she likes enough to buy. Suspect that will take us well into the new year.

I still feel very tired and always seem to drop off about 5pm – but only for 10 minutes today. Then I get to bed well before midnight and never feel like sleeping until I've had a chat on FaceBook, done a bit of writing and generally relaxed. As it's now approaching 2am again, I think I ought to get my head down as the effort of getting Alan out of the house by 10.30am will be a bit of a challenge!

25th November: Not a good start to the day again. Alan didn't get to sleep until about 5.30am – presumably because he had wound himself up so much about Dodgy Doc! Anyway, he told me to cancel the appointment as he didn't feel well enough to go and also to ask Gill if she had time to come and give him a shower as the bed was soaked yet again.

I made a quick trip out to the doctors' surgery to return their nebulizer – duly cleaned and polished!

I seem to have washing everywhere and still finding more to be done! Think it will keep me going all this week. Before I had finished the rotation between washing machine, tumble dryer, conservatory airer and ironing basket ... Mr. Tesco arrived with the shopping order. By the time that was all forced into cupboards and fridge it was almost time for Gill to arrive.

The chemist delivery lady arrived with the new medications for Alan's nebulizer and as per usual on the one I didn't recognize, I sat down to read the fact sheet. "Let your doctor know and special care should be taken if this medication is to be used by someone who ... (a) has any problems passing urine ... and (b) a man who has prostate problems. So where do we go from here? I spoke with the doctors' receptionist who tells me we are unlikely to get a call back from the doctor until between 7 and 8 o'clock tonight. I tell her I will phone the secretary later and see if she can get an answer for me.

Then, as Alan has decided that he would like to have a week in the Cottage Hospital so that I can have a bit of a rest, he asks me to phone the palliative care nurse to see if this is within her remit to organize. Manage to get her on the phone quite easily – which makes a change – and she will liaise with the doctor to see what can be arranged. Whilst I've got her on the phone I query the nebulizer medication with her. She will phone the doctor and get back to me. As she hadn't phoned by 3pm then I know the phone is not going to ring as that is her daily finish time.

As we don't have an answer to the question, we decide that the new meds will not be given until we hear from someone ... whenever that may be. This new nebulizer which arrived on Saturday is way too noisy for my liking. It's as though the cover is not attached to the guts and it rattles very loudly. Surely it's not meant to be like this? Only way to find out is to phone the manufacturers and let them listen to it over the phone. They agree and are very apologetic ... totally unacceptable ... exchange it. As we now can't be without it, the only way around the situation is to order and pay for a second unit and when that has arrived, pack up and return the first machine for a refund. The second machine will be delivered tomorrow! Nothing ever seems to be quite right for us!

When the phone range at 8.50pm the last person I was expecting to hear on the other end was the doctor! However, that's who it was! She advised that if we had any fears about the new medication, not to take it and she would discuss it with us when she visits on Wednesday. With reference to the respite week, she has put Alan on the waiting list and feels that advantage could be taken of this time to sort out the ECG monitoring and getting Alan onto a new regime of medications for his COPD. Hopefully there will be a bed available within the next couple of weeks or so.

With the thought of going into hospital again and how he struggled with his old little phone last time he was in, I suggested to Alan that perhaps he would like a new Smartphone to play with. Yes, he thought that would be a good idea ... so another chunk of money has been thrown at Amazon today to buy him a Samsung Galaxy which should be here in a couple of days. He'll enjoy that ... if I can teach him how to use it!

So I feel as if I've had an afternoon of retail therapy from my armchair because I also found a remote control for the PS3 which will be more helpful than the game controller thingie, and a banana pillowcase covered in Union Jacks ... which will be a laugh when he goes into respite again as he takes the banana pillow with him!

There is nothing planned for tomorrow ... but we never seem to get through a day without something or other unexpected happening. Wonder what it could be?

26th November: La Bella Italiano came to see Alan again today and she has decided that as things are becoming so complicated he will be best served if he is admitted to the Cottage Hospital for a week ... this way he can have x-rays done, ECG monitoring, COPD drugs introduced again, tweak heart meds in an attempt to get heart rate down, and finally get his BP under control.

There's no panic involved so she is waiting for the private room to become available again as she knows that with the PTSD problems he will be better sleeping in a room on his own. I get the feeling this will happen within the next week ... may even be this weekend. It just seems that so many things have changed at the same time (typical to happen when Doc M is on holiday!) and it's difficult to control everything at the same time. The added complication now is that the nebulizer treatment is giving him 'the shakes' - not just in his hands, but all over. The dose has been immediately halved.

Apart from that there's nothing much happening on The Hill base camp ... other than Alan's new phone is delayed until tomorrow. He seems to be getting quite excited about it and was quite disappointed today!

28th November: Just a bit fed up on the back end of down in the dumps tonight. Alan has been unwell all day and topped it all off with another seizure type episode late afternoon. The colour drained from his face in an instant. Phoned doc to see if there was a bed available at the Cottage Hospital ... but no, not today. We have to go there tomorrow for Alan's infusion, so I'll have a packed bag in the car, just in case. Things do seem to be changing here quite quickly and disturbingly, but I keep hoping he will bounce back like he's done before. It's actually very difficult to know what to think at the moment. All he can tell me is that he feels totally rubbish, wants to curl up in a corner, and the 'big bang' is getting close. No one deserves to suffer like this and I feel dreadful as there is nothing I can do to help ... I just feel that it's so unfair.

29th November: It's been a day of two halves ... as they say. Started off quite well at noon! Alan felt OK whilst we went to the hospital for his infusion. They took four ECG readings one minute apart and you would swear they were from four different patients .. the only constant was his heart rate! Also had the chest X-ray done. Still no bed but in any event there are no doctors on at the weekend, so there would be little point in him being there. But all of this took its toll and by the time we got home he was totally knackered, fell asleep for a while - and felt dreadful when he woke. Started to shake and I thought he was heading for another seizure ... but no. He went to bed early and straight to sleep. He has just woken for tea and tablets but I don't think he'll be awake long. He said to me today 'if they can't sort me out in here (hospital) then I don't think I will ever get out'. His head must be in a very black place, poor man.

30th November: The end of yet another month ... time is just rolling on at horrendous speed even though we are stuck within our own walls 99% of the time.

Yet again we had a day of two halves. Alan woke this morning feeling absolutely dreadful, and yet again the bed was soaked from top to bottom. We had planned to go to Coalbrookdale visiting Brummie today, but there was no way he could even drag himself out of bed at this stage. He stayed in bed all morning and slept the majority of the time. He finally woke at about 1pm and felt somewhat better and decided to get up ... not dressed – just up! He tells me that he feels it's unfair that I have to spend so much time on my own and that he must make the effort to spend time with me. I was well into the ironing when he got up, but if there's any excuse I can easily be persuaded to stop! There's always tomorrow morning! I have a washing machine full of wet towels and an awful weather forecast for tomorrow, so yet again they will have to be dried indoors.

We spent the afternoon in the lounge and I gave Alan a lesson on his new phone! I think we will have to have several before he gets the hang of it. It may be a Smartphone but all he wants it for is making and receiving calls ... and even that is proving a little difficult! Repetition, repetition, repetition!!

Alan enjoyed his tea for a change and was happy to be up until about 9pm when, after watching 'Frost', I turned over to the X Factor ... that was his prompt to decide he would be better off in bed!

I'm not even going to try to wake him in the morning – just let his sleep take it's natural course and hopefully he will feel better for it. I have to admit I'm feeling stressed both physically and mentally and am finding it very difficult to become enthused to do anything. If only we could just have a couple of 'good' days then I would hope these feelings would change.

30th November/1st December: Rough weekend for Alan. He has spent most of his time in bed feeling dreadful. We feel it's a real shame there hasn't been a bed available for him in hospital but hopefully we will hear something early in the week. No visitors. No phone calls. Very quiet time but gave me chance to catch up with some ironing!

2nd December: Alan took his time getting up this morning and was happy Gill was coming to help him with his shower as he had suffered mega sweats both nights at the weekend. He felt well enough to be dressed and spend the afternoon in the lounge.

Quite late on in the afternoon, the phone rang. It was our solicitor dealing with the litigation against Dodgy Doc. She told us that she had received a call from his insurance company. It's good news! Certain admissions have been made and they are prepared to immediately pay the interim payment (without prejudice) which was requested way back in May! They do not want papers put into court and want to sort out the tail end of this matter as quickly as possible. We were both listening to the phone call and absolutely gobsmacked that they didn't try to negotiate this payment downwards. They informed her that Dodgy Doc was now co-operating – we had realized how obstructive he had been throughout the GMC case, so it was no surprise to find out he had acted in the same manner throughout this case! She explained to us that we still had a way to go and she still wanted to obtain a Urologist's report prior to a conference in January, where our Barrister, expert witnesses, and ourselves could go through everything and, presumably, come up with a final figure to be requested as compensation.

When the call ended a cheer went up from both of us ... and then I burst into tears. A massive weight has been lifted. All the time and effort I've put into this for the best part of three years ... the research, the challenges, the GMC., etc., etc., have all paid off. I can't tell you how happy we both are tonight. Finally, we feel that justice is about to be done!

Even the interim payment is a life changing amount of money which will allow us to employ whatever help we need for Alan in the future. It also covers the outlay we have had on the bathrooms being refurbished and all the equipment we have already bought.

Total vindication ... at last!

3rd December: Alan woke feeling really unwell and to add to all his other ailments, he was also being sick. I phoned Gill to cancel her call. I also phoned through to the surgery to see if a bed had become available. The secretary told me she would get back to me. By lunchtime Alan felt well enough to sit in the kitchen and have a bowl of soup but was soon ready for bed again. He'd not been back in bed long and was using his nebulizer when Doc M arrived ... his first day back at work after sunning himself in the Caribbean! He was not exactly up to date with the situation but checked Alan over and feels that another chest infection is brewing and considers he would be better off in hospital for a while. As there is a bed available we can get ready and go straight away.

I hadn't packed a bag as Alan had asked me to do so I was running round finding everything he would need for a few days. We got down to the hospital by about 5pm ... just in time for tea! Amazingly, by now, he is feeling quite bright and is in the mood to be joking with everyone!

As usual there is a ream of paperwork to be completed and I was specifically asked to take Alan's 'Do not resuscitate' form into the hospital. I didn't think that sounded too good, but apparently this should be with the patient when admitted to hospital. Alan was happy for me to leave just after 7.30pm as he seemed to be getting tired by this time.

Of course, I had quite a few phone calls to make, but still managed to get to bed quite early. I would really love to know why I can't sleep when I'm so tired ... but that's how it seems to be recently.

4/5th December: Bit of a typical time in hospital for Alan ... the medications aren't right, they don't have certain tablets even though I offered them our stock, the TV is not working, they don't allow patients to share the hospital Wi-Fi, patient opposite is non-communicative, none of the promised tests done ... bored out of his mind! Great!

I got up early to make sure I was down in Kidderminster before everything got too busy. I was looking for a mobile broadband Wi-Fi router on a pay as you go basis. The one I was after was sold out so the expected £34.99 turned into £59.99 – but, if it helps to keep Alan happy in hospital, then it's worth having.

Givvi went to visit him for a couple of hours this afternoon and set up his Wi-Fi gizmo, which raised his spirits – they had had a good session of joking and laughing, causing their usual mayhem. By the time I arrived for evening visiting he was still in a very good mood and we escaped to the car for a cigarette. Doc M is duty doctor tomorrow morning so perhaps we'll learn a bit more.

As I've not slept well for a couple of night, I've taken a sleeping pill and hopefully that will do the trick.

6th December: I was rudely woken up by the phone … it was Alan! Just after 10am and he had already been seen by Doc M who without laying a stethoscope on him announced that he was ready to go home … end of! So suffering badly from sleeping pill hangover I pull myself together well enough to be at the hospital by noon and immediately start my packhorse act and load up the car yet again. Alan is always very keen to get out quickly once he has been told he can go and in actual fact there were no hindrances today. Even the drugs were handed over quickly.

He's happy to be back at home and we share the thought that this exercise has been a complete waste of time for both of us and that we must make enquiries about respite care in a care home through Continuing Health Care. The big problem is that our McMillan nurse is on maternity leave and as yet we've not had a visit from her replacement. A quick phone call to the CHC team gave us the information we needed about which care homes they use for respite care. If Alan is entitled to six separate weeks a year of respite care, then we have already missed out on 6 opportunities. .. but if you're not told about these benefits, how can you make use of them?

One of the care homes is in Bewdley – just 20 minutes away – and from what we can find on the internet, looks very nice. I've requested a brochure and at some time we will make an appointment to visit. We can then request a visit from the replacement McMillan nurse and try to put wheels in motion.

Janet turned up mid-afternoon – oh dear, I had forgotten to ring her and let her know not to visit Alan in hospital! We never discuss our case against Dodgy Doc as she is still his secretary ... but I have told her on the phone about our success. As my best friend I would like her to be pleased for us .. but she's not able to do that ... in fact she has always been somewhat disapproving of everything I instigated in this respect. Yet she has managed to separate things in her mind and has been nothing but supportive to us both throughout Alan's illness, and for that I will be eternally grateful. I'm hoping that when she retires next May, we may finally be able to have a long talk about things.

Jo and Jason were due to visit Alan in hospital this evening but came here instead and we had a lovely Chinese meal and a very enjoyable time. We watched 'The Jungle' and by then Alan was ready for his bed. I've been fighting the tiredness all day, but as soon as I get into bed, I'm wide awake again ... and suffering very badly! Indigestion! When will I learn that as you get older you must eat spicy food much earlier in the evening? Where did I put those Rennies?!!

7th December: Just a quiet and very pleasant day! No pressures to do anything and it's just been nice to be able to sit together and have a good chat. More days like this would be good!

8th December: A quiet day where I watched Alan going downhill again and by the time bedtime came around, yet again he was feeling quite unwell. Here we go again!

9th December: Here on The Hill we are back to square one after just a couple of days back home. The bed, the breathing, the unwell feeling. I've racked my brain trying to think what is happening and the only thing I can come up with is Alan's mattress. It was supplied by Social Services nearly three years ago to reduce pressure on his mets. I know I'm clutching at straws! Over time we have learned how sensitive he is to certain meds and chemicals and I'm just wondering if, as the foam degrades, harmful toxic fumes are being given off. I'll take it off today and leave it off for a week or so and see if things improve. I'm sure he'd rather have a little more Oramorph for the pain rather than be suffering like this.

10th December: We've had a really bad 'do' here this morning on his return from the loo. Closest we've come to losing him, I'm sad to say. Just could not get any breath, chest heaving, etc., etc. Straight onto nebulizer followed by oxygen - must have taken half an hour before he was breathing properly again. He's also had another 'fit' an hour or so before when he was in bed. He's totally wiped out and asleep now. Have cancelled Gill for today and my appointment for tomorrow in Worcester. Can't possibly leave the house at the moment, and also can't hand the responsibility on to someone else. What a b*stard all this is! Dry bed this morning!

Have spoken with Doc M ... little or nothing else can be done - other than giving him the oxygen first rather than the nebulizer! I'll get it right one day!! Unfortunately something we are going to have to learn to live and deal with. As he said, he could jump straight in the car and come to the house when this happens again but the episode would be over before he got here ... same with ambulance. He would like me to try and get his SATS if and when it happens again. He said that he must sleep with oxygen on as this will help. All I can do is more of the same. Bugga!! But at least he's now aware that everything is not as hunky dory as he thought it was on Friday.

Yet again I've had to cancel my bone scan due tomorrow – just don't want to leave Alan on his own or with someone else at the moment.

11th December: Alan has slept the clock round today. I went to bed just after 10pm and within five minutes he was awake! Feed me, feed me! Sandwiches, cakes, tea, tablets, powders and potions!! Once all that is dealt with, it's nebulizer time, before setting him up on oxygen for the night! What an exciting life I lead! All I know is that I'm dog tired and would love to have about 12 uninterrupted hours of quality sleep!

I found a white feather in the hall last night and this evening I've had the sensation of butterfly wings stroking my arm whilst I was making a cup of tea. Just wondering if it's my Dad trying to help me along at the moment.

We have the new Palliative Care Nurse coming on Monday and there is an outside chance she may have the Palliative Care Consultant with her. I'm going to request one night's cover and at least four hours extra per week from CHC - then perhaps I could get one good night and have some hours to get out to do things which need to be done! On average I'm only getting 3-4 hours' sleep at the moment. I have spoken to her on the phone and asked her to find out about the nursing home respite which we apparently qualify for under CHC. Hopefully she will have some news on that when she visits.

I managed to get to the surgery to pick up Alan's medications ... I think we qualify to open a branch of Boots' Pharmacy now!

Please, please, let tomorrow be better than today!

12th December: Giv arrived at mid-day so that I could nip into Kidderminster for an eye test and organize some new specs with the frames I have bought on line. Alan has been in desperate need of oxygen and nebulizer this morning. Gill came whilst I was out for his shower but I was back before she left. Alan had been very unstable in the shower and was back on oxygen immediately afterwards.

Having settled him into the lounge Giv took on the job of staining the new shelves for Alan's bedroom whilst I started getting the Christmas tree up and making an effort with the decorations. I just can't get enthused about it this year even though he will be having such a landmark birthday on Boxing Day. I really must pull myself together and get into the swing of things! I've bought Alan a Diesel watch and a book about the Dog Unit for his birthday. He keeps telling me he doesn't want anything, but I can't let his 65th pass by unmarked in some way. I have all the gear to make him a birthday cake, but if I run out of time I'll use the Christmas cake I've already bought! Good to have a Plan B!

The motor scooter has been brought into the house again as Alan is suffering too much getting from one end of the bungalow to the other. It's a bit of a pain in a confined space, but needs must!

13th December: Friday the 13th ... doesn't bode well, based on previous experience!

Our favourite blood sucking nurse turned up early this morning ... well, early for us!! She was in a good mood as was Alan ... all smiles and laughter. The mood continued throughout the morning and there was hilarity in the bathroom during shower time as Alan managed to soak Gill almost to the skin! However, after yesterday's near fall in the shower, today we had to get him onto oxygen as soon as he left the bathroom. Seems so strange that he can get so utterly breathless when someone else is showering and drying him ... he doesn't have to do a thing!

After lunch I finished putting up the decorations whilst Alan was varnishing some shelves for his bedroom unit. Even sitting doing this little job exhausted him and I had to take over in the end!

The computer decided to have a hissy fit so I needed to do a bit of work with that to try and clear the problem. When it was working properly again an email arrived from our solicitors to confirm that the interim payment had been received in their office, would be banked on Monday and as soon as cleared will be BAC transferred to Alan's account. That will look good when his balance suddenly increases from £4.64 to a level never seen in his account before! I wonder how long it will take someone from the bank to be on the phone with all sorts of ideas as to what should be done with this new balance? The smile on Alan's face said it all ... at last we have it in black and white that the money is on its way. Total vindication for us both. No amount of money will put right what happened to Alan ... but this goes some way to showing that justice has been done. At least we now have no worries if Alan should need funded support services any time soon. Hopefully we will be able to get an increase in his Continuing Health Care funding ...

we will be speaking to the new Palliative Care Nurse when she calls on Monday.

I have also spoken to the respiratory nurse today as I feel we need to restructure our oxygen supplies. She will be coming to see us on Wednesday.

After tea I said I would finish off the varnishing work on the shelves. Alan made his way from the kitchen to the lounge and by the time he got there was gasping and air grabbing again. Immediately put him onto oxygen as this episode was on a par with the one he had on Tuesday, but his recovery time today seemed to be longer. When his breathing had returned to a comfortable and manageable level he then went on to the nebulizer. What I hate is the panic in his eyes and how frightened these episodes make him. As before, when the whole episode is over he is completely wiped out and the best place for him is bed ... but of course we have to wait until he feels capable of making the distance. I always feel happier once he is in bed ... somehow it seems safer for him to be there than anywhere else.

So that's two major and about four minor episodes in the last four days. The rate of increase is frightening, but we just have to continue to cope with them. I do hope tomorrow can be episode free.

14th December: We both had the luxury of sleeping in late this morning ... how nice is that!! The day has been fairly quiet and uneventful. Alan watched the Harry Potter film whilst I finished off the varnishing of the shelf units for his bedroom. Hopefully we can get them finished off tomorrow so that he can sort out all his Buddha's.

He really enjoyed his tea today – which makes a change – but was ready for bed by 7.30pm and was dozing most of the evening.

A quiet, uneventful day ... just as we like them!

15th December: The job of getting the shelving units finished for Alan's bedroom seems to have been hanging around for weeks and weeks. Finally today I managed to get them all put together and installed in his bedroom. All that needs to be done is for the shelves to be fixed down with pins or nails from one of those automatic gun things, which we have ... if only we could find the pins!! Hopefully he will have a flash of inspiration and remember where they may have been put!

The effort for him to try and help me with this today has meant that he has been on oxygen more than usual and when we had finally finished and went to sit in the lounge his heart rate was a massive 146! The strain on the heart must be horrific.

The rest of the day has been quite peaceful but we are both very tired. Alan decided to go to bed at 8pm so that I could watch the final of the X Factor ... he can't stand the programme! The result was as predicted with Sam Bailey, a prison officer, becoming the winner. Elton John was also on the show and I'm convinced he was p*ssed as a f*rt! He had a visible prompter by the side of him and when he got up from his piano he could hardly stand. Disappointing to see him performing like that.

So another new week starts tomorrow ... I wonder what it will bring. Hopefully a bloated bank balance by the end of the week!

16th December: Such a busy day and yet I'm not too sure I've achieved that much!

We were both awake quite early and I've been on the go since 7.30 with cups of tea ... tablets, etc. Alan then decided he wanted pea and ham soup for breakfast! Who am I to argue? Strange man!!

We had received a letter from the Department of Work and Pension with reference to the new PIP benefit which is replacing the old DLA payments. They want to re-assess Alan as it is a new benefit. What part of 'terminally ill' did they not understand from the first claim? The first stage of this re-assessment takes the form of a 20 minute phone call ... just so many questions! To top it all they want another DS1500 form completed by Doc M so that the matter can be dealt with under their special rules which is the speedy service, otherwise it can take up to 26 weeks to process new claims. I have spoken to the surgery and hopefully this will be organized within the next couple of days.

As lunchtime approached and I stopped my tidying up efforts, I asked Alan what he would like to eat. Rice pudding! Strange man!!

The new Palliative Care Nurse, Sam, called in with one of her students. We had a chat on the phone a few days ago about the possibility of respite care for Alan. She confirmed today that Alan qualifies for six individual weeks of nursing home care, fully funded, in any period of 12 months. It's good news and bad news ... as we weren't told about this earlier. We have already lost out on the six sessions which we could have had in the past 12 months – and they would have been really useful considering what we've been through! I have also requested a further four hours per week for help in the house and sitting duties. We should know the answer by Thursday.

I phoned the doctors' surgery to get the results of Alan's regular 4-weekly blood tests which have been totally uninteresting for over two years, so you tend to get a bit blasé over them. Well there was a bombshell today! His PSA figure has increased 4-fold in four weeks and his ALP figure by 10%. Now this could be a blip, or as the result of an infection ... or it could be the start of the main event with the prostate cancer whereby it has become hormone refractive and his treatment is no longer working. But we will need to get another couple of results before we can establish what is happening. Alan has done exceedingly well in his response to this treatment in that it has held the cancer back for the best part of two and a half years. It's responsible for his heart failure ... but held the cancer at bay! You just can't have everything, can you?

Late afternoon I've had to start moving furniture around as Alan is becoming very uncomfortable on the corner unit. I've brought one of the reclining chairs out of the conservatory and re-jigged the lounge to fit it in. Hopefully he'll be happier now.

I just feel today that I've been on the go non-stop all day and am thoroughly tired and weary. Really looking forward to my bed. But then Alan would like me to deal with his toe nails ... so up I get again to start yet another little job. One of his nails is sore and he says he will deal with it himself. Oh, he did that all right! Stabbed the toe with the pointy scissors!! The blood was everywhere! I didn't laugh ... honestly!! I've put him back together with a couple of plasters and the thumb off a medical glove. His walk to the bedroom tonight was hilarious ... at the very least you would think he'd had a leg amputated! No doubt all the dressings will come off overnight and I will have a blood bath in the bed to contend with tomorrow! C'est la vie!!

17th December: All of a sudden I don't seem to have enough hours in the day! I'm not up to date with anything ... especially the ironing of bedding! I think I have at least four sets waiting to be dealt with!

Alan's breathing continues to get worse and has to use the oxygen far more often. He is now getting very concerned about It. I spent the afternoon making steak and kidney pies to last us all winter ... well, not quite, but it seemed a lot! Guess what we're having for tea? ... and I'll still have four left to freeze down!

The washing machine is very sick ... sounds as if it has a bag of nails inside it. Had several attempts to call in the service engineer but couldn't get through on the phone. Have sent a message from their website. Luckily it's still under warranty.

By the end of the day, I'm just so weary – hopefully I'll sleep a bit better tonight.

18th December: A day of mayhem. I had decided it would be mince pie day and started on the pastry early. Alan attempted to get onto the edge of his bed to start his getting up process and was immediately hit by a massive breathing incident. What a great start to the day ... not! The sweating continues and his bed is soaking wet.

Georgie arrived to lend a helping hand and first job was the bed. She then worked her way right through the bungalow whilst I carried on cooking. I've asked her to come back tomorrow as well so that she can attack the clothes ironing.

Gill arrived to help Alan with his shower and on checking the damaged toe decided that it is infected so we're going to have to take great care of that! Alan emerges from the shower puffing and panting just as his respiratory nurse arrived! She has re-jigged our supplies so that we have what is useful to us ... not what they think Alan needs!

By 2.30pm we are alone at last. Time for lunch and then collapse in the front room. The mince pies have been 'tested' and it would seem that I have excelled myself this year! Melt in your mouth, mince pie heaven ... but they have given Alan violent indigestion! He should know that would happen ... always does, but he can't resist them!

We had the delivery today of a laser star field, which projects stars and clouds onto the ceiling. What a fabulous 'toy'. Absolutely mesmerizing and soothing. The plan is that it will help Alan get off to sleep more readily. As it has an auto switch off and we don't have to worry about it, I'm hoping it will work for him

The weather has battered us badly today and the power has gone off about four times ... not for long, but long enough to trigger all the electronic clocks to re-set themselves! What a pain that is to re-set them all!

We had a chat on the phone with Brummie in New Zealand ... all's well there with wonderful weather. He'll be gone for another six weeks or so. Sure the time will soon pass.

I've dropped a line to Doc M tonight as he's not seen Alan for a couple of weeks and really he has no idea how he is at the moment. Hopefully he will call in tomorrow afternoon.

19th December: Georgie and I spent the morning ironing ... so we're nearly up to date – just one set of sheets left which aren't dry yet.

Alan has been 'wiped out' all day ... so very tired. His big toe seems somewhat better than yesterday. After his shower with Gill all he could manage to do was sit in the lounge and fall asleep. We waited until after 4pm hoping that Doc M would put in an appearance, but disappointingly he didn't materialize. Alan was quite upset and starts to think he's been abandoned. I would have liked to have seen a call every couple of weeks as the surgery is less than five minutes down the road ... but obviously priorities have to be made within the time constraints the doctors are working under. However, Alan is a dying man and we both need support on a regular basis.

Alan had the most dreadful pains in his chest this afternoon – he truly thought it was a heart attack. However after a glass of coke and a couple of ant-acid tablets it became very apparent this was indigestion!

We were expecting a delivery of oxygen today ... but that hasn't arrived either!

By 8.30pm neither of us can keep our eyes open so both head for bed. Hopefully we will both have a better night.

20th December: Not a good day all round.

Roberto was here at the crack of 8.30ish with the oxygen order as submitted by the respiratory nurse - which, as usual, was all wrong! I give up!

Alan asked me to cancel Gill and shower as he feels so rough. Waited in all morning in case Doc M called after morning surgery ... but no. When Alan got up his big toe looked even worse so I asked Gill to come up and have a look at it. She's going to contact the District Nurses to tell them about it, but has re-dressed it for the time being. Alan has slept in the chair for the rest of the day and I have felt myself sinking lower and lower. Got weepy on phone with a friend tonight, about lack of response from Doc M really ... jeepers is there no time in a day for a five minute phone call? I know there is nothing he can do ... but a bit of support would be appreciated - I'm his patient too, and just at the moment I'm finding life very difficult to cope with!! I just feel very isolated – partly due to location and partly due to not feeling able to put pressures on those closest to me - Giv and Janet. Moan over!! No doubt I'll be in a better mood again by tomorrow – I tend to bounce well!

21st December: Alan had a comparatively good day as we had a visit from Giv and Percy during the afternoon. They managed to get all the burning done in the new incinerator. I don't know what it is about having a fire but they love to do it every time they come over.

As Alan was in the mood we had a takeaway Chinese which was absolutely beautiful. I also managed to remember to replace the gas cylinder for the lounge .. the first one having lasted 47 days. If we carry on like this it will work out far cheaper than burning logs all winter. OK, so it doesn't look so pretty ... but what the hell! Convenience is the key!

Alan called me 'The Black Witch' again tonight and I've asked him not to continue with this so called joke as it upsets me, but which then led the conversation back to all the events of that dreadful day in September and caused both of us to become somewhat agitated. Later in the evening he asked me if I 'wanted him here'. He'd overheard some of the phone conversation with Janet earlier when I got quite tearful. He truly doesn't seem to understand that although I love him to bits and would do anything for him ... I am tired and I do need a rest, but I now feel that emotional blackmail is being put in place so that he doesn't have to go into the nursing home for respite care. I can't win. If he goes into respite, in his head I will be pushing him out ... and if he doesn't go then I'm going to end up feeling chewed up and spat out.

22nd December: A thoroughly miserable day all round. Alan didn't feel well enough to get up this morning and when he finally decided to get up all he did was have soup for lunch and then slept in the chair all afternoon. He enjoyed his tea but was soon ready for bed.

During a very brief conversation later in the evening I asked him what was wrong and was I the problem. Absolutely not! He is thoroughly 'f*cked off' with how he feels and has worked himself into such a state about the fact that Doc M has not been in touch. I've told him I will make the phone call in the morning. What I don't want is for him to fall out with Doc M ... he is our lifeline and we desperately need him on side. I've given Alan a sleeping tablet otherwise he's going to lie awake all night again.

I don't like days like today, and wish we didn't have so many rough days rather than good ones.

23rd December: Got on the phone first thing to sort out a few things with Doc M's secretary for Alan's infusion which is due later in the week. She will get back to me. I was hoping he would phone during the morning ... but no.

Gill came to do Alan's shower quickly followed by Janet who had volunteered to sit with Alan for the afternoon whilst I went to Kidderminster for last minute shopping, collect new specs, and visit the nursing home recommended as first choice for Alan's respite.

The weather couldn't have been worse ... torrential rain and strong winds. The supermarket was blitzed but I think I managed to get 90% of what I went for. Called in to collect new specs which are lovely and I feel that I can see so much better and I look more like myself again! Called back in at the nursing home on the way back but, to be honest, I was somewhat disappointed. It's definitely more of a residential home for old people and I know Alan wouldn't like it. Staff seemed very pleasant and a homely feeling, but under CHC funding Alan wouldn't get a room with en-suite and may even have to share. Can't see that working! I'll have a look at the next one on the list after Christmas.

When I got home all was well apart from the fact that neither Janet nor Alan knew how to switch on the gas fire. Oh, dear!! Anyway, they had got on fine and hadn't killed each other ... which has to be a bonus!

24th December: At long last Doc M came on the phone at lunch time. He was most apologetic that he'd not been in touch earlier but had missed the email until his secretary had put it in front of his nose earlier today. After explaining how difficult our situation has become, he became most concerned about how we were coping. He says that Alan should not be walking around and should use the scooter whenever possible. We also talked about the extra blood test and he has authorized this for early January. If the cancer is now progressing he feels that even if Alan would agree to chemo, his heart wouldn't cope with it, but a bit of targeted radiotherapy might be an option. He cannot prescribe secondary hormone therapy and Alan would need to return to the Oncologist for this ... if I can get him there.

I then passed the phone over to Alan and he said he could tell from Doc M's voice that it was obvious he now fully understood how worried we are about Alan's heart and breathing. As he can't get up to us at the end of the week, Doc M will come and see us on New Year's Eve to give Alan his Zometa infusion. He has suggested increasing Alan's daily morphine dose in an effort to keep the pain levels down as they have been increasing quite quickly over the past 4-5 weeks.

Alan is much happier to have spoken with him and all's well with the world now! I was beginning to worry that it was going to upset our Christmas as Alan had been so upset he had not been in touch.

I've been making stuffing from scratch today ... just hope it turns out OK. I can hardly lift the turkey now that it's stuffed and said to Alan I can see me basting it on the kitchen floor!! By tradition I will cook the turkey overnight ... it's not Christmas unless the smell of cooking turkey wakes me!

I have managed to bake a birthday cake for Alan today, without him realizing, and will have to get up early in the morning in an attempt to get it iced and finished before he wakes. Fingers' crossed! Must also get a bottle of champagne in the fridge tomorrow .. I've dug out the champagne flutes in readiness – can't remember the last time they saw the light of day!

We have been waiting all week for the promised interim payment from our legal case to hit Alan's bank account .. it was promised before Christmas. No sign of it as yet! Never mind, we know it's on the way.

25th December: I was up at 4.30am to ice Alan's birthday cake. I have never used fondant icing before so it was a matter of trial and error ... but luckily it has turned out to be of very acceptable quality! I've hidden it away in the conservatory, cleaned up the kitchen and got myself back to bed by 6.30am. Eventually dropped back off to sleep until Alan buzzed me at about 10.45am. By this time the turkey is cooked so we are able to have hot bacon rolls by using the rashers which have been protecting the bird!

I was able to give Alan a print off of his bank account with the interim payment sitting there waiting to be cleared through on the 27th December. Happy Christmas!! He's never seen so much money in his bank account before!

Alan managed to surface by about 1pm and the intention was to have a lazy day in front of the TV. All was well for about an hour and then suddenly after clearing his throat, Alan went into a nasty seizure again and passed out immediately. All I could do was hold the oxygen mask in front of his nose until he came round. This took 2 or 3 minutes and he didn't have a clue what was going on. Yet again this episode rendered him totally exhausted and needing to sleep ... which he did for the rest of the afternoon.

To be honest this put us both off our Christmas dinner and neither of us enjoyed it very much. What a shame after all that trouble.

However, this is the third Christmas day in succession that has gone wrong for us and I'm not at all sure we are going to get another chance.

Having seen this seizure today there was absolutely no prior notice that something was going wrong and I am wondering just how many may be happening when Alan is in bed on his own. He would have no idea it had happened as there is this overwhelming need to sleep immediately afterwards. I checked his heart rate at the time and it had increased by some 15 beats per minute above the number it had been an hour or so before.

This situation combined with the cancer numbers now heading north are a cause of great concern to me as I feel that events are stacking up against him with only one undesirable outcome at the end of it. I have no idea how long his poor heart will be able to cope with these pressures.

Tomorrow Alan will be 65. A real achievement considering the prognosis we were given almost 3 years ago. I'm just hoping he is well enough to enjoy the day.

26th December: What a lovely day we have had ... quiet, but special. Alan has not felt this well in weeks. He had no pain ... no seizures ... not too much oxygen. He was stunned by Giv's beautiful painting and was very surprised by the cake ... and he certainly wasn't expecting a Diesel watch from me! He has decided to treat himself to an iPad mini2 Retina, so I have already ordered that and a cover. The only 'downer' on the day was that Percy has gone down with flu and had to stay in bed at home ... but I sent him a food parcel to compensate! We needed today to be a good one ... just in case - and we've achieved that! He's gone to bed a happy bunny tonight ... and so have I!

27th December: As is our luck you must realize that there has to be a 'payback' for such a good day yesterday! Alan has been so tired today and feeling really rough. Can't really do anything other than go with the flow. Having said that, I too have been unbelievably tired today

– woke up feeling very drugged! We both had a nap in the afternoon and Alan felt ready for bed by 6pm.

Unfortunately after only getting to sleep at 1.30am, Alan buzzed for me at 3.30am convinced he had just had another seizure. However, I'm more inclined to feel this was a dream because that overwhelming need for sleep was not present as far as I could see. He said that it was not psychosomatic, but somehow I feel there is a bit of that in play.

Once woken, I'm awake until 7.30 and then managed to get another couple of hours sleep! Almost too tired to function this morning!

28th/29th/30th December: Three days of almost continual sleep have descended on The Hill. Alan feels very poorly and is not really interested in food or drink. We have struggled through the weekend and on Monday morning tells me that he feels he ought to be in hospital. The lead GP from the surgery called in at around lunchtime and decided that Alan was not 'acute' ... there was nothing for him to treat ... and perhaps Alan would be better off in a nursing home!!! There may well be a bed available tomorrow at the Cottage Hospital, which they will reserve for Alan. However, he did mention a brand new nursing home in Ludlow – I'll have to have a look at that! There was also an almost snide remark about being able to afford to pay! (Seems Dodgy Doc must have let it be known that we had received an interim payment!) Doc M is due tomorrow afternoon for the Zometa infusion. We'll start again and go from that point I think.

If I had been able to get Alan out of bed, it would have needed to be changed about 3 times a day, but this, it would seem is perfectly acceptable – so we have been told! His sweating is out of control. I've still not been able to change the bed today but it must be done tomorrow. Hopefully Gill will be here at lunchtime and she will help me.

Three nights in the past four Alan has buzzed me at some time between 3am and 5am needing help. Only problem is, once the issue is resolved he goes back to sleep quite easily ... I very rarely do and therefore am surviving on just two or three hours of sleep a night. Can't go on like this forever!

31st December: Luckily Alan feels somewhat better today – thank goodness. It's been a busy day!

We had a very gratifying and productive hour with Doc M today. He turned up 4 hours early which wasn't a bad thing as he saw Alan struggling to get back to his bed for the infusion and his total lack of breath after a 20' journey. Then he sneezed and coughed at the same time and passed out on the bed ... all these things Doc M has never seen before. He is going to recommend to CHC that we have a night sitter for a minimum of 4 nights a week. He doesn't like the sound of the CHC chosen nursing home for respite and wants Alan in the brand new purpose built unit just 5 miles away (but there may be an issue with what county it is in!). He has confirmed our thoughts that Alan's on the slippery path downhill and also confirmed that one more increase in PSA will see us back in the Onco's office! He said that it's only because Alan is a stubborn old b*stard (his words) that he's lasted this long! I got a kiss and a hug at the front door as he left. We were both very pleased with his visit.

Georgie had to sit and wait in the kitchen until Doc M had gone – then she was able to get on with the work in hand. Then the Tesco driver arrived with the grocery delivery which always takes a while to put into cupboards. Georgie and I just about managed to get Alan's bed changed before she ran out of time and before she had moved her car off the drive, Gill had arrived for his shower! Phew! In the middle of all of this chaos the washing machine engineer phoned ... he had not been told I had cancelled the call! Oh dear, never mind!

Tried in vain to get in touch with Sam, our Palliative Care Nurse, but she's off till next week. She is the only one able to sort out the CHC to get these changes sorted, so I've left a message that we need to see her as soon as possible. Let's strike whilst the iron is hot.

371

My ladies group on FaceBook for Prostate Cancer Support is having a change of name overnight so I have all the pictures ready for uploading. Hopefully it will go without a hitch. After a democratic vote, the group will become 'Prostate Sisters' Accord' ... PSA for short.

A busy New Year's Eve!

2014: 1st January: A day to relax ... no Gill ... no visitors ... just take it easy. Alan doesn't want to get up and stays in bed until it's time for tea! That consumed and the final part of Harry Potter watched, then for him it's time for bed again! I wasn't far behind him!

2nd January: Dentist. Just how do you break a wisdom tooth on the back edge? It is just about the most awkward place for Pete the Prod to attack and injections right in the join of top and bottom jaws are somewhat uncomfortable. After waiting several minutes for me to 'freeze down' the drilling begins ... and stops abruptly!! "You didn't give me a 'horse dose', did you?" So the dreaded needle re-appears and wriggles towards the second nerve which has been totally unaffected by the first jab! Second attempt with the drill is much more acceptable. New crater created and filled successfully. I spend the next couple of hours dribbling quite uncontrollably! Only porridge for lunch!

Alan has been well, but very tired and very 'windy'. He has managed to stay awake most of the day!

3rd/4th January: Just horrendous weather all over the country and the floods are back. There are many times that we appreciate living on this hill. When it arrives, snow is short lived by comparison to what these poor people with flooded houses have to contend with – my heart goes out to them at times like this. We are due a couple of days respite only to be hit again on the 6th.

My new iPad Air arrived on Friday afternoon. It's lovely! But I must now stop upgrading and be happy with what I have. Alan is also getting into his mini iPad which he showed no interest in it whilst he felt so poorly.

I had a couple of parcels to get away today but arrived at the local post office just as the collection driver was leaving and who refused to wait! Fuming I ran the gauntlet to two other post offices trying to beat the cut off times in different areas. I failed miserably! Emails of apologies duly sent to recipients.

Again, Alan has felt quite well in himself, but has this overwhelming tiredness to deal with along with the breathlessness. The only answer is for him to sit quietly and do nothing other than essential trips to the loo, after which he needs to go on oxygen!!

We're expecting visitors for lunch tomorrow, so must be up early-ish to try and make the place look presentable!!

5th January: Maz and Pip came to visit today and brought Brummie's dog Nugget with them. It turned out to be quite a comical day other than the fact that Alan was unwell and spent 90% of their visit in bed. Brummie always misses his dog so I sent him photos on FaceBook with this letter ....

"Dear Mum and Dad ... today I've been to visit The Hill and what an adventure I've had! I went to find Uncle Ed (Alan) who was in bed. He was being sick and sleeping, but I did enjoy rolling around on the duvet! I met a huge Buddha sitting on the window sill. I didn't like him so I barked and growled at him until I was distracted. Aunty Cath gave me a chicken dinner and shortbread biscuits ... yummy. This was my reward for sitting quietly whilst they had their dinner! It was so good that an hour later I had another one! Auntie Maz took me outside on my lead ... but Uncle Pip forgot so I had a really good run around the garden in the dark. It's big, isn't it!! Uncle Pip seemed a bit out of puff when he caught up with me! I've been running round this big house and liked it so much I marked it as my territory ... all over the base of the big clock in the hall. Oh dear, I got shouted at!! But all was forgiven when I ran round the house like a burst balloon and then danced around Auntie Cath till she got those lovely biscuits out again! Uncle Ed got up and came into the lounge during the evening so I was able to jump all over him and the furniture. Then I followed Auntie Cath into another room ...

she didn't see me as I explored around the bed ... then the light went out and the door was shut. I was soon heard as I gouged the door with my claws!!! I've had a lovely day and I think you should bring me here again! Your beloved, but abandoned, Nugget. x"

Stupid ... I know ... but then Brummie is a daft bugger anyway! Three weeks before they are due home but he sounded most unhappy on the phone the other day and was talking about trying to get an early flight home. Oh dear!

6th January: Phone calls were the priority today ... especially to Sam our PC nurse to explain what Doc M is recommending in the way of respite and overnight care for Alan. She will have her work cut out with the CHC panel ... they will not authorize spending money if they can possibly get out of it. Doc M may need to fight for us and if that fails then I shall wade in with both feet until someone listens to me.

Alan still very 'windy' today and the oxygen has come out three or four times, but generally he didn't seem too bad today – providing he sits still and doesn't attempt to do anything.

The place from where I bought the iPad last week agreed to my cheeky request for a partial refund as I could have got it cheaper elsewhere but the projected delivery wasn't as quick. However, as it turned out with the late delivery I had, I could have used the cheaper company and got it here in the same amount of time. So a refund of £30 is coming my way!! Result!

With Alan being up overnight I ended up having just over an hours sleep! So the last three nights have been three hours, two hours and one hour. I'm knackered!

7th January: Quiet day for both of us today. I think we are both too tired to get excited about anything! The district nurse came in this morning to do the extra blood test we need to have done. Results tomorrow.

Not feeling great Alan was in bed by 5.30pm and almost immediately asleep. He wanted nothing to eat so kept the supplies of tea going even though each one was left to go cold! By 8pm I'm almost on my knees so decided to go to bed. Unbelievably I went straight to sleep in a coma-type state and woke up at 3am.

Alan had been calling me and I'd not heard him. In his head he was back in the caravan and couldn't find the toilet, the result of which is that we had an accident in the bedroom! Never mind ... worse things happen at sea!

Both of us went straight back to sleep and by 7am I really felt as if I'd had a good night.

8th January: Alan has woken up soaking wet from sweat, yet again, and is feeling dreadful. He is coughing and spluttering – there is obviously a lot of rubbish on his chest. He has slept most of the day soaking the bed about every three hours. He is not drinking enough because he is asleep and his output is down to 'not a lot'! If this continues overnight again, I will need to contact Doc M tomorrow because he is so obviously dehydrating at speed and we may have to organize a hospital visit for an IV to be fitted so that he can be re-hydrated over several hours. We have started the antibiotics from our own stock today and I've emailed Doc M to let him know.

The blood test result shows a drop in PSA from 3.6 to 2.4 which has to be good news, but we still need the results of another test in two weeks' time before we will have a clearer picture how things are progressing. I'm hoping for another good night's sleep ... please!!

9th January: Having slept through till about 6am I suppose that was not a bad night. However, Alan is absolutely soaking wet yet again and I am concerned about how dehydrated he may be. I left a message for Doc M at 8.15am with a request that he phones back at some point during the morning.

Spoke with Doc M and got instructions to stand over Alan at least every hour and make him drink a glass of water! You can take the water to the horse, but you can't make him drink it!! Three hours later and only half a glass consumed, Doc M phoned again for an update. He decided to visit.

Alan was asleep when he arrived so he was rudely awakened and told in words of one syllable that if he didn't drink he would end up in Worcester hospital as no bed available locally. Alan swore and cursed but eventually got the drink down him! Steroids have been increased, antibiotics doubled, add Paracetamol into the mix to bring down his core temperature and hopefully stop the sweating. I have to report in tomorrow morning. He whispered to me on the way out that he has earmarked a bed for Alan locally if he should need it tomorrow ... but just wanted to scare the **** out of him at the thought of going in to Worcester! Strangely enough, no sweats this afternoon. Wouldn't it be wonderful if he was dry in the morning?!! So with all the extras, he's currently on 32 tablets a day ... unbelievable! He managed to get up for a couple of hours this evening and ate half a meal ... better than nothing.

Already he is looking forward to his shower tomorrow as we have had to cancel Gill for the past couple of days.

10th January: I've had a disturbed night but ended up oversleeping until 11.30am. Oh dear, never mind! Alan is a little brighter ... bed is wet again ... and he doesn't feel well enough for his shower. I have left a message for Doc M saying that I think we can cope here OK for the weekend and that Alan doesn't need to be admitted locally.

During the afternoon we had a very surprising phone call from Sam, our PC nurse. She had faxed the Continuing Healthcare people just yesterday afternoon with our new requests and she had heard back from them today! They have approved funding for two overnight sitters so that I can get some sleep and also have approved the funding for the 'cross county' care home in Ludlow for Alan's respite care sessions.

This is absolutely brilliant news – especially as the nursing home is only six miles from home and is brand new and purpose built. The photos we have seen look great ... just like a nice hotel. We are hoping Alan's first respite week could be at the end of this month.

It was lovely to have some good news for a change and even lifted Alan's spirits enough for him to get up for the afternoon!

11th/12th January: Very quiet weekend as Alan continues to improve. Weather was dreadful. We both have problem teeth and will be on the phone first thing Monday morning to get us both appointments!

14th January: Had to cancel dentist last minute as Alan had a mega major 'do' which left him totally wiped out and me not far behind him! Lots of chest pains with it this time too. Good job Pete the Prod is very understanding about us cancelling on a regular basis. Still have to get over to see Doc M this afternoon to get a new supply of antibios for us to share! Hoping to get respite and night sitters organized for next week and his rest home stay for the end of the month. Just feel shattered!!

Appointment with Doc M was fine and he had new student, Elizabeth, with him. He said I did the best thing to take antibios for my gum problems and has prescribed two more sets of the tablets so that we have plenty of stock for Alan.

15th January: Have managed to book Alan into respite for the week of 27th January ... his Zometa and Zoladex for that particular week will be moved to the following week. All of this is dependent on the assessment carried out by the head nurse of the nursing home during a home visit which should happen next week. The other extra hours come into effect next week - night sitters, etc.

In other news I've had to put a call in again for Doc M to phone as Alan is on his way downhill again. I've increased the steroids back to where they were a few days ago but need him to confirm whether or not to double up again on the antibios - I've got stock here so could do it if that's what he wants done. I don't think for one minute he will see a need to come out to visit today.

I have a lady coming in on Sunday to give me a quote for deep cleaning the whole house from top to bottom as really it's only had a 'lick and a promise' for the best part of three years now! Alan asked me what I wanted for my birthday ... and that's it!! ... apart from new purple stripes (in my hair) next week!

16th January: Alan managed to get out of bed by about 12 noon and strangely enough he was in the kitchen having cup of tea with Georgie and myself and was quite jovial. He went to the study for half an hour on the computer and then suddenly he put himself back to bed feeling as rough as a dog and very sick! So that's it for the day, I suspect! He was soon fast asleep with a hot water bottle. He changes faster than the weather! I never know whether I'm on foot or horseback! Doc M confirmed doubling antibios was fine. Alan's just called me down to the bedroom and we've got one of those rigors going on again! Even his teeth are chattering! Blanket, tea, new hot water bottle! What's the betting the next thing today will be a soaking wet bed?!!!

I win!! I was right!! Within two hours of the rigor this afternoon he was hanging legs out of the bed and all the bed clothes off, soaking wet in a major sweat! How the hell are you supposed to treat someone who changes like the wind? Hair appointment now the week Alan's in dock. No car tomorrow ... in for service. They're collecting at 9am. Washing machine man due ... as is Givvi with Gill later. Usual Friday chaos on the hill!! Won £25 on lottery when tickets were checked yesterday!!

17th January: A busy morning with Givvi ... managed to get so much done by way of clearing out the spare room and getting the majority of boxes into the roof. Many of Alan's tools and 'bits' have gone back to the garage and suddenly the place looks a whole lot clearer.

Gill arrived early but Alan was not feeling well enough for his shower and went back to bed where he stayed for the remainder of the day.

18/19th January: As so often seems to happen these days, Alan has not felt well enough to get up and has spent the whole weekend in bed, with the exception of the hour when Janet came to visit. Although I did fetch us a Chinese meal on Sunday evening, even that couldn't tempt him and most of it was left. Wonder what the new week will be like?

20th January: It has made a nice change to have Alan up and about today. He enjoyed his shower and spent the afternoon in the lounge watching television. We had a long discussion about what sort of car we think we ought to be buying this time next year and at the moment we have come up with a Mitsubishi ... the specs are wonderful when compared with other manufacturers.

Alan also announced that he intends to stop taking some of his medications. I've tried to talk to him about this but he is adamant ... he just feels that his life revolves around pills and he's had enough! Nothing I said was going to change his mind!

21st January: Bloods due to be taken today – important for us as this test will show us what, if anything, is happening with the cancer.

If the numbers are up – then we're in the proverbial, but if they are down then we can breathe again for a while. However, after waiting all morning for the nurse to arrive I phoned the office only to be told the test had been moved to Friday! Why? Don't know! I explained that the test results were needed before Alan's infusion which is due on Thursday and dates should not be altered on a whim! However, they were not to know that the infusion has been postponed for a week and that a Friday test this week will actually be OK. I've asked for an explanation but haven't got one yet.

Again, as Alan feels unwell, I have had to cancel Gill for today. Unfortunately this is becoming a regular event.

I spoke with Doc M on the phone and he has decided to change the antibiotics which Alan is taking. I should have collected them late this afternoon ... but I fell asleep so will have to get out early in the morning!

Tomorrow will be quite busy. Gill is due and is bringing a lady called Bev, who will be one of our night sitters. She will be coming for the first time on Thursday night. During the afternoon we have the assessment being carried out for the nursing home. Let's hope it all goes well.

22nd January: Well, life on The Hill has been a whirlwind of merriment today! I had to whiz over to the surgery first thing to pick up new antibios for Alan which Doc M prescribed yesterday ... more horse pills! Georgie, my little helper arrived at 11 to spend a couple of hours with the hoover and dusters. Gill arrived at 1pm so that Alan could drown her in the shower. 2pm but late was Becky who will be lady doing the first overnighter tomorrow and 2.30pm one of the nurses from the nursing home arrived to do an assessment to make sure they could cope with Alan! He passed the test - heaven only knows how! ... and he is allowed to take the scooter!! The home is known locally as "The Palace"! Have still not had chance to get down there, but looking at the specs, nothing has been overlooked.

It's very difficult to know what bug it is that Alan has ... he's being treated as if it's a chest infection but he's not rattling or shifting rubbish from his chest, but he feels awful and has done so for about four weeks, hasn't been dressed since Boxing Day and in the past two weeks he's probably been up three times. Consequently he is as miserable as sin tonight and I've been criticised for asking how he feels more than once over a period of about three hours!

Alan should have had a PSA blood test today, but the nurses, in their wisdom, decided it would be OK to change vampire day to Friday!

I checked with them Monday to confirm they were coming Tuesday - yes - and then they didn't turn up. With new antibios in the system don't see that we can fully rely on the result we'll now get - which is a shame as I've said before we think Alan's numbers are beginning to climb and we needed this result to be the confirmation of what is happening. So we'll now have to wait a further four weeks before we know for sure. Oh ... and I'm still fighting a battle with Hotpoint about this washing machine ... 18 months on and they still won't play ball ... I'll get there in the end ... I'll email them into submission!!!

Alan called me back into see him just after midnight ... he was reduced to tears about how ill he feels. So we have sat and chatted for well over an hour, had another drink, and he's tired now so hopefully he will sleep OK ... but that means I have to get on to Doc M again in the morning as these new antibios have had such an immediate adverse effect on him. So here we are again - almost 2am and now I'm wide awake!! Definitely taking a sleeping tablet at 10pm tomorrow night!

23rd January: Life on The Hill ... Part 101: A day of two halves!:

First Half: This morning we had an unexpected visit from Alan's PCN who spent an hour with him and assessed that he would not be fit to go into respite next week. This infection is proving so difficult to shift that she feels the visit should be delayed by at least three weeks. She had a private chat with Alan about how he felt and what her thoughts were, and later she and I sat for some time on our own. It was her opinion that it may be that Alan doesn't get through this infection and asked if we had EOL (end of life) kit in the house - no we haven't - she will organize it. Obviously I had a few tears coming to terms with what I had been told. It's not as though I wasn't aware that this was going to happen one day ... but we all live in the hopes that 'one day' won't actually arrive and I think it is the suddenness of the reality that hits you like a brick. Anyway, she left with the intention of speaking to Doc M and asking him to call in.

Givvi arrived, and Gill, who has given him a bed bath today.

Again, both of them shocked and upset at the thought of what has been discussed. I have cancelled the respite bed ... cancelled the oxygen supply to the home ... cancelled the spring cleaning.

Second Half: Doc M arrives with student and gives Alan the once-over. He is in total agreement with postponing the respite visit. However, he considers the care he is getting at home cannot be bettered by the hospital so there is little point in moving Alan, but having said that he can't see the need just at the moment. If Alan became dramatically worse, then, of course, he would move him into hospital if needs be. At this point he doesn't consider that Alan is in any danger of not overcoming this infection and has arranged to come in on Tuesday to give him his Zometa and Zoladex.

Dressing Room Conference: What the hell is going on? There is nothing worse than being left so uncertain ... but it would seem that we have no choice other than to live with it ... but it is most unsettling for the emotions. My thoughts are to go with Doc M's opinion as he knows Alan so well. First overnight stay by Becky. I took heavy dose sleeping pill and was out of it by 10.15pm and knew nothing till 9.45 next morning! Wonderful!

24th January: Felt very 'over dosed' today and certainly don't think I should be driving the car ... but I have no choice. Prescriptions need to be collected and Alan would like 'something nice' from the bakers! Whilst I was out the District Nurse called in to take blood samples and then left the sleeping beauty to continue his sleep! After all of yesterday's mixed emotions, I'm not surprised that Alan is not too bothered about getting up today. However he did manage his shower with Gill – and managed to spend a couple of hours in the lounge during the afternoon.

Gill arrived just before 10pm as she is on night sitter duties, and apart from getting up for a drink at 2.30am I managed another good night's sleep. I'm sure this is all going to help.

25th/26th January: No real improvement in Alan during Saturday but Sunday started off looking quite promising and he was up for several hours. He enjoyed his scampi and chips for tea but was then very tired and was off to bed early. He went off to sleep so quickly that I totally forgot about his evening pills!! Oh dear ... never mind!

27th January: Alan is obviously feeling somewhat better and his tongue must have been in the knife drawer all night. He's in a feisty mood and is actually making some nasty, totally unnecessary remarks. He thinks it's clever ... to me it's hurtful – so I told him. He just seemed agitated much of the day. He went back to bed mid-afternoon and slept for several hours and was much more amenable when he woke up!

However, later in the day we have both suffered with the same upset stomach which was quite unpleasant and we have come to the conclusion it must have been yesterday's scampi ... shame really as it was beautiful!

I've had to order two new batteries for the mobility scooter ... disgraceful really when you consider it is only 15 months old and may have travelled a total of half a mile in that time. When these new ones are fitted they will remain 'on charge' permanently ... the only way to avoid premature death apparently! The scooter suppliers wanted almost £100 for a pair whereas searching eBay I found them for £38 – guess who got the business?

Making plans for the ladies FaceBook group meeting in March, I've ordered some pin badges today. Hopefully they will be appreciated. The proof from the manufacturer looks very promising.

28th January: Turbulent Tuesday!! Doc M has been with his two lady students to give Alan his Zometa and Zoladex ... hands on experience in field medicine!! Another issue has now raised its ugly head. Alan's liver numbers have been somewhat odd for a couple of months and Doc M suddenly realized this afternoon that he is not gaining weight round his middle ... he reckons he's full of fluid! Two lines of thought .. the heart is just not coping, or more likely at this stage is liver mets and the possibility of the beginnings of liver failure. Oh, joy .. as if we didn't have enough to play with already!! The med students have been very amused by the antics ... the one starting the infusion nearly passed out when Alan feigned collapse - she thought she'd let an air bubble through. Alan and Doc M can be very cruel to students when they get together, and the room was filled with uncontrollable laughter. I think Doc M is going to have a discussion with the German Maid as to whether she should drain his abdomen (she is an abdominal consultant) and that would need to be done down at the Cottage Hospital. Wait and see time again!!

Have found out tonight that the German Maid is on annual leave until next Monday. There will be no progress with the possibility of draining the fluid this week. However, we have decided to chat with Doc M tomorrow (not quite sure how or when as I'm out) to ask for the most appropriate scan of the liver to be done. Whether or not anything other than draining can be done, we'd like to know what it is we're dealing with. After this afternoon's frivolities and Doc M squirting saline all over Alan's chest and face to raucous laughter (payback time for Alan's tourniquet joke on Doc M in the hospital), I have started calling him my 'water babe' ... to which I was told 'you can f*** right off'!! He's got such a lovely way with words!!!!

I have sent Doc M a nice email asking if Alan can have a scan of the liver and for him to arrange with the German Maid to carry out the draining procedure. Always wise to put requests in writing.

29th January: Off to the hairdressers this morning. We have a new lady to 'sit' with Alan ... Rhianna ... a very bubbly blonde who is covering Georgie's shift for today.

I had to have a new girl at the hairdressers ... I didn't particularly like her but she made a fair job of my new purple streaks, cutting and finishing. Not sure yet whether I would use her again or not. Plenty of time to decide.

I got back home to find virtually none of the housework done as Rhianna and Alan had hit it off so well, they had spent the whole time chatting and drinking tea. No problems really as she will become one of our overnight sitters shortly and it's better to have someone in the house who you feel comfy with.

We had a phone call very early afternoon from the Imaging Department at the local hospital. They have an appointment slot for Alan on Friday afternoon at 4.40 pm. Wonderful! Someone has worked some magic as we were told there was a 2-3 week waiting list even for urgent scans! They gave me a list of instructions about not eating and only drinking water for six hours prior to scan ... that'll go down well!!

I've telephoned Dawn, Doc M's secretary, to thank her for working her magic in getting the appointment and to let her know how much we appreciate her efforts. Always oil the wheels!

This afternoon we've had a visit from Jo-Pot and Jason who both work full time but visit whenever they can. Alan was asleep in bed when they arrived but I woke him later so that we could all have a Chinese meal ... and very nice it was too.

Not late to bed ... we're both very tired.

30th January: The main story of the day was the visit by the washing machine engineer ... again! Having made a video of the noise it was making, at least he had a fighting chance of identifying what was wrong. After dismantling most of the works, I was embarrassed to witness the removal of Alan's comb, almost toothless, from the inside of the machine. My mission to get the company to replace this machine over the past two years suddenly disappeared! Bugga!. They will claim this has been the problem all along even though my initial complaint, which has continued, is that the machine does not get washing clean. He put the machine back together including a new heating element as it is so difficult to make a good seal replacing an old unit. The old unit looked OK and he checked it with his little meter thingie and it appeared to be in working order. We have to assume that the water has been coming up to temperature since we had the machine, although you wouldn't think so!

However, during the weekend I have done several loads of washing and the difference in the wash quality has been immediate. Stains and marks have disappeared and ageing tea towels which have been greying over time, suddenly have their colour lifted several shades! It would seem my problems from day 1 have been that the original heating element could not possibly have been working properly and therefore all the washing has been done at temperatures not much above freezing. No wonder nothing was clean! Hotpoint have insisted over five visits that their computer testing equipment showed up no faults, but I have always argued that testing the machine for two minutes does not guarantee that sufficient water or correct temperature is being reached. I feel another phone call coming on!!

31st January: Well the scan went well this afternoon after I managed to drag him from his bed!! Of course we know nothing other than 'you should contact your doctor in a week to 10 days'. What a joke! However, I do know that the electronic reports are done virtually straight away and should be on Doc M's computer by late on Monday. I have spoken to Janet, my secretary friend, and she will keep her eye out for the report coming through ... put it in front of the German Maid (Doc M's day off Monday) and ask her to ring us just to let us know if there is anything significant there. Then we can talk it through with Doc M on Tuesday. Picked up fish and chips on the way back ... absolutely gopping, so they went straight in the bin and then Alan fell asleep. So he's in bed and settled and Gill is due in at 10pm. I'll take a half dose sleeper tonight and try to get a second good night.

1st February: After much anticipation of seeing Brummie following his long trip to New Zealand, it was very unfortunate that he, too, has succumbed to a chest infection and Lynn to a dreadful cold. All visits have to be postponed until everyone is clear of infection. However Alan was only capable of being out of bed for about half an hour to eat his meal and is generally feeling very low in view of the scan which was done yesterday. Monday seems so far away!

2nd February: This particular date always upsets me somewhat. It is my son's 41st birthday. Spencer, who I have not seen now for a full five years, and prior to that particular visit on my 60th, I hadn't see him in nearly 10 years. Relationships may break down, but the love a mother has for her child will never wane. I have missed out on the pleasure of two grandsons whom I've never met and Spencer has missed out on what have been the happiest years of my life. All very sad.

Giv and Perce came over to visit but having to see Alan in bed as he was not feeling well enough to be up and about other than for 15 minutes in the kitchen to have some lunch. He decided to spend the afternoon in the lounge, but could hardly keep his eyes open and slept most of the time. When he was ready to go to bed the process of getting there was almost impossible .. he has no strength in his legs and had to stop 4 or 5 times in the short distance to the bedroom. Once in bed he slept for a very short while before waking and staying awake all evening. I just wish he could stay awake whilst we're in the same room!

3rd February: Apprehension is the word of the day as we anticipate pretty devastating news about the scan later today. I've not slept well having been up twice during the night to make drinks. I just can't envisage this having a good outcome.

Just after 9am the phone went and it was my friend Janet at the surgery. Much to our delight the scan is clear. Nothing showing in the liver and no fluid in the abdomen! However, Alan is full of bowel gases!! Now officially named "Fart Arse"! This gave us a huge lift today. Will speak to Doc M when he's back at work ... he's going to have a field day with this news!!

Have spoken to Palliative Care Nurse and requested another two nights be covered by sitters. She will put the request in and be in touch as soon as she knows.

Alan had an appointment at dentist to deal with a small filling. It was a nightmare to get him there – told me not to take the portable oxygen as there would be some at the surgery, but that was not when we needed it! He needed it in the car! Just a few steps to get him into the surgery and he was on the point of collapse. After having his tooth dealt with the return journey was even worse. I really don't think we're going to be able to do this again.

4th February: Alan has now decided that he wants to go into respite next Monday, 10th February, so I have spent the day checking with the home, ordering oxygen supplies for him and generally putting things in place that will be needed.

5th February: My birthday ... now a fully qualified pensioner at 65 with a licence to be obnoxious, push into queues, and vent my wrath on whom so ever should upset me! Also the release of bodily gas is now acceptable, apparently, and even expected! No need to clamp the cheeks together in company anymore!!

Today was a very big 'non-event'. Alan did his best to be up and about whilst Givvi and Percy visited, but then soon after his tea he was ready for bed and I spent the whole of the evening on my own. Never mind ... it's only another day. But I think I will introduce him to moonpig.com so at least he could choose his own cards!

6th February: An opportunity to relax for a couple of hours as Janet had asked me out to lunch. We stayed close to home and went to The Crown at Hopton Wafers – nice food but very quiet. Gave us the chance to have a chat though. She has bought a little cottage way out in the countryside outside Leominster, and she is looking forward to moving in soon. We also talked about her retirement from work which she has been planning for over two years now, having stayed on longer than expected in an effort to get extra funds behind her to boost her pension. Although counting the weeks, she has still not mentioned her plans to anyone at work. She has worked for the NHS for nearly 30 years, the majority of time in our local surgery. No doubt it will be a shock to all concerned when she hands in her notice.

It would seem sod's law has been in action whilst we were out. Alan passed out in the shower leaving Gill to deal with him on her own. She grabbed the oxygen bottle from the kitchen which promptly ran out – so she had to get him to the bedroom to use the supply there. Unbelievable – the first time I've been out socially in 15 months and this has to happen!

I called in to see Doc M to get some sleeping pills to help whilst we have the night sitters. Unfortunately, the ones he has given me seem to be totally ineffective, so I'll have to let him know next time I see him.

7th February: Today was the long awaited visit from Brummie and Lynn after their trip to New Zealand. It was really good to see them after this amount of time. As Brummie still has no car Maz and Pip were good enough to bring them down and luckily Alan was far better than the last time they saw him a month ago. They left after a couple of hours which is just about the maximum time that Alan can cope with visitors these days. Oddly enough it was warm enough to sit in the conservatory ... the first time we've done that in mid-winter!

Once he had eaten his tea, Alan was very much ready for his bed. Rhianna is our sitter for tonight and hopefully she will have few or no problems.

8th February: The day when no one is due to call at the house. I've taken advantage to get some more washing done now that the machine seems to be working for the first time in 2 years! The rest of the day we spend quietly together watching films. We decided we would have a lazy day tomorrow as well ... don't intend to get up till lunchtime!

9th February: Alan did not emerge from his bed until 1pm and was falling asleep in the lounge for the next couple of hours. At 4pm he wanted to go to bed and slept until 11.30pm. I was then up and down till close on 2am before he finally settled again. Unfortunately it would seem by the sound of his chest that the infection has not gone away, but has just been lying quietly in the background for a week. I immediately gave him a double his dose of steroids and started him on another course of antibiotics – these have always been Doc M's instructions rather than waiting to speak to him. As he is always day off on a Monday, that would mean best part of two days before I can speak to him, so we felt it was better to act quickly and try to get on top of things.

10th February: Whether he felt well enough or not Alan was determined to get into the nursing home today for his week in respite care. Gill came in and showered him at 1pm and helped me get his scooter into the car. It had taken me all morning just to make sure he would have everything he would need .. one large holdall, one flight bag, one freezer bag and one carrier bag plus his banana pillow! We arrived there just after 2pm.. The only thing I had forgotten was his shower sponge!

"The Palace" is on the outskirts of Ludlow, next door to a motel and a pub! It is very new and is akin to a hotel inside. All the rooms are large with their own en-suite shower room. There is a locking safe in the wardrobe and two locking drawers in the furniture .. plenty of room for everything he has taken. The admission admin was a total shambles. They took photos of his elbow with the bedsore and another couple of bruises he has (thin skin due to steroids, we think). They wanted a complete itinerary of what he had taken with him.

Alan's drugs are always a bit of a problem! During all his hospital visits the drugs' regime has never been correctly achieved, so this time I decided to dispense the daily doses into appropriate purpose-made containers. Well, what do you know? I can't do right for doing wrong!! The management wanted to know that Alan could identify every pill, knew what they were for and when to take them. Their names and description had to be written down and then Alan had to sign to say that he would self-medicate during his stay and be responsible to locking them in the safe. I do hope he gets it right – I can't do any more. For over three years now Alan has trusted me to dispense his pills for him and has never had to identify any of them. He recognizes the pretty ones, but several of them are white Aspirin-looking tablets of varying sizes with no chance of identification if you're not used to handling them. We'll just have to see how he gets on!

I left him at 5.45pm tucking into his evening meal. I did try to phone him later in the evening but the phone was already switched off. I can only hope that he has a good night.

11th February: Have to thank Givvi for all the work she did in Alan's bedroom today .. half packets of biscuits, lighters, cigarettes, tissues - that have all made their way down the back of the bed! She's cleaned all the skirting boards and the carpet and the whole room looks like a new pin - all done whilst I'm trying to sort out 'stuff' on the phone. Great help! The rest of the place is ***** but at least he has a lovely bedroom to come home to!!

He's settled in well, facilities lovely, food good (but not enough for him) ... but there is a definite lack of bodies – staff! No-one has time to be with you, even for just five minutes! He was asked this morning if he needed help with showering and dressing ... yes, please ... As of 7pm when I left, he was still waiting! The response time to buzzers is disgraceful - we're talking 10-15 minutes, if you're lucky. If Alan was to buzz it would be because of a breathing problem and in need of urgent help ... he'd be dead before they got to him. I need to speak to someone during office hours, so that will have to wait until tomorrow. Without his scooter he would be confined to his room as it is a big place with long corridors - so he's happy to get out in to the garden where staff have shown him the place to hide whilst having his ciggies! I took him some 'munchies' to keep him happy this evening, and I've come home with a list of requests for tomorrow! So far ... so good!! Sleeping tablet for me tonight - one that works! I was up three times making drinks last night - couldn't switch off!

12th February: I had a really good night's sleep after taking a tablet. Phone went at just after noon .. woke me up!

It was Alan! He's fine apart from the lack of service! No shower yesterday. No shower today. He slept in the clothes he was in as no-one came to help. Buzzer response times still very poor (for others, not him). I have phoned the home and spoken to the nursing manager and have lit the blue touch paper! I explained that should Alan be buzzing, it will be a breathing problem, and if they want to leave him 10 minutes before responding .. he will be dead. I think she understood! Should she not react to all I've told her by the time I visit tonight, then verbal lashings will follow! I've slept ... I'm alert, and I'm certainly ready for them! The price being paid for this week's care is not to be sniffed at and in reality the service should be first class in all respects. I know it's not our own money involved ... but that really isn't the point!

The weather is still dreadful with water lying on the roads everywhere. Too dangerous for Jason and Jo to make the trip this afternoon, apparently, so I will have to go in early ... kill two birds with one stone!

By the time I got to the home just after 3pm and spoke with the manager, everything requested had been put in place! I argued there was little point in home assessments being undertaken if no one was going to read the notes! When I got to Alan's room there were three members of staff with him sorting out! He now has a neck buzzer and everything else will be done. I'll be here for a couple more hours and then back home. Collars have been felt and flooding apologies have been received! Time will tell ....

We managed to have a very pleasant few hours together .. I picked up a Chinese on the way home and was back in the house before 7pm.

Another tablet tonight and I really should be catching up on all the lost sleep of recent weeks!

13th-16th February: As the days went on Alan settled in and was far happier other than the fact that not one of the staff seemed aware of what was wrong with him. There were several discussions with staff, a chat with the deputy home manager, and finally I think we have got across the points which needed to be highlighted. This was always going to be his most difficult visit and I'm sure things will be a lot different next time he goes there in a couple of months' time.

There is no doubt that this is the very best option we have for respite, as far as we know. Alan met a lady who had searched for weeks within this area for the best nursing home for her son, suffering with MS. She had seen some awful sights and some homes she had not even got in through the front door. She could not believe her luck when she found "The Palace". All the fees are very similar so therefore it makes sense to be at a nursing home which in every respect appears to be a high class hotel with nurses and carers – free access visiting – communal or private dining – large rooms all with en-suite – lounges and cafeterias – and in the summertime, lovely gardens which are easily accessed. There is no doubt that we would ever find anything better.

17th February: I fetched Alan home and although he has enjoyed himself, he is glad to be back. Only downside of the day was when the heating stopped working and there is a warning light visible on the boiler. In the pitch black and pouring rain I made my way to the oil tank in the garden and carried out my trusty 'broom handle' test! As I suspected we have no oil!! With the system switched off, I have left and emergency request for oil on the supplier's answerphone and hope they can deliver tomorrow.

18th February: No oil, no heat, no hot water. Had a quick word with the oil suppliers and they will do their best for first thing tomorrow after which I can get our service engineer in to service and reset the boiler. By tomorrow night we should be back to normal .. hopefully.

Apart from Alan suffering very bad pains in his back and being very breathless at times, he has had a good day but got very annoyed with me when I fell asleep for an hour late afternoon. Bottom line is, this is a regular time when I feel tired, but once through it I can be awake till 2am easily. I can't help it .. it's just how it is for me at the moment!

We managed to stay up until 11pm tonight ... haven't done that for months.

19th February: We've had a very odd day! Out of the blue Alan has had just a wonderful day!! Full of life, humour, good mobility .. bit on the breathless side, but nothing to get excited about. He had his nebulizer whilst still in bed. Showered, dressed and still feeling good. He had three or four shots of Oramorph yesterday and he needed one this morning too. His tail bone is really playing up this week. So what was so very different about today to make this happen? We racked our brains and really didn't come up with anything. By mid-afternoon and with a sitter in, I was ready to head off to town when I realized that I'd not taken any of my tablets today ... and guess what? I had totally forgotten to give Alan any of his meds this morning too as the oil delivery and the heating engineer had arrived at the same time - totally throwing my routine to pieces! Makes you wonder though, doesn't it?

20th February: As suspected, there was no chance of two good days on the run! Alan has been very tired again, has needed plenty of Oramorph, is breathless again and the pain in his back is not receding. Givvi has had a very unsettling couple of days and she's been on the phone in tears a couple of times. I really wish I could just get in the car and go to visit her. She could do with her Mum at times like this and it makes me feel so guilty that I can't drop everything and go to see her.

Becky, our Thursday night sitter, arrived a little early and it was nice for her to be able to see Alan still up and about. So again I have a night off and don't have to worry about anything – have to make the most of it!

21st February: Alan has been in a lot of pain today, refusing to take extra pain meds and he's being grumpy into the bargain. After having his shower he decided it was time to clean brasses again – how many times does this job have to be done? I always end up having to finish off the job and do the clearing up. I wouldn't care if I never see another piece of brass ever again!

This afternoon we have test driven a new Mitsubishi car which Alan wants to buy for me. It really is beautiful and much more sensible for us in view of all our present medical issues. He has ordered one! It's due to be delivered during the first week of April. I suggested we left this until later in the year, but he says he wants to see us enjoy it a little before he's gone. He tells me it will last me a lifetime. He has wanted to see some benefit from the money he has been awarded .. and you can't blame him really. It's every girl's dream to have a car bought for her .. how exciting!

Giv and Perce came over for the evening and I cooked us all a Chinese which everyone enjoyed.

Luckily we have a night sitter again as I am just so physically tired today, I certainly need to get my body into bed.

End of Year 3: During the last week of February we experienced some bad days .. and some even worse! The daily routine is always very much the same but I am finding I have less and less time to carry out essentials within the house as Alan depends on me more and more for every little thing he needs.

All the brasses were produced again and re-polished and all we need now is half a day of sunshine so that they can be put outside and sprayed with lacquer. Then they will never have to be touched again. Yippee! Then there was the arrival in the post of two huge wooden Buddha heads .. 14 inches tall, which needed some attention before being polished and now Alan is toying with the idea of sinking a gemstone in each forehead! Any of these jobs end up being mine these days as he has no breath to actually do anything, shaking hands, and very little patience! I am rapidly becoming a 'Jack of all trades'!

The end of year blood tests disappeared in the system, so fresh blood was taken on 28th February. The results are not too encouraging – last half a dozen have looked like this in the PSA department ... 0.6; 1.9; 3.6; 2.4; 2.5; 3.8 ... and therefore we now have an established upward trend. We are assuming that very soon (presumably after one more test with an increased result) Alan will need to see the Oncologist again to have something extra prescribed in an attempt to reduce the figures and continue with the fire-fighting.

Alan continues his fight on both fronts but it looks as if the Prostate Cancer is now progressing, and the indications are that his heart is also deteriorating. These first three years have been horrendous and I can't foresee that changing in year 4 .. but we can but live in hopes!

Chapter 24: Looking for closure in Year 4

3rd March: Not a good day! Alan has suffered two seizures today and has been on the point of fainting a couple of times. Usual story – his blood pressure is in his boots and his heart rate climbing up the scale. Had to insist he laid on his bed with his legs raised and taking oxygen until his blood pressure rose to a more acceptable level. These seizures always wipe him out and he falls asleep immediately afterwards. I've made the call for Doc M to visit in tomorrow.

4th March: At 1am I've just been up attending to another 'do' with Alan. One biscuit crumb went down the wrong way and all hell broke loose! He's already had two or three incidents during the day! Doc M came out in very compassionate mood today .. feels the upward trend in PSA will need to be looked at by the Oncologist, but think we'll wait for next test. We're keeping a close eye on things so it's not going to get away from us.

As I saw Alan clasp his chest at the start of one of his seizures yesterday, Doc M now has the confirmation he wanted that these 'events' are a direct result of a heart event rather than lack of oxygen to the brain (just a very subtle difference). He is now convinced Alan is having mini heart attacks and that heart's deterioration is gathering pace confirmed by the almost permanent swollen ankles and hands. The breathlessness is worse than ever .. he can only walk two steps without stopping to control his breathing. So to help with this situation we have an electric wheelchair being delivered tomorrow.

The desktop computer has decided to die and many hours have been wasted attempting to resurrect it. My last resort was to re-format it and start again. 36 hours after the breakdown I am back at the same point .. it's not working. After several more hours it becomes obvious that a Windows update has totally wiped out an essential piece of software. Once the update is uninstalled, hey presto, we're back working. So much work. So much time wasted ... and all so unnecessary. However, this has all made me very aware of the problems we're having with the internet and our wireless connection, so have ordered a new adaptor and high speed cable to try and improve matters.

5th March: The wheelchair delivery was an hour late and the poor old guy – so called 'engineer' – had no chance of getting this into the house on his own. Whilst helping him I managed to get my little finger well and truly pinched and blistered – ouch! It looks great and I'm sure it will help Alan a lot within the house. May have to move some furniture a bit to accommodate it but will be worth it!

Alan was feeling somewhat better this morning and decided today was the day to lacquer all of the brasses we have been continually cleaning for almost two years in preparation for this. Wednesday is always my 'helping hands' day and gives me a bit of time to get out to the shops, etc. By the time I have everything done and manage to get out I have just over an hour before I run out of time. Next week things will be different … I keep saying that!

Alan was so tired after his busy day getting the brasses done, he was in bed by 6.15pm and slept all evening which gave me a bit of a chance to install more bits on the computer.

6th March: Big day for us today – our solicitor is due to visit to explain the current situation with our litigation case and to take instructions from Alan.

Unfortunately Alan feels most unwell and is staying in bed. His shower has been cancelled.

Margarita, our solicitor, arrived on time and after a full explanation and consideration of the situation, Alan has instructed her not to settle the claim until after his death as the claim could be worth twice as much then .. unless an offer is made which can't be refused! She asked him outright how long he felt he had left .. his response was 'three months'. There is no doubt that he is going downhill, but I truly hope he's wrong on this.

After she had left, Alan managed to get up for a couple of hours but was dozing the whole time. Once he had eaten his tea, he was off to bed again. I got to bed about midnight and Alan was on the buzzer before 5am – reckons he's not been to sleep yet. Becky should have been working tonight but she had such a nasty cough and cold we had to send her home.

So here I am, again, at some ungodly hour, wide awake and alert listening to Alan snoring his head off as he has finally got to sleep.

7th March: A busy hectic day – not sure where the time went but I knew I was looking forward to 10pm and the arrival of Rhianna who does our Friday night sleep in. Time to hand over the responsibilities for a few hours .. take a sleeping tablet and have a good night's sleep .. with a lie in on Saturday morning.

8th March: I seem to have spent the whole day doing something for Alan, in particular picture frame edges to use on the base of the huge brass lions which have now been lacquered and eventually ready for display. More work to be done on these tomorrow. Did manage to get one load of washing on the line as the weather has improved somewhat. Alan has knocked himself out today and is so very tired ended up in bed very early.

I spent several evening hours trying to get the desktop computer back to a working level. There is definitely a problem with the version of Windows Vista pre-installed on it so have opted to buy a copy of Windows 7 in the hopes that will put a few things right.

It was 3am before I managed to fall asleep and Alan was on the buzzer by 6am! I'm taking the opportunity to watch several episodes of 'House of Cards' .. really enjoying it!

12th March: Legal Team meeting and conference call in Birmingham. Alan felt he didn't want to attend as he would lose his temper – good job really as there were two flights of stairs! - I don't know where to start ... so I'm not going to say much other than it was a very frustrating meeting. I kept my cool for nearly an hour during the conference call with the two 'expert' witnesses talking to our Counsel who was in the room .. then I had to challenge each of them on a couple of points. The GP specialist tells us that the PSA test is a useless tool in the diagnosis of PCa, but later contradicts himself, and that ED naturally occurs in men of a certain age! Nothing to do with Prostate Cancer! Oh, and NICE have no guidelines on PSA tests. Good job I had a copy of the NICE guidelines with me stating any man aged over 50 is entitled to an annual PSA test if he requests it! The Onco specialist refuses to accept 3 different countries' findings on the relationship between HT and heart problems, even though published in BMJ and American Medical periodicals, totally dismissing one study which involved 76,500 PCa sufferers over a nine year period. She also insists that every Gleason 9 tumour (untreated) has a doubling time of 8-12 weeks - no more. She said that Alan did not have cancer in 2005 or in 2007! How the hell does she know? Good job these are only 'opinions' rather than fact! At one point I was sat there with my head in my hands. Both Alan and I knew there was a major problem with something back in 2005 and no-one knows their body better than the patient. I've argued my corner, but did ask Counsel, after the phone call ended, what planet they found these two specialists on!! The GP specialist is going to be replaced – will find another one who doesn't want to sit on the fence! We may have to get a Cardiologist involved if we can't squeeze an immediate offer out of the other side. Both the solicitor and Counsel said "this just doesn't feel right" - referring to what these experts had come up with! Our solicitor said that if Alan's treatment was documented in a newspaper article, the public would be absolutely horrified. So it's the waiting game again I'm afraid.

13th March: Givvi came to help me this morning. She cleared out and cleaned the whole of the conservatory. What a great help it was. I managed to clear the rest of the bedding ironing before Gill arrived. She had not even got Alan into the shower before Brummie and Lynn arrived. Lovely to see them again, but Alan was really too tired to cope. Doc M returned my call and has agreed Alan needs to go back onto the augmenting antibiotics along with an increase in steroids. This damn chest infection will be the death of him one day.

Becky the night sitter is here tonight .. at least I know I won't have to get up at 4am or some other stupid time just to make a cup of tea! Sweet dreams!

14th March: The slightest movement today has caused Alan severe breathlessness and the need for oxygen. It's becoming more and more distressing. Hopefully when the anti-bios kick in this will improve.

19th March: Feeling guilty tonight that I've not been writing our continuing story, but the fact is that the past few days seemed to have rolled from one to the next without notable changes. Alan is continuing with the antibiotics and there does seem to be an improvement in his chest. The daily routine doesn't change much and nothing exciting is happening.

Today with the help of Rhianna much of the housework has been done including some windows and curtains – but it has used up all my respite hours for the week and I didn't even get out of the door!! Yesterday was all about cleaning silver candlesticks and wall plaques! I never seem to be able to do anything that I would choose to do.

This evening I have spent some time making preparations for the Ladies day out next week in Stratford upon Avon. All the mugs have been delivered but were not boxed. It's surprising how long it takes to make up just 25 of these mug boxes! They are now all packed up with the little extras inside. However, this ended up taking a couple of hours and even though Alan was in bed, he queried why I had not been down to see him, what had I been doing and was I now finished! He really doesn't like me having something of my own to do! Still waiting for the ribbon bookmarks to arrive which have been in the post over a week now ... apparently. I paid for them on the 7th but it would seem they didn't get into the post until the 11th – second class too! The girl who has printed them seemed a little unwilling to help a couple of days ago, but if they have not arrived by Friday then she will have to make them again and get them in the post a bit smartish.

25th March: Started off such a good day. New car has arrived at the garage and can be delivered on Friday. I managed to get a good enough deal on the motor insurance and Motability have agreed to take their car back 10 months early – so that will disappear next Wednesday. All good.

Then we had a phone call from one of the district nurses trying to organize Alan's next respite care home visit as the Palliative Care Nurse has gone off on a week's leave without telling anyone – well not us! Alan is going back to the same home, for the same length of time, and has already been told that he qualifies for six visits a year. This will be visit number 2. Continuing Heathcare, in their wisdom, are asking for the care home to produce a costing! Is it really likely to have changed significantly in eight weeks? What a waste of peoples' time. I bet you we will get to Friday of this week and still not have it confirmed.

Janet phoned this evening .. had a good chat about the house she is planning to buy and the piece of land she is trying to sell. Then we got onto the medical stuff and I said we were due to see Doc M on Thursday as Alan was to have his Zometa infusion. I had phoned last Friday and spoken to Dawn (his secretary) who confirmed she would put Alan on the visiting list for that day. Well ... Doc M is on leave this week ... seems he's not even told his secretary!! She is not in the office tomorrow, so will speak to Jan and see what she has been able to sort out – I need to get blood results tomorrow as Alan may have to go back to the Oncologist if his numbers have climbed again.

Tomorrow is my day out with the Ladies .. hopefully that will go to plan!

26th March: Having taken great care to book the carers for today and getting extra hours, I managed to get away on time at 10am to get to Stratford-on-Avon for mid-day after picking up Givvi in Worcester. There was a dozen of us at the pub, so we had a very cosy extra-long lunch. Everyone had a lovely time. The ladies gave me a huge display of flowers and they had all been pleased with their little gifts and the mugs I had designed. They would like to use the same pub again – The Old Thatch Tavern – as everything was first class.

During a phone call with Janet that evening we have arranged for Alan to have his Zometa treatment next week when Doc M is back at work.

Alan's blood results today are not encouraging and actually confirm what had been concerning us for several weeks. His PSA has risen again to 4.2 having doubled in about seven weeks and his ALP has made a huge jump from 63 to 104 in the same seven weeks. This all points to the cancer 'being active and on the move again', in which case we will need to see the Onco again soon – no doubt this will all be at the top of the agenda when we see Doc M.

28th March: Today saw the arrival of my long awaited new car which Alan has bought for me! Maisy! She's a beautiful pearlized cherry red, Mitsubishi ASX 4-D with a 2.3 auto diesel engine … just the right tool for living up on this hill during the winter! Now we should be able to escape whatever the weather. Can't wait to get out in her!

1st April: Doc M is on his first day back at work after a week's holiday .. spending time at home delivering lambs! The weather was so lovely today Alan had been sitting outside for an hour in the sunshine, so Doc M did his infusion in the garden! Very pleasant afternoon. We discussed Alan's numbers and Doc M will contact the Oncologist for advice on the likely next step to be taken in the cancer treatment.

2nd April: Returned Insignia to the garage .. still with 150 miles of fuel in it! I had desperately tried to use up as much as I could over the last few days! Although I had cleaned out the inside of the car and it certainly needed a good wash, as it was pouring with rain all morning up until I set off, the garage had to have it back dirty! We are still waiting to hear any progress from the Continuing Healthcare team in respect of Alan's next visit to "The Palace". We've had to change the dates again as there was so little time to give Gill notice for the girls. We have decided he should go in on Easter Tuesday, 22nd April, for one week. He will have his new electric chair to use which he is looking forward to. He seems much happier about going in this time and I have made a comic poster to put on the door so that the staff will have no excuse in knowing what is wrong with him and what help he requires. Hopefully they will have changed their ways somewhat at the home ... but if not, then we'll pull him out of there.

3rd April: Bit of a red letter day! My new car has been here almost a week and today it got its first outing. Alan wanted to call in at Brightwell's, the auction house in Leominster, and then to B & Q to pick up some more shelves for his bedroom. Weather wasn't great but it was a nice trip out. I can see it's going to take me quite a time to get used to all the different controls in the new car!

6th April: I am just totally knick-knacked. Alan decided he wanted the three new shelves in his bedroom done today. Well, I know he can't deal with it anymore, so guess who got the job? Whilst Giv and Perce were over yesterday sorting out the garage, I had three 1.2mtr shelves and 18 bracket pieces to stain .. three times each. Even after Giv left I was on my feet for another three hours. Then of course he wants feeding! Today started well ... huh ... he buzzed me at 8.45am having spilled a complete cup of tea over the bed. Therefore, no lie in .. had to get up.

First job was to put the two halves of the shelf brackets together. Got the wall marked up and holes drilled for two of the shelves. Disaster! Two holes go at the top and one at the bottom ... guess who had done it the other way round? I managed to get over that by drilling other holes below the double ones and filling in the ones above. It won't show by the time I'm finished!! Had to do a bit of clever manoeuvring with cocktail sticks in the holes but two shelves up and one to go tomorrow. In the middle of it all he wanted feeding ... and at the end of it he wanted feeding! Then he's ready for bed - which I changed whilst the pie was cooking .. and he then tells me not to be long before I go to bed.

When am I meant to wind down .. perhaps even get the washing in the machine or what's already dried, ironed? Housework .. forget it. It's a full time job being his carer .. let alone taking on the DIY stuff as well? I think I may be in Tramadol heaven shortly, my back feels 106!!

8th, 9th, 10th April: After a good visit with the Palliative Care Nurse on Monday afternoon Alan became very tired during the early evening. He went to sleep about 8pm and apart from the odd half hour awake he has slept for some 63 hours! How does he do that!

I asked Doc M to visit on 10th and he feels that the dreaded chest infection is back .. or never went away in the first place. Alan will have to continue on antibiotics as a permanent fixture and take increased numbers of steroids initially to try and get rid of this. We've also heard that Alan has an appointment with the Oncologist on 14th and Doc M is insisting on hospital transport in case Alan has not improved by then.

14th April: Today has been interesting. Ambulance transport was on time and dropped us off at the cancer unit at Kidderminster Hospital. Flinders! What a name for a huge doctor with his hair scraped back into a pony tail about a foot long!! When he looked at all the notes he was quite surprised that Alan had made it this long!!

Well, there's good news and there's bad news .. as we expected. He thought Doc M's timing of the referral was excellent in view of Alan's heart complications and thought it was a wise move even though Alan's numbers are still low. Decisions have been made .. Alan cannot have chemo (not that he would have agreed to it anyway) ... reckon it would kill him stone dead! RT is not the answer in this case . He is not well enough to tolerate Abiraterone. Enzalutamide? Not well enough for that either, and anyway requires chemo first - so that's also off the list. The obvious thing we had all considered was Casodex. No! Apparently that doesn't behave well with Cyprostat! The list of options is fast running out!! Then the Registrar pulled the rabbit out of the hat ... double the daily dose of Cyprostat. We weren't expecting that one!

Should have the same results as would have been expected from Casodex Return in three months. Not a lot going for him treatment wise when this fails but for the time being just keep fire-fighting is the message we were given.

Now I know for many others given this news it would be totally devastating, but our approach is a bit unconventional and Alan's comment was - hope the heart heard they'd given him 3 months!! On the question of HT being the likely cause of the heart failure ... yes, most likely (as we thought) .. but the most likely culprit would be the Cyprostat rather than the Zoladex - another surprise!

It's all good .. we're happy enough tonight and have had one of those silly half hours recalling little memories and laughing till we've cried .. jaws aching, the full works! Magic!!

15th April: Oh dear .. only me!! Here - have a giggle at my expense!!

Life on The Hill Part 667: Alan has slept most of the day and really didn't want any tea. So I quickly prepared a ready-made macaroni cheese for myself. Quite enjoyed it. He wants ice cream .. so I have a cheap version Cornetto, the sort with choc sauce and nuts on top. Suddenly I'm aware of a very hard bit of nut in my mouth ... wrong! Tooth! A whole one ... snapped straight off at gum level!! Right at the front at the top, no. 2 tooth.

So I'm now sitting here doing a very good impression of Nanny McPhee. The upside, of course, is that I can now smoke and type with both hands with the ciggie stuck in the gap!! However, there was a shard still attached which was giving me an injection on the inside of my lip every time I moved my mouth ... I can fix that! Out comes the Dremel!! Sorted! I'm off to see Pete the Prod tomorrow ... wonder if he could stick it back together with superglue?!

Couldn't make it up, could you?!

17th April: We had a new gardener/maintenance man start work for us today. He seems keen enough to get his new business off the ground and was recommended by Postie Lin. However, his equipment is not up to the job and he ended up having to use our mower. We'll have to get the ride on mower checked over and then he can use that and he will get the work done in half the time.

News back from Continuing Healthcare team .. we have been refused any extra night sitters as they consider there is no significant change in Alan. The fact that Doc M wanted the extra nights so that I could get more rest seems to have carried no weight at all. How to be made to feel worthless in one quick phone call!!

18th April: Alan has been a real waspy Mr. Grumpy today

and all I can think is that he is in more pain but refusing to admit it. I have been doing some work on walking sticks he wants to complete but with the shaking hands with which he now suffers very badly at times, he has no hope of doing these things himself.

Becky, one of our night sitters, in tonight, so I shall be taking a sleeping tablet and hope I can get some proper sleep.

19th April: Ah ... now we know why Mr. Waspy Grumpy was around yesterday! Alan didn't wake up till 2pm complaining bitterly about his throat. One look in the mouth, which now resembles the top of a meringue pie, confirms the oral thrush is back ... only twice as bad as last time. When I can get him to stay awake long enough I can start treating it! ... and yes, I did have a good night ... eight glorious undisturbed hours - such a novelty!!

All Alan has wanted today has been drinks of tea, ice cream and sleep, so I've seen very little of him!

20th April: Easter Sunday and we are due to visit Givvi and Perce for lunch. However, I had a problem getting Alan to wake and an even bigger problem getting him out of bed and dressed. Within 10 minutes he announced he was not well enough to go, so his bed was made and he was back in it and asleep in the next 10 minutes! Such a shame as I had been really looking forward to a half day out and actually got very upset about it.

Givvi and Percy had gone to a lot of trouble for us and instead of the lovely turkey dinner she had prepared I ended up with a bowl of porridge!

Alan did not surface for the rest of the day.

21st April: Alan has had a bit more life in him today .. just enough to have a shower, be dressed and sit in the conservatory. His throat is still painful and it is now affecting his voice. Tea and ice cream have been the favourites of the day again, although he did manage to have some beans on toast – first he has eaten in three days.

I am hoping he will be well enough to go into the care home tomorrow for respite .. I desperately need a break! The biggest challenge about tomorrow will be getting the new wheelchair into the back of the car! We've bought the ramps but will I master how to use them? If not the chair has to be stripped down into four parts ... and so far I've only managed to get it into three!

I have most of Alan's bits and pieces ready on the spare bed .. I'll pack it all in the morning. What am I talking about .. it is morning – 5.45am and I've not had a wink of sleep yet! Hungry and ready for breakfast!!

22nd April: Although Alan still has raging oral thrush, he is determined to go into respite today. I spent the morning getting everything into bags – we had vowed not to take as much as last time, so how on earth have we ended up with four bags plus two cylinders of oxygen?

Having spent a fortune on ramps, I was instructed not to deconstruct the new wheelchair but to power it up the ramps. However, this has to be done in reverse otherwise it would be impossible to reach the controller! After a few well-chosen words and several bruises the chair was eventually in the car! The bags were piled into any available space and before I could catch my breath, Alan had set the house alarm and was ready for the off!

Ten minutes later I was unloading everything in reverse order at the rest home! There was so much sweat involved you

would have thought I'd just emerged from a sauna! We were both pleasantly surprised at how the atmosphere in the home appears to have changed. Everyone is more friendly and attentive. Alan is room 13 which is a garden room with access directly to the outside gardens .. what a bonus!!

Having put everything away and set up the TV and tea making equipment, I was ready for home! Let's hope this all goes to plan!

23rd April: Givvi arrived early to help me reorganize the furniture in the conservatory and lounge. Took several hours of pushing and pulling involving plenty of sweat, but the re-arranged rooms look much better. All I need is a couple of new lights and a rug. Will start searching for them on the internet and then talk to Alan about what we will buy.

I've had an appointment with the dentist to have impressions taken .. first appointment in a series of four to get this new plate made. That all went without a hitch.

Alan has settled well in "The Palace" ... a resident he met last time, Miranda, was very pleased to see him again. She had a stroke 11 years ago when she was only 54 which took her speech and use of one side. She too rides around in an electric wheelchair and no doubt the two of them together will be lethal! It's amazing how much can be communicated when one half of the conversational couple can't talk. They get on really well.

24th April: Ian, our new gardener, arrived before 9am. Today's job was fence painting. At the moment, he is only working for us for three hours a week so it will take some time to catch up on three years of 'neglect'. I went off to the hairdressers during the afternoon to get my colour put back in.

Arrived later than hoped down at "The Palace" but Alan seems to be quite content and had spent the afternoon sitting outside in the sun. This throat seems to be somewhat better and he had enjoyed a visit from his Palliative Care Nurse and a student. I spent a couple of hours with him by which time he was very tired. He is certainly enjoying this visit far more than he did the first.

25/26th April: The majority of my time during these two days has been frustratingly spent in vain attempts to get the carpet shampooing machine to work. I have stripped it down and checked all the moving parts and all seems well ... but it will not dispense the shampoo mix. Having wasted far too much time, I've given up on the thought of cleaning carpets.

Alan was particularly tired during my visit on Saturday and I got him into bed well before 7pm and he was ready to settle for the night. He asked if I would visit during the afternoon on Sunday and hopefully the sun would be shining so we could spend some time outside.

27th April: I arrived at "The Palace" at 3pm to find Alan asleep on the top of the bed still in his dressing gown. The staff informed me that he has not eaten anything since Saturday lunchtime. He did not wake up for more than five minutes during the 3 hours I was with him. I collected up as many clothes as possible and packed them to take home. I left him asleep just before 7pm.

28th April: I telephoned the home at 10am to ask how Alan had been overnight. They tell me that he is unwell and they are considering calling in a doctor and carrying out a urine test. I told them I would get straight in the car and make my way there.

When I arrive Alan is obviously very unwell. I declined the home's offer to call out a doctor. With Alan's complicated medical history it would be totally unfair to expect an outside doctor to be able to make any useful assessment. On days when Alan feels as bad as this the only place for him is in his own bed. I told the staff that I would be taking him home immediately and managed to pack up his room in about 10 minutes flat!

Having loaded the car with the help of the staff Alan managed to get to the car in his wheelchair which I abandoned at the home for later collection. I forgot one of the oxygen cylinders too!

When we arrived home, Alan told me that he felt so ill he thought he was dying. How awful it must be to feel like this. I was soon able to get him into his bed and comfy and there he stayed for the rest of the day until about teatime. He wanted to get up and have something to eat .. so feeling a bit better.

I tested his urine and his glucose level seems to be 'off the scale' so I telephone Doc M's secretary to voice my concerns. She will let him know before his visit tomorrow.

Neither of us has slept well .. I think the last cup of tea I made was at 4am. I really wish that night-time sleep came easier to us both.

29th April: Alan slept until very late morning but was up in plenty of time for Gill to come in for his shower. He's missed her over the past week. He didn't want lunch and was happy with drinks alone. Doc M arrived very late to give him his Zometa and Zoladex and we talked about the possibility of Alan having high glucose levels. He will instruct the District Nurse to call tomorrow morning to take bloods for tests. He feels Alan may have steroid induced diabetes which will be treatable and Alan may begin to feel somewhat better.

He also checked his calf which is very, very sore and thinks it is phlebitis rather than DVT. Chances are, I think, that it is a varicose vein and we'll just have to keep a close eye on it. Last item on the agenda

411

today is Alan ingrowing toe nail. Doc M says he will return on Thursday with the right tools to deal with it … oh dear!

I asked Doc M about Dihydrotestosterone levels and their possible effects on feeding Alan's prostate cancer even though his PSA level has dropped. Not surprisingly he has no idea of the significance of this or the fact that Alan's body hair is re-growing. This surely indicates that testosterone in one form or another is circulating the body again which is not good news on the cancer front as it will feed the cancer and add to the speed of any progression. I must do some more research to try and find answers.

30th April: Bone density scan for me today. Had to go all the way to Worcester and was given the results letter immediately to hand over to Doc M. Everything has deteriorated in the past 4 years especially my left hip and the part of my spine which had surgery. Well, I'll just have to learn to live with it!

1st May: Doc M arrived as promised armed with sharp scissors to deal with Alan's in growing toe nail. Although we had had Alan's toe covered in Emla cream and cling film I don't really think it made much difference as he screamed the place down! But it's done now and we are looking for a different 'foot' lady as we never had a problem before. Can't afford to have to go through this sort of thing on a regular basis.

We also got the results of the HbA1c blood test for diabetes. I don't think any of us needed three guesses to know how it would turn out. The numbers are horrendous … 98 mmol/mol, which equates to 11.1%, whereas the target figure is 31 or 5%. Doc M has prescribed a drug called Metformin which he tells us will bring the situation under some sort of control and hopefully make Alan feel less tired and allow his legs to work a little better! However, he tells us that the generally accepted daily testing will not be required … my feelings are that he has no great expectations of this situation improving much and that Alan already has enough to cope with. He has not even suggested any changes to his diet – which would be very difficult having told Alan for the past 3 years to eat what he likes, when he likes. Somehow I can't imagine Alan on a diet of peas, grapes, strawberries and bananas .. never going to happen!

2nd May: The only notable incident of today is that Alan had been very troubled with spinal bone pain yesterday. He took two small doses of Oramorph between 6pm and 9pm which took the edge off things. Then during the night he took 3 more 5ml doses. He slept really well! He had trouble getting up in time for Gill to shower him and was talking 'gobbledigook' ... obviously floating some 6 feet above the rest of us! He spent the rest of the day totally pain free .. but asleep mostly! Even trying to get him to eat his tea was quite comical!

Payment of Alan's benefits has suddenly stopped and during a conversation with the benefits' office it would seem he has been taken off the system! An urgent enquiry will be made and they will contact us early next week. Good job we're not wholly dependent on these payments otherwise we would be 'up sh*t creek without a paddle'!

I also phoned Onco, Dr. C's secretary to ask her to check if he would like a Testosterone test added to the blood test to be carried out before his next appointment. She will phone back next week.

3rd May: Alan continued to sleep most of the day and was still in slumber-land when Giv and Percy arrived as arranged. We had hoped to take them out for a meal to celebrate their 5th anniversary tomorrow .. but those plans had to be put aside. We had a Chinese meal from the local takeaway which was lovely .. made a nice change.

4th May: It would seem that Alan had a very bad night suffering from nightmares and consequently spent all of this beautiful sunny day dozing in the conservatory and was in bed before 7pm. Very quiet day for me!

5th May: Another Bank Holiday! .. and another very sleepy day when food was of no interest – other than ice cream. However, Alan's right leg, the one in which we are told he has phlebitis, decided to swell up past his knee and was huge by comparison to his left leg. His ankles and feet have been swelling for some time, but this is something new. I found some compression socks which he has worn for the afternoon and evening which seems to have stopped the aching that he had been experiencing. He has decided to keep them on overnight, but I will still need to phone Doc M in the morning ... after all, this could still be a clot, which I'm assuming cannot just be left to its own devices.

6th May: Reported Alan's leg to Doc M whose secretary immediately requests and urgent ultra-sound scan to ascertain whether or not this is a DVT. She hopes we will get a phone call today calling us in to the hospital. Doc M called up during the afternoon to prescribe some blood thinning tablets. Alan yelped as his leg was examined .. it really is very painful. Not sure he will be impressed by an ultra-sound scan with the probe being rubbed up and down the painful bits. As it happens we didn't receive the call so will have to wait until tomorrow.

Alan obviously felt very unwell around lunch time as he was fractious with Gill and me ... she's not really been on the receiving end before and was quite surprised by it all.

Having managed just about an hour's sleep last night, I'm hoping that tonight will be a little more restful. However, I find this latest problem more worrying than some of the others. The last thing I want to see happen is this clot (if that's what it is) break up rather than disperse.

Did he step on a Robin or shoot an Albatross? Can't believe this is all happening to him in such a short space of time.

7th May: What a nightmare this turned out to be! Phone calls I had waited in for all day yesterday came in the 20 minutes Alan was on his own as I had to get to the dentist and Maria was not arriving until 11am. When I got home he couldn't remember what had been arranged although he did remember who had called. Well, that's something I suppose! Spent the next half hour recalling folks.

The most important call was one for him to go for his scan today at 2.20pm. As Alan looks and feels so poorly today I phoned the doctors to arrange ambulance transport on a stretcher. Had a phone call back to say this was all confirmed and to be ready by about 1pm. Alan had decided he was not well enough for a shower so that was cancelled.

2pm - no transport has arrived. Have put scan on hold with hospital until I can take advice from Doc M who will be back in his office at 3pm. Struggled to get Alan dressed this morning as he is so unwell today (and being sick just to add to things) and I put him back in bed fully clothed! Will have to keep him in bed, I suspect, in case it is a clot and it decides to go wandering around - but I can see us ending up on a 999 to A & E if that's the only way! I could do with a Valium!

2.25pm Doc M was on phone ... during conversation ambulance arrived! Decided to go for scan then paramedics decided that 2 of them wouldn't be able to get Alan into ambulance - would need 3 of them (he weighs 16st.). So we didn't go for scan!! Transport went away! Doc M feels we must find out exactly what the problem is in the leg, so I phoned the Imaging Dept. to re-schedule. Can't do that! They will speak to Consultant tomorrow morning and I must phone 10.30a.m to see if they can fit him in tomorrow ... and depending on how he is, as to whether we go through this nightmare with ambulances again ... or I just pour him into the back seat of the car if I can get him up the 3 steps we have to get to the drive. He's been in bed all day ... half a piece of toast and two spoonful's of soup. Refusing to take Oramorph even though he is still in considerable pain. He got snappy. I got snappy back 'cos I've had it up to my eyeballs today ... and have a serious case of telephone ear!!!

Benefits office - he's fallen off the system at the end of three years of DLA payments. He does qualify for PIP and we have a letter telling us about increases ... BUT the letter telling us that he qualified for PIP was never issued ... and that's the piece of paper that generates the payments!! Phone call expected tomorrow a.m. Already two payments behind!

Alan woke at 10.30pm wanting rice pudding ... when he's finished that, I'll settle him down again and then I'm off to bed! Tomorrow is going to be hugely better than today ... please!

8th May: Scanning department phoned at 9.15am ... can we be there by 10.15am? When I stopped laughing, I asked if there was anything later ... 11am! Even that's going to be a challenge.

I think we may have got there on time had he not virtually collapsed as I was getting him to the car ... setting him up on oxygen and calming him down. We managed to get behind every Sunday driver on the road and when we had about eight miles to go he started vomiting ... pulled in, dealt with that. Off we go again then three miles out he was vomiting again. Arrived on department at 11.05am. I had to buy tissues and water at the little shop and when I returned they had taken him in for the scan. Seems if you're looking for a clot in the calf you only scan groin to knee! Yes, I wondered about that too! We double checked, but that's what was done. Apparently they would detect 'back pressure' in vein if there was a clot anywhere. Not convinced personally ... but who am I to say?! Had real problems getting him back from car into house ... then had to change bed as soaked again ... and he's gone straight to sleep. Palliative Care nurse due this afternoon and I have already spoken to Doc M on phone. Alan can stop taking the blood thinners now - they may be the cause of the vomiting. I am not doing this again ... if they want him anywhere then someone else will have to do the fetching and carrying 'cos I'm cream crackered now!

The hospital was 45 minutes away in traffic today even though it's only 20 miles. It's done now, but as I said before, if he's this poorly on another occasion, they will have to send transport if they want him in a hospital. I've been concerned all afternoon that no scan of the calf was done, but Alan tells me he could 'hear' the scan - like deep sea diving sounds (!) - so I have to assume that it was the sonic Doppler (?) test which sends a sound wave the complete length of the leg vein ... and if no echo comes back then there is no clot. I feel more at ease with it now. They said there was no thrombosis, etc., in his leg. Good news, but it's still painful and he is still feeling very poorly. His mobility is down to about 8' before he is gasping for breath, leaning on the wall and his legs begin to bend. Seems to me it's not going to be too long before he is confined to bed if this keeps up. He sat in the lounge for an hour tonight so he could inspect the new rug ... but then wanted to go back to bed. Again he's not had a meal ... can't tempt him with anything. He's had one mint this morning and an individual trifle this afternoon. My turn to sleep tonight .. Becky will be here at 10pm.

Benefits office - apparently a letter has been sent out today but she couldn't access it to tell me what it says .. but she did mention the word 're-assessment'! I told her if that is correct to expect my call on Monday so that I can give her a definition of 'terminal' as they obviously don't know what it means!!

12th May: Frustrating times on The Hill: I've had to have a quiet word with Alan today. He is in far more pain and I have tried to explain that 1 x 5ml Oramorph is just not going to deal with it. I said to him that he always knew that things were going to get worse. He said to me that he didn't ever imagine it would be this bad and that morphine just doesn't do it for him! Never likely to if you don't increase it along with the pain levels. I'm going to have to get Doc M in to review and to talk to Alan in words of one syllable about pain management, as I've told Alan I'm not prepared to just sit back and watch him in this sort of pain. So that issue is 'work in progress'.

Benefits: Have not yet received last Thursday's letter. I was quite shocked today when they phoned us!! However, what they have done is beyond belief. As of today, Alan is three payments missing ... all of the same amount and could quite easily be paid into the bank account. But being the Department of Work and Pensions it's not that simple ... DLA and PIP are paid in advance and we have to go right back to 19th February qualifying date (paid in on 12th) when he changed from DLA to PIP (both amounts exactly the same). They tell me they have paid everything into the bank on 8th May for the period from 19th Feb to 18th May (due on 11th May) and then we will have to pay back everything other than the 3 weeks they owe him ... but the amount they have told me they have paid in does not correspond to what it should be for that period ... it's short. So I have now had to calculate what the payment should have been ... what the shortfall is ... and therefore what has actually got to be repaid. They are phoning back tomorrow at 11am to see if we can get figures to match!!! As of 10 minutes ago, nothing has yet turned up in the bank!! Give me strength!! Watch this space!

14th May: I have a new smile today! All done ... no more visits to the dentist! Roots with hockey sticks on the end didn't help but all went well ... felt as if my eye was being dragged out, let alone a couple of teeth! No pain and plate fitted perfectly immediately after the two extractions. Lisping a bit, but only to be expected. It feels very strange ... last had something like this when I was 13 and had an old fashioned brace attempting to re-position my dog teeth ... 'attempting' being the significant word – it never did work!

The expected benefit payment finally found its way into the bank and we were expecting one letter confirming everything ... but we actually received four! That must mean four people trying to justify their position in the Department of Work and Pensions! Having spent about half an hour on the phone with one of their nice ladies, we have agreed upon a figure which has to be repaid to them after she confirmed what amount they were actually paying. I must have bamboozled her well as it would seem we are ending up almost £100 better off than we should have been. Makes a nice change to get one over on 'the system'!

Alan was unwell, no shower or sitter today .. will stay with him myself as Tesco delivery was due this afternoon. Actually he improved during the day and finally admitted he was pain free on just an extra 10mg of Zomorph. However, he did ask me to source a ripple air mattress so we agreed with one we found on eBay and hope that will help him in bed and whilst sitting in a chair. If it works in both locations then I think we will have to invest in a second one rather than stripping the bed every day in order to use it on a chair! Becoming sore is an increasing problem with his lack of mobility.

17th May: The benefits Alan was owed did finally turn up in the bank a couple of days ago but we now have to wait for a further letter to give us instructions as to where to repay two-thirds of it as an overpayment. Their system is so complicated – no wonder they have to employ so many people.

Alan has felt much better the past couple of days. We have increased his morphine very slightly so that he is virtually pain free and I feel that the Metformin has now kicked in properly. He is not so tired and his legs are not letting him down in the same way as they have been of late. I haven't noticed his hands shaking quite as much either. Seems to me that excess glucose in the system could be responsible for quite a few problems he's been experiencing for over 12 months. We should have looked at the possibility of diabetes many months ago ... hindsight is a wonderful thing, isn't it?

The guy who cut the hedge called in today to quote for cutting our grass as I'm none too sure about the one who is currently doing it. Anyway it's too small a job for him ... so the hunt continues. I've also left messages with three local domiciliary services companies in an effort to find a regular cleaner .. no doubt they will phone back next week.

Best day of the year so far, weather-wise ... it's been beautiful all day.

18th May: Saturday was such a brilliant day on so many levels ... we had wall to wall sunshine .. Alan was feeling so much better and managed a trip across to our garage and a short walk on the grass ... and we had a guy come and mend the tractor mower so that it is working again. Ready for use or sale!

Then Sunday has to arrive! Why is it that there always seems to be a price to pay for a good day? When he got up Alan asked me if he was 'grey'. At the time all I could tell him was 'no'. He looked OK to me, just a bit dark round the eyes. However, within an hour he was being very sick and was by then certainly very grey! Unfortunately this then set the tone for the whole day as he felt completely rubbish. Such a shame as the weather was glorious again.

I'm not sure what it is about weekends, but it seems we don't have good ones! Quite a busy week ahead so I'll live in hopes that he starts to feel better again.

20th May: The ripple air mattress has arrived and appears to be a really good buy at way less than £100, when most of this type has a starting price of £700 or more. Even if it only lasts a year its cost will only be about £1.50 a week which is a small price to pay for comfort.

Blood samples taken this morning .. we're keeping our fingers crossed that the new medication routine involving Cyprostat will have paid dividends.

21st May: Happy, talkin', talkin', happy talk!! You won't need three guesses to know who has a PSA figure 43% LOWER than 4 weeks ago when the contrived 'option 6' of doubling Cyprostat tablets was started! Well, yippee doo!!

Alan has started on Fentanyl patches today in an effort to reduce his tablet intake .. it will make a difference of 6 tablets a day, which he's pleased about. Not sure how they will work out but hopefully there shouldn't be a problem.

We had 'Natalie Nails' visit today. Our previous 'foot' lady appeared to be the cause of Alan's in-growing toenail so we decided not to invite her back. However, Natalie was an absolute gem and makes the other one look like a butcher. She has spent an hour gently trying to reach the root of this toenail problem and has got close .. but has decided to call back on Tuesday to complete the job. Alan can't get over how different it feels already.

Alan says that the mattress feels strange .. so does any new mattress .. but the fact that he hadn't switched it off during the night implies to me that he was sleeping well on it!! We'll see how tonight goes.

So, a good day all round .. made even better by such wonderful sunshine!!

22nd May: After such a good day yesterday it is disappointing to watch Alan becoming unwell again by lunchtime today. In fact after his shower he went to sleep in the chair wrapped up in a blanket and there he stayed until he asked to go to bed at 8pm.

23rd May: Becky, the night sitter, woke me at 6.30am to tell me Alan was quite unwell, his bed was soaking wet with sweat and everything needed to be changed ... oh, dear – I only did this yesterday. Alan tells me that he has been up during the night a couple of times with diarrhoea. Once back in a clean and dry bed, Alan went straight back to sleep and in all honesty hasn't woken all day until he called me during the afternoon having totally mistimed a trip to the bathroom! Oh joy! Cleaned up and back in bed, Alan immediately went back to sleep after taking two Imodium.

The night sitter arrived at 10pm and I gave her explicit instructions that if Alan had diarrhoea again, he was to be given one Imodium tablet. I woke about 1.30am and got up to make a drink. The Imodium tablet packet on the kitchen table has just one tablet left in it. There were 6 tablets at the start, Alan took two earlier .... so where have three disappeared to? I spoke with Alan who was also awake by now and he told me that when he buzzed for a cup of tea earlier, she had brought him the tablets!!!

I'm fuming and daren't wake her as I'm likely to lose my temper, but I have written her a stern note and will have to report this to her boss. Hopefully these extra tablets are not going to cause us problems this weekend ... but it is another Bank Holiday and we have no access to Doc M should we have major problems. I'm so angry I don't think I will get back to sleep tonight.

24th May: The night sitter left me a note telling me that Alan had asked for the tablets! I have my doubts! We had only spoken just before I had gone to bed about Alan becoming dehydrated and confused ... even without this current bug, he very rarely knows what day it is, let alone what meds he should be taking. Would she have complied if he had made repeated requests for Oramorph? If these people are not going to follow my instructions then there is little point in them being here as all trust would be gone. I will need to resolve this issue with Gill when I next see her.

Alan has continued to sleep all day. All I could do for him this morning was to wipe his face with a flannel as he looked so sweaty. All day I have topped up his water supply and made the occasional cup of tea. He managed to take some of his medications and wanted cornflakes. The breakthrough came about 7pm when Alan woke up feeling somewhat better and decided that he would like some trifle. We've been able to have a chat this evening and he's had a bit more to eat and drink.

However, by midnight he has asked me for his bowl (feeling sick) so I have set up another buzzer by the side of the commode in his room – just in case! I'm keeping my fingers crossed for a quiet night, but not particularly hopeful.

25th/26th/27th May: Alan has continued to sleep most of the weekend. He's obviously very unwell but being a Bank Holiday we have no access to Doc M and it's pointless asking anyone else to make an assessment on Alan these days.

I phoned and asked that Doc M called out to see him on Tuesday afternoon and yet again Alan has been hit by a mega chest infection on top of the local bug. The plan is to hit it hard with 'augmenting' antibiotics in the hopes of a speedy recovery.

I would normally have made a trip to Malvern today to visit Dad's grave as it is his birthday, but sadly I've had to call it off in view of how Alan is. Luckily, Giv was able to pick up my flowers and take them over to the grave for me. I think this is the first time in 12 years that I've had to miss the day and to be honest was very upset about it and had several bouts of tears during the day ... but I'm sure he would understand.

28th May: Thankfully Alan is much improved today. He still wasn't feeling able to have a shower, but Gill was able to give him a bed bath. He had managed to shave himself sitting in the kitchen before she arrived. His new foot lady, Natalie Nails, also called in to double check on his in-growing toenail which she has now successfully dealt with. We've had a very pleasant afternoon and evening even though the weather has been terrible again. Alan ate a good meal tonight .. the first in probably a week and managed to stay up until 10pm. Hopefully tomorrow he will feel even better if we've broken the back of this bloody chest infection.

Alan has recently commented that when he was diagnosed three years ago, he had no idea that he would end up like this. I think he envisaged that his treatment would work for some indeterminable time which would then be followed by a progressive decline until his death. It never occurred to him that he would spend well over two years being virtually tied to the house, unable to walk many steps and have such debilitating breathing difficulties. I can't tell you how totally p*ssed off he is with this whole situation. He's a bit like a rubber ball .. he keeps bouncing back!

29th May: Zometa infusion day again. Alan not feeling great this morning but gave in to the thought of having a shower so that his hair could be washed. He decided that he would be dressed and sit in the conservatory to wait for Doc M. He arrived a bit late (as ever!) along with young Tom, his current 3rd year student. All went well with the infusion but whilst I was making a drink, Doc M came and spoke to me in the kitchen. He had been somewhat surprised that Alan's PSA and ALP numbers had dropped again – I don't think he had been expecting that. He jokingly told me that he had already written and destroyed three eulogies as Alan was obviously not 'going anywhere' soon! As always there was much frivolity and laughter during the visit and young

Tom, who appears to be a bit straight laced, was aghast with most of the banter. Never mind .. he'll learn one day that the best medicine is laughter!

30th May: Another quiet day – shower cancelled – and Alan slept most of the afternoon. He managed to eat some tea but was ready for bed by 8pm and asleep by 8.05pm!! Poppy is on duty tonight and we had to wake Alan at 10pm to give him his medications. Hopefully he will get back to sleep without too many problems.

1st June: Since when did paying for an eBay item via PayPal become a matter of life and death? Important enough to drag me out of the shower? ... It's my only five minutes of solace in the whole day. I should have had my shower before he woke up!! ... but then he gets grumpy because I'm upset and raise my voice! Unbelievable!!

The sun has been shining and Alan felt quite well. Time to get in the car and go out for lunch!! Can't remember the last time we did this. Very enjoyable!

2nd June: After the reaction I got yesterday when we were out and I mentioned our anniversary today ... I thought it best just to keep my mouth shut today. Mind games get played here from time to time and I've had enough of them. We're too old and life is too short to play with peoples' emotions like this.

Alan has had another good day and has spent his time trying to locate things he can't remember where they were put. This has involved numerous very breathless trips up and down the hall between bedroom and study. Don't think he succeeded in finding anything – but the exercise should have done him good!

Tomorrow I must face the paperwork I've been avoiding for the solicitors .. a Schedule of Loss and an updated statement – not looking forward to that.

3rd June: The anniversary of Dad's death .. 12 years. Time passes so fast – sometimes it feels like only last year. I miss him dearly.

We're now paying the price for having two good days! Alan has been very sleepy all day and although he managed to stay awake for half an hour he has gone back to bed without eating   anything complaining of severe stomach ache .. quickly followed by the return of the dreaded s****s!   So he's back in bed asleep again now with commode returned to its bedside position, mobile buzzer in place by the commode and control panel in my pocket.

I finally finished the paperwork by lunchtime and have emailed it all off to the solicitor. I've been somewhat blunt in my statement, but they can like it or lump it - they're not living with this 24/7:365 - time for me to have my say, especially if it's going to end up in Court.

Chloe, my hairdresser arrived just before 6pm to find me asleep in the conservatory and then I found Alan had put himself back to bed and was ready for basting with his electric blanket on the highest setting! She has trimmed his hair – nothing drastic first time around – give him chance to have confidence in her before she cuts it to the sort of length which suits him – maybe next time!   Will have to put a reminder on the calendar in about 8 weeks' time … he'll get used to it!

The question now is … will Alan be well enough to leave with someone else tomorrow afternoon whilst I snatch a couple of respite hours?   I may have the answer to that question two minutes before the carer is due to arrive!!! I really need to get to the shops in Kidderminster but it all depends on how he will be feeling.

4th June: Helping hands in the form of Maria arrived on time to whisk her way through the housework … Gill came to do Alan's shower .. and Poppy arrived at 2pm for Alan sitting. The weather was dreadful and it took me the best part of 3 hours just to get down into Kidderminster for a couple of things in B & Q, get some specs repaired and drive back home. Ridiculous!

5th June: As the day has progressed Alan has been getting worse with runny nose, sneezes, coughing, etc., etc. Will phone docs in the morning!

6th June: I'm off to the docs to pick up yet another course of the augmenting antibios and if he's not improving by the end of the weekend I have to add in the ever faithful Doxycycline twice a day. He's sneezing all over the place and his nose is running well - sounds like a good head cold on top of everything else! Let the 3x a day pill battle start again ... oh, how he hates me for it! In other news, had my sleeping tablet last night but still woke to his buzzer at 2.30am - didn't hear Becky's feet go down the hallway so I got up myself ... only to find that I had dreamt it - again!! Struggling to keep my eyes open this morning! Sun is shining on The Hill.

Surgery closed early today so I've missed picking up tablets. Friend Jan has got another script signed and will deliver to chemist so that I can collect tablets this afternoon! Phew! Jan retires in 3 weeks and I'll miss her being there - but I've already trained up the other secretary so my very useful contact will continue!!!!

I'm at screaming pitch tonight. After struggling to get the meds from chemist - he doesn't want to take them! I nearly got wiped off the face of the earth by a local lorry on a bad hairpin bend on a steep hill. He didn't want his shower so Gill sat with him whilst I went to the chemists. He's had a skull pain up the side of his eye socket (mets?) all day and the chicken I cooked for tea was so tender it has hurt his gums and given him toothache! (I'll make sure it's like Ghandi's sandals next time!) Add that to the constant heart burn today followed this evening by quite significant chest pains, the runny nose, sneezing, coughing, inhalers, oxygen and regular pain ... he's been an absolute delight to be with today! Ha ha, bloody ha!! Looking forward to the weekend? You must be flippin' joking!! Roll on 23rd June when he's next due to go into "The Palace"!

8th-13th June: As Alan's chest infection takes hold again he has spent most of the week in bed and asleep. Doc M was back to work on Tuesday and I spoke with him on the phone. He made certain suggestions with regards to Alan's medications and we'll be able to put all of them in place on Wednesday. He has suggested stopping all antibiotics and introducing 'Actimel' drinks until Alan's stomach gets itself back to normal. His steroids have been doubled for three days which will be followed by 3 day reduction pattern.

By Friday we have improvement! Alan is feeling much brighter and gets up quite early. The weather is lovely and he has spent the whole day in the conservatory. Hopefully he will continue to improve now as the isolation I've felt over the past couple of weeks is so depressing.

14th June: Today I have become the queen of Buddhist pendants. Alan has bought new medallions, neck chain and jump rings. It has been my job to assemble everything as per instructions. No matter what I may have to do, during his waking hours Alan can almost always find something to keep me away from what I'm meant to be doing in favour of little jobs he wants completed.

His ingrowing toenail is causing problems and we are bathing it daily in the hopes we can reduce the infection. Unfortunately it is so painful he is reluctant to let anyone touch it … but I can see that there will be more work to be done on it if it doesn't improve quickly. This has been going on several weeks now and has never improved … only got worse!

Alan tells me he has bone pain everywhere today. It's sometimes difficult to determine how intense the pain is as Alan is not good with pain, but he has convinced himself that the bone mets are increasing and this is where the pains are coming from. He's either right or the new Fentanyl patches are not working as well as the morphine tablets have done in the past. We'll just have to see how this situation progresses.

16th June: With every expectation of Alan being admitted into "The Palace" for respite care on 23rd and both of us being primed up for it to happen, we were surprised to get a phone call today from our Palliative Care Nurse advising that the respite won't be happening as the home does not have the 'nursing capacity required'. She has been told to phone back to try and rearrange in two weeks' time.

Neither of us can believe this. Alan knows that I'm ready for a break and he's fuming .. well, so am I really. There was so much I was hoping to do but now the whole set of plans I had is on hold.

In other news the grass has been cut .. finally .. not well, but it looks slightly tidier than the 'field' effect we had been living with!

Alan seemed quite a bit better today and he's been pottering around and getting me doing all sorts of little jobs. His toe is considerably better as well!

17th June: Gill arrived with her 'shadow' this lunchtime ... Lisa. She is an experienced carer and reading between the lines I think that Gill is going to substitute her in for the showering at least twice a week. Gill has been tempted to take up a position as a District Nurse on a part time basis and although 'Sovereign' is her own business she feels compelled to keep up to date with her nursing skills and this will be one way of achieving that. Time will tell.

I visited "The Palace" to enquire about Alan's respite time only to be told exactly as I had heard from Sam, the PCN. However, as I was leaving I bumped into their head nurse, Fiona, who quickly grasped what upset this situation had caused. She is going to look into the feasibility of getting Alan in and intends to discuss this with the home manager. Hopefully we will have an answer by tomorrow.

Toni, our friendly blood sucker, arrived unexpectedly this morning ... we had totally forgotten it was blood sample day! Fingers crossed for good news tomorrow!

18th June: All bad news here today! Alan's PSA has increased from 2.0 to 6.3 in just 4 weeks indicating that the primary tumour is growing at a rapid rate. However the ALP figure which indicates activity of tumours attacking the bones had dropped which indicates that the Zometa treatment is working really well. If this rate of increase is repeated at the next blood test, then I think we are in real trouble as the medics have nothing more to offer Alan by way of treatment for the primary tumour.

Have had phone call from head nurse at "The Palace" ... absolutely no chance of getting Alan in next week – and this is the ongoing situation for 'months'. Not sure where we go from here as this is the best nursing home in the area and I wouldn't like to see Alan in any other locally. For the time being at least it would seem we have to do without any respite! I think we need to see Doc M!!

19th June: Doc M arrived for another hilarious session this afternoon. Chest infection and cough .. no more antibios but keep up the steroids dose for a few more days. Toilet problems .. are being blamed on Metformin, the diabetes drug – so little can be done about that, other than keep some incontinence pads on hand! Pain issues .. increase the Fentanyl patches from 37 to 50mg as from today – done. Rise in PSA .. ignore it till next test – knowing Alan it will drop again! Respite care .. no offer of putting Alan into Cottage Hospital so I need to get to work on Plan B.

Plan B involves finding another brand new nursing home within a reasonable distance. I have found one in Kidderminster which looks beautiful and have made an appointment to view tomorrow afternoon. They take CHC patients and should have a vacancy very soon ... sounds promising.

"The Palace", apparently, realizing that they cannot fill the place charging £1200 a week have dropped their fees, been in touch with all the local services and, of course, that is why all the rooms have been filled so quickly! So you never know, Plan B, if it works, may become Plan A!! This location would add 20 miles to the round trip when visiting – not a problem really!

Alan has stayed up chatting with Becky our Thursday night girl until 12.15am! I don't think he's been up this late for about 4 years! Hopefully we will all sleep well.

20th June: We were both hoping for great things today, with the visit to a new nursing home in Kidderminster. New shower lady, Lisa, arrived early so that we had a good chance of getting out on time. However we were dogged by slow traffic and by the time we got to the end of the Bewdley by-pass we were in nose to tail traffic all the way into Kidderminster.

This nursing home, referred to by us as "The 19th Hole" is similar to any new nursing home, I suspect. It looks very much like "The Palace" inside . BUT it was alive ... buzzing. Loads of staff and patients about – having coffee; sitting outside in the sunshine; having a joke with each other and staff members. We were shown around the home and everything is on a slightly smaller scale than we have seen at "The Palace", but still totally acceptable. There is a 12 seat cinema and hairdressing salon. In the coffee lounge there is an abundance of cupcakes to lust over. Patients are even given a choice of what colour room they would like to be in ... blue, pink, green, lemon, lilac or peach. The bedrooms are very well equipped and each has its own en-suite shower room. We were very impressed.

They would be quite happy to accept Alan as a CHC patient, in fact they already have five patients who are CHC funded staying in the home this week ... so the home's costs should not be a problem. Alan actually feels quite excited at the prospect of going there. We hope to know later next week when it will be, but most likely by the third week of July – not too long to wait.

21st/22nd June: I spent Saturday making an early start for being ready to have the carpets cleaned on Tuesday. I started moving all the small bits of furniture into the spare room and piling it all onto the bed! Alan, in the meantime, was pottering about, but not feeling great so did spend a fair amount of time just sitting in the chair. He has decided that the Fentanyl patches are to blame for how he feels and therefore he wants to revert back to the Zomorph pills as from Sunday! Who am I to argue?

Sunday arrives and I do more of the same .. clearing away what I can .. hoovering the carpet and washing down skirting boards. This concentrated effort of work is killing my back and I'm in considerable pain, but it has to be done.

We were just deciding what to have for tea when the doorbell rang. I went outside from the conservatory to see a lady at the front door who I had never met before .. but instantly recognized! It was Sheena .. one of the ladies from my PSA FaceBook group! She comes from Arbroath in Scotland, had been in Leicester for the weekend, and had detoured in our direction as they were going to travel back to Scotland up the west coast. She had no address, no telephone number but headed in the direction of Ludlow knowing that we lived close to the top of the hill and had two flag poles! Once she was close she recognized the view so just kept going till she found the flag poles and the name of the house on the fence!

Sheena and husband Graeme spent a lovely couple of hours with us. Made my day! It was such a surprise and so unexpected – makes the meeting all that more special in a way!

23rd June: My goodness .. 12 years today since Mother died – have been so busy today that I didn't even think about it till I got into bed. Twelve years! Frightening how quickly time passes.

On the phone first thing this morning to Palliative Care Nurse to get her organized with arranging Alan's stay in "The 19th Hole". She will have to go through the motions with CHC and will contact us later in the week when she's managed to get things sorted.

I continue with more of the same in clearing rooms and cleaning skirting boards whilst Alan spent the afternoon playing with Nitro Morse and a Buddha! My back is still complaining and I'm finding that I can't stand for long without being in terrific pain. Can't wait to get this work out of the way and finished.

24th June: Ian, the guy who has been cutting the grass recently, arrived this morning for the money I owed him from last week. We had a very short discussion about the quality of his work – which he thought was absolutely fine – and I told him we would have to part company. I told him we have no-one to take over the work but that he had left the garden in a totally unacceptable mess and we could live without seeing it like that. Givvi wondered if he had had a helper called Stevie Wonder!!! So, yet again, I'm asking everyone if they know anyone who knows how to do a proper job. We could end up with a very chic and fashionable 'natural' field-like garden!!!

The carpet cleaners arrived just after 10am and got to work straight away. I still had even more bits of furniture to move in my bedroom and in Alan's. However, Alan decided not to move from his bed till 11.30am. He got up to use the loo, so I dashed into the room and starting piling everything on the bed so that he couldn't get back into it. By the time I have finished, I feel physically exhausted. It takes them till 2pm to get the work done and in the meantime Gill came in to do Alan's shower.

Once everyone had gone, we were able to sit in the conservatory. Alan is still coughing badly which is causing him to vomit and then feel really tired. We both fell asleep this afternoon! When I woke up I had to start the job of putting the bedrooms back to normal so that we could both get in our beds tonight. The rest of the house can wait until tomorrow! My back just won't cope with any more today. However, Alan doesn't seem to accept/understand how much I'm suffering at the moment and has accused me of being a 'moaner' .... It's becoming blatantly obvious that I'm not allowed to be ill or suffering in any way. Well, he's in for a big shock when I can't move or do anything for him – then we'll see who does the moaning!

25th June: Maria, my helping hands, arrived on time and we spent most of her time with us today getting all the furniture out of the spare room! I decided to clean the samovar and then wish I'd never started on it! It's a fabulous piece of Old Sheffield Plate but very intricate to clean. Alan not feeling great and stayed in bed the whole morning only getting up in time for Gill to arrive for his shower. However, the NHS Podiatrist also arrived at 1pm and wanted to inspect his feet. She was somewhat brutal and caused quite a bit of pain .... but she had managed to relieve the pressure being caused by the ingrowing toenail. She is available 'on demand' every four weeks and tells us that we must take great care of this particular nail otherwise it could become very troublesome!

Gill had Alan in the shower before the Podiatrist left and just before 2pm our new sitter, Debbie, arrived. She seems to be a lovely lady just about to hit 50 and who could talk the hind leg off a donkey!

Postie Lin had told me the sheep were out and about so I feel obliged to go and mend the front gate rather than have an invasion! Once finished, I closed the gate and one of the slats immediately fell off .. ********! I managed to get that screwed back in place. Now, finally, I can get in the shower. It's my afternoon off but I didn't manage to get out of the door till 3.15pm and have to be back by 5pm! Hardly worth the effort, but I picked up some bits at the DIY store, Tesco's, and then filled up the car. Got home with five minutes to spare!

During the evening I could see that Alan was wilting and I took him to bed about 9pm. He was well settled by 11pm. I went to bed in the hopes of sleep ... but the first buzzer went off at 2am – I hadn't even got to sleep at that stage! Alan's toilet problems have returned with a vengeance. So yet again, I dig out the Imodium tablets and set up the commode in the bedroom. He called me again at 4am and 5.30am. I made yet another cup of tea at 7am and then he finally went to sleep properly. I slept till 9am!

26th June: I cancelled Gill for today – it was obvious Alan was not going to be fit enough for a shower. Whilst he slept this morning I took advantage of the quiet time and washed all the delicate glass pieces we have .. two pairs of lustres and a beautiful table centrepiece. Managed to complete the job without breaking anything. Result!

During his waking moments Alan is coughing, spluttering and getting short of breath. Very miserable for him. La Bella Italiano called in as Doc M has been off sick all week. She was here to do his Zometa infusion. He could hardly wake up! We had a long discussion as to how Alan was feeling and she made some suggestions by way of changes to the drugs' routine in the hopes that it would help Alan to feel better.

La Bella Italiano has suggested stopping the Metformin and restarting a different drug on Saturday which is not known to upset stomachs in the same way. She also suggests he goes back on to Doxycycline once a day permanently. I had already upped his steroids to 8 this morning, which she OK'd and restart the usual reduction routine. She had had to phone Doc M to find out how the Zometa should be administered and arrived here without one of the needles she needed! "Have you got any needles, Cath?" Well, it just so happens that after Doc M's continual forgetfulness I do have a supply of needles ... and syringes! She's left me with new supplies - a cannula, pre-injection skin 'deadener', butterfly needle and swabs!!

It's been one of those days when Alan has become very emotional as he just wanted to curl up in a corner and fade away. I just wish I knew what the trigger was which causes this dreadful yo-yo effect that he suffers. I sat with him this evening - candles and smellies burning and the night-sky light we have in his room, and just had a good chat, but he was so close to tears much of the time. Really sad to see him like this. Let's hope the string on the yo-yo is shorter tomorrow!

27th June: ..... and I've ordered my first ever iPhone .. a blue 16gb 5c on a great deal. Free phone .. unlimited calls .. unlimited text .. 2GB of data for under £24 a month! I love having new toys to play with and have been lusting over an iPhone for years. It is being delivered on Monday.

28th/29th June: Although feeling somewhat better, Alan has been very tired over the weekend .. in fact we both stayed in bed until after noon on Sunday. During the afternoon we amused ourselves with Buddhas and walking sticks which needed to be fixed, stained .... whatever!!

30th June: Janet has been in my mind much of today .. it's her very last day at work and I'm sure she will find it very difficult to walk out of that door this evening after working in the surgery for 29 years and one month ... it's a lifetime!

Respite confirmed for Alan to go to "The 19th Hole" on 9th July for a week. Must get labels sewn into his clothes and shorten all his jogging pants – job for next weekend I think!

Shower by Lisa today .. she needs to get in her hours before finishing work tomorrow for her holiday. Giv had arrived earlier and was busy having fires in the garden and constructing a new chair we have bought for the study. The 'old' chair is going to have a new throw and cushion so that it can be used in Alan's bedroom as somewhere a bit more comfortable to sit as there's not enough room for an armchair in there. I've also had to order a bed cradle as the one supplied by social services only lifts the duvet about 3" – they don't supply the adjustable type! They've never got anything suitable for us to use and we always end up buying our own! Alan needs this to keep the covers off his in-growing toe nails which are still giving him problems.

Brummie and Lynn turned up on an unexpected visit just after lunchtime. It was lovely to see them after so long and definitely lifted Alan's spirits. He misses not being able to see them more often, but now that Brummie also has questionable health issues, we are dependent on him feeling well enough to make the drive down here.

New phone was meant to arrive today. I phoned them at 4.45pm and kicked off big time .. now promised for tomorrow. Within 5 minutes the delivery driver was on phone as he was lost! Oops!

Wonder if I will get a second one tomorrow?.. I'll be signing D. Duck if I do!!

Remember all the trouble we had with the local Hospice and the 'kidnap' incident? ... well it's happened again! They've obviously learned something (but not enough) as they called the police this time, who went and rescued the lady from her niece! ... but why did they let her off the premises instead of calling the   police first? Beats the hell out of me!! All reported in the Shropshire Star newspaper!

I went to bed still playing iPhones and trying to get it just how I want it and trying to find out how to activate the damn thing!

1st July: Well, it's Janet's first day of retirement and she visited this afternoon feeling a bit like a lost soul. She's not used to sitting and resting and feels she needs to be doing something. There is work to be done at the cottage – no doubt this will keep her busy for a few weeks.

Alan's quite well today although still extremely tired and can fall asleep at the drop of a hat. Not eating particularly well and early to bed! His bedroom looks complete with chair and bed cradle in situ – don't think there's much more we can fit in that room!

Have broken my new specs – will visit opticians tomorrow. I was attempting to clear greenery away from the path and patio as I want to get all the paths and patio cleaned whilst Alan is in respite.

2nd July: Drama on The Hill! Alan wanted a drill out of the garage late afternoon and decided to come across there with me. Big mistake .. big, big mistake. As we set off to come back across to the bungalow, his recently damaged ankle gave way and he went down like a sack of spuds on the driveway! Not a soul in sight to give me a hand! I grabbed the walking frame out of the garage and with my help he managed to climb back up but it was a very precarious journey back into the kitchen. On oxygen I cleaned up the nasty wound on his wrist but he is complaining of pain in his side - lower rib/liver type area.

Phoned 999 and paramedics arrived within 15 minutes or so. They were with us best part of two hours running all sorts of tests - mostly fine, but ECG very odd and confusing (good job I had warned them this could be the case!). They didn't want to take Alan to A&E but called the out of hours doctor and after having a long conversation with said doctor, he advised them to give him 2 Paracetamol!!! Doc will come out later this evening. Paramedics left about 7.45pm and I got us something to eat. Doc's driver phoned to say hoping to leave Kidderminster at 8pm then en route to us. However, 10 minutes later Doc had emergency in the opposite direction and driver will phone when they are on the way to us. No phone call as yet - it's 10.45pm, Alan's in bed and I'm ready to go too. At 11pm I'll ring O-O-H and tell them to cancel the call ... he can see one of our own doctors tomorrow afternoon. ... and, after all that, the drill wasn't in the garage!!! It must be in the house somewhere!

On a brighter note, from the tests they did we've found out his sugar levels have dropped significantly in the time since dx .. so that's all good! Down from 11 point something to 8.8.

3rd July: Phoned surgery for home visit, explaining the situation ... all arranged. An hour later Doc M was on the phone to check how things are going and I'm told I can give him whatever Oramorph is needed to keep the pain in check .. and that he won't be doing a home visit as he has so much to catch up on from his week off sick and before he finishes for a holiday tomorrow evening!! Alan went absolutely 'skits'. As I said to Doc M - you may not need to see Alan .. but he needs to see you. However, he has other priorities today.

Head nurse from "The 19th Hole" got lost but finally arrived to do Alan's assessment for next week. We had her in stitches and she's learned everything she needs to know ... sounds as if it is going to be a very different experience from "The Palace" - for the better, I hasten to add.

We had a phone call to let us know that Becky, our night sitter, has a cold and did we want her to come ... NO - not if it's anything catching!! Keep away! Trouble is they had no-one to cover .. but Poppy has agreed to come in on her day off so I should get some sleep.

On a brighter note .. whilst searching everywhere in the garage for this soddin' drill, I found where the mice have been nesting so I know where to put the poison down - this is our second family of illegal immigrants to have taken up residence! Little b*stards ... I'll get some more stuff tomorrow but I can't see us ever getting rid of the pesky little blighters altogether.

Can't find the drill - reckon somebody's nicked it!

4th–8th July: It may be Independence Day in the US but there are no celebrations here .. just a quiet time with Alan resting as much as possible. He has been taking regular amounts of Oramorph to quell the pain from his damaged rib. However, by Monday it is obvious that perhaps we have been a little generous with this drug and Alan is talking gibberish and for all intents and purposes he is 'stoned'. We immediately reduced the amount and cut down on his normal tablets of morphine to re-balance the situation. By Tuesday he is back with us and although he won't actually admit to it, he is looking forward to going into the nursing home tomorrow. He knows that I badly need a rest and we have high hopes this will be a better home than "The Palace" in that they will cater more appropriately for his needs.

9th July: Respite Day 1 - gone in a blur of activity and swear words! Spent the morning packing bags ready for the off and checking all present and correct. (Actually it turned out not to be!!) Loaded electric wheelchair into the car via the ramps we bought for the job and fitted the luggage in around it including banana pillow and just one Buddha! Shower done, lunch devoured .. off we go then.

Arrived at the nursing home to a welcoming party - handed over bags - unloaded wheelchair. Press button to get it going - nothing! It's only been on charge for the past 24 hours! Twiddle this, turn that, unplug, re-plug. Nothing! Monumental swearing. Reload useless piece of **** back into the car ... four months old and it won't work! Unpack in room - lovely view by the way - quick coffee, back home. Unload heap of junk and replace with electric scooter. Can I find the receipt for the wheelchair? Of course not - well not in the two minutes I have to phone them and get back on my way to Kidderminster. Could be this, could be that ... back over to the garage, dismantle the whole thing and try everything they've told me. Nothing! More swearing but get back in car and head back to the home.

Then I got collared by the staff who wanted to know *everything* other than Alan's inside leg measurement. He's been body checked, had photos taken of bruises (he told the staff that I'd done them ... thank you Alan!!) and a portrait photo for his file. Room is lovely .. his tea looked very nice - I've had one cup of coffee, one cigarette and headed for home again. Got in at 8pm! I have a list of the forgotten items to take with me tomorrow - I even forgot his DNR certificate .. but more importantly, his Lynx!! Perhaps things will go a little better tomorrow when I start again!!

10th July: Respite Day 2 - gone in a blur of activity and swear words ... again! You won't believe this! Alan had been out for a final ciggie last evening and was on his way back to his room when he encountered a problem.   Every doorway has a keypad. The other side of the door (i.e. inside the ward area) there are three zombie-like faces looking at him! Scared the **** out of him. However, he has to go in through the door but then the three who are in gaga-land are trying to escape. He tries to hold them back and refuses to tell them the code ... so they all pin him against the wall leaning and pushing on him until a member of staff found them.   What they have managed to do is aggravate the rib injury ... and frighten him to death!.

He got very little sleep as next door leaves TV on all night at full blast and one of the others in gaga-land is off 'over the rainbow' at the top of her voice. So this morning he is like a bear with a sore head - had the manager down to his room and vented his wrath. Then he got on the phone to me - tearful, upset and should he take Oramorph for the pains? He wanted me there straight away but luckily Givvi was already on her way.

I arrived at 5pm and Alan's in considerable pain again so after discussion with our surgery we have called in the out of hours doc who arrived about 7.30pm. Actually this is the first doc he has seen since the fall! He is badly bruised and the rib is very likely fractured but he wants nurses to take control of Oramorph which then creates another set of paperwork headaches! I could go on but I won't ......

The staffing levels at "The 19th Hole" are far superior to those at "The Palace". Alan has two nurses fussing over him all day rather than care assistants. I think we both feel far more confident that they are doing a 'proper job'.

The incident with the Alzheimer's patients is very unfortunate but has been brought about by a set of circumstances which is soon due to be rectified. The home has three storeys and opened just last September. There have not been enough residents to utilize all three floors and therefore permanent residents occupy the lower ground floor, and the Alzheimer's patients are currently on the same floor as those with nursing needs. Next month the top floor will be opening – staff are currently being recruited. The Alzheimer's patients will stay on the ground floor and patients requiring nursing care will be catered for on the top floor. This should eliminate the type of problem we have experienced. I'm just hoping that this unfortunate incident won't make Alan retreat into his room and become isolated.

I got home at 9pm and have had cauliflower cheese and chocolate. Batteries for wheelchair are being dealt with and should be here by Tuesday! Alan's due to come home on Wednesday morning! Only us .. every time - you just know there is going to be something go wrong!! Knackered now!

11th July: Well, I've been awake since 3am, now on my third cup of coffee and ready to attack the ironing before I go to this Palliative Care Seminar at 11am. Can't wait to see that Hospice woman again - there just may be another 'pinning to the wall' incident and I can assure you she will end up looking like an envelope - flat!! Looks like another nice day in the making!

When I arrived to visit Alan today he was sitting in the reception area waiting for me. We sat in the coffee lounge but hardly enough time before the start of the seminar. The hospice woman had seen Alan before I arrived so she didn't ask me the question about how he was. What a shame as I was truly ready for her.

The talk about palliative care concerned a new team which had been put together to devise a form which would be filled in by all elderly, sick or palliative patients on which their end of life decisions would be recorded ... along with so many other personal details it becomes an object of intrusion. The plan is that these forms will be placed in a folder and made available to any medical clinician required in the treatment of the patient. Why do they need to know whether you have chosen burial or cremation? What possible difference could it make to the treatment being received? Why does a paramedic need to know whether you have a financial power of attorney in place? They don't, do they? Intrusive!

Alan was out in the garden when I came out of the meeting and yet again I was criticised for chatting to people I don't know – other carers who have to contend with similar issues as me. Why does he need to do that? Is he jealous that the two minutes I spent with them should have been with him? Anyway I get us both a drink and he seems to calm down. One of the nurses brought him his soup as starter for his lunch and all he managed to do with it was dip in a slice of French bread. Any other time he would eat tomato soup without a problem ... but not here! He's not eating at all well as he reckons the food is not good ... personally I think he's in the mood to do anything which will create a 'problem'.

For the past couple of years I've been asking Alan to have his eyes tested and get new glasses but he has refused on the basis that there is no point in wasting the money as he is dying! However, today, he is suddenly insistent that he has to have an appointment for tomorrow, just so that he can 'get out of this place' for an hour or so as he feels cooped up. I manage to get an appointment with SpecSavers for 2pm Saturday. He hasn't given a thought to the fact that I may

PHUKET TO EVEREST - DANCING IN THE RAIN

already have plans. His selfishness is increasing and frankly he is behaving like a spoilt brat. Perhaps I am to blame for this as from the beginning when we thought time was so short, I have overindulged him in virtually every whim he has had. Well, I think it's time to bring him into the real world again and put a stop to this 'me, me, me' attitude. It will be a battle.

12th July: Without time to do much other than have a shower and get ready I was on my way to the home by just after mid-day. When I arrived Brummie and Pip were already there and very impressed with the home and the amenities. They told Alan how lucky he was to have found such a lovely place to stay. I think that they have read him the riot act before I have arrived in the way he is not allowing me any time to myself and that he is defeating the whole object of this respite week.

We headed off into town to get to the opticians and they set off back to Telford. The eye test went well, but even in such a short time Alan is just so tired. He sat down outside the shop whilst I went to fetch the car and we made our way to the other opticians, Blink, where he chose a pair of red and black frames for his new specs. Hopefully they will be ready before the end of the week.

On the way back to the home he said how nice it was to get out for an hour, to which I responded that he was only in the home for a week and that he had given no thought to the possibility that I had plans for today. Then with such sarcasm he retorts ... "oh YOU have plans for today" ... as if I had no right! I was told I could drop him off at the home and not come back till Wednesday! So I said to him ... "and then you get nasty."

Back at the nursing home he tells me to go home, but as he has no cigarettes I need to go back to his room and roll enough for him for the next couple of days. I make him a cup of tea and he lies on the bed with his eyes shut. Half an hour later, not knowing if he is dozing or not, I told him that we were going to find the lift where he could access the downstairs dining room and garden. He followed like a lamb. As soon as we got downstairs to the residents area he was immediately into conversation with one of the staff as if butter wouldn't melt in his mouth. Just goes to prove that any nastiness is only directed at me! So now that he knows how to access this area I feel that I can leave him having done everything I can.

Having told him that I will not be visiting on Sunday I made my way back home after a quick visit to The Range for a bit of shopping. Bought a kebab and chips for my tea and switched off for the whole evening. I was so looking forward to a good night's sleep ... but the kebab heartburn was horrendous and little sleep was had!

13th July: I was awake early and able to finish off the ironing of five sets of bedding. Jason, a young man from Ludlow, came up to look at the situation with the grass cutting. I also spoke to him about having a step created outside the conservatory as he has been a 'bricky' for years. I will speak to Alan before making a decision ... but we're backed into a corner really as we don't know of anyone else to do the work! I was also expecting the 'gate man' to arrive, but he was a no show.

The kitchen floor was in a dreadful state and took quite a bit of time and effort to get it looking anything like decent. Only problem is that I have upset my back and will need to sit down for the rest of the day. I've had a nap, done nothing, had a curry for tea and generally feel as if I've been very lazy. Still, that's what it's all meant to be about! Tomorrow, I just want to change my bed and re-make Alan's. Don't intend to do much more other than get a Tesco order ready so that it can be delivered on Tuesday.

14th July: Overslept mega-style today. Postman woke me at 11.55am! Janet arrived within 5 minutes to help with some housework. After a quick shower we went out to the local pub for a bite to eat ... and then Alan was on the phone. I could tell from his voice that he was very upset and the excuse for phoning was that he only had 3p left on his phone. I told him I would be with him by 4pm.

Back at home I managed to top up his phone and get an order in with Tesco before it was time to head off for Kidderminster, not knowing quite what I was going to find.

Alan was in a bad way and told me that I just didn't understand. Well if you don't talk to me and tell me what you are feeling, how the hell can I ever understand. I suggested we went for a coffee in the gardens and have a cigarette. It was then that he started to open up on what had been happening. He had become very upset during the morning when talking to a 90 year old lady who was worried about her house and garden and the money she was paying out to have work done. She explained that she had lost her husband when they had both walked to their local post office and as they left the shop, they both tripped and fell. Unfortunately, her husband died there and then. They had been together over 70 years and she was totally lost without him. Alan offered to go and check that the garden was being done properly, but she got called away to the hairdresser and that's where the conversation had ended. He was in bits relating the story. Add this to the fear he has been feeling about being in such close proximity with the dementia patients who, although looking frail, have great physical strength which he experienced on the first night, then I can appreciate why he is ready for home.

It's a no brainer! I packed up his room within minutes throwing things into any bag I could lay my hands on ... loaded everything into the car and got him out of there as quickly as I could. We had spoken briefly to the home manager whilst having coffee and told him this was probably going to be our plan for the day. He understood. He knows there has been a problem. Alan has nothing but praise for the staff but felt isolated and lonely. He had not spoken to anyone since I left on Saturday until he was chatting to the old lady this morning – other than staff, that is.

Delighted to be back home we have enjoyed a Chinese meal together and he has gone to bed a happier man. I'm sure he will be sleeping much better tonight ... and I will not be waking him in the morning – give him a chance to catch up!

So no rest for me! I think I'm more knackered than I was the day I took him into the home! Oh, well – c'est la vie – I'll get over it!

15th July: It's our 19th wedding anniversary ... and at least we are going to be able to spend the day together! A very laid-back day when I have unpacked everything from the home at my leisure. Alan stayed in bed most of the morning and seems quite good in himself when he finally gets up.

The first phone call of the day is one we have been waiting for ... from our solicitor Margarita. She has finally had a response from Dodgy Doc's legal team giving details of his admissions with regard to negligent treatment, and at last we have an offer on the table. The amount offered, we all feel, falls short of the mark as, so far, our claim calculations put us at quite a bit more. We have been asked to consider what is on offer, what increase we should ask for if we want a speedy conclusion. Our immediate reaction was to attempt to achieve something in between, but we will discuss this later in the week with Margarita. There are several points in the offer letter which need to be challenged and corrected.

It has taken us 23 months to get to this point and we now know that we are very close to a conclusion. That's all we want now – closure, so that we can get on with the rest of our lives together. It's not really about the money, but acknowledgement that Alan was badly let down by Dodgy Doc, that he was negligent, and this is what he has admitted right back to 2005 and again in 2008 – the very dates we had argued vehemently should be brought into question. The letter quotes 'his regret' for not offering tests and investigations at that time ... but still no apology! I am going to pat myself on the back for this achievement as all of the research into the medical aspects of this case have been carried out by me and without this work being put in we would not have ended up with this result. I know Alan is grateful for what I have done in this respect and congratulates me time and time again. I know I have done my very best to achieve justice for him and hope now that he will be able to put this all into one of his little boxes at the back of his head.

445

I would dearly love to share this news with Janet (Dodgy Doc's secretary before she retired) but I'm not at all sure how she would take it, even though she has been so supportive of us both over the past three years. She really is a very special friend and I don't want to rock the boat between us ... but as it is the elephant in the room, one day it will need to be discussed.

Our 19th anniversary turned out to be very memorable and exciting ... one we won't forget.

Alan continues to look physically well and his sense of humour has definitely remained intact, as this Bombay Sapphire Gin 'infusion' shows, set up for the benefit of Doc M's new student in July 2014. Breaks the ice, and lets him know he's come to the mad-house.

Chapter 25: Time to Reflect

The past three and a half years of Alan's and my life can only be described as a nightmare, struggling from one disaster to another. This time has challenged us on so many levels and it is only strength of character that has brought us through this ... not unscathed ... but still together. There have been medical, mental and trust issues along the way and we both know there will be more challenges to face during the time we have left together.

I have a feeling that the cancer stability which we have 'enjoyed' for the past couple of years will soon be coming to an end and the disease will then continue to progress through till the inevitable end. I will continue to devote my love and life to Alan to give him the best possible time ... in comfort, without pain, or in fear of the future.

Our experiences may have broken many a loving couple but I have always refused to give in ... even through the dealings with the GMC and then with the litigation case. It was always my contention that Alan had been wronged and badly let down by his doctor and when, after a year of waiting, no apology was forthcoming, I had to try and get justice for him ... for the pain and suffering he has endured with every piece of bad news handed to us along the way. I knew in my heart that I was right, and now with two positive results, I feel I have been vindicated in my actions. Alan's concern has only ever been to secure my future without him so that I will be able to continue to live in comfort without the financial worries suffered by many other pensioners.

Along with keeping this diary, my work and research into Prostate Cancer and heart failure issues, have helped me keep my sanity, especially through the countless sleepless nights. We have managed to achieve some re-education of several medics along the way which, it is hoped, will change their attitude when dealing with other patients. Several students have benefited from Alan's desire to help them learn by treating a live patient.

The ripple effect of all the circumstances surrounding Alan's illness has been profound and has caused very deep concerns for Givvi and Percy, Janet, Mark and Lynn   without whose support, life would have been very much more difficult. It has also introduced us to some very caring people who have taken us into their hearts and lives ... Gill, who has looked after Alan every weekday for showers; Sam, our stand-in Palliative Care Nurse who has done a superb job helping in counselling terms and organizational skills;   our District Nurses and Cottage Hospital staff, but most important in this list has to be Declan, our young and enthusiastic GP who has devoted huge amounts of time caring for Alan and without whom, neither of us would have survived as long as we have. Affectionately known as Buddha Doc ... he will never be forgotten and I will never be able to find a way to thank him for what he has done for us both.

I must also mention the love and support of 80 ladies in my FaceBook group, Prostate Sisters' Accord, most of whom I have never met, but who have always been there to listen, support and advise. These ladies all share a common problem – Prostate Cancer – and therefore understand the intricacies of the disease, its treatment and possible consequences. They understand the need to vent and cry and we have all supported each other on a daily basis. It is a whole family of friends – worldwide!

I will continue to keep my diary of events during whatever time Alan and I have left together but feel that the biggest part of this journey from Phuket to Everest is complete and memorable.

The final part of the journey will be of indeterminable length, even more harrowing and upsetting, as it reaches its inevitable conclusion, but the events of the past few years have made me stronger to be able to cope with the future ... a future which will eventually see me in a life on my own. I'm not relishing the thought of this final mile but will be strong enough to face it.

"Life is not about waiting for the storms to pass ..
it's about learning to dance in the rain

449

and that's what we will continue to do for as long as possible!

14th August: *Alan has accepted Dodgy Doc's insurer's third offer of a six-figure sum in full and final settlement of his claim. We were due to lodge papers in Court on 3rd September so this was a very timely ending to the case.*

THEY THINK IT'S ALL OVER ... IT IS NOW!

Our legacy and first port of call on return from the Far East
the memorial stone dedicated to the Army Dog Unit Northern Ireland,
located at the National Memorial Arboretum, at Alrewas, Staffordshire.

This memorial was instigated, sourced and installed by the two of us on
behalf of the original Army Dog Unit Northern Ireland Association which
we had formed back in 2008.

Appendix: What he means to me (first written 1996)

I will always want to remember my time with Alan, but I can imagine that as time goes on and the memory fades somewhat, that I will forget some of the details. It is for that reason that I want to get this down in writing so that in years to come I shall be able to recall it all more clearly.

It would be pointless starting this at the exact time when we met as the circumstances of the previous few years has some bearing on how things happened. I think a précis of these events is called for.

A convenient starting point would be my birthday in 1992. I was having a week's holiday from my job as a security officer with Tesco - I had taken this particular week in the previous three years. My husband of nearly 23 years, Selwyn, had not bought me a present, as in several previous years. The usual excuse was, no time, no money and no imagination. I can't even remember whether he had bought me a card. However, we went out for the day and he bought me a velour track suit from one of the chain stores and we then went to my parent's for lunch. Looking back, I can remember that the conversation seemed to revolve around Paddy Ashdown, the politician, who had just admitted to having had an affair. My father was disgusted and damning. How could he be trusted in any responsible office if he couldn't be trusted with women? Dad explained that he was a one-woman man and could not understand the mentality of anyone who could act without self-control, behaving no better than an animal! Selwyn seemed a little sheepish, (no pun intended) but nothing that I thought about until much later.

Selwyn is a talented musician and at that time was playing in a duo. They were playing the following night, but for whatever reason, I was not going with him. On the following Sunday morning we were taking the children to the local car boot sale and on the way there I lit up a cigarette and opened the car's ashtray, which he had emptied on the morning of my birthday. I was horrified to see it almost full of butt-ends which were not of the brand which I smoked. Selwyn was a non-

452

smoker. My mind went into overdrive and by the time we got back home I was at bursting point. Having sent the children to their rooms, I confronted him about the possibility that he was seeing someone else. This man, who I had trusted implicitly, then pulled the bottom out of my world. He was deeply involved with someone and had been for some considerable time. Various reasons were offered, some of which contained an element of truth.

I asked him to leave that day, which he did, but by the Thursday he was back asking to be forgiven. He had finished the affair and wanted us to be back together. We both made a supreme effort for the next few months, but it was like walking on glass the whole time. In our own way we did manage to put many of our grievances to rest and I think that we were both glad that we had tried to make things work. At the end of six months, Selwyn became very restless and secretive. It was obvious he was now regretting his original decision. He contacted her again, with my knowledge, and it was finally decided that we should go our separate ways.

I immediately started divorce proceedings and spent a lot of time re-vamping the house. I handed Selwyn his decree absolute on what would have been our 24th wedding anniversary.

At this point I feel I must mention Beryl, a medium I contacted through a close friend and neighbour. Just after Selwyn left, I went to see her and she told me many things relating to his affair. Strangely enough, when I had first seen her some two years previously, she had gone into great detail about an affair that my son was having with a dark haired married woman, and that this affair was going to cause tremendous problems. As my son was all of 17 at the time I had totally dismissed it, but on later questioning she had seen the affair involving someone shorter than me and had assumed it must be my son (she was not aware that Selwyn was a good 6" shorter than me.) So I had been warned! On this second visit to Beryl, she described a man with whom I would become involved, who used to wear a uniform. She also mentioned that there was a diamond ring coming my way. There was talk of a hospital ... an operating theatre, doctors in 'scrubs' ... along with loads of other bits and pieces. I made a notes and kept them.

During my birthday week's holiday in February 1993, I was reading through the "lonely hearts" section of a local magazine and spotted someone, who by the wording of their advert, sounded interesting. I telephoned the contact number and left a brief message and my phone number. Nothing happened and after a couple of weeks, I thought no more about it. However, during the second week of May (yes, that long!) the phone rang one evening and this gorgeous voice was on the other end. There had been many reasons why the caller had taken so long to ring me but would I still be interested in meeting up for a chat and a drink. We arranged to meet the following Sunday night at a pub which was about equi-distance from each other's homes.

Sunday, 16th May, 1993, soon arrived and I got myself made-up and dressed casually, but smartly. I had never done anything like this in my life before. I had been told to look for a black Saab in the car park. I think I arrived two or three minutes early, and the black Saab was already parked up. My stomach was unbelievable. Butterflies? I think I must have had the complete flock!

This was Alan. He was obviously as nervous as me and we went into the pub where we didn't stop chatting all evening. We showed each other pictures of our children, and talked about everything imaginable. The evening went by far too quickly. I was very taken with this quietly spoken, very personable man. At closing time he gave me his phone number and said it was up to me whether I made contact again - but I had already decided that I would like to see him again, and that I would leave it to him if he wanted to get in touch. We went outside to the cars and he quite shyly kissed me goodnight and the instant I responded to this, it actually took several minutes before we parted.

The phone didn't ring on Monday night. I went to bed feeling quite disappointed. I'd been on a high all day in anticipation. I fretted at work all day Tuesday but was rewarded by the call that evening. We had another long chat and arranged to meet at the same pub on Thursday but then carry on somewhere else for a meal. Givvi was quite concerned that I was going off with a strange man, on my own, into the countryside, in his car! Anyone would have thought there had been a role reversal!

We went off into the countryside to one of his favourite pubs which served excellent meals. I was not allowed to pay for anything. He did take a £5 note off me for drinks, but gave it me back, saying that the barman wouldn't accept it! Alan has such a wonderful, playful, sense of humour and during the evening I warmed to him rapidly. We just didn't stop talking and laughing. We drove back to the original pub where I had left my car and decided to have a last drink there. Was this pub ever dead that night? It was terrible. Quite innocently, I said to Alan that I'd got a bottle of wine at home if he would like to come back. So the two-car convoy made its way back to Worcester. He made pleasantries about the house, I got the wine out, put the music on and we were able to settle down on our own. Both children were out, Givvi at a band practice, Spencer on duty all night with the police.

At this point, I think I must have had a total brain storm. I wasn't drunk, but I was very much enjoying the session we were having on the settee. We'd been in the house all of 15 minutes! You know what it's like when you do something totally out of character which even shocks yourself? Well, this was it for me! I sat up, took hold of Alan's hand, and said "Come with me" and promptly led him upstairs to the bedroom. The music was still going, all the lights left on and the bottle of wine on the table. What the hell was I doing? Once Givvi had come in and settled in her room we were able to carry on for the next couple of hours. I often think back to that night and wonder whether I had "tart" written across my forehead. Between 2 and 3 in the morning I told Alan that I must get some sleep as I was going to work next morning. Unbeknown to us, when Spence had arrived home at 6 o'clock and seen the mysterious car with Irish number plates parked outside, he'd run a check on it through the police computer trying to find out who was with me!

Alan and I had arranged a date for the Saturday night. I would drive to Kidderminster, park up at his flat, and go out for the evening. He had asked me to stay the night. We had a great evening out, even though we were both struggling to keep our hands off each other. We had a taxi back to the flat and spent what can only be described as a non-stop, totally memorable, sleepless night. I was totally hooked. I don't think I shall ever forget that night. He had an art-deco electric fire, painted white, but with a kaleidoscope lighting effect which changed colour every few seconds. Very sensuous. It only took that one night for Alan to remove all my inhibitions, although there were several embarrassing moments still to come for me!

During the next couple of weeks we spoke on the phone daily and Alan spent most of the nights at the house with me. We decided to have another night in Kidderminster and went to a few of the local pubs and finally ended up at the Chinese take-away to take back to the flat. That was the last time I ever spent the night there. I have very fond memories of the place. The following morning whilst getting ready to come back to Worcester, Alan gave me a gent's heavy gold signet ring, in the shape of a shield, to wear. There was a diamond mounted in the centre. Remember Beryl? The other thing I should have mentioned was that Alan had served in the Parachute Regiment for nine years! I dissolved into tears. - It had been such a long time since anyone had been so spontaneously kind to me. He thought he had done something wrong!

Within the next week or two we had the most fabulous day out in Brean, near Weston super Mare. The weather was glorious and we spent our time in the sand dunes and walking out to a wreck in the sea, which Alan was trying to convince me was a pile of rocks. We went on the pier at Weston and went on the very vicious little ride at the far end. The ride was so violent I remember being jolted about and hitting my knees on the bolts holding the car together. In the evening we carried on down to Burnham on Sea, where we found this great little pub and had a smashing meal before heading back to Worcester.

I was having great difficulty in concentrating at work and my arrest rate had fallen dramatically. It was also at this time that the problem with my back started with a vengeance. I had been x-rayed in April following a bad bout of trouble in March, but it showed nothing. Now the problem was so bad I was bed ridden. Through work it was arranged for me to see a specialist privately and it was decided that I would have to have my back manipulated under anaesthetic to try and solve the problem. Alan was with me the whole time. It was obvious within days that this hadn't cured it. My specialist wanted me to have an MRI scan and all the arrangements were made to go to the Priory in Birmingham. Alan had explained to me that he was due to visit Portugal for a week and was leaving the day after my appointment in Birmingham. He took me to the jewellery quarter that day and bought me a beautiful opal and amethyst ring - a going away present, he called it. The scan was done and Alan took me home and we said our goodbyes. I was going to see the specialist the following week for the results of the scan. Little did either of us realize what was going to happen next.

When I got up the following morning, it was obvious to me that something had gone drastically wrong with my back. How I drove to the doctor's I shall never know. The pain was indescribable. It was suggested I got to the private hospital to see if my specialist could see me straight away. I managed to drive the few miles to the hospital and I walked into reception in floods of tears. The girls told me to get straight back home and they would get the specialist to phone me. By now I was on large doses of pain killers and feeling sick, but also floating a bit! The specialist phoned me after the scan results had been faxed to him and told me he would operate two days later. Alan phoned me from the airport, but I couldn't bring myself to let on what trouble I was in - how could I upset his holiday plans? He said he should be back by the following Thursday and would see me soon after that. How I cried when I put the phone down - facing this lot on my own.

I think that was the longest weekend I can remember. I had to phone the doctor from bed to ask if I could double up on the pain killers -

I was on another planet by now! Their effect was now lasting less than 2 hours and I just didn't know what to do with myself and there was nothing anyone could do for me. Spence wanted to send for an ambulance in the early hours of Sunday morning, but I'd only got to get through one more day before the operation.

On the Monday morning my Mum and Dad took me to the hospital for 10 o'clock and just as I was settling into the room the pain was back with full force and I was given a pre-med immediately. Suddenly the pain was gone - I couldn't believe the feeling of relief as I fell asleep. The next I knew I was on my way to theatre. On waking, I felt as if I had had a lump of lead implanted in the middle of my back. I couldn't move and had to stay flat on my back until the next morning. But it was all over - or so I thought. I wasn't at my happiest with Alan being away, but Thursday would soon come. I behaved and did everything I was told and was released on the Wednesday afternoon. Thursday came and went without a phone call. I was upset. Friday came and went without a phone call. I was even more upset. When, by Saturday night I had still heard nothing, I was beginning to get really worried. So on Sunday, and contrary to all the advice I had been given, I got in the car and drove to Kidderminster to track down Alan's sister, Wendy. Her address was on some paperwork Alan had left with me.

She was shocked that I had turned up on her doorstep and as far as she was concerned Alan would not be back until the following day. I had quite a long chat with her. She knew of my existence from Alan as she used to be his confidante and he had told her quite a lot about me. She seemed a genuine lady and we got on well together. I left a note at Alan's flat that I was concerned as to where he was and that I was worried that I'd not heard from him. The phone call came Monday lunchtime - I said I'd got a surprise for him and he said he would come straight down. He was totally speechless when he put his arms round me and I said "mind my back" and showed him what had been done. The line of staples holding my back together was a bit of a clue! There was guilt written all over his face.

During the next couple of weeks, I was aware that things between us were deteriorating. No phone calls when promised, broken dates, not wanting to be alone together for too long. I didn't know what I'd done wrong. It all came to a head at the beginning of August when Alan suggested that we call it a day. I had previously told him that I loved him, but he was frightened of any commitment and it would be better to end it. Better for whom? I was devastated. My world was upside down again. We gave each other back the gifts we had exchanged. I was in tears. He drove away in tears. I retreated back into the security of my own four walls. I was still off work after the operation, my mobility was not so good and the days were long. Then one week later the phone went - it was Alan again. Could he see me? We met up the following night at a local pub.

Alan then told me such a lot of things which he had never discussed before and the fact that he was in a serious financial mess. I suggested that if things were that bad, then perhaps he should declare himself bankrupt and start life again without all the debts hanging over him. I was asked to give him a bit of time and space to sort things out - a couple of weeks, or so. He brought back the diamond signet ring for me - he would be back!

I became quite strong again in my mind at this time, but was not prepared to sit at home waiting and actually made a wrong decision that the best thing to do would be to get back to work. Within three days I was in serious trouble again with my back and was off sick again. I spoke to my boss and the specialist and the only way I was to be allowed back to work was on "light duties". As a store detective, there was too much risk of further injury, especially when arresting suspects who may turn violent – a risk the Company was not prepared to take.

For the first two weeks apart, I didn't expect to hear anything from Alan but as the days and weeks went on I was very upset and did a lot of private soul searching and crying.

I decided to go and see Beryl again. I found it hard to believe what she was telling me. She queried whether he was still married. I knew his divorce was well under-way as he had shown me the papers at the flat. She told me she could definitely see a wedding ring and that I ought to find out more about his financial situation. She's never been wrong, but I didn't want to believe it, or couldn't make sense of what she was saying. She also told me that I would go to the jewellery quarter again (not knowing I'd already been once) choosing another ring. I was quite confused.

I carried on working the best I could but the pains in my back and leg meant I was still on pain killers all the time. Sometimes I would be walking round work like a zombie. I always had a bottle of the strongest tablets I had been prescribed in my handbag - until one Wednesday, early in September. For some reason, I had forgotten to put the tablets in my bag. By lunchtime I could hardly walk so I decided to come home during my lunch hour to collect the tablets. I wonder about fate sometimes. As I walked into the house that day, the phone was ringing. *"Hello, Kate. This is Wendy, Alan's sister. Have you seen him lately?"* I said that I hadn't and briefly explained what had happened. She then went on to tell me that he was flying out to America that day.

"Forever?", I asked.

"No, just for a holiday."

My immediate reaction was "well, he must have found someone with money then!"

"That's right" she said. I just couldn't believe it. I must be naive, but it hadn't occurred to me that there might be another woman involved. *"Well, who do you think he went to Portugal with?"* she said. I had to get back to work. I thanked Wendy for letting me know. At least I knew where I stood.

Again, I was devastated. All this was doing my weight the world of good. I was actually beginning to look half decent! One thing I had always said about Alan, was that he gave me back my confidence that I was "fanciable" and was attractive to the opposite sex. But on that particular day, that was the last thing on my mind.

Still, I coped. I always have to. Life goes on. But it's a bitch. So you think of the positive things - own home, own car, good job. What more could you want? Alan! I was just getting over that phone call when some two weeks later Wendy phoned again. "Has Alan been in touch?" I said that I'd heard nothing. She had discussed the next bit of the conversation with her partner and they both felt that I should know that Alan had married whilst in the States. How much more had I got to endure? My love for this man was not dying. I burst into tears. How could this have happened so quickly? I really had thought that I meant something to him. I asked if I could visit her rather than talk on the phone. She was able to fill in a lot of the gaps and at last I was able to put things together in my head. We both wondered if he would ever contact me again. She told me a little bit about Madge and from what I was hearing there couldn't have been a more perfect miss-match if you'd tried. But I had no alternative other than to accept what had happened.

Yet again, I had to cope. I always have to cope. I put on a brave face and got on with work - not a lot else. I would come home and stay in, only seeing very close friends occasionally. I really didn't want to do anything. And my back was getting no better. So, I got on with things, worked longer hours, always helpful to the customers, did some decorating, and spent evenings reading the few letters that Alan had written to me at various times.

Less than three weeks after Wendy's last call, I was at work on 14th October when a tannoy message asked me to go to the reception area. This was unusual - they usually ask that you phone them. I got to reception to be told there was a phone call waiting for me - "put it through" I said pointing to the phone on the wall.

"The gentleman said to ask you first if you want to speak to him. It's Alan." I asked for the call to be put through to an empty office upstairs - and I ran. My heart was in my mouth. It was wonderful to hear his voice again. Why couldn't I rant and rave, and hurl abuse at him for the way I had suffered? I just couldn't. Alan was totally unaware of all the info I had got from Wendy. We talked for about half an hour. He wanted to see me again and I agreed to meet him on the following Sunday evening - three days later.

After the phone call had ended, I dissolved into tears again. This man has been married exactly four weeks and he wants to see me. A close workmate's reaction was "well, I hope you told him where to go". All my friends thought I had gone completely insane. I was on cloud nine - a totally different person again. How I got through the next three days is difficult to say, but the letter that arrived from Alan the following morning certainly helped.

Unfortunately, this was the very week when I had arranged to see a couple of other guys. I went along, had a couple of drinks with them and a meal, but I was only making mental comparisons all night - and none of them came anywhere near the person with whom they were being compared! In fact, I even told one of them that I was involved with a married man and wasn't prepared to jeopardize that relationship. He must have thought I was odd!!

On Sunday, I was so excited. I was like a wound up spring. I couldn't concentrate on anything. We were meeting at 7.30pm which meant I could leave home at 7.25pm and still arrive early at the pub! I was visiting a neighbour that afternoon and at 4 o'clock I said that I must leave to get in the shower. *"But you're not seeing him until 7.30!!"*

"I know, I know". Shower, hair, make-up, perfume, dressed - by 6 o'clock! Went back and knocked neighbour's door. "How do I look?"

"Great, but you're not meeting ..."

"I know, I know!" What can I do for an hour or so? What am I going to say? Is he going to tell me?

462

Over the previous three days, I had thought long and hard about what I wanted to happen. It didn't matter to me what other people thought - all that mattered was the two of us. I had made my decision. I just had to wait now to see what Alan actually wanted of me.

I arrived in the pub car park 10 minutes early - I just couldn't contain myself any longer. As I drove in, Alan was already waiting! We both got out of the cars, held each other and kissed. I was crying - but it seems I do a lot of that! It was several minutes before we were both composed enough to actually go into the pub. As late on as Alan getting the drinks at the bar, I made the decision as to which way I was going to approach this - basically, like a bull in a china shop! He put the drinks on the table and sat facing me. The Scottish landlady started chatting to us, and we thought she'd never go. It was probably only for a couple of minutes really. Anyway, I thought, here goes - do or die. I took hold of his hand, looked him straight in the eye and said "I know where you've been. I know what you've done. Basically, I don't give a shit. You get one more chance with me - and this is it!"

He was totally and utterly gob-smacked. Tears welled up in his eyes. He knew what a dreadful mistake he'd made with this marriage but I told him that for as long as I could cope, I wanted him in my life and if that meant being his "bit on the side", then that's what I would have to be. We did only manage the one drink in the pub that night before we both decided we would rather be somewhere else. That's right - back to my place and straight back to bed. What a reunion! Naughty, but very nice!

We were now in daily contact again. I was still at work so Alan would travel down most days just to spend an hour with me at lunch times. He decided that he must get out of the situation he was living in and it was decided that he should move in at the end of October. I excitedly waited for the day to arrive.

My honesty lets me down sometimes! I have always had a very close relationship with my parents and they had been especially supportive during my divorce. When I had been given the news about

Alan's marriage, I had told them. Big mistake! Big, big mistake. Huge! I think this was the biggest mistake ever. But then, how was I to know that he was coming back to me? On Givvi's birthday at the end of October, they were due to visit ... and so was Alan. When they arrived, I had to tell them that I was seeing him again. There was a look of total disbelief from them both ... and silence. They left very quickly that day. Alan arrived with a gift for Givvi and the rest of the day was fine.

Alan moved in at the very end of October, but was uneasy somehow. A couple of days later, Spence phoned me at work asking if I knew that Alan had gone again. All his things had been taken from the house. I was totally confused and devastated yet again. What the hell was going on?

Alan told me that the timing wasn't right. I was still not prepared to give up hope and we continued to see each other whenever we could. The second attempt at the move was made at the end of November. All the possessions and clothes were moved in again. During the first weekend after the move, Alan went to see his children. He phoned me whilst he was out. Madge had been burgled and had phoned the children to try and find out where he was. He would have to go and see her.

You know the knots you get in your stomach that make you feel sick when something horrible is going to happen? Whilst he was still on the phone, I got the knots. He felt sorry for her having to cope with his disappearance and the burglary. He moved most of his belongings back to her house, again, and for several days I was in touch with him by phone asking him to remove the remainder.

A couple of days later, he finally came to visit me. I couldn't cope. Let's finish the whole thing. We had a long tearful talk. I told him that I would have made him a great wife, but was obviously not going to be given the chance. Again we parted, and again we were both still crying as he drove off.

464

I could hardly believe it when at work the next day I was told that he was on the phone for me. *"I can't do this"* Alan said. *"We have got to be together, but I'm going to have to work out how and when."*

Much to my parent's disgust, we continued to see each other as often as possible and we were in daily contact by phone. He would leave the house and go to the local phone box so that we had five minutes together each day.

I was not looking forward to Christmas. Spencer would be working nights with the police and as Givvi had already left home, and she would have arrangements made with her friends. But most of all, Alan would not be with me. However, he did manage to phone me on Christmas day, singing down the phone the Stevie Wonder song "I just called to say I love you".

Boxing Day is Alan's birthday and he was hoping that we would be able to spend some time together. However, at lunch time he rushed in, explained that he was only meant to be out collecting his children to go back to the house for dinner; so he wouldn't be able to stay long! I was so upset ... but then, when you are the "other woman" you have to accept what little time is available, or not bother at all. Strangely enough, through all that upset, Giv managed to take a photo of us together that day ... one of the best photos we've ever had together! And It is said 'the camera never lies' .... oh, yes it does!!! It doesn't show the pain and turmoil of the whole situation ... but portrays a happy couple who are obviously in love – without a care in the world!!

The next hurdle to get over was New Year's Eve. Yet again I was going to have to be on my own. Alan was committed to working for the evening in Madge's son's pub in West Bromwich, but he had promised to phone me in the early hours of New Year's Day. All my friends had their own arrangements for the evening, so I decided to meet up with a band that I knew, Marmalade, who were playing at a nightclub in Birmingham. As I was driving, there was no chance of having a drink but at least I was forcing myself to go out. Just after midnight, I started the drive back home and as I approached the West

26th December, 1993

Bromwich junction I was wondering how Alan's evening had gone. Up ahead on the motorway, I could see several cars, one in particular didn't appear to know which lane it wanted to be in. Well, I'm doing 85 to 90 in the middle lane and as I approached these cars it occurred to me that I recognized the wandering Metro. It was Alan's (which for one reason or another happened to be registered in my name). Madge was driving and Alan appeared to be slumped in the passenger seat.

As I got to the point of overtaking them, she suddenly decided to pull out in front of me! I swerved out into the outside lane, narrowly missing the Metro. I stared at her as I passed and flashed my hazard lights when I pulled back in. Obviously Alan would recognize my car if

466

he was awake. Can you imagine the situation had there been a crash and the police had been called? When checking on both vehicles they would find them both registered in my name - and Madge knowing absolutely nothing? The mind boggles! Alan and I have often laughed about the incident since.

At the beginning of January I was due to see my specialist again as he had told me he was unable to make a decision on a course of action until six months had elapsed since the last operation. Again, Alan came with me for the appointment and it was decided that the operation would have to be repeated. The date was fixed and I continued at work for another week, not knowing at that time that it would be my last ever days working for the Company.

By now the weather was not good but Alan had told me that he would be with me every day at the hospital. And he was. But the comical thing is that the Metro was very bad on cold starts and on a couple of the mornings, Madge had actually had to push start it! If only she had known what she was doing, I'm sure she wouldn't have been quite so willing to help!

Now that I was at home all the time after the operation, it was so easy for Alan to be with me on a daily basis. It was wonderful. I would phone him in the mornings after she had gone to work and make sure that he was awake. He would travel down for the day and get back home before she arrived home at about 4.30pm. We decided to decorate the lounge and dining room. It took about two weeks in all and the results were great. I was still not able to go back to work as my back was probably even worse than it was after the first op. I finally took advice from the Company's Occupational Therapist, who came to the house to talk to us about the best options for me. It was decided to apply for a Full Medical Discharge and pension. The Company asked for a detailed medical report from my specialist who confirmed to them that I would have to totally rethink my lifestyle and that I would never be fit enough again to carry out my duties as a retail security officer.

Finally, the decision was made to give me a full medical pension and a generous cash bonus of a year's salary.

I was now able to make certain decisions about work on the house that needed to be done. I also found that I was in a position to repay the second mortgage that I had taken out to pay off Selwyn for his portion of the house. I needed a new roof on the extension. The patio doors needed to be double glazed and I had two faulty gas fires which needed to be replaced. I was also advised to have a new bed to help support my back. We started looking around for the things which were needed and making arrangements for the workmen.

Alan had told me that Madge intended to visit relatives up north for a few days and that he would have to go with her. He didn't dare tell me that, in fact, she had arranged for them to go to Turkey for a week! During that week, I waited for the phone to ring and after three days came to the conclusion myself that he was actually out of the country. It transpires that he must have had such a dreadful time out there, with her, that on his return he had definitely decided to make the move. On the day that the roof was being done and the gas fires were being fitted there was total chaos, so that seemed like the best time for Alan to borrow a van and move everything he owned in one go! Fish tank and all!

I admit to being a little wary, but in my heart I knew that this time it would be right for us. Alan did everything he could to convince me that this was his last and final decision on the matter. He changed his address on everything so that everyone knew where he was, except Madge. Obviously, there were loose ends to tie up with her and I admit that I was a little uneasy about his visits to see her. Their divorce could not even be started until the middle of September and I did understand that there was a need to keep her "sweet" until everything was finalized.

No-one north of Worcester in Alan's circle of friends knew anything of the affair and this also included his children. He took them out several times on their own to talk to them about the situation and they were finally brought to the house to stay over one night. It was a

468

little tense for them being brought to a strange house to stay with a stranger, but all things considered it went fairly well.

Alan took advice from a local solicitor with regards to his divorce, but it was decided that we should go it alone with the court. I prepared all the papers for him after he had discussed and agreed with Madge how the divorce would run. He had previously given her an address where mail could be sent but she had obviously taken the trouble to try and find him, unsuccessfully, and when the divorce papers arrived on the doorstep, she knew for certain where he was. She also seemed to know quite a bit about me, too! The info must have come from the wife of one of Alan's now ex-friends, with whom we had had a meal some 12 or more months earlier. Anyway, things were now moving with the divorce.

At the end of October, Givvi was getting married to Lee. Alan and I were convinced it was the wrong thing for her to do but she is so headstrong and we gave her all the support we could. Alan even went to the wedding with her in the car as her surrogate father as Selwyn had let her down. Alan and I got engaged on that day.

In November we decided to book a holiday. Something to look forward to in the new year. We got a bargain to Turkey, even though Alan had not enjoyed himself there in the company of Madge, he had been very impressed with the place. We would be leaving on 8th May. It was at this time that I asked Alan if we could get married on 6th May and have the holiday as a honeymoon. That agreed, we decided to tell the children about this at Christmas.

As Christmas approached it was lovely to be able to make arrangements for all the children to be together. By now, Sam and Rebecca had accepted the situation and were quite happy to visit. We had an excellent time at Christmas and Boxing Day was extra special to me, to be with Alan on his birthday. We announced our intention to get married in May and everyone seemed happy about this.

The decree nisi came through on 9th January, and it was also on this day that Alan decided to tell me that he thought we were rushing things and wanted to postpone the wedding. He didn't want to be seen getting divorced and remarrying straight away, like the last time. I was very upset, but decided that I wouldn't mention marriage again for at least six months or so. His decision had stemmed somewhat from Sam, who had told his dad that he didn't want him to get married. It transpires that Sam thought that I would take his dad away from him.

Another reason for the postponement was Spencer's attitude towards his own role within the house. Basically he made very little financial contribution, his room was like a tip and his attitude towards Alan became worse when we told him of the postponed wedding. The final straw came on my birthday when, after being off work for three days, Spencer failed to even produce a birthday card for me. He had been 'too busy' to go to the shops, which are all of 50 yards from the house! Alan was upset and made his feelings known. Spencer was asked to leave by the end of the month, owing us money since before Christmas. He was not impressed by the fact that I would not climb down on this decision and is still holding this grudge against me.

It was about this time when Alan's decree absolute was nearly due that I suddenly received an anonymous letter through the post. It was obvious to us both that it was from Madge, but when challenged, she denied any knowledge of it – obviously! Unfortunately for her, there were certain aspects of the letter which related to her alone. She had always referred to me as "Cathy", something I have never been called by anyone and she always made the same mistake in our address when she had written to Alan. We realized that she wanted to cause disharmony by putting a "spanner in the works", but on checking with the Court we were told that she had stopped the divorce proceedings, telling them that she and Alan were reconciled! Alan visited her immediately and he stood over her whilst she wrote a letter of retraction which he delivered to the Court. Alan was then able to obtain his decree absolute on 21st February, 1995.

470

After Spencer moved out, we undertook the task of clearing his room and decorating again. This became the room that Rebecca uses. Sam then wanted to know when "his" room would be done. So that was the next task. Alan then decided that the bathroom, hall, stairs and landing needed to be done ... and this is how the weeks went by. When all this work was done Alan had still got the bug for decorating and our bedroom was next on the list. It was whilst we were decorating this room and using a back bedroom to sleep in that Alan told me there was a present for me in the kitchen. I had not long been in there making a drink and had not seen anything obvious. I was told that it was in the area of the notice board.

I went down to make yet another drink and could find nothing but we do have a calendar on the notice board – so I flicked through the pages. There it was! 15th July marked "Today's the Day". I was ecstatic. I know that marriage means different things to different people. To Alan it's not that important, a piece of paper, but to me it really is very important, and he knows this. I knew that he was doing this for me to make me happy. As it happened, I really didn't know what to say to him at the time!

When we had originally decided on a May date, I had designed wedding rings, and we were having them made in the Birmingham Jewellery Quarter. We had been backwards and forwards having alterations made, but they were now ready and we had them at home. They were designed to look like brickwork (for building a life together) and we had diamonds taken from my Nan's ring set into the rose gold. They are so unusual - we never expect to see anything else like them.

The saga with my parents had continued all this time, but Alan had decided that enough was enough, and it was mutually agreed that we should go and see them. Alan was prepared for a showdown with Dad, but had the wind taken out of his sales completely when Dad turned round, caught hold of his hand and said *"Hello, Alan, mate. How are you?"*. It was as if we had been in a time warp for some 18 months. Why did we all have to go through it? There really had been no reason.

I just wished they could have believed me when I said that Alan and I would be together one day.

Now that the house was decorated, and the peace had been made in Malvern, we were able to enjoy our "funnymoon" in Turkey. It was the most wonderful holiday I have ever had, not that I've had that many. The weather was terrific. We spent a lot of money thoroughly enjoying ourselves. We made love two or three times a day and enjoyed each other's company completely. We will have to go back there one day. On our return from holiday Alan decided to paint the outside off the house, back and front, whilst I was trying to organize the wedding.

All the arrangements came together on 15th July, 1995, when we married at Worcester Register Office with our friends and families around us. The reception at "The Swan" at Whittington went off without a hitch and the buffet they had provided was excellent. It was a memorable and emotional day for me.

I now look forward to spending the rest of my life with the man who taught me what life is all about, whom I have loved dearly since very early on in our relationship, who never fails to surprise me and who, I know, loves me.

What does he mean to me?
Alan means everything to me. He is my life and world.

Our Wedding Day - 15th July 1993